KU-444-344

Rangers

POCKET ANNUAL
1995-96

Edited by
Andy Graham

W·O·R·D·S·O·N·
Sport

Rangers Pocket Annual 1995-96

Copyright © Andy Graham – 1995

ISBN: 1-898351-34-1

Typeset by Bruce Smith Books Ltd

All photographs supplied by

Cover Photo: Brian Laudrup by Empics

The right of Andy Graham to be identified as the Author of the Work has been asserted by him in accordance with the *Copyright, Designs and Patents Act 1988*.

This is not an approved nor an official publication of Glasgow Rangers Football Club.

First published in 1995 by
Words on Sport

All rights reserved. No part of this publication may be reproduced, stored in a retrieval system, or transmitted, in any form or by any means, without prior permission in writing of the publisher, nor be otherwise circulated in any form of binding or cover other than that in which it is published and without a similar condition including this condition being imposed on the subsequent purchaser.

Words on Sport Ltd
PO Box 382
St. Albans
Herts, AL2 3JD

Registration Number: 2917013

Registered Office:
Worplesdon Chase, Worplesdon,
Guildford, Surrey, GU33LA

Printed and Bound in the Great Britain by
Bell & Bain Ltd, Glasgow

CONTENTS

Introduction
A great club deserves a great pocket annual. Read on. 7

1994-95 Season Review
The season in perspective, month by month, fact by fact. 9
Gazgow Belongs to Paul 14
Gers' Diary 1994-95...17
Results Roundup 1994-95 40
The Season – Match by Match 42
The blow by blow account of every match in 1993-94. Note the scorers, subs and match facts. Watch the top of the table change game by game and record this season's result for comparison.

Season's Records 1994-95
Attendances 139
Player Appearances 140
Bookings...141
Dismissals...143
Suspensions 143
Penalties...143
Scorers..143
Referees..144
Reserve Tables 146
Premier Milestones...147

Quotations – Rangers on Rangers 151

Player by Player
All your favourite players for 1995-96 profiled in detail....................................157
Full backgrounders with career and current form analysis, previous clubs, appearance record and estimated value.
They Played Their Part 195
New Arrivals 206
Davie Cooper Obituary 209

Premier Division All-time Records
Scottish League..272
League Cup..275
League Cup Winning Teams..291
Scottish Cup 294
Scottish Cup Winning Teams...316
European Cup 321
European Cup Winners' Cup..332
Fairs/UEFA Cup..340
European Roundup..345
Country by Country 346
Club by Club 347

Scottish Player of the Year 348
Scottish Young Player of the Year 348
Scottish Football Writers Player of the Year 348
Record-breaking Attendances 349

3-Year Form and Fixture Guide 350

Disclaimer

In a book of this type it is inevitable that some errors will creep in. While every effort has been made to ensure that the details given in this annual are correct at the time of going to press, neither the editor nor the publishers can accept any responsibilities for errors within.

If you do notice any mistakes then please write in and we will try and rectify them for future issues. In addition, if there are other areas of information about Manchester United Football Club that you feel should be included in future editions then please let us know of your choices.

Champions Again and Again!

Acknowledgements

Thanks to: Doug Baillie, Ron Scott, David Walker, Scott Fyfe, Stephen Halliday, Gary Keown, Danny Stewart, Anton from the Scottish Football League, Kenny MacDonald, Ray Spiller, Mark Clements and his Weekly News sports team – Banda, Brains, Beaker, Lilo, Fryman, Kano and Victimised. I appreciate the help you gave me.

Also worth a mention are Brid, Nick Puckey and Stephen Robertson, who all encouraged me at different times, and various flatmates including Andy, Daniel, Debbie and Pie, who had to put up with some wild moodswings during the writing and editing of the book!

Last but not least, I thank my mum and dad. Without them I doubt it would have seen the light of day.

Enjoy 1995-96.

Introduction

Throughout football, the global game, there are very few – if any – clubs who can claim to have the sort of standing Rangers do. Their continual success and massive support, in a tiny country by worldwide standards, is a source of envy for rivals right over Europe. Put simply, they are one of the continent's biggest clubs.

Over the years, they have produced footballers whose achievements have been unique. Jim Baxter, Davie Cooper, Ally McCoist and now Brian Laudrup have become household names by way of their efforts in the famous blue jerseys.

However, it is not solely their exploits on the pitch which have made Rangers a very special institution. There is not a club in the land which treasures its history to the extent it does; any visitor to the famous Ibrox Stadium on the south side of the Clyde in Glasgow is immediately aware that this is no ordinary football ground – but a place of real historical significance.

What makes Rangers the force they are, though, is the special marriage between the traditions of the club and a foresight unmatched in UK soccer. Nobody else had an all-seater ground with a capacity in excess of 40,000 before Rangers; nobody else could lay claim to a Pools operation which generates the amount of money Rangers' does; nobody else in Britain could now seriously hope to attract 45,000 crowds for the visits of clubs the size of Partick Thistle.

For the last few years, Rangers have dominated Scottish football with an iron grip. This first great edition of the independent Rangers Soccer Annual chronicles another season of success, match by match, blow by blow, goal by goal. But it contains much else besides – all the records, facts and statistics associated with a truly unique football club.

As the pages unfold, follow, follow on through the story of 1994-95.

The Season Reviewed

Champions again, but a disappointing season – albeit with mitigating circumstances. That could be the only just description of 1994-95 for Rangers, who predictably proved far too good for Scotland, but sadly not up to scratch in the real testing ground of Europe.

Perhaps it is a measure of how far the club has travelled since the appointment of Graeme Souness in 1986 that a league title won by the proverbial street is treated as something of an anti-climax. Just nine short years ago, seven games won in a row would have been treated as some sort of achievement, far less seven titles.

Now, it seems, that nothing less than a European Cup win will appease the fans, and after the outlay the club has made on new players and their fabulous Champions League run of 1992-93 – it is not too much of an expectation.

So it would be fair to say that the capitulation against AEK Athens in August, in the preliminary round of the Champions' Cup, cast a massive shadow over the campaign before it had even got under way in earnest.

In 1993-94, the disappointment of a first round exit to Levski Sofia was bitter enough, but the feeling was that it had taken a late, freak goal, against a severely under-strength Rangers, to execute the elimination. There could be no similar excuses about the Athens debacle. Rangers were outplayed, and on reflection, lucky to lose by only three over two legs.

Admittedly, there were factors which contributed. Being asked to play the first leg before the league term had even started put the side at an immediate disadvantage. And, although his subsequent performances were less than impressive, one can only wonder if the absence of Basile Boli through suspension was the first, very early, nail in the coffin of the European run, as well as the Frenchman's Glasgow career.

Nevertheless, Rangers were fortunate to lose by only two in Athens. Had it not been for an inspired performance by the reinstated Andy Goram, a result which was truly embarrassing might have been recorded. The two goals by Dimitrios Saravakos were worthy reward for the Greek champions, who looked a fine side.

A fortnight later, there was a genuine air of anticipation in Scotland that the two-goal deficit could be overturned, much of it based on AEK's dismal away statistics in European competition. It quickly became evident, however, that those statistics would be rendered meaningless as the visitors displayed an incisiveness and fluency which could not be matched by Walter Smith's men. Toni Savevski's first-half strike merely rubber-stamped the exit and left a packed Ibrox thoroughly subdued. The Greeks' failure to impose themselves on the Champions League only rubbed salt into the wounds.

Has any good come from another European disaster? There certainly seems to have been a return of realism following two first hurdle exits, and an appreciation, even in hindsight, that the efforts of the 1992-93 vintage were even more remarkable than they seemed at the time. If ever there was any doubt, Rangers now know that they can afford no passengers in continental competition and that it is absolutely imperative that they get the blend and tactics right from the start. 1995-96 will be vital one for the club on the foreign front; yet another failure would surely jeopardise their chances of landing more of the soccer world's big names.

It would be foolish and wrong, even, to write the entire campaign off simply because of that early slip-up. The league win, while by no means a procession of thrilling football, was emphatic enough and attained despite a crippling catalogue of injuries which would have destroyed clubs of lesser character.

No less than 33 players were used on Premier duty, almost an average of a new one every game, and it is a tribute to the resolve of every single individual who pulled on a Rangers shirt in 1994-95 that at no stage did the destination of the title flag look in doubt.

However, whilst acknowledging it was a team effort, one man put in the sort of contribution which will be talked about in years to come. In a league which at times can be depressingly stale, Brian Laudrup was a genuine breath of fresh air, offering a regular taste of the marvellous skills fans on mainland Europe expect as part of their regular diet. In 33 League games, his indifferent performances could be counted on one hand, and more often than not – and probably more often than manager Smith would like – he proved the single difference between the collection of three points or one.

In a season when Scottish football tragically lost one of its great entertainers, Davie Cooper, through a brain haemmorhage, it was absolutely fitting that the Danish superstar should so effectively fill the role that Coop did for so many years at Ibrox. For fans honed on the likes of Willie Henderson, Jim Baxter and Willie Johnston – but more used to more workmanlike, if successful performers in recent seasons – Laudrup was a wonderful blast from the past. His two player of the year awards, from the scribes and his fellow pros, were as deserved as they were inevitable.

The League campaign got under way with a 2-1 win over the club who were to prove, nominally at least, the closest challengers through the course of the season, Motherwell. Mark Hateley, and Duncan Ferguson, with only his second (and last, as it transpired) league goal for the club, were the marksmen.

Yet another Hateley strike and an own goal from David Byrne gave Rangers a 2-0 win at Partick, and ensured that they were the only club with a 100% record after a mere two games.

That was quickly to be shattered, in a desperately disappointing Old Firm clash at Ibrox. Coming the Saturday after the European exit, Rangers' lethargy could have been forgiven against any other Scottish side, but the fact that Celtic were well worth their 2-0 win made the defeat all the more galling.

Two successive home defeats was almost unheard of in the modern era, and the vultures were ready to swoop. When Rangers went out of the Coca-Cola Cup to Falkirk the following midweek the knives really were out.

With whispers of an Ibrox crisis in the air, the team responded in the only manner possible with a comprehensive 3-0 win over Hearts on September 11, handily enough in front of a live TV audience. The flag chase was back on track thanks to a brace from Hateley and a first of the season for Gordon Durie. Revenge was then wreaked on Falkirk, as the Bairns were dispensed with through a 2-0 victory at Brockville.

It was the two big money foreign signings who claimed the glory, Laudrup and Boli, and the latter's goal should have been a significant one. It was his first game back after comments attributed to him had been published in France, in which he unkindly criticised the club and the manager. Walter Smith went out on a limb to claim Basile had been misquoted, and everything seemed rosy as he returned with that splendid goal. Everything was far from rosy, though, and that strike merely papered over a few short-term cracks rather than start to solidify his place at the club.

A tempestuous game at Pittodrie followed, ruined by the erratic refereeing of Les Mottram. A contentious penalty, scored by Billy Dodds, was to provide Aberdeen with a point after Hateley and Craig Moore's first for the club had given Rangers the impetus.

Hateley and Laudrup kept the ball rolling by scoring the goals which sunk Dundee United 2-0 at Ibrox, before the second league reverse arrived at Easter Road.

Yet again it was Basile Boli who was in the headlines, with a goal then a red card as Hibs came back to triumph 2-1.

Rangers, whilst still looking good enough to win the League, were still decidedly shaky at this stage of the season and their next performance served only to confirm this. David Robertson and Charlie Miller scored to defeat Kilmarnock 2-0 but it was, on the whole, a less than satisfactory match.

Miller was just one of a number of new faces who began to express themselves at Ibrox at 1994-95, and this, as much as the injury crisis, almost certainly played a part in the general inconsistency. However, the youngster from Castlemilk, Craig Moore, Alan McLaren, Gary Bollan and Alex Cleland will all feel the benefit of having a season in the first-team under their belts.

With the first quarter of fixtures completed, it was time to cross swords with Motherwell again, but with less success. Despite John Philliben's own goal, the Lanarkshire club ran out 2-1 victors on their own patch.

With two defeats in three matches behind them, and the memory of their August drubbing against Celtic still fresh in the memory, Rangers then entered the second derby of the season with a lot of questions to answer. They did just that.

The 90 minutes at Hampden, screened live on TV, would be a contender for their best performance of the season, as Laudrup ripped the Bhoys to shreds with a showing which was as fruitful as it was flamboyant. One goal didn't really do him justice, but with another couple from Hateley to savour in a sensational 3-1 win, there was little room for complaint. The early-season debacle had been avenged completely.

Tellingly, this win launched Rangers on a 15 match unbeaten run, by far their best spell of the campaign, and a period in which they did enough to confirm that a seventh championship would be theirs.

A 3-0 romp home romp over Partick Thistle was sealed (Miller, Hateley and Laudrup), quickly followed by two 1-1 stalemates with Hearts (away) and Falkirk (home), in which Hateley was the scorer in both.

A rare Friday night fixture at Ibrox, caused by the scheduling of the Coca-Cola final there on Sunday, saw Aberdeen dispatched and the champs back to their winning ways. Ally McCoist's solitary goal in the game was to prove his solitary goal in an injury-afflicted season.

Another televised match continued Rangers' love of the cameras as they turned in a devastating three goal salvo, without reply, against Dundee United, at Tannadice. Pieter Huistra, Laudrup again, and Ian Durrant, welcomed back into the fold after an unhappy stint on loan to Everton, were the heroes.

A first goal for the club from McLaren and another from Laudrup saw off Kilmarnock's challenge in a 2-1 success at Rugby Park, before two decisive wins over the Christmas holiday period.

Hibs and Motherwell were the two clubs who were leading the chase on the league leaders, but they were to be found wanting on Boxing Day and Hogmanay respectively.

2-0 may not seem like a walkover, but Alex Miller's side were simply steam-rolled on December 26. Captain Richard Gough and Hateley got the goals, but it was the chances that were missed which were the story of one of the most one-sided matches at Ibrox in recent seasons.

New Year was seen in in fine fettle too, with the Steelmen given a lesson in what winning championships is all about at Fir Park. Stuart McCall, Durie and Laudrup proved deadly enough to have Alex McLeish conceding the title at an early juncture, after watching a 3-1 defeat.

Sky TV chose to launch their coverage of Scottish football with Rangers' next Old Firm clash, the traditional Ne'erday knees-up with Celtic, which had a bizarre feel on January 4.

Sadly, the satellite station's billing of it as the biggest and best derby in the world fell a bit short of the mark, as Ian Ferguson and Paul Byrne shared the goals in a tame 1-1 draw.

A 1-1 (David Robertson) draw with lesser Glasgow rivals Partick Thistle was next, before collection of three points became the norm again. Pieter

11

Huistra, on his last appearance for the club, made it a dream send-off with a double in the 3-2 fightback at Falkirk, McCall getting the other. Then Miller ditched Hearts at Ibrox with the only goal of a poor match.

By now, it was a question of by how many points rather than if, and the performances were beginning to tail off again, which was perhaps the best excuse for a lacklustre 1-1 draw with the soon-to-be relegated Dundee United, Robertson again netting.

The other north-east side in trouble at the bottom for the most part of the season then ended the unbeaten run. It was Roy Aitken's debut as Aberdeen manager, and his players, not unexpectedly, gave him 110 per cent to get him off to a flying start with a valuable 2-0 home win.

As the run-in drew in, a nervy Rangers finally got rid of Killie 3-0 – Durie, Laudrup and Durrant – before a couple of draws halted the momentum. McCall was on target in a 1-1 with Hibs, then Maurice Johnston inspired Falkirk to a share of the spoils on his first appearance for the Bairns at Ibrox in a 2-2 draw. The ever-reliable John Brown and Laudrup made the scoresheet.

A rare League defeat at Hearts, 2-1 (Laudrup), concluded a disappointing spell, but four consecutive wins wrapped up, then toasted, the title in true champion style.

A Durie effort after 12 seconds then a McLaren free-kick finished off Dundee United 2-0 on Tayside, then, in one of the most attractive matches of the season, Aberdeen fell 3-2 at Ibrox.

Again belying its lowly status, the Dons made a real go of it, but Durrant, Hateley and Neil Murray, with his first ever goal on Premier business, made sure that the long trip up to the Granite City was an unhappy one.

Anti-climactically, the title was confirmed as Celtic, the only side who could mathematically catch Rangers, slipped up at Pittodrie the following Saturday, but at least it meant there was a party atmosphere for Scottish TV cameras to capture at Ibrox on Sunday April 16, as the champagne flowed and Hibs were yet again the sacrificial lambs, this time by 3 goals to 1. Durrant, Durie and Alexei Mikhailtchenko were the men to be thankful to.

Miko secured Rangers' final win of the season with the lone goal in another TV match at Kilmarnock, before the traditional end of season fizzle-out with losses at home to Motherwell (0-2) and more disastrously at Celtic (0-3).

It was left to Aussie Moore to score the last goal of another title-winning season at home to Partick Thistle on the concluding day, but three minutes from the end, Alex Taylor popped up to deny a final three points.

So, despite a winning margin of 15 points, it was an up and down season, with plenty of wins, but few real high spots. There were no wins in Edinburgh, against either Hibs or Hearts, or at Aberdeen – usually the supporters' three favourite away trips. And that glorious 3-1 Hampden walkover apart, the Celtic clashes were a let-down, with the club's oldest rivals taking seven of the available 12 points.

Nonetheless, the League season did throw up a few stars. Andy Goram, when fit, proved he was the best keeper in Britain, if not Europe, and McLaren was a steadying influence on a defence which looked rocky at times. Moore and Miller, both still teenagers, suggested they have big, big futures and Laudrup, of course, was dazzling.

The domestic cup front was short-lived. The Coca-Cola Cup was surrendered weakly, to round off those three dismal home defeats in August, in a 2-1 loss to Falkirk. The match was notable only for Brian Laudrup's first goal for the club. Rangers had beaten Arbroath 6-1 (Hateley 2, Duncan Ferguson 3, McCall) to reach the third round.

The Light Blues only lasted two games in the Scottish too. A twice postponed fixture against Hamilton got played at the third attempt, and Rangers aptly managed three goals (Boli, Trevor Steven and Laudrup) to Accies' one. But, and it was no consolation that the match was a treat for the neutral fan, Hearts sent four past Ally Maxwell in the fourth round to end the involvement. What made it all the more galling was that Rangers had pulled back from 2-0 down, thanks to Durie and Laudrup, only to succumb again.

On the transfer front there were departures for Gary Stevens, Steven Pressley, David Hagen, Dave McPherson, Pieter Huistra, Fraser Wishart, Ally Maxwell and most sensationally Duncan Ferguson. The club's £3.75 million gamble on the big man never really paid off and although he has shown some inspired form at Everton, there could be little doubt that Walter Smith probably made the right decision of accepting a profit on a player who had done little to rid himself of his 'too hot to handle' label.

In came McLaren – in the deal which took Hagen and McPherson to Hearts – and Cleland and Bollan in a double swoop from Dundee United. All will have their parts to play in achieving more success.

And with Gordon Petric, Stephen Wright and Paul Gascoigne now on the books few would dispute the club's determination to keep ahead of the chasing pack. 1994-95 was no classic campaign for Rangers, but the main objective was attained, the League title, and that Celtic record of nine-in-a-row moves ever closer. The hope at Ibrox must be that there's something else in the trophy cabinet when number eight hopefully comes in!

GAZGOW BELONGS TO PAUL

On July 11th, it finally happened, almost two months after the speculation started. Paul Gascoigne signed on the dotted line and was paraded in front of 2000 euphoric fans on Edmiston Drive.

Sure, there had been blips and hitches on the way. Chelsea were interested. Leeds were interested. Aston Villa were interested. Then, at the last moment, Manchester United were rumoured to be interested. But it mattered little, as it was Rangers who captured one of the most prized signings of the summer. The deal was confirmed at £4.3 million, eclipsing the previous highest transfer fee paid by Rangers, and indeed, any Scottish club – the £3.75 million for Duncan Ferguson.

And there can be little denying that the man at the centre of attention, Gazza himself, is expected to deliver far more than Big Dunc managed during his time at Ibrox, and more immediately as well. Judging by his effervescent performance at the press conference, he certainly seems up for the task.

"I'm ready to make up for all the lost time *now*," he bubbled, referring to his disastrous injury blighted time in Italy with Lazio, following his move from Tottenham.

"People have said for years that I can't find the form of 1990, but I've spent most of that time injured. I'm 28, but I still feel like a boy. In football terms, I feel like I'm still only 25, because I have hardly played.

"I just want to get on with playing football and enjoying it again and I know I'll do that at Rangers. I've only been here for one morning and already I feel very settled. It usually takes players *months* to feel like this."

Optimism running high, then!

But just what was it that caused Rangers to splash out such a phenomenal sum in the first place? For those who have been on the moon for the past five years, Gazza has been the highest profile British player of his generation; a genius, but a tormented genius, failing to live up to his potential through misfortune and self-destruction.

After making his League debut with Newcastle United – where former Geordie legend Jackie Millburn prophetically said he would be the best in the world – the bright lights of London proved an attraction, as he was tempted to follow the example of another Toon Army favourite, Chris Waddle, and sign on for Spurs. After a sensational World Cup of 1990, where Gazza, labelled "daft as a brush" previously by manager Bobby Robson, ran the England midfield on their march to the last four, he came into his own at White Hart Lane. He single-handedly took the north London men to the FA Cup final that season, and scored a succession of fantastic goals, including a free-kick, against Arsenal's David Seaman at Wembley, in the FA semi, which is talked about to this day. It was form which attracted the attention of sleeping Italian giants Lazio. But his season was to end in tears, just as his World Cup had done. And while Gazza had been genuinely unfortunate against

The Magician!

Germany in the World Cup semi, picking up an unfair booking which would have precluded him from the final, his Wembley woe in the English game's showpiece was all his own undoing. A disastrous tackle on Gary Charles of Nottingham Forest, which could have seen him sent off, instead contributed to badly damaged ligaments which were to rule him out of soccer for a year.

The move to Lazio went ahead, but Gazza was not to kick another ball for a year, because of his career-threatening injury. His time in Serie A has been well-documented, a succession of downs with only the occasional, very slight up. There was one glorious equalising goal in a Rome derby for Lazio, but on the whole, Italy became a case of what might have been for Gazza. Broken legs, broken cheekbones, belching, sendings-off, recurring weight problems and an over-zealous press all took their toll.

Obviously, therefore, shelling out £4.3 million for Gascoigne is a real risk for Rangers. He is obviously being seen as the missing link who can propel them to a European success, or at least qualification for the Champions League, something which has eluded them for two seasons. On that stage he would come into his own, and the move would be deemed a massive success; the sales in replica shirts, interest from English TV and spin offs from UEFA would see to that. The draw, against Famagusta of Cyprus, should ensure an easy path – defeat would be the worst result of the club's European history. But a couple of early defeats there, and will Gazza still be interested? Sceptics would have you believe he will not be keen on wintry nights at Kilmarnock or Partick Thistle, and are beginning to question the wisdom of the move.

Don't bet on it.

Like Brian Laudrup last season, he will thrive on the confidence a winning team provides, and that more than anything else, will keep him enthusiastic about the supposedly mundane fixtures.

Similarly, English commentators' suggestions that he will be wasted in Scotland and no longer an automatic choice for the England side are way off the mark.

Laudrup played some of his best international football ever last season; and it was no coincidence he was in a side which played to his strengths, and made him feel very much at home. That will be the case with Gazza too.

Anyone with any doubts should listen to the warcry he arrived at Ibrox with.

"I want to win things and enjoy myself here. I want to win the championship 10 times in a row because I know what that means. I feel that is what I am going to do and if I feel as happy as I do now after my contract finishes in 1998 and the chairman and manager are happy, I'll sign another contract."

The Gazza era has just begun.

Diary 1995-96

July

4th Around half of Rangers' squad start pre-season training at the city's Bellahouston Park. Centre of attention is Andy Goram, transfer–listed at the tail end of the previous season over attitude and fitness problems.

8th The rest of the first-team squad, including summer signings Brian Laudrup and Basile Boli, arrive at Ibrox to get their training under way.

12th Manager Walter Smith dismisses rumours that ill-health is going to force him into general manager's job at Ibrox, with Kenny Dalglish taking over as team boss!

14th Doctors announce that seriously ill, hard-drinking former Rangers star Jim Baxter is to get a liver transplant at Edinburgh Royal Infirmary.

19th Former Rangers and Dundee star Andy Penman dies after being unwell for some time with a kidney complaint. Penman stayed at Ibrox for six years after signing in 1967. Meanwhile, Rangers fly back from their training camp in Italy.

20th Rangers are drawn against AEK Athens in the preliminary round of the European Cup. A Champions League place with AC Milan, Ajax and either Casino Salzburg or Maccabi Haifa awaits them if they are successful.

21st It emerges Basile Boli is suspended for the European Cup opener with Athens, after bookings picked up with previous club Marseille. Secretary Campbell Ogilvie and security officer Alistair Hood fly out to Greece to discuss arrangements for travelling fans.

23rd Jim Baxter has his liver transplant in Edinburgh and begins his battle for life.

25th Andy Goram will miss Rangers' pre-season tour of Denmark and Germany, it is announced. The injury plagued 'keeper is to undergo rehabilitation on his thigh injuries. Alexei Mikhailitchenko, Colin Scott, Craig Moore and Duncan Ferguson are also ruled out. The club urge fans not to travel to Greece, in the belief that the Nikos Goumas Stadium could be a volatile prospect for travelling supporters.

27th Rangers launch their tour with a 1-1 draw against Aalborg in Denmark. Mark Hateley scores. Rangers sign 36-year-old 'keeper Billy Thomson from Motherwell for a fee which will be decided by tribunal. Danish TV station TV1 announce they will cover several of

Rangers' games during the forthcoming season because of the interest stirred up by Brian Laudrup's move.

28th   Rangers agree a deal with Maccabi Haifa for Oleg Kuznetsov. Euro opponents AEK Athens approach Dundee United with a view to a warm-up match prior to their match with Rangers.

29th   German side Kaiserslautern overcome Rangers 1-0 thanks to a goal from Martin Wagner. Alexei Mikhailitchenko undergoes a cartilage operation in London. "Follow Follow", a play charting Rangers' history, starts at Glasgow's Kings Theatre.

August

1st   Rangers draw 1-1 with Danish first division side Ikast. Basile Boli scores his first goal for the club – but Pieter Huistra breaks his nose and Dave McPherson has to go off with a wound above his right eyebrow which requires five stitches. AEK's attempts to arrange their friendly with Dundee United fall through. A Rangers XI, including Ally McCoist and Duncan Ferguson, beat East Fife, Kevin Fotheringham hitting two with Super Ally getting the other.

2nd   A unique commercial alliance between 11 British football clubs is announced at Ibrox. The enterprise will try to encourage companies to make more use of the business facilities at football stadia.

5th   Sampdoria turn a 2-0 deficit into a 4-2 victory against Rangers in the Ibrox International Tournament. Mark Hateley and Trevor Steven are on the mark for the home side. Newcastle beat Manchester United 6-5 on penalties, after a 1-1 draw, in the other semi-final. Reports suggest that AEK are on £13,000 a man to beat Rangers in their Euro tie – the Light Blues are on a staggering £20,000 each!

6th   A David May own goal is enough to give Rangers victory over Manchester United in the 3rd-4th place play-off, but the biggest talking point is Eric Cantona's sending-off for a wild lunge at Steven Pressley. Alex Ferguson slams Rangers fans for their abuse of his side claiming, "They are stuck in the past." Sampdoria beat Newcastle 3-1 in the final.

7th   Billy Thomson loses two goals as a young Rangers slump 2-0 at Berwick.

9th   Andy Goram is taken off the transfer list as Rangers prepare in Athens for their European opener. "He knew why I put him on the list and his response has been great," says Walter Smith.

10th   Disaster as Rangers fall 2-0 against AEK in front of 30,000 fans in Athens. A new defensive formation of Gary Stevens, Richard Gough and Steven Pressley has a miserable evening and is lucky just to concede two. On a tempestuous night, Rangers' team-bus is bottled, and the RFC aeroplane is stranded at Athens airport for three hours waiting to return home. 10 fans are convicted of theft in Italy after a shoplifting spree en route to the game.

11th   The Danish FA threaten to invoke FIFA rules and suspend Brian Laudrup from the opening two weekend fixtures of the season, after the Danish players threaten not to turn up for their fixture with Finland on August 17. Rangers slam AEK for their fans' behaviour in Athens, and UEFA pledge an investigation into the firing of flares into the section allocated to Rangers supporters.

12th   Andy Goram is outstanding as Rangers beat Motherwell 2-1 in the opening league fixture. Brian Laudrup plays as the Danish row is sorted out, and Mark Hateley and Duncan Ferguson get on the scoresheet. Ally McCoist suffers a calf injury which will rule him out for at least a month.

16th   Scottish Television announce exclusive rights to screen Rangers' European matches live, starting with the home clash with AEK.

17th   Duncan Ferguson scores his first-ever hat-trick and Mark Hateley his 99th and 100th goals for the club in a 6-1 Coca–Cola Cup win over Arbroath. Stuart McCall gets the other, but boss Walter Smith chooses to watch Brian Laudrup and potential signing Marc Reiper in Denmark's international with Finland. Laudrup scores in a 2-1 win.

18th   Rangers are drawn at home against Falkirk in the second round of the Coca-Cola Cup. Pieter Huistra flies to Germany for signing talks with Duisburg. Marc Reiper announces his desire to join compatriot Brian Laudrup in Glasgow, saying "There have been English clubs interested in me, but Rangers are bigger."

19th   East Kilbride awards Ally McCoist a Certificate of Meritorious Achievement in recognition of his contribution to the town.

20th   A 2-0 win at Partick Thistle on league business is achieved thanks to an own goal from David Byrne and Mark Hateley.

21st   It's claimed again that Rangers will be on an incredible £20,000 a man to defeat AEK and progress to the Champions League.

22nd   Walter Smith calls on the Rangers support to make Ibrox as intimidating for AEK as Athens was for them. "I hope Rangers fans give the same as the Greek fans did," he stresses.

24th   An early exit from Europe, as AEK win 1-0 at Ibrox for a 3-0 aggregate. Walter Smith draws heavy criticism for playing Basile Boli in an unfamiliar right-back role. Toni Savevski scores the goal which deprives Rangers what could have been up to £6 million earnings from the Champions League.

25th	Walter Smith pledges no wholescale changes after a European disappointment. Chairman David Murray is equally frank, admitting "I don't know what the answer is." However, he hints that the planned seating of the corners at Ibrox, to take the capacity over 50,000, may now be scrapped as players become a priority.
27th	David Murray and Walter Smith are subjected to the most vitriolic abuse either has heard in their time at Ibrox as Rangers slump 2-0 to Celtic in the first Old Firm game of the season. On a happier note, the Bhoys' fans are allowed back into Ibrox again, and there is negligible damage to seating after the previous season's excesses.
29th	Tabloid newspaper reports claim Rangers are to hold a summit after the disasters of the past week. Ian Ferguson, Andy Goram, Stuart McCall and David Robertson are named in the Scotland squad for the forthcoming European Championship match against Finland, while Steven Pressley is in the Under-21 squad. Denmark call up Brian Laudrup for their match with Macedonia.
31st	Yet another defeat as two goals from Richard Cadette take Falkirk through to the quarter-finals of the Coca-Cola Cup. Brian Laudrup scores his first goal for the club, but it is of little consolation in a shocking 2-1 loss.

September

1st	News arrives back in Scotland of criticisms of Rangers made by Basile Boli in the French press. The defender is alleged to have said, "It was crazy to use two centre forwards who play the same way," on Walter Smith's decision to play Duncan Ferguson and Mark Hateley against AEK Athens. Boli added, "You can't go about winning an important game by having a laugh in the dressing room half an hour before kick-off," and complained at being played in a right-back role.
2nd	Rangers order Basile Boli back from a break in France to explain his comments. "We won't be needing any interpreter," says manager Walter Smith ominously. UEFA fine AEK Athens £25,000 after fans threw firecrackers during their home match with Rangers.
5th	Boli arrives back in Scotland to face the music.
6th	Boli and his wife have a two hour meeting with Walter Smith, after which the manager announces the French star will be back at Ibrox with his lawyer for more talks. Neil Murray and Steven Pressley play in the Scotland Under-21 side which loses 1-0 to their Finnish counterparts in Salo. Stuart McCall is one of five Scotland stars who have their wallets, cash and cards stolen from their rooms in Finland.

7th	Andy Goram and sub Stuart McCall feature in Scotland's 2-0 win in Finland, watched by boss Walter Smith. Brian Laudrup plays for Denmark against Macedonia in a 1-1 draw.
8th	Basile Boli is staying at Ibrox, Walter Smith announces. The club claim that his interview in the French press was not properly translated into English by the Scottish media. "With the evidence now, there's not really any action that the club could take."
11th	Rangers get back to winning ways with a comfortable 3-0 victory over Hearts. Hateley (two) and Durie are on target.
12th	Brian Reid begins a week-long trial with Portuguese outfit Uniao Leiria. Trevor Steven undergoes an exploratory operation on his calf injury.
13th	Steven Pressley is put up for sale after refusing a three–year contract, claiming he wants regular first-team football. Duncan Ferguson is booked and has a prolonged argument with the referee in the tunnel after the match as Rangers reserves draw 2-2 with Hearts at Tynecastle.
16th	Andy Goram signs a new four-year contract with the club, and thanks the team-mates who stood by him when he was transfer listed in the summer. "Ian Durrant and Ally McCoist gave me the boost that I needed when were in Toronto for Durranty's stag party in the summer."
17th	Falkirk fall 2-0 to Rangers with back-in-favour Basile Boli and Brian Laudrup on the mark.
19th	Incredibly, Basile Boli is again credited with critical comments of Rangers in the French media – and says he will only stay at Ibrox for two years.
20th	No comment from the club as they play down the latest Boli controversy. Gary Stevens is linked with Sheffield Wednesday and Japanese outfit Grampus Eight.
22nd	Walter Smith launches his biography "Mr Smith" and admits that Rangers' loss against AEK "certainly put pressure on me personally."
23rd	Ally McCoist is included in the squad for the league match with Aberdeen, after successfully recovering from a calf injury.
24th	A 2-2 draw at Pittodrie, Mark Hateley and Craig Moore scoring, is overshadowed by erratic refereeing by Les Mottram and an alleged incident between a fan and the big English striker after the game.
26th	It is revealed Ibrox is on the shortlist of venues for the season's European Cup-Winners' Cup Final.

| 27th | The SFA confirm that Gordon Durie picked up the equivalent of a red card in the tunnel after the match against Aberdeen, and will be suspended from Rangers' next match, against Dundee United. |
| 28th | Rangers secretary Campbell Ogilvie claims TV evidence should not be used by the SFA to decide disciplinary measures following the stormy clash at Pittodrie. |

October

1st	Dundee United get their comeuppance for defeating Rangers in the Scottish Cup Final in May, with a 2-0 defeat at Ibrox. Mark Hateley and Brian Laudrup hit the mark. But the day is dominated by correct rumours that Duncan Ferguson and Ian Durrant are on their way to Everton.
3rd	Durrant and Ferguson arrive on loan deals at Goodison for one and three months respectively. The former's supposed permanent deal does not materialise amid doubts over his fitness. But Durrant insists he is 100 %; "I've played over 100 games in Scotland in the last three years so I don't feel my fitness is a problem."
5th	Ferguson makes his debut for Everton, but they crash out of the Coca-Cola Cup at Portsmouth after a 1-1 draw leaves them 4-3 behind on aggregate. Nevertheless manager Mike Walker says, "I thought the big fellow showed a lot of quality." Durrant stays on the bench throughout the 90 minutes.
6th	Ally Maxwell picks up a training knock on his ankle to become another Ibrox casualty.
8th	Basile Boli scores – but is sent off as Rangers lose 2-1 at Hibs.
9th	Ally McCoist calls on Ian Durrant to forget about a transfer to Everton and stay at the club he loves. "Ian's one of the fans own. Guys like me, John Brown and Ian Ferguson are fans as well."
10th	David Robertson and Stuart McCall fail fitness tests and are withdrawn from the Scotland squad for their European Championship match with the Faroe Islands.
12th	Andy Goram plays in the 5-1 win over the Faroes, while Brian Laudrup features in the Danes' key 3-1 success over Spain. Two stars on their way out of Ibrox are Pieter Huistra, who goes on trial at QPR, while Gary Stevens completes a £350,000 move to Tranmere.
14th	It is revealed that Rangers are a total of £8 million in debt, but chairman David Murray stresses there is no need for worry – the club has a facility for a £14 million overdraft.
16th	Kilmarnock are the latest Ibrox victims, losing out 2-0 with Charlie Miller and David Robertson on the mark.

17th	Walter Smith dismisses suggestions that Ally McCoist's career is under threat after his latest injury problems. "He would be the first player to have his career threatened by a calf strain," raps the boss.
18th	Captain Richard Gough signs a new three year deal which will keep him at the club until he is 35, as Steven Pressley prepares to move to Coventry in a £750,000 transfer.
19th	Pressley arrives in Coventry and admits, "My Ibrox days are over and it's sad. I've been at the club since I was 12." Rangers' move for Alan McLaren for £1 million plus Dave McPherson and Neil Murray goes on hold – as the Rangers players want financial guarantees from the Tynecastle club.
20th	No move on the McLaren deal. Manager Smith says, "They are trying to get their choice of players, so it's their problem." Falkirk full-back David Weir emerges as the club's latest transfer target.
21st	Duncan Ferguson's trial for headbutting is postponed again after his solicitor has to go to Australia to visit a sick relative. Pieter Huistra returns to Glasgow to play in Rangers' league match with Motherwell due to the lengthy injury list.
22nd	A John Philliben own goal is Rangers' only consolation as they lose 2-1 at Fir Park. Meanwhile, the club's accounts show that failure to reach the Champions League in 1993-94 cost them at least £4 million.
23rd	Rangers are believed to have offered Dave McPherson and Neil Murray £400,000 as an enticement to go to Hearts. Brian Reid is also thought to be in the reckoning for a switch to Tynecastle.
25th	The McLaren saga ends as the Scotland international signs for Rangers in a deal which sees Dave McPherson travel along the M8 to Hearts, and is valued at £2 million. "I'm coming to place that has ambition," says McLaren. "Hopefully my ambition matches theirs."
26th	Ibrox is used as a venue for the Coca-Cola Cup semi-final between Celtic and Aberdeen. Celtic win 1-0.
27th	Aberdonian defender David Robertson admits he was hounded, spat on and pelted with coins by some by Dons' fans at the above game as he attempted to sit in their end, the Copland Road stand. The Scotland international was forced to move.
28th	Rangers confirm former Celtic manager Lou Macari has slapped a cash arrestment on the club's accounts preventing any money being paid to his former side.
29th	17-year-old youngster Brian McGinty is called into the Rangers squad for the second Old Firm match of the season, as an alternative to the struggling Ally McCoist.

30th   No sighting of McGinty, but a scoring wondershow from Brian Laudrup and two goals from Mark Hateley grant Rangers a deserved and exhilarating 3-1 success. Alan McLaren makes his club debut. Laudrup is named Tartan Special Player of the Month, while Charlie Miller takes the Young Player's award.

November

1st   Ally McCoist fires a hat-trick as Rangers christen Huntly's new floodlights at Christie Park. Pieter Huistra and Brian McGinty also score as Rangers win 5-2. Rangers field a strong side: Goram, Wishart, Robertson, Moore, McLaren, Boli, Hagen, Murray, McCoist, McGinty, Huistra.

Basile Boli hits the tabloids again, with suggestions that German club Muich 1860 are keen to take him to the Bundesliga. "I don't know about this," insists Walter Smith.

Fraser Wishart, meanwhile, explains that he hopes his recall for the Old Firm game could lead to a move away from Ibrox. "I hope Sunday's game proved to any interested parties that I'm still more than capable of playing at the highest level."

2nd   Ian Durrant returns to Glasgow after his failed loan move to Everton. He managed only four and a half games for the Merseyside club, and featured in one win, against West Ham.

Ally McCoist cheekily tries to claim his hat-trick against Huntly takes him past the magical 300-goal barrier for Rangers, but is forced to admit, "I would love to count them, but I don't think the club will let me."

5th   A convincing 3-0 win over Partick Thistle keeps Rangers at the top of the Premier League. Laudrup, Miller and Hateley score.

6th   Rangers learn that they will lose Brian Laudrup on international duty with Denmark in January, when he will miss matches against Partick Thistle and Falkirk. However, he will be free for the Old Firm clash with Celtic on January 4. Denmark are competing in the Inter-Continental Cup in Saudi Arabia.

7th   Andy Goram, Alan McLaren, David Robertson and Stuart McCall receive the call from Craig Brown for the European Championship clash with Russia. Charlie Miller earns his first Under-21 recognition, alongside Neil Murray – but a knee knock at training is to count him out.

8th   Mike Walker is sacked as Everton boss, but Duncan Ferguson will not be ending his loan spell and returning to Ibrox. "We'll be advertising for a new manager, but Duncan will remain an Everton player until January 3 at least," says Goodison chief executive Jim Greenwood.

9th   Mark Hateley converts a penalty, but John Colquhoun equalises as Rangers and Hearts draw 1-1 on League duty at Tynecastle.

10th   Joy Royle is appointed Duncan Ferguson's new boss at Everton.

11th   Gordon Durie finally makes his comeback after a persistent hamstring problem in a 1-0 Premier Reserve League defeat to Partick Thistle. However, he picks up a head knock and receives a booking which leaves him just one yellow card away from another SFA suspension.

13th   Alan McLaren reveals how he has written to Hearts fans to thank them for the support they gave him during his years at Tynecastle. Ally McCoist is given the freedom of home town East Kilbride – then announces he and wife Allison are to have their first child. Secretary Campbell Ogilvie calls for a resurrection of the loan deal scheme in Scotland to allow their young players to get experience in other clubs' first teams.

14th   Rangers hold their AGM and David Murray announces plans to install giant TV screens at Ibrox which will allow ticket-less fans to watch away games in comfort. Craig Moore is hit with a two-match SFA suspension for the forthcoming fixtures against Aberdeen (home) and Dundee United (away).

Goalkeeper Andy Goram is splashed all over the front pages again, as wife Tracey files for divorce.

15th   Neil Murray plays in Scotland Under-21s' 2-1 win over their Russian counterparts at Broadwood.

16th   Goram stars in Scotland's 1-1 draw with Russia, as McCall and McLaren also start. David Robertson is an unused substitute. But there is disaster for Brian Laudrup and Denmark in Spain, as they crash 3-0.

19th   Nicky Henderson is on target to peg back Rangers as Falkirk manage a 1-1 draw at Ibrox. Mark Hateley is the Light Blue marksman.

25th   Another home win, as Ally McCoist gets his 299th goal for Rangers in the 1-0 success over Aberdeen, in front of 45,072, the biggest home gate of the season to date. Typically, he claims it is his 300th! But Mark Hateley picks up a worrying ankle injury.

27th   Ibrox is the scene of mass jubilation, as Raith Rovers defeat Celtic 6-5 on penalties, after a 2-2 draw, to lift the Coca-Cola Cup.

29th   Richard Gough continues his comeback from a toe injury with 90 minutes in Rangers' 2-2 Premier Reserve League draw at Pittodrie. Kevin Fotheringham scores both Rangers' goals.

1st Fringe player David Hagen leaves Ibrox for Premier rivals Hearts. Manager Walter Smith explains, "David needs first-team football. He wasn't going to get it at Ibrox."

4th An emphatic 3-0 League win over Dundee United is captured by the TV cameras. Laudrup, Durrant and Huistra all score. Walter Smith denies that Ian Durrant will be moving to Arsenal for £1 million. "The last time I spoke to George Graham was 10 months ago, when he phoned me to enquire if we could provide opposition for Tony Adams' testimonial," says the gaffer.

5th Another goal for Duncan Ferguson for Everton, against Leeds, intensifies speculation that his loan deal will be made permanent.

6th Ferguson, who is costing Everton a whopping £35,000 a week, seems almost certain to move south. Goodison boss Joe Royle says optimistically, "We are making progress."

7th Rumours suggest that Leeds United and Arsenal are preparing bids for Fergie too. Meanwhile, he is named in the Scotland squad for their Euro qualifier in Greece, as are David Robertson, Andy Goram, Stuart McCall and Alan McLaren. Charlie Miller and Neil Murray are in the Under-21 travelling party. Marc Rieper's chances of coming to Ibrox are buried as he signs for West Ham for a year.

8th Brian Laudrup is officially named in the Denmark squad for the Inter-Continental Cup in Saudi Arabia.

10th Alan McLaren scores his first goal for the club, and Brian Laudrup is on the mark too, as Rangers beat Kilmarnock 2-1 in a League match at Rugby Park.

12th Big Dunc is on his way! Everton shell out an incredible 4.26 million for the wayward hit-man. It amounts to over half a million profit after it is revealed that Rangers only paid Dundee United £3.75 million when he arrived in the summer of 1993. More money was due, but Fergie did not make enough appearances for the club.

13th The man of the moment joins up with the Scotland squad, and announces. "I've always been confident in my own ability, and I've shown that with the moves I've made." Chairman Murray, meanwhile, dismisses speculation that Rangers are set to sign Aberdeen's Scott Booth. "I can categorically say we have no interest in Aberdeen players," he stresses.

17th Neil Murray captains Scotland's Under-21s to a 2-1 victory over their Greek rivals in the Nikos Goumas Stadium, where Rangers crashed to AEK Athens in August. Charlie Miller makes his Under-21 debut. Scottish TV announce they will televise Rangers' clash at Aberdeen on February 12. Celtic reserves beat Rangers reserves 1-0 in a Reserve League Cup clash at Broadwood.

18th   Disaster as Andy Goram picks up a torn calf muscle in Scotland's 1-0 reverse in Athens. There's a wobbly performance from Alan McLaren, but Stuart McCall does his usual power of work.

19th   Former manager Graeme Souness announces that he is to sue an English paper who made allegations of improper transfer dealings during his time as boss at Ibrox.

Henry VIII (Ally McCoist), Popeye (Pieter Huistra) and Al Capone (John Brown) are among the characters who surface at Rangers' annual fancy dress Christmas party.

20th   Walter Smith confirms that Goram's injury could keep him on the sidelines for a couple of weeks.

22th   Raith Rovers' Steve Crawford becomes the latest player to be linked with a move to Ibrox. David Murray re-confirms plans to fill in the corners of Ibrox with seats and giant TV screens, similar to those used at the Coca-Cola Cup Final and at Arsenal's Highbury. The capacity would rise to 51,000.

23th   The SFA are expected to have to fork out close on £10,000 to Rangers for Andy Goram's injury.

26th   A canter for Rangers as they easily beat Hibs 2-0 at Ibrox. Richard Gough and fit-again Mark Hateley are the marksmen.

27th   Danish TV station DR1 announce they will televise the Old Firm showdown on January 4 – the first Scottish match to be televised in Denmark.

28th   Pieter Huistra is linked with a move to the megabucks J-league in Japan.

29th   Huistra clinches a two-year contract with San Frecce Hiroshima. The deal is expected to make him a millionaire, and will net Rangers £500,000 , a £200,000 profit on a player they signed from Twente Enschede in August 1990.

31st   Another match, another win, this time 3-1 at Motherwell. Stuart McCall, Brian Laudrup and Gordon Durie all but finish the Steelmen's League challenge, as the Light Blues go ten points clear.

January

1st   Alexei Mikhailitchenko meets up with Oleg Kuznetsov in Ukraine, after his former Ibrox team-mate's unhappy time in Israel. He has returned to his homeland as Macabbi face up to the reality of being unable to pay his wages.

4nd	Ian Ferguson's first-half opener is cancelled out by a Paul Byrne equaliser as the New Year Old Firm clash, delayed until the fourth for live transmission on Sky TV, ends in a 1-1 draw.
6th	Walter Smith rules out a loan move to Israel for perennially injured Ukrainian Alexei Mikhailitchenko.
7th	A league debut, in a match to forget, at Firhill for Brian McGinty, as an under-strength Rangers and Partick Thistle fight out a 1-1 draw. Andy Goram departs early with a calf injury.
8th	Brian Laudrup, captaining Denmark for the first time, is on the mark as they beat host nation Saudi Arabia 2-0 in the Inter Continental Cup in Riyadh. Dundee midfielder Morten Wieghorst, regularly linked with a move to Rangers, scores the other.
9th	Manager Smith reveals Goram is expected to be out for a month with his injury, while Mark Hateley is to see a specialist in London regarding his ankle problem. Duncan Ferguson's trial for his alleged assault on Raith Rovers' John McStay whilst playing for Rangers is postponed for the third time in eight months after legal arguments at Glasgow Sheriff Court.
11th	Celtic manager Tommy Burns admits he asked Rangers boss Walter Smith for advice before signing Dutch player Pierre van Hooydonk.
12th	A tabloid report suggests that Mo Johnston is wanted by Walter Smith as a short term answer to his striking injury crisis. It is dismissed immediately by the manager.
13th	Manager Smith explains why Johnston will not be coming to Ibrox. "We did give it serious consideration, but ultimately felt it was not a step in the right direction." Closest title rivals Motherwell and Hibs draw 0-0 at Fir Park, and the Easter Road side's Michael O'Neill concedes, "The title is in Rangers' hands now." The Light Blues are 14 points clear. Brian Laudrup skippers the Danes to Inter Continental Cup success with a 2-0 win over Argentina, while Greek Under-21 defender Angelos Vilanakis is banned by UEFA for five matches after spitting on Charlie Miller in December.
14th	Two goals from Pieter Huistra in his last game for the club help clinch an exciting 3-2 win at Falkirk. "I couldn't have written a better script," he stresses.
16th	Manager Smith admits that he is in the market for three new players, including a right-back and a midfielder – but not one newspaper has accurately guessed the identity of the players he is chasing!

19th	It emerges Dutch striker John van Loen has been offered to the club by a Dutch agent following Pieter Huistra's departure, but manager Smith indicates that he is not interested in any deal.
21st	A first minute Charlie Miller goal is the prelude to a dire 90 minutes as Rangers edge past Hearts 1-0 at Ibrox.
22nd	Brian Laudrup's Danish international team-mate, Morten Wieghorst of Dundee, is again rumoured to be on the way to Rangers. Wieghorst first came to the fore when playing for Lyngby against the Light Blues in the European Cup of 1992. Another exotic name filling space in the tabloids is Augustine Okacha, a Nigerian with Eintracht Frankfurt, who would cost in excess of £3 million.
23rd	Graham Stuart of Everton becomes the latest player to be linked with a move to the club.
25th	Ally McCoist and wife Allison parade their new son, Alexander, for the cameras for the first time.
26th	The 'right-back' and 'midfielder' referred to by Walter Smith earlier in the month are Alex Cleland and Gary Bollan of Dundee United, who sign on at Ibrox in a combined deal worth £750,000.
28th	A waterlogged pitch KO's Rangers' Scottish Cup tie with Hamilton at Firhill. The match is re-scheduled for Tuesday, January 31.
31st	Crocked Ibrox star Scott Nisbet admits he is preparing for a new career as a referee. "I'm just keen to put something back into the game I love," he explains. Yet again, the weather counts out the Scottish Cup tie with Accies.

February

1st	It emerges that Marseille's desperate need for cash has saved Rangers £200,000 following their agreement to pay another instalment of Basile Boli's transfer in advance.
2nd	Another comeback for Ally McCoist as he scores twice for Rangers' reserves in a 3-0 win over Hibs' second string.
4th	David Robertson is on target as Rangers have a 1-1 draw with Dundee United at Ibrox. But another injury for Ally McCoist to his hamstring – sees him KO'd for a suspected six weeks.
6th	Goals from Trevor Steven, Basile Boli and Brian Laudrup are more than enough for Hamilton Accies as the clubs' Scottish Cup third round tie is played at the third attempt.
11th	Swedes Jonas Thern, of Roma, and Jesper Blomqvist, of Gothenburg, become the latest players to be linked with a move to Ibrox.
12th	Roy Aitken, in charge of Aberdeen for the first time after Willie Miller's dismissal, makes it an unhappy Sunday for the Light Blues

by steering his Dons to a 2-0 victory in a live TV game.

14th　Pieter Huistra makes a dream start for San Frecce Hiroshima with the opening goal in their 2-1 friendly win against Aussies Wollongong City. Rumours about Jonas Thern coming to Glasgow appear unfounded as Roma say he will be staying at the club.

15th　Mark Hateley becomes the latest victim of the rumour factory, as tabloid papers suggest he is en route to his first club, Coventry as assistant to new boss Ron Atkinson.

16th　Rangers return from their four-day mini-break to Monaco, designed to give the players a bit of sunshine prior to their cup clash with Hearts.

20th　One of the best matches of a dismal Scottish season holds little comfort for Rangers, who exit the Cup at the fourth round stage to Hearts. In a 4-2 defeat, Brian Laudrup and Gordon Durie are 'Gers marksmen, while Hearts thank John Robertson, Kevin Thomas and ex-Gers Dave McPherson and Colin Miller for their progress.

21st　The tabloid rumour mill loses its sense of reality as Walter Smith is tipped to succeed sacked George Graham as Arsenal boss. Smith won't even comment on the suggestions and laughs them off. Back in the real world, Mark Hateley and Andy Goram face doctors in London to see if there is any hope of playing again before the end of the season. Hateley's groin and Goram's calf strain are causing concern.

22nd　Rest is the diagnosis for Hateley's problem – but it is revealed that his spell on the sidelines could be as long as six weeks. Goram, however, will have to be operated on, and will miss the rest of the season.

23rd　Gary McAllister is named as the latest Rangers transfer target, as part of the club's bid for European success in 199596. It is confirmed that preparation for the continental campaign will no longer include a trip to the Italian training camp of Il Ciocco. Kenny Dalglish thanks the club for their part in Blackburn's 2-1 win over Wimbledon – they allowed the Lancashire outfit to use their protective pitch covers amid heavy rain.

24th　It is reported that McAllister would miss out on a £500,000 testimonial if Leeds were prepared to sell before the end of his contract in 1999.

25th　John Brown inspires Rangers to a 3-0 win over Killie at Ibrox. There are goals from Gordon Durie, and both Brian Laudrup and Ian Durrant from the penalty spot.

26th　It's David Platt of Sampdoria's turn to become linked incorrectly with a move, as is Tomas Skuhravy of Genoa. At least Smith makes the trip to Italy to watch the latter, but he is not impressed. Richard

Gough learns that he is not even in Craig Brown's list of 70 names for visas for Scotland's upcoming European clash with Russia. "If I'm not included in Craig's list of 70 players, that looks like it's it for me," admits the captain.

27th   Chairman David Murray pleads with fans to be patient as more and more names are linked with the club. He says, "We'll be out every weekend looking for the guys Walter needs, but we don't want to buy for the sake of it." Andy Goram, meanwhile, has his long-awaited operation on his calf.

March

1st   Brian Laudrup tells the club newspaper that leaving Rangers to sign for Barcelona would have been a big mistake.

3rd   Leeds United knock back a £2.5 million bid from Rangers for Scotland captain Gary McAllister. However Elland Road chairman Leslie Silver says, "It's up to Rangers if they want to try again."

4th   Maltese keeper David Cluett completes a week of training at Ibrox, in the hope of attracting a transfer to a Scottish side.

5th   Stuart McCall fires Rangers into the lead against Hibs at Easter Road, but a Keith Wright equaliser gives Hibs a 1-1 draw.

7th   Aberdeen full-back Stephen Wright is tipped to follow the trail blazed by David Robertson in 1991 by signing on at Ibrox in the close season.

10th   Fraser Wishart leaves to join Hearts for £50,000 – a year after turning down the Tynecastle club!

12th   A John Brown header and a Brian Laudrup penalty are cancelled out by two Colin McDonald goals as Falkirk – inspired by new signing Maurice Johnston – steal a point at Ibrox. The Bairns' young full-back Graeme Hamilton is sent off. Alan Smart, chased out of Inverness Caley by boo-boy fans, has made such a splash at Preston North End that he is said to be attracting the eye of Rangers.

13th   Walter Smith says Rangers' injury crisis has been so severe during 1994-95 that he has still to field what he considers their first-choice line-up.

14th   Rangers' backroom man Billy Kirkwood is listed as favourite for the manager's job at Dundee United after the Tannadice side sack Ivan Golac.

15th   Walter Smith flies to Sweden to check on Gothenburg's Jesper Blomqvist in their European Cup clash with Bayern Munich. It also emerges that Queen's Park Rangers' Les Ferdinand has been watched by Ibrox scouts too.

18th	Another success for Hearts over Rangers, this time 2-1. John Robertson and John Millar net for them; Brian Laudrup, inevitably, for Rangers.
20th	Stuart McCall and Alan McLaren are called into the Scotland squad for the match with Russia in Moscow. Gary Bollan and Charlie Miller make it into the Under-21 party, but Neil Murray misses out through suspension.
22nd	Scottish football is shocked as Rangers legend Davie Cooper collapses after a brain haemorrhage whilst filming a TV coaching series for children at Broadwood Stadium, Clyde.
23rd	Davie Cooper dies at 9.45 am. Scotland is plunged into mourning.
24th	Scotland captain Gary McAllister announces that the team will play with black armbands in the match with Russia and that it will be dedicated to Cooper.
25th	Minute silences are observed around Scotland for Cooper as hundreds flock to Ibrox to lay scarves at the shrine which has evolved between the Copland Road and Main Stands. Stuart McCall is pulled out of the Scotland squad with an Achilles injury, with reports claiming Rangers were ready to pull him out and risk a massive SFA fine even if he'd failed a fitness test.
27th	Rangers stars are in attendance as Davie Cooper is laid to rest in his home town of Hamilton.
28th	Billy Kirkwood, as predicted, leaves Ibrox to take over the manager's job at Dundee United. Charlie Miller scores and Gary Bollan also plays as the Scotland Under-21s record a fine win over their Russian counterparts in Moscow. However, Miller is booked and will miss the young Scots' match in San Marino.
29th	Alan McLaren plays a key role as Scotland secure an excellent 0-0 draw against the Russians. Brian Laudrup features for Denmark in their poor 1-1 draw with Cyprus – and is slated by the Danish press. A young Rangers side win 5-1 at Cowdenbeath to mark the opening of the Blue Brazil's new £500,000 stand. Neil Caldwell, John Douglas, Lee Dair, Brian Reid and Lee Robertson all score as 1500 pay to watch.
30th	National boss Craig Brown tips Charlie Miller for a full Scotland call-up before too long. "At the moment he is the first in line to move into the big squad out of a fine group of youngsters." Plans are announced for Scott Nisbet's testimonial on May 1. Rangers will play a Rangers international select including the likes of Ray Wilkins, Graham Roberts, Nigel Spackman and Terry Butcher. But there will be no number 11 in the select side – after the death of Davie Cooper, the first ex-Ibrox star approached to play.

1st   The tragedy of Davie Cooper's death is recognised in England, where ex-Bear John Spencer wears his own black armband in Chelsea's 1-1 draw with Newcastle at Stamford Bridge. Back in Scotland, Gordon Durie sets Rangers on the road to a comfortable 2-0 victory over Dundee United at Tannadice with a remarkable goal in only ten seconds. Alan McLaren scores the other in what is Billy Kirkwood's first match as United boss after leaving Ibrox.

2nd   Scott Nisbet is told that he's too young to have a hip replacement, the only treatment which will ease the pain of his pelvic injury. And even if he did have it now, it would have to be repeated in later years.

3rd   The Daily Record, Scotland's biggest selling daily newspapers launches the Davie Cooper Appeal to raise funds for research into the brain disease which took Cooper's life.

4th   Mark Hateley resumes training after his long injury absence. It is reported that Stoke City have watched Ally Maxwell in a 1-0 reserve win over Hamilton Accies, after he was dropped from the weekend win on Tayside. Stuart McCall will NOT need an operating after receiving damage to his cartilage in that Dundee United clash.

5th   Edinburgh businessman Ian Russell becomes Rangers' first ever associate director. His loan of £1 million will entitle him to wear a club blazer and tie, sit in the directors' box for matches and fly with the official club party on European trips, for a spell of five years. Another four are being sought by the club. "Football clubs, especially one as ambitious as Rangers, must look at a wide range of methods of increasing their revenue," explains chairman David Murray. However, Mr Russell will have no say on board decisions and will not attend board meetings. David Murray also claims that there will be more additions to the playing staff over the summer. Two or three big names, or five or six players, are his target.

7th   Ibrox is used for the Scottish Cup semi-final, where Hibs and Celtic draw 0-0 in a tepid game broadcast live by Sky Television.

8th   Rangers all but clinch the championship with a 3-2 home win over Aberdeen, which puts the Dons in very real trouble of relegation. Duncan Shearer and Billy Dodds score for the visitors, but these goals are cancelled out by Mark Hateley, back in the first team after his lengthy absence. A revitalised Ian Durrant is on the mark, as is substitute Neil Murray, a replacement for Basile Boli, who dislocates his shoulder. It is Murray's first-ever Premier Division goal for Rangers.

9th	London Police ban Rangers from playing Gary Mabbutt's testimonial at Tottenham on August 4. Mabbutt says, "I'm disappointed. I wrote to Rangers because Richard Gough is a good friend." The decision is taken because of trouble on Rangers' last excursion south of the border, against Sunderland.
10th	The transfer stories start about Basile Boli. German giants Bayer Leverkusen are believed to be willing to pay £1.5 million for the Frenchman at the end of the season.....
11th	But wait! Another side allegedly enters the Boli transfer circus. Turkey is claimed to be Baz's destination, with Fenerbahce keen to take him there. And his fee has gone up £500,000 in 24 hours, with it now appearing to be £2 million required for his signature! On a more immediate note, his injury from the weekend is not as serious as first thought, and he should return for the championship party against Hibs. Andy Goram and Ally McCoist will also return before the end of the season. Walter Smith confirms that he will shortly be having contract talks with Ian Durrant, Alexei Mikhailitchenko, Ally Maxwell and Colin Scott.
11th	Ibrox is used for the Scottish Cup semi-final replay between Celtic and Hibs. Celtic win through 3-1. Walter Smith travels through to Bolton to run the rule over Wanderers' highly-rated centre-half Alan Stubbs in a 0-0 draw with Luton at Burnden Park. Davie Cooper's memory is to be recognised by his first and last club, Clydebank, who announce they will name their new £3 million stadium after the tragic star.
13th	It appears that it is Brian Laudrup AND Basile Boli who the Turks want. They would willingly splash out £4 million for the Dane, according to reports. Borussia Dortmund become front runners in the chase for Boli.
14th	Laudrup announces that he wants to stay at Ibrox despite the Turks' interest. "There is no way Fenerbahce interest me. I don't want to go and I will not be leaving Rangers." Ali Sen, the Turks' supremo, is undaunted and will watch the Light Blues against Kilmarnock. Plans to rip up the seats the multi-coloured Govan, Copland Road and Broomloan stands are revealed. Ibrox will be an all-blue, 51,000 capacity. And the Ready For The Future initiative is unveiled. Season ticket holders will be asked to cough up £399 a head to guarantee a seat for 10 years. It will generate £5 million for new players for the challenge ahead in Europe. Admits Murray, "We are at a crossroads as a club. We could be seen to be stagnant." And, on a day of big

news, it is confirmed that plans are afoot to show the away legs of European fixtures on screens at Ibrox.

15th   Celtic lose 2-0 at Aberdeen, thereby ending any even slight mathematical chance of Rangers not winning the championship.

16th   It's a title party as Rangers beat Hibs 3-1 in yet another live TV match, on Scottish ITV. But it's a close run thing, and it takes late, late strikes from Ian Durrant and Alexei Mikhailitchenko to get the champagne corks popping with gusto as Gordon Durie's early opener is cancelled out by Michael O'Neill. Says Richard Gough, "I am just so proud and honoured. In ten years time, it will probably sink in just how remarkable it is to win seven titles in a row. It's been all the more memorable because we have gone through a transitional period and won with a greater margin than ever. Losing in Europe, then against Falkirk in the Coca-Cola Cup and Celtic in the league in the space of a week was hard to take. When things like that happen doubts do cross your mind. But the boss brought in good pros and we all had the pride to battle back."

17th   There are whispers that Rangers have bid £2.5 million for Jesper Blomqvist, and that Brian Laudrup has spoken to the player in a bid to persuade him that his future lies in Scotland.

18th   Rangers clinch the BP Youth Cup with a 2-0 win over St Johnstone at Hampden with goals from Brian McGinty and Steve Boyack.

19th   A third bid for Liverpool's Neil Ruddock has failed, it is disclosed. The bid is believed to have been close on £3 million pounds. "He is going nowhere," says Anfield boss Roy Evans.

20th   Alexei Mikhailitchenko scores his second goal in successive games as Rangers beat Kilmarnock 1-0 in a satellite TV fixture at Rugby Park. Ally McCoist and Gordon Durie pay their way into the crowd, but it's Scotland McCoist is focusing on. He is hoping a couple of first-team games before the end of the season will put him in the reckoning for Craig Brown's squad's trip to Japan at the tail end of the season. Meanwhile, Scott Nisbet's testimonial will see Graeme Souness return to management as boss of the former Gers. "You can never say never in football, but I do not envisage being a manager again after this," says Souness.

23rd   A young Rangers draw 2-2 with Queen of the South, but of more importance is the return of Andy Goram, who looks set to figure in the first team before the end of the season. Craig Moore and Lee Dair score.

24th   Gary McAllister is again named as the man who will be arriving at Rangers in the close season by the Scottish tabloid press. Trevor

Steven is alleged to be the bait, while Colin Hendry of Blackburn, Stephen Wright and Stevie Crawford are yet again named as targets.

25th Gary Bollan and Neil Murray play in the Scotland Under-21 side which scrapes a 1-0 European Championship win against San Marino. The winner is scored by ex-Ger Steven Pressley.

26th Alan McLaren is the sole Rangers representative in the Scotland senior side which wins 2-0 against San Marino's first team.

28th Scotland boss Craig Brown warns crocked keeper Andy Goram that he now considers Jim Leighton to be his first-choice goalkeeper. "It's now a matter of Andy having to displace Jim again when he regains his fitness," says Brown.

29th A disappointing day at Ibrox, where Rangers crash 2-0 to Motherwell. Dougie Arnott and Shaun McSkimming score for the Lanarkshire club. Basile Boli is watched by representatives of Fenerbahcei. Walter Smith confirms "We've had a couple of enquiries about him."

30th Graeme Souness, who will manage the ex-Rangers select in Scott Nisbet's testimonial, admits he was wrong to want to sell him when he was in charge at Ibrox. "I look back now and think I'm glad I didn't sell him," admit Souness.

May

1st Fenerbahce chief Ali Sen admits that his interest in Basile Boli has waned following the Frenchman's poor performance in the 2-0 defeat against Motherwell. "I was interested in the Boli of yesterday, not the Boli of today. Unfortunately, yesterdays mean nothing in football."
Scott Nisbet's testimonial attracts a crowd of almost 30,000 and sees the first team beat the ex-stars 3-2.

2nd Brian Laudrup is confirmed as the Scottish Football Writers' Footballer of the Year. He says, "I'm right at home here and it's a tremendous honour to become the first foreigner to win the award."
Frank Bruno pays a visit to Ibrox to publicise his fight at Glasgow's Kelvin Hall on May 13.

3rd It emerges that John Carlton, a Rangers fan from Rutherglen, was cautioned by police for an impromptu, but good-natured, pitch invasion during Scott Nisbets's testimonial.

4th Rangers are formally linked with Paul Gascoigne for the first time. The injury-blighted England star looks certain to leave Lazio in the summer and Walter Smith is believed to be interested. The Rome club's supremo Sergio Cragnotti confirms, "Rangers are one of the few clubs who have made genuine inquiries about the player."

5th	Despite official denials from Gazza's agent, Len Lazarus, and from Rangers' assistant manager Archie Knox, it is understood that a fee of almost £4.3 million has been agreed between Lazio and the Ibrox club, and the move is dependent on the player himself. Gazza would stand to earn around £1 million a year. But Lazarus insists, "It is absolutely not true to say that Paul Gascoigne is about to sign for Rangers at any minute. Neither he nor I even know if he is leaving Italy."
6th	Gazza makes his first comment on the move proclaiming, "I've got to admit that Rangers are a massive club and come strongly into my thoughts. And remember they are playing in the European Cup next season." Walter Smith says, "We have reached agreement with Lazio and I have spoken to the player." But a fly in the ointment could be England boss Terry Venables, who is keen for the player to move to England. Meanwhile, 8000 are at Ibrox to watch a 1-1 Premier Reserve League draw between Rangers and Celtic. Lee Robertson opens the scoring for the Light Blues in the 52nd minute, but sees Charlie Nicholas hit an equaliser with 17 minutes left.
7th	A heaviest defeat of the season at Hampden, as Rangers crash 3-0 in the final Old Firm match. Celtic's scorers, in front of a disappointing crowd of 31,025, are Pierre Van Hooydonk and Rudi Vata, with Craig Moore, in his first Glasgow derby, scoring an unfortunate own goal.
8th	It is revealed that the Department of Employment are only willing to give Alexei Mikhailitchenko a six month work permit, while Rangers want to give him a new one-year contract. The Gazza saga rumbles on, too, with the player reported to be in Sardinia thinking about the move.
9th	Gazza returns to Rome, but gives Lazio officials no decision on whether he will be joining Rangers. Alan McLaren is the only Rangers player selected for Scotland's friendly matches in Japan with Japan and Ecuador. Barcelona pull out of the race for Swede Jesper Blomqvist, leaving Rangers favourites to sign him. And an injury crisis which sees 31 players at the club unfit forces Walter Smith to play oldies Terry Butcher, Bobby Russell, John MacDonald and Gordon Smith in a reserve match at Clydebank, which is lost 1-0.
10th	Duncan Ferguson is found guilty of assault at Glasgow Sheriff Court after head-butting Raith Rovers' John McStay in a League match during the 1993-94 season. Sentence is deferred. Ferguson says in court: "It happened very quickly. I saw McStay turn to square up to me and I intended to square up to him." McStay admits he does not want Ferguson to go to jail, but that is the real possibility – the

37

offence happened when the former Rangers player was on probation. Meanwhile, the club announces it will pull out of the Scottish Reserve League West in 1995-96, because they don't have enough players to compete in the four leagues they are currently operating in.

12th   It is claimed that Jurgen Klinsmann turned down £30,000 a week to sign for Rangers in order to return to Germany with Bayern Munich, after deciding to quit Tottenham.

13th   Fresh reports that Gazza has given his word to David Murray and Walter Smith, who stayed in his villa in Rome, that he will be playing for Rangers next season. The fee is now put at £5 million. The league season is wound up with a 1-1 home draw with Partick Thistle. Craig Moore scores; Alex Taylor equalises. There are league debuts for Neil Caldwell and, as a sub, Paul McKnight.

Strangely, Caldwell is to be freed by the club, as is young goalkeeper Neil Inglis.

14th   Walter Smith reveals that Ally Maxwell has knocked back a one-year deal and will sign month–to–month contracts alongside Brian Reid, John Morrow and Lee Robertson. Following the departure of Billy Kirkwood to manage Dundee United, John McGregor will be assisted in coaching Rangers' reserves by John Brown – although Bomber will remain registered as a player.

15th   It emerges that Ibrox chief scout Ewan Chester has watched Seville striker Davor Suker. Ian Durrant, thought to be on his way out of Rangers during the season, confirms a new three-year contract. Paul Gascoigne is alleged to be seeking compensation from Lazio for the remaining two years of his contract – which could force Rangers into offering even more money.

16th   Walter Smith hits out at UEFA's method of seeding clubs for the Champions League, which means that yet again will Rangers will be forced to play preliminary matches. "We are working on the premise that we will be in the first round again," admits the manager.

18th   Espanol's Romanian Florin Raducioiu is the latest target for Rangers – and there appears to be some credence to this latest rumour. Chairman David Murray admits, "There was a meeting in Barcelona and we have agreed a price." But there's more trouble brewing over the bid for Paul Gascoigne, still not settled, with Lazio threatening to keep him out of football for a year if he does not sign for Rangers. The English international is squabbling over a £1,000,000 pay off he believes he is entitled to. Italian press claim that Walter Smith, in the country to supposedly tie up the deal, is furious.

Bench Talk!
Archie Knox
&
Walter Smith

20th	With Gazza heading back to England for the funeral of his grandmother, Chelsea reveal they are willing to match the deal Rangers have agreed with Lazio. There's joy for ex-Gers Duncan Ferguson and Paul Rideout at Wembley as Everton beat Manchester United 1-0 in the FA Cup Final – Rideout scores the winner.
21st	Alan McLaren features in the Scotland team which records a dismal 0-0 draw with Japan in Hiroshima.
22nd	Ex Rangers boss Graeme Souness is surprisingly linked with a move to Turkey to coach Galatasaray. Says Souness, "At Rangers I managed the club with most fanatical fans in Scotland. It was the same in England with Liverpool. Now it could be the same again if I come to Turkey."
24th	Yet more reports that Gazza will be definitely be coming to Rangers. Walter Smith flies to London to meet Lazio president Dino Zoff with David Murray, hopeful of tying up the deal. Alan McLaren plays in the Scotland side which defeats Ecuador 2-1 in Japan.
25th	Gazza has signed! Or has he? The deal itself is not complete, but it appears that he has given his word to Smith and Murray that he will be coming, and the transfer will be completed soon. David Murray is quoted as saying, "The only thing left to sort out is the matter of compensation - but Gascoigne will be coming to Rangers". It is confirmed that Rangers will not be seeded in the 1995-96 Champions League - but Blackburn, with no European pedigree, will. And at Glasgow Sheriff Court, Duncan Ferguson is sentenced to three months in jail for his assault on John McStay in a Rangers v. Raith Rovers match in April 1994. He is released pending an appeal.
26th	Part of the deal to take Gascoigne to Rangers could involve Lazio participating in the pre-season Ibrox International Tournament. Leeds, believing they were to be having talks with the player, admit they are outraged by his decision. Says Ellan Road supremo Bill Fotherby, "It's disappointing that we've lost out on him without having the chance to speak to him."
31st	Paul Gascoigne confirms, "I have not signed for Rangers yet. But I do expect to be up in Scotland soon and hopefully I'll be able to let the fans know what's happening as soon as possible."

June

3rd	Ally Maxwell, after refusing a new deal at Ibrox, claims the fans want him to stay. He stresses: "Since it became known that I intend to go, I have been approached by hundreds of fans wanting me to stay."

4th	Gazza, although he is still not signed, arrives at Ibrox to make his first public appearance. After seeing the famous Blue Room, the awe struck England star admits, "No wonder it only took me a couple of minutes to decide to come to Rangers." David Murray says, "The fee is £4.3 million. Paul's happy. We have agreed terms in principle and for personal reasons he'll sign at the start of July."
6th	Florin Radicioiu admits he will be coming to Ibrox. He is quoted as saying: "I want the Scottish people to know that I am delighted to be signing for Rangers. I am thrilled at the opportunity of playing beside players like Laudrup and Gascoigne and I am looking forward to doing it in the Champions League." It appears that Borussia Dortmund have dropped plans to launch a bid for Basile Boli, as they opt to look for a striker rather than a defender. Alan McLaren plays in Scotland's 2-0 win over the Faroe Islands in a European Championship qualifier.
11th	It is claimed that Gazza's signing could add over £4 million to the clubs' off-field earnings per annum. Commercial boss Bob Reilly confirms, "There's no doubt this could be one of the best signings the club has ever made."
12th	David Murray talks to Italian agent Antonio Caliendo as the on-off Florin Radicioiu deal hits another hitch. However, it is understood that the transfer will still go through.
16th	Ally Maxwell leaves the club for £150,000 to sign for Dundee United, claiming to have made the move in a bid to get back into the Scotland reckoning.
17th	Mark Hateley on his way out at Ibrox. That's the buzz on the grapevine as Gazza, Laudrup and Radicioiu look set to occupy the non-Scottish spots next season.
25th	QPR boss Ray Wilkins responds philosophically to his failed bid of £750,000 for Gers midfielder Ian Ferguson. "If I was Walter, there's no way I'd have let him go either."
28th	Reports that Paul Gascoigne could be tempted to go to Manchester United instead of Rangers are dismissed. Lazio claim United would have to buy him from Ibrox, while David Murray dismisses the reports as nonsense. "The deal is done as far as we are concerned," stresses a Lazio official.
29th	Basile Boli to return to France? That's the latest speculation as Olympique Lyon are earmarked as potential buyers.

6th	Aberdeen's Stephen Wright becomes, after Gazza, the second signing of the summer. Out of contract at Aberdeen, the Scottish international full-back claims he was not offered new terms. But the fee is set for tribunal, as Rangers bid £800,000 - the Dons want £2,500,000. "He is a valuable addition to our squad," says boss Walter Smith. But there is still no movement on Florin Radicioiu's proposed transfer from Espanol.
8th	David Murray admits he is tiring of the Radicioiu saga. "This deal is getting a little bit boring for me just as I'm sure it is for every other Rangers supporter. Let's hope that something materialises over the next few days."
10th	He's arrived AT LAST! Gazza is paraded in front of thousands of adoring fans in Edmiston Drive and pledges to take Rangers to the utopia of ten titles in a row. "I know what that means," says the new hero. And the enthusiastic England star even finds time for a double training session. But as one star arrives, another is on the way out. Basile Boli, despite proclamations that he wants to stay, is told that he has no future at the club. Roy Aitken, meanwhile, blasts the club for their £800,000 bid for Stephen Wright. "It fell way below our valuation," raps the Dons boss.
13th	A good week continues as Rangers get lucky in the European Cup draw and land Anorthosis Famagusta. "It's a relief that we haven't got one of the top sides in the tournament," admits Walter Smith.
14th	Florin Raducioiu's deal is stalling because of a payment the player believes he is entitled to from Espanol, but the club are still hopeful it will go through. The club are in conciliatory mood with Aberdeen as well, and look set to agree on a fee for Stephen Wright. "We hope to work something out," says Walter Smith.
14th	The Euro tie will be live on Scottish TV it is confirmed. Basile Boli is back in France seeking a move. But most importantly, Gazza scores in the first match of the 1995-96 season, a 4-0 closed doors win over Stirling at Forthbank.
16th	Another goal for the Geordie, alongside strikes from Brian Reid and David Robertson, seals a 3-1 win over St Mirren. But there's an injury disaster for Ally McCoist, who has nine stitches inserted in a knee gash and may miss the club's trip to Denmark.

The Season
Match by Match

Results Summary

Date	Type	Opponents	Scores		Scorers	Att
Jul-27	F	Aalborg	A	1-1	Hateley.	-
Jul-29	F	Kaiserslautern	A	0-1		-
Aug-01	F	Ikast	A	1-1	Boli.	-
Aug-05	F	Sampdoria	H	2-4	Hateley, Steven.	27,282
Aug-06	F	Man Utd	H	1-0	May OG.	30,186
Aug-10	CL	AEK Athens	A	0-2		30,000
Aug-13	L	Motherwell	H	2-1	Hateley, D. Ferguson.	43,750
Aug-17	CC	Arbroath	A	6-1	Hateley 2, D. Ferguson 3, McCall.	4,665
Aug-20	L	Partick Th	A	2-0	Byrne OG, Hateley.	15,030
Aug-24	CL	AEK Athens	H	0-1		44,789
Aug-27	L	Celtic	H	0-2		45,466
Aug-31	CC	Falkirk	H	1-2	Laudrup.	40,697
Sep-11	L	Hearts	H	3-0	Hateley 2, 1 pen, Durie.	41,041
Sep-17	L	Falkirk	A	2-0	Boli, Laudrup.	12,778
Sep-24	L	Aberdeen	A	2-2	Hateley, Moore.	21,000
Oct-01	L	Dundee Utd	H	2-0	Hateley, Laudrup.	43,330
Oct-08	L	Hibs	A	1-2	Boli.	12,118
Oct-15	L	Kilmarnock	H	2-0	Miller, Robertson.	44,099
Oct-22	L	Motherwell	A	1-2	Philliben OG.	11,160
Oct-30	L	Celtic	A	3-1	Hateley 2, Laudrup.	32,171
Nov-01	F	Huntly	A	5-2	Huistra, McGinty, McCoist 3.	3,500
Nov-05	L	Partick Thistle	H	3-0	Laudrup, Miller, Hateley.	43,696
Nov-09	L	Hearts	A	1-1	Hateley pen.	12,347
Nov-19	L	Falkirk	H	1-1	Hateley.	44,018
Nov-25	L	Aberdeen	H	1-0	McCoist.	45,072
Dec-04	L	Dundee United	A	3-0	Laudrup, Huistra Durrant.	10,692
Dec-10	L	Kilmarnock	A	2-1	McLaren, Laudrup	1,283
Dec-26	L	Hibs	H	2-0	Hateley, Gough.	44,892
Dec-31	L	Motherwell	A	3-1	McCall, Laudrup, Durie.	11,269
Jan-04	L	Celtic	H	1-1	I. Ferguson.	45,794
Jan-07	L	Partick Thistle	A	1-1	Robertson.	19,351

44

Date	Type	Opponents	Scores		Scorers	Att
Jan-14	L	Falkirk	A	3-2	Huistra 2, 1 pen, McCall	13,495
Jan-21	L	Hearts	H	1-0	Miller.	44,231
Feb-04	L	Dundee United	H	1-1	Robertson.	44,197
Feb-06	SC	Hamilton Accies	A	3-1	Steven, Boli, Laudrup.	18,379
Feb-12	L	Aberdeen	A	0-2		20,000
Feb-20	SC	Hearts	A	2-4	Laudrup, Durie	12,375
Feb-25	L	Kilmarnock	H	3-0	Durie, Laudrup pen. Durrant pen	44,859
Mar-04	L	Hibs	A	1-1	McCall	12,059
Mar-11	L	Falkirk	H	2-2	Laudrup pen., Brown.	43,359
Mar-18	L	Hearts	A	1-2	Laudrup.	9,806
Apr-01	L	Dundee United	A	2-0	Durie, McLaren.	11,500
Apr-08	L	Aberdeen	H	3-2	Durrant, Murray, Hateley.	44,460
Apr-16	L	Hibs	H	3-1	Durie, Durrant, Mikhailitchenko.	44,193
Apr-20	L	Kilmarnock	A	1-0	Mikhailitchenko.	16,086
Apr-29	L	Motherwell	H	0-2		43,576
May-07	L	Celtic	A	0-3		31,025
May-13	L	Partick Thistle	H	1-1	Moore.	45,280

Rangers' Pre-Season Friendlies

Given the disaster which was to follow in Europe, Rangers' pre-season build-up was perhaps an accurate reflection of their inability at the time to deal with continental sides, whether from the top drawer or one or two levels below that.

The high profile tournament at Ibrox obviously attracted all the headlines but, in fact, the whole show got on the road, appropriately enough, in Denmark, from where Walter Smith had gone searching for one of his expensive close-season purchases, Viking international Brian Laudrup. Aalborg, a Danish league side, were the opposition on a sweltering night on July 27 when temperatures touched 80 degrees. Not surprisingly, Laudrup was the focus of attention for the eager crowd, his appearances back home now limited to his run-outs for the national team in the Parken stadium in Copenhagen. And it was a start to savour for the signing from Fiorentina, as he was unquestionably the star man in an outing which appeared little more than a *breaking-in* exercise for the Glasgow men.

The game, as indeed all the pre-season warm-ups were, was intended as a tester for what Rangers might expect in Athens, and although the quality of the opposition was not nearly as strong as AEK, the heat and Aalborg's match-fitness, having started their League programme, made it a worthwhile test. Indeed, Aalborg proved they were no slouches as they breached the Ibrox rearguard after only 14 minutes. In a move beginning on the left, Pedersen slipped the ball to Madsen, who eluded Richard Gough and Dave McPherson, before completely deceiving Maxwell, chipping beautifully over him. Andy Goram had been left at home to improve his fitness after his problematic previous season, and it was not the start his deputy would have wanted.

Rangers' response was immediate, and born of embarrassment at their slipping one behind. After David Robertson had been fouled, Laudrup swept over a free-kick for Mark Hateley to comfortably side-foot the ball home from a couple of yards.

That was the end of the scoring, but the Scots had plenty of opportunities to record a morale-boosting victory. McPherson had a 25-yarder saved by Gill, then Durie had a close-range effort brilliantly blocked by the Danish 'keeper.

After the break, Rangers introduced as many new faces as they could in a bid to give everyone a run. Most notable of the substitutes was Basile Boli, who made his first appearance in a blue jersey. In fact, it was the big Frenchman, looking a menace on his forays upfield, who came closest to claiming an opening win for the visitors, when his header from a Laudrup free-kick was well saved again by Gill. Obviously, at this stage, the result was not all-important and Walter Smith's men settled for a 1-1 draw.

Match two, though, saw the side slip in Germany to Kaiserslautern. A 1-0 defeat, admittedly even at this premature part of the term, was warning of the problems which would face them at European level. However, it was a useful exercise in terms of raising match fitness against an undeniably talented Bundesliga team.

Watching was their forthcoming European Cup foe, Dusan Bajevic, manager of AEK Athens. He left, however, claiming he had learned virtually nothing. *"I will have to watch Hateley and McCoist again, because they only played together for 15 minutes,"* he lamented. *"It was obvious that Rangers were not particularly serious. They, like us, are looking for physical preparation, rather than results at the moment."* Of course, McCoist's contribution to the matches would be non-existent anyway, due to injury.

The strike which decided proceedings came from German World Cup star Martin Wagner in 19 minutes. Two minutes later, the Germans thought they had added another when Kuka slipped the ball under Maxwell, but a linesman flagged for offside and the advantage remained at one. Incredibly, seven minutes later, the Scots also had a goal chalked off when Durrant was adjudged to have fouled Kaiserlautern's Roos when heading home McPherson's cross. Encouragingly, Rangers' fitness levels obviously improved as the 90 minutes progressed and they began to create more opportunities.

An Ian Ferguson header, a Laudrup shot into the side-netting and a Hateley header were the closest they came, but there were enough signs in the last half hour to suggest that the standard which would be required to reach the Champions League was attainable, if not within immediate reach.

By game three, the media back in Scotland were beginning to give the results closer scrutiny, and the third successive fixture without a win did not pass without comment in the press. The encounter with Danish league side Ikast was a definite step-up in terms of competitiveness, as Rangers were to find to their cost in a bruising 1-1 draw. Both Pieter Huistra and Dave McPherson picked up worrying knocks with the Ibrox International Tournament on the horizon. The Dutch winger suffered a broken nose after colliding with Ikast 'keeper Rindom after only 18 minutes, while four minutes from the end, McPherson had to leave the pitch with an eye gash which later required five stitches. Big Mac had been involved in a running feud all game with his marker, as had captain for the night, Stuart McCall. Indeed, the casualty list may have been even higher had an elbow from Danish defender Kent Hansen connected with Gordon Durie. The ex-Spurs man was understandably livid at the challenge, and remonstrated at length with the perpetrator, but the referee decided to let both players off with a warning, rather than resort to producing any cards.

Amongst all the rough stuff, there was at least one bright spot for the touring side, when Basile Boli notched his first goal for the club. A cross from the left from Trevor Steven was met on the head by the French international, who directed his glancing header low into the net. The cult figure obviously enjoyed his first strike for the Rangers side, and celebrated elaborately. That counter was a welcome equaliser after Billy Thomson, signed earlier that week and making his debut for the Light Blues, had slipped while going for a ball from Sorensen, allowing Ove Hansen to chest the cross and volley it into the net.

Two draws and a defeat were not the statistics Rangers would have looked for when they embarked on their tour, and although it had achieved its aim of getting

47

the players up to an acceptable sharpness, it really served as a useful warning that the side which had dominated Scottish football for the previous six seasons was nowhere near its peak form – something it would have to find for the vital double header with AEK Athens.

Aalborg 1   Rangers......1

1	Ally	Maxwell	11	Brian	Laudrup
2	Stuart	McCall		*Subs*	
3	David	Robertson			
4	Richard	Gough		Gary	Stevens
5	Dave	McPherson		Pieter	Huistra
6	John	Brown		Ally	McCoist
7	Trevor	Steven		Basile	Boli
8	Ian	Ferguson		Neil	Murray
9	Gordon	Durie		Neil	Inglis
10	Mark	Hateley		Ian	Durrant

Score Sheet

J. Madsen
14 min – 1-0

Mark Hateley
18 min – 1-1

Kaiserslautern ..1   Rangers......0

1	Ally	Maxwell	10	Ian	Durrant
2	Dave	McPherson	11	Gordon	Durie
3	David	Robertson		*Subs*	
4	Richard	Gough			
5	John	Brown		Gary	Stevens
6	Stuart	McCall		Steven	Pressley
7	Trevor	Steven		Basile	Boli
8	Ian	Ferguson		Billy	Thomson
9	Brian	Laudrup			

Score Sheet

M. Wagner
19 min – 1-0

Ikast 1   Rangers......1

1	Billy	Thomson	10	Ian	Durrant
2	Gary	Stevens	11	Pieter	Huistra
3	Neil	Murray		*Subs*	
4	Basile	Boli			
5	Dave	McPherson		Richard	Gough
6	Steven	Pressley		David	Robertson
7	Brian	Laudrup		Mark	Hateley
8	Stuart	McCall		Ally	Maxwell
9	Gordon	Durie		Ian	Ferguson

Score Sheet

O. Hansen
65 min – 1-0

Basile Boli
70 min – 1-1

Richard Gough

Rangers

Sampdoria

(2) 2

(1) 4

Friday 5th August 1994, Ibrox   Attendance: 27,282

RANGERS

1	Andy	GORAM
2	Stuart	McCALL
3	David	ROBERTSON
4	Richard	GOUGH
5	Dave	McPHERSON
6	John	BROWN
7	Trevor	STEVEN
8	Ian	FERGUSON
9	Ally	McCOIST
10	Mark	HATELEY
11	Brian	LAUDRUP

Subs

12	Basile	BOLI
13	Ian	DURRANT
14	Ally	MAXWELL
15	Gordon	DURIE
16	Neil	MURRAY

SAMPDORIA

1	Walter	ZENGA
2	Michele	SERENA
3	Marco	ROSSI
4	David	PLATT
5	Pietro	VIERCHOWOD
6	Sinisa	MIHAILOVIC
7	Attilio	LOMBARDO
8	Vladimir	JUGOVIC
9	Alessandro	MELLI
10	Mauro	BERTARELLI
11	Riccardo	MASPERO

12	Giulio	NUCIAIRI
13	Stefano	SACCHETTI
14	Fausto	SALSANO
15	Giovanni	INVERNIZZI
16	Maurizio	SALA

Match Facts

• Rangers sported their new third-choice, lilac *'European'* kit... for the only time against European opposition, because of the subsequent Champions Cup exit to AEK Athens.

Score Sheet

M. HATELEY 4 min – 1-0

T. STEVEN 31 min – 2-0

M. BERTARELLI 36 min – 2-1

V. JUGOVIC 57 min – 2-2

A. MELLI 65 min – 2-3

M. BERTARELLI 90 min pen – 2-4

Referee:
Mr. J. McCluskey (Stewarton)

Ibrox International Tournament – Match 1

A Game Of Two Halves

An unfamiliar-looking Rangers took to the pitch wearing their new lilac strip for the first time, then proceeded to turn in a 90 minutes which was in a similarly unfamiliar Jekyll and Hyde style. For a side looking for a confidence-boosting display in the immediate run-up to their Champions Cup tie with AEK Athens, it was not the ideal result, but Walter Smith's men did enough early on to suggest the fluency they were seeking was not too far away. More worryingly, though, there was frailty in defence which they would be able to ill-afford when the real stuff got under way. Perplexingly, it all had started so promisingly, and for those fans who chose to attend and the others who opted to watch the match on satellite TV in the pubs of Glasgow, there was a near perfect start when Brian Laudrup fed Ally McCoist who, in turn, provided a cut-back for Mark Hateley to sidefoot past Walter Zenga after a mere four minutes. A second could and should have been added in a comical move when Laudrup hit a post, had a follow-up effort blocked by the former Italian international goalkeeper, then Hateley proceeded to miskick entirely just a couple of yards in front of goal. However, Rangers did confirm their ascendancy with a second on 31 minutes, and Laudrup was again the provider. His ball from the left took a deflection off Rossi and fell ideally for Trevor Steven to chest it down and double their advantage. At this point, thoughts of European Cup glory must have been filtering into the minds of even the most pessimistic Teddy Bear, so in control did Rangers look over one of the best outfits on the continent.

Those thoughts would have been entertained for only six minutes, though, as the Genoa side set about putting matters right. A Melli header off the woodwork had posted warning of their intentions, before Bertarelli was given acres of space to fire past Andy Goram.

That goal seemed to rattle Rangers, and the second 45 minutes saw only their opponents playing with any great purpose. The equaliser arrived when Jugovic dragged the ball past Ian Ferguson and fired a breathtaking drive beyond Goram on 57 minutes. Rangers' embarrassment was complete eight minutes later when their 2-0 lead became a 3-2 deficit as Platt pierced their defence with a through ball for Melli to stroke home.

The fourth and final nail in the Ibrox coffin came in the last minute from the penalty spot, after McPherson had fouled Platt. Bertarelli converted for his second of the night, and to complete a scoreline which had scarcely seemed possible an hour previously. The booing which echoed round Ibrox was hardly a fitting reward for an Italian side which had entertained all present with some exhibition football, but a sharp reminder to Rangers that expectation at the club had reached unprecedented levels and capitulations like what had just been witnessed simply would not be tolerated.

In the second match of the evening both Newcastle and Manchester United fielded weakened sides, but managed to serve up a watchable spectacle. In a 1-1 draw, Eric Cantona levelled a Darren Peacock opener, before the Geordies clinched a final berth when Swiss World Cup star Marc Hottiger's penalty put the lid on a 6-5 shoot-out win.

Rangers (1) 1
Manchester United (0) 0

Saturday 6th August 1994, Ibrox | Attendance: 30,186

RANGERS

1	Ally	MAXWELL
2	Gary	STEVENS
3	Neil	MURRAY
4	Basile	BOLI
5	Steven	PRESSLEY
6	Craig	MOORE
7	Ian	DURRANT
8	Gordon	DURIE (†73)
9	Ally	McCOIST (*86)
10	Duncan	FERGUSON
11	Pieter	HUISTRA

Subs

12	Richard	GOUGH
13	Brian	REID
14	Billy	THOMSON
15	Kevin	FOTHERINGHAM (*86)
16	David	HAGEN (†73)

MANCHESTER UNITED

1	Peter	SCHMEICHEL
2	Chris	CASPER
3	Lee	SHARPE
4	Nicky	BUTT
5	David	MAY
6	Gary	PALLISTER
7	David	BECKHAM (*46)
8	Paul	INCE
9	Dion	DUBLIN (†46)
10	Mark	HUGHES
11	Simon	DAVIES

12	Steve	BRUCE
13	Keith	GILLESPIE
14	Brian	McCLAIR
15	Eric	CANTONA (*46)
16	Ryan	GIGGS (†46)

Match Facts

• A first appearance on first-team duty for youngster Kevin Fotheringham.

• Eric Cantona received his fourth red card in a year.

Score Sheet

D. MAY 42 min O.G. – 1-0

Referee:
Mr. A. Waddell (Edinburgh)

Ibrox International Tournament – Match 2

Rangers' May Day As Cantona Sees Red

A match which should rightfully have been billed as the *Battle of Britain* proved nothing of the sort, as both Walter Smith and Alex Ferguson opted to put out sides far-removed from their strongest starting XI's. However, United's cavalier Frenchman Eric Cantona came on in the second half and decided to conduct his own private battle against Steven Pressley, which ultimately saw him dismissed for the fourth time in a year. Disappointingly, that flashpoint proved the major talking point in what was undeniably a low-key affair.

From a positive viewpoint, Rangers finally recorded their first win of the season, at the fifth time of asking, when David May put through his own net in 42 minutes. An own goal was hardly the way Walter Smith would have liked to get off the mark, and most of the personnel involved were unlikely to feature in Athens, but it was still an important result. The thought of Rangers travelling to Greece without having recorded a solitary victory in their warm-up games was not an encouraging one. The goal which decided the fixture seemed to ideally suit the lacklustre pace the game was played at. It was definitely not in the classic category. Gordon Durie showed a welcome turn of pace on the right flank and delivered a cross which seemed destined for Duncan Ferguson – or at least that's what United's recent signing from Blackburn, May, thought. So preoccupied was the newcomer with Big Dunc, that he somehow managed to divert the ball past Schmeichel when attempting to clear for a corner.

In an equally dull second half, Rangers almost added to their tally when Hagen supplied McCoist, and Super Ally, the only Ranger to start both games in the tournament, fired a shot against the post.

Such was the lack of real commitment from both sides, Cantona's ability to get himself worked up enough to be sent off came as a real surprise. After a brush with Pressley nine minutes from time, he picked up a yellow card after trying to shake hands with the young Ranger as referee Waddell waited to lecture him. That looked an injustice, but there could be no condoning his actions a minute later when Pressley was the target of a vicious two-footed tackle, which he luckily managed to skip over. The intent was clear, however, and Cantona had to go. It was a nasty incident, and soured even more the relationship between the two British champions. All afternoon, United had been subject of great hostility from the Ibrox crowd, but this contretemps brought matters to a head. United manager Ferguson subsequently criticised the Light Blues fans, describing their actions as '*stupid*' and '*pointless*' then fanned the flames even more by refusing to condemn his wayward French striker. *"When he feels an injustice has been allowed to pass, he tries to correct it,"* offered Fergie by way of explanation. It didn't wash.

Not surprisingly, the final became almost of secondary importance after Cantona's indiscretion, but, for the record, Newcastle also discovered the folly of scoring first against Sampdoria. Andy Cole fired them into an eighth minute lead, but two strikes from Attilio Lombardo and another penalty from Bertarelli emphasised the standard the Geordies would have to reach in the UEFA Cup, if they wanted to make a real impression.

AEK Athens
Rangers

(1) 2
(0) 0

Wednesday 10th August 1994, Nikos Goumas Stadium.   Att: 30,000.

AEK ATHENS

1	Eliae	ATMATSIDIS
2	Emmanouel	PAPADOPOULOS
3	Christos	KASSAPIS
4	Stylianos	MANOLAS
5	Refik	SABNANTZOVIC
6	Michail	VLACHOS
7	Dimitrios	SARAVAKOS
8	Toni	SAVEVSKI
9	*Timour*	*KETSBAIA (*9)*
10	Vassilios	TSARTAS
11	Christos	KOSTIS

Subs

Vassilios	*DIMITRIADIS (*9) (+84)*
Georgias	*AGOROGIANNIS (+84)*
Vaios	KARAGIANNIS
Vassilios	BORBOKIS
Vassilios	KARAGIANNIS

RANGERS

1	Andy	GORAM
2	Gary	STEVENS
3	David	ROBERTSON – *Booked*
4	Richard	GOUGH
5	Steven	PRESSLEY – *Booked*
6	Stuart	McCALL
7	Brian	LAUDRUP
8	Ian	FERGUSON
9	*Gordon*	*DURIE (*77)*
10	Mark	HATELEY – *Booked*
11	Neil	MURRAY

12	John	BROWN
13	Ally	MAXWELL *(gk)*
14	*Ian*	*DURRANT (*77)*
15	Dave	McPHERSON
16	Ally	McCOIST

Match Facts

- AEK had never previously faced Scottish opposition in Europe, but had crossed swords with Liverpool, Derby County, Nottingham Forest and QPR.
- Brian Laudrup made his Rangers debut, while Gordon Durie played his first European match with the club.

Score Sheet

D. SARAVAKOS 45 min – 1-0

D. SARAVAKOS 70 min – 2-0

Referee:
Mr. P. Mikkelsen (Denmark)

European Cup, Preliminary Round – First Leg

Greek Tragedy

In an unprecedented move, Rangers kicked off their competitive season with a European fixture – and one which was to prove one of the most important of the campaign. A poor performance and disastrous result left Walter Smith's men with a monumental uphill task if they were to qualify for the financially rewarding Champions League. Certainly, Rangers' lack of match action was a contributory factor in their loss, but that took nothing away from an AEK side who had been unfairly underrated by virtually everybody in Scotland, on account of their national side's dismal efforts in the World Cup Finals.

In a highly charged and intimidating atmosphere, the visitors were overrun – and their fans almost overpowered, as fire-crackers were launched into their area by the volatile home contingent. Calm was what required as things went completely against Rangers, and it was heartening for the Light Blues that possibly the most nerveless man afield appeared to be Andy Goram, who kept his men in the match for long spells of a one-sided first half. Dimitrios Saravakos (twice), Vassilios Tsartas and Christos Kostis were all denied by the rejuvenated 'keeper, but he was powerless four minutes into injury time when Saravakos finally got the goal he had threatened for 49 minutes, firing home through a wall of players and beating Goram all ends up.

The second half simply continued in the same vein as the first, with Walter Smith's new-look defensive formation of Stevens, Richard Gough and Steven Pressley appearing particularly uncomfortable. How Smith must have wished the suspended Basile Boli was available. Goal two, when it came, was no great surprise, and the scorer again was the tricky winger Saravakos. He converted at the second attempt, after originally beating Gough to the ball, then watching the heroic Goram beat out his first attempt.

Such was the Greeks' superiority, two or three more goals could have been added, while Rangers had just one effort which could even modestly be described as a half-chance. Even then, Gordon Durie and Brian Laudrup delayed far too long when in the clear, and a last-gasp tackle prevented any real danger for Athens goalie Eliae Atmatsidis.

The frustrations so obviously felt by the Scottish champions became particularly evident as potentially damaging bookings were picked up by Pressley, Mark Hateley and David Robertson. And, at the final whistle, relief more than anything else was the emotion on display, as the team survived a missile attack which scraped past sub Ian Durrant – and an even heavier defeat which would have killed off their European aspirations in one, torrid evening. Captain Richard Gough summed up the mood when he commented on the on-field proceedings, *"We know we were a little fortunate to escape having lost only 2-0, so I look upon the result as a moral victory."*

	Home	Away	Total
European attendances	–	30,000	30,000

Rangers
Motherwell

(1) 2
(1) 1

Match Two

Saturday 13th August 1994, Ibrox   Attendance: 43,750

RANGERS

1	Andy	GORAM
2	Neil	MURRAY
3	David	ROBERTSON
4	Richard	GOUGH – *Booked*
5	Basile	BOLI
6	Dave	McPHERSON
7	Ian	DURRANT
8	Stuart	McCALL – *Booked*
9	*Ally*	*MCCOIST (*30)*
10	Mark	HATELEY
11	Brian	LAUDRUP

Subs

12	Steven	PRESSLEY
13	Ally	MAXWELL (gk)
14	*Duncan*	*FERGUSON (*30)*

MOTHERWELL

1	Stephen	WOODS
2	Rab	SHANNON–*Booked/Off*
3	Rob	McKINNON
4	John	PHILLIBEN – *Booked*
5	Brian	MARTIN
6	Chris	McCART
7	Paul	LAMBERT – *Booked*
8	Billy	DAVIES
9	Tommy	COYNE
10	Phil	O'DONNELL
11	Steve	KIRK – *Booked*

12	Paul	McGRILLEN
13	Ray	ALLAN (gk)
14	Alex	BURNS

Match Facts

• Duncan Ferguson took just one game to match his 1993-94 League tally of one goal.

Score Sheet

M. Hateley 44 min – 1-0
T. Coyne 47 min pen – 1-1
D. Ferguson 86 min – 2-1

Referee:
Mr. A. Waddell (Edinburgh)

Bell's Premier Division

		P	W	D	L	W	D	L	F	A	Pts
1	Hibernian	1	1	0	0	0	0	0	5	0	3
2	Aberdeen	1	1	0	0	0	0	0	2	0	3
3	Partick Thistle	1	1	0	0	0	0	0	2	0	3
4	**RANGERS**	**1**	**1**	**0**	**0**	**0**	**0**	**0**	**2**	**1**	**3**
5	Celtic	1	0	0	0	0	1	0	1	1	1

All's Well That Ends Well

Rangers kicked off their defence of the Premier Division title with a welcome, if not entirely convincing, defeat of the side who pushed them closest for most of the campaign before, Motherwell. The Steelmen were under new management, with Alex McLeish in charge after his move from Aberdeen, but it was the Light Blue new boys, Brian Laudrup and Basile Boli, who were the real focus of attention. Both had played in the pre-season tournament, but were making competitive home debuts in this match. Indeed, the Dane turned in a display which swept away a lot of the gloom which had followed the debacle in Athens.

Proceedings got under way with the familiar presentation of the League Championship flag, but it was the action on the pitch the fans were more interested in, and they were not to be disappointed. Unfortunately for the Ibrox support, much of the play was going in the wrong direction initially, and it took three marvellous saves from the back-in-favour Andy Goram to keep the scoreline level. Then, with a minute to go before the interval, the goal the 43,750 crowd had been baying for finally arrived, from a familiar source. The head of Mark Hateley has proved its worth time and time again, and it was his trademark ballistic effort, from a dazzling Laudrup cross from the right, which got Walter Smith's men up and running for the season. Disastrously, the lead was to last only two minutes of the second half. World Cup striker Tommy Coyne, a man known only too well to Rangers from his time with Old Firm rivals Celtic, converted a penalty after captain Richard Gough had been penalised for climbing on Brian Martin. In an open game, both sides had chances after this, and it looked as if it might be heading for stalemate, before Great Dane Laudrup took control. In a quite sensational run from the halfway line, he brushed past three Motherwell defenders, before forging an open path for Duncan Ferguson to accurately place his shot in goalkeeper Woods' far corner for what proved the winner. Three points were at stake for the first time in Scottish league encounters, and they were safely tucked away – but not without a cost.

Ally McCoist, blighted by injury problems in 1993-94, lasted only 30 minutes of the new season when yet another knock took its toll. A badly strained calf muscle increased the star striker's frustration following a pre-season in which he'd finally attained the sharpness which had evaded him the campaign before. Indeed it was a bruising match, for the Super Ally injury aside, there were no less than six yellow cards, and the second Ibrox dismissal in a week, after Cantona's red card in the International Tournament. 'Well's Rab Shannon, booked early on for a foul on Laudrup, was sent packing after 38 minutes for a dangerous aerial challenge on the other new boy, Boli. The new FIFA rules and regulations obviously contributed to the high crime count, but a competitive encounter was the ideal reminder that the Scottish season was going to be a very different kettle of fish from the silky World Cup of the summer. It also served notice to the rest of the Scottish Premier that Rangers, even without injured stars like Trevor Steven and Gordon Durie, were the team to beat yet again.

	Home	Away	Total
Attendances	43,750	–	43,750

Arbroath
Rangers

(1) 1
(3) 6

Match Three

Wednesday 17th August 1994, Gayfield Attendance: 4,665

ARBROATH

1	Derek	JACKSON
2	Brian	MITCHELL
3	James	RAE – *Booked*
4	Craig	FARNAN
5	Stuart	ELDER
6	Malcolm	MURRAY
7	*Ian*	*DOWNIE (†82)*
8	Colin	McKINNON
9	*John*	*REILLY (*59)*
10	Steven	TOSH
11	Justin	McGOVERN

Subs

12	*John*	*BROCK (*59)*
13	Robert	DUNCAN *(gk)*
14	*Steve*	*FINLAY (†82)*

RANGERS

1	Ally	MAXWELL
2	Stuart	McCALL
3	John	BROWN
4	Richard	GOUGH
5	Basile	BOLI
6	Dave	McPHERSON
7	Craig	MOORE
8	Ian	FERGUSON
9	Duncan	FERGUSON
10	Mark	HATELEY
11	*Ian*	*DURRANT (*73)*

12	Steven	PRESSLEY
13	Billy	THOMSON *(gk)*
14	*Neil*	*MURRAY (*73)*

Match Facts

- Rangers scored six for the first time since beating Alloa 6-0 in the 1993-94 Scottish Cup.

- Duncan Ferguson scored his first ever senior hat-trick.

Score Sheet

M. HATELEY 1 min – 0-1
D. FERGUSON 19 min – 0-2
C. McKINNON 20 min – 1-2
S. McCALL 42 min – 1-3
M. HATELEY 55 min – 1-4
D. FERGUSON 74 min – 1-5
D. FERGUSON 84 min – 1-6

Referee:
Mr. S. Dougal (Burnside)

Coca-Cola Cup Second Round

Hateley Marks Up A Ton

From Athens to Arbroath in seven days possibly wasn't the most exciting of prospects for the Light Blue legions, but they saw a match which was significant for two reasons. Both Mark Hateley and Duncan Ferguson reached personal milestones in an otherwise run of the mill fixture, which was perhaps best demonstrated by the fact that manager Walter Smith chose to miss the game. The boss preferred, instead, to run the rule over potential signing target Marc Rieper, who was featuring for Denmark in a 2-1 international win over Finland in the Parken stadium in Copenhagen. In fact, an absent 'Ger in Angus, Brian Laudrup, scored the Danes' first goal. Rangers were not expected to have any trouble against Arbroath, and so it proved. From the very start they were on the attack, and it took them a mere 44 seconds to open their account. Mark Hateley scored his 99th goal for the club with a typically strong header from a perfect Ian Durrant cross. It was a personal triumph for £4 million man Duncan Ferguson. After matching his previous season's tally on Saturday with his solitary strike against Motherwell, big Fergie made it two for 1994-95 with a super solo effort. He held off Jim Rae and Craig Farnan before beating 'keeper Derek Jackson with a splendid flicked shot. Rangers received a shock immediately they'd gone two up – the home side pulled one back. Yet again, for back-up 'keeper Ally Maxwell, after a few errors during the season before, it was a counter which did not paint him in the best light. He flapped at a speculative cross, with captain Richard Gough seemingly in his way, and as his defenders dithered with their attempts to clear, Colin McKinnon raced in to convert. Basile Boli started wandering up the pitch menacingly, while young Aussie Craig Moore looked the part in an unfamiliar midfield role and Ian Durrant was sprightly in a wide right berth. The third, when it came, was no surprise. A Duncan Ferguson knockdown from a Durrant cross found its way to Stuart McCall, who comfortably scored with his head. That goal dispelled any lingering thoughts there may have been of a possible shock, and Rangers were very much in the control in the second half, although Arbroath did come close on two occasions. Maxwell was equal to the task, however, as he denied Tosh twice, the second time pushing a great effort on to the bar. The milestone strike for Hateley came on 55 minutes, with yet another powerful header from an accurate Craig Moore cross. It marked a century of goals from Big Mark in his four seasons with Rangers, a ratio of 25 per campaign.

All that was left for Duncan Ferguson to ensure it was his name which dominated the daily papers' headlines the next morning. His second goal was a beautiful left-foot drive following a pinpoint McCall ball, then he completed his first ever senior hat-trick with a storming close-header, from yet another Moore cross. All in, it was a satisfying night's work from a strong, if not full strength, outfit and a memorable one for the strike pairing of Hateley and Ferguson, who posted notice they could perhaps form an effective pairing in the correct circumstances.

	Home	Away	Total
Coca-Cola attendances	–	4,665	4,665

Partick Thistle
Rangers

(0) 0
(1) 2

Saturday 20th August, 1994, Firhill — Attendance: 15,030

PARTICK THISTLE

1	Craig	NELSON
2	David	BYRNE – *Booked*
3	Bobby	LAW – *Booked*
4	Willie	JAMIESON
5	Grant	TIERNEY
6	Derek	McWILLIAMS
7	Alex	TAYLOR
8	*Albert*	*CRAIG (†76) – Booked*
9	Roddy	GRANT – *Booked*
10	*Isaac*	*ENGLISH (*78)*
11	Chic	CHARNLEY

Subs

12	Ian	CAMERON (*78)
13	Kevin	BUDINAUCKAS (gk)
14	*Tom*	*SMITH (†76)*

RANGERS

1	Andy	GORAM
2	Stuart	McCALL
3	John	BROWN
4	Richard	GOUGH
5	Basile	BOLI – *Booked*
6	Dave	McPHERSON
7	Craig	MOORE
8	Ian	FERGUSON
9	Duncan	FERGUSON
10	Mark	HATELEY
11	Brian	LAUDRUP

12	Ian	DURRANT
13	Ally	MAXWELL (gk)
14	Gordon	DURIE

Match Facts

- Mark Hateley scored his fourth goal of the season, every one a header!

- David Byrne's own goal was the first for Rangers since Alloa's Willie Newbigging put through his own net in the Scottish Cup fourth round tie at Ibrox on February 1994.

Score Sheet

D. BYRNE 8 min og – 0-1
M. HATELEY 77 min – 0-2

Referee:
Mr. B. Tait (East Kilbride)

Bell's Premier Division

		P	W	D	L	W	D	L	F	A	Pts
1	**RANGERS**	2	1	0	0	1	0	0	4	1	6
2	Hibernian	2	1	1	0	0	0	0	5	0	4
3	Aberdeen	2	1	1	0	0	0	0	5	3	4
4	Celtic	2	1	0	0	0	1	0	3	2	4
5	Partick Thistle	2	1	0	1	0	0	0	2	2	3

Byrne Blow For Thistle

Rangers became the only side to start the League season with two straight victories as they were given a helping hand at their city neighbours. David Byrne was sinner for Thistle, putting through his own net after only eight minutes, setting Rangers up for a confidence-boosting win prior to their European engagement in midweek.

If it wasn't the most comfortable of wins, it was still a deserved one. Thistle, for all their huffing and puffing, didn't really do enough to merit a point despite manager John Lambie's view afterwards that, *"We knocked them up so many times, it was untrue."* The performance was typical of many Rangers had produced in their previous six championship campaigns – purposeful and efficient, without ever having to push themselves to superhuman efforts to pick up the points. One man, though, who seemed ready to go to war, if necessary, was the ever-combatant Basile Boli, who was yellow-carded after a tackle which almost dissected Thistle striker Roddy Grant. Grant went into the book for retaliation, and other bookings were collected by the unfortunate Byrne for dissent, Bobby Law, also for dissent, and Albert Craig for tripping Brian Laudrup.

The goal which settled the visitors' nerves was a strange one. Ian Ferguson would have claimed the *'Fantasy League'* assist with his cross from a Craig Moore throw-in, but it was indisputably Englishman Byrne's as the ball spun off his thigh and beyond despairing 'keeper Craig Nelson. Despite Rangers' overall control, the closest the first half saw to another goal was when Chic Charnley set up Alex Taylor from a corner, and the ex-Dundee United man hit Goram's crossbar with a thunderous shot. Walter Smith's men were, despite all their hard work, somewhat awkward, with Mark Hateley holding court in the centre up front, Duncan Ferguson periodically charging in from the left and Brian Laudrup, yet again the most creative player, producing occasional flashes on the right, despite more subdued form compared to his opening day supershow.

Nevertheless, the grafting nature of the Light Blues' game conjured up a second, clinching strike 13 minutes from time. Mark Hateley got his bid for a second century of goals under way with an unstoppable header from a magical Laudrup cross. Thistle, to their credit, kept plugging away and were denied the consolation goal their fans would probably have claimed they were worth when, right on the full-time whistle, Goram managed to keep out an effort from Grant with his legs.

Not surprisingly, the victory pleased manager Walter Smith, who had watched his men toil at Firhill in recent seasons. And he found particular satisfaction in the display of one of his summer signings, Dane Brian Laudrup – and suggested there was more to come from the exciting Scandinavian.

"It is difficult to involve Brian as much as we would want, but he showed his worth again," enthused Smith.

	Home	Away	Total
Attendances	43,750	15,030	58,780

Rangers
AEK Athens

(0) 0
(1) 1

Wednesday 24th August 1994, Ibrox   Attendance: 44,789

RANGERS

1	Andy	GORAM
2	Stuart	McCALL
3	David	ROBERTSON
4	Richard	GOUGH
5	Basile	BOLI – *Booked*
6	David	McPHERSON
7	*Gordon*	DURIE (*63)
8	Ian	FERGUSON – *Booked*
9	Duncan	FERGUSON
10	Mark	HATELEY
11	Brian	LAUDRUP

Subs

12	*Ian*	*DURRANT (*63)*
13	Ally	MAXWELL
14	Steven	PRESSLEY
15	Neil	MURRAY
16	David	HAGEN

AEK ATHENS

1	Eliae	ATMATSIDIS
2	Georgias	AGOROGIANNIS
3	Emmanouel	PAPADOPOULOS
4	Stylianos	MANOLAS
5	Refik	SABANANTZOVIC
6	Michail	VLACHOS – *Booked*
7	Dimitrios	SARAVAKOS – *Booked*
8	*Toni*	*SAVEVSKI (*75)*
9	Christos	KOSTIS
10	Vassilios	TSARTAS (†86)
11	Christos	KASSAPIS

12	Vaios	KARAGIANNIS
13	*Harilaos*	*KOPITSIS (†86)*
14	*Stavros*	*STAMATIS (*75)*
15	Vassilios	KARAGIANNIS
16	Nicolaos	MIRTZEUN

Match Facts

- Rangers' loss denied them around six million pounds worth of Champions League earnings.

- It was the eighth time in European competition, since 1956, that Rangers had exited at the first hurdle.

- The last time Rangers failed to score, either home or away, in a Euro first round tie was against Real Madrid in 1963, when they fell 1-0 at Ibrox, then slumped 6-0 in Spain.

Score Sheet

T. SAVEVSKI 43 min – 0-1

Referee:
Mr. Leif Sundell (Sweden)

European Cup Preliminary Round, Second Leg

Gers Doner For

The pre-match hype had suggested that Rangers were on the verge of their greatest ever European comeback, overturning a two goal deficit for the first time in their history. Sadly for the expectant spectators, it all proved wildly inaccurate as Walter Smith's side produced a thoroughly disappointing performance, which saw them deservedly knocked out of the continent's most lucrative competition before it had even begun in earnest.

Confidence was high as the match kicked off, but it didn't take long for the supporters to fully appreciate the size of the task facing their heroes. Quite simply, AEK yet again proved they were a quality side. They caused no end of problems for the Light Blues, particularly down their left-hand side, where Basile Boli had been chosen to operate in an unfamiliar right-back role. The Frenchman appeared comfortable going forward, but unable to cope with the pacy Greeks' lightning breaks upfield. Indeed, most of the visitors' attacks in the opening 45 minutes came through alarming gaps in the channel Boli was meant to be protecting. However, it would be unfair to single him out for special mention as regards the end of the Euro dream. Brian Laudrup failed to get over a telling cross all night, while Mark Hateley and Duncan Ferguson as often as not got in each other's way, rather than provide the fearsome aerial presence the Greek manager, Serbian Dusan Bajevic, had worried about.

Indeed, the only Ger to show his true form was Andy Goram, and in a disappointing opening period, how it was required. Toni Savevski was denied by the Scotland international, while Christos Kostis three times looked set to score, before fate conspired against him. The inevitable could not be delayed though, and when a poor David Robertson clearance found Kostis, he picked out Vassilios Tsartas, whose cross was eased past Goram by Savevski. An away goal, and that was that.

A sign of Rangers' frustration had been the first-half bookings for Basile Boli and Ian Ferguson, for fouling Saveski and Dimitrios Saravakos respectively. Things got no better after the interval, as the realisation that the job in hand was a million miles beyond Rangers sunk in. Athens had numerous chances to add to their tally – the Light Blues a solitary opening to get off the mark. Even then, Mark Hateley, when through, found the ball on his less-favoured right foot and shot tamely into the side netting. Boli also forced a save out of Eliae Atmatsidis, but the fact his token effort warranted mention was proof enough of the bluntness of Rangers' attack.

Afterwards, a philosophical Walter Smith was succinct in his appraisal of his outfit's failings. *"I'm disappointed, but we didn't do enough in terms of creating chances and we can have no great complaints. AEK were the better team and deserved to win over the two legs. It ended up all very predictable for us up front and their defence handled it well."*

	Home	Away	Total
Attendances	44,789	30,000	74,789

Rangers
Celtic

(0) 0
(1) 2

Saturday 27th August 1994, Ibrox   Attendance: 45,466

RANGERS

1	Andy	GORAM
2	Stuart	McCALL
3	Steven	PRESSLEY
4	Richard	GOUGH
5	Basile	BOLI
6	Dave	McPHERSON
7	*Ian*	*DURRANT (*77)*
8	Ian	FERGUSON – *Booked*
9	Gordon	DURIE
10	Mark	HATELEY
11	Brian	LAUDRUP

Subs

12	*Duncan*	*FERGUSON (*77)*
13	Ally	MAXWELl (gk)
14	Craig	MOORE

CELTIC

1	Gordon	MARSHALL
2	Peter	GRANT
3	Tommy	BOYD
4	Mark	McNALLY
5	Tony	MOWBRAY – *Booked*
6	*Pat*	*McGINLAY (*87)*
7	Mike	GALLOWAY – *Booked*
8	Paul	McSTAY
9	*Simon*	*DONNELLY (†84)*
10	Andy	WALKER
11	John	COLLINS

12	*Charlie*	*NICHOLAS (†84)*
13	Gordon	MARSHALL (gk)
14	*Brian*	*O'NEIL (*87)*

Match Facts

• Celtic wore numbers on their backs for the first time in the season, following a Scottish League directive.

• The result stretched Celtic's unbeaten run on League business at Ibrox to three matches, the Light Blues' last win coming on January 2nd, 1993.

Score Sheet

J. COLLINS 45 min – 0-1

P. McSTAY 47 min – 0-2

Referee:
Mr. H. Williamson (Renfrew)

Bell's Premier Division

		P	W	D	L	W	D	L	F	A	Pts
1	Hibernian	3	1	1	0	1	0	0	6	0	7
2	Celtic	3	1	0	0	1	1	0	5	2	7
3	**RANGERS**	**3**	**1**	**0**	**1**	**1**	**0**	**0**	**4**	**3**	**6**
4	Falkirk	3	1	1	0	0	1	0	5	4	5
5	Aberdeen	3	1	1	0	0	0	1	6	5	4

Derby Disaster

The end of a dismal week for Rangers was capped by a woeful performance in the opening Old Firm game of the season. Paper talk of a crisis at Rangers seemed premature, but there was no denying that the cracks which had first appeared at the tail end of 1993-94 had not been papered over with the purchase of Boli and Laudrup. Perhaps testimony to the extent of the shambles was the defensive set-up, which saw centre-halves Steven Pressley and Dave McPherson operating at left-back and right-back respectively. From the very start the rearguard struggled, and Rangers could have been one down in only eight minutes when a Paul McStay shot was blocked and Pat McGinlay saw his re-bound effort well saved by Goram. Yet again, the Scotland number one was in inspired form, and he denied a resurgent McStay with a splendid push over the bar from an 18-yard effort. After Ian Ferguson had diverted an Andy Walker flick on to his own bar, however, the writing really did seem on the wall, and the inevitable happened just one minute before Rangers could reach the sanctuary of the half-time dressing room, when John Collins, for the second successive time at Ibrox, scored an exquisite left-foot free-kick. A mere two minutes after the break, the contest was over. McStay finally did what he'd looked likely to for most of the first half, and fired a fierce 25-yard strike, from a Grant pass, in off the post. There could have been more goals. McStay, totally dominating a Rangers midfield for the first time in an Old Firm game for years, hit the post again, although this time the ball landed safely, rather than in the net for what would have been a humiliating third counter. In contrast, the home side's closest brush with the scoresheet came when Ian Ferguson saw his header deflected over Gordon Marshall's crossbar by Mike Galloway. For Boli and Laudrup, making their Old Firm debuts, it was a traumatic experience. The Frenchman, back in the centre of defence after his unhappy experience against AEK Athens in the previous match, was unable to form a workable partnership with Richard Gough, while the Dane, so promising during pre-season, failed to deliver on an occasion when it really mattered. Indeed, his crossing was by and large wayward.

For a support reared on such relentless success, a second home defeat in four days was extremely unpalatable and there were more than one or two dissenting voices towards chairman David Murray and manager Walter Smith from the Main Stand at the final whistle. More worrying than the result, though, was the unavoidable fact that Rangers had been outplayed by their most bitter rivals.

Conceded Smith, *"Our standard of possession is not good enough. We have not created enough chances to warrant winning."*

On a more pleasing note, while the team was in disrepair, the ground remained intact. Celtic fans, banned for the previous Old Firm derby at Ibrox for vandalism, damaged only six seats.

	Home	Away	Total
Attendances	89,216	15,030	104,246

Rangers
Falkirk

(0) 1
(1) 2

Wednesday 31st August 1994, Ibrox   Attendance: 40,697

RANGERS

1	Andy	GORAM
2	Stuart	McCALL
3	David	ROBERTSON
4	Richard	GOUGH
5	*Dave*	*McPHERSON (*81)*
6	Craig	MOORE – *Booked*
7	Ian	DURRANT
8	Ian	FERGUSON – *Booked*
9	Gordon	DURIE
10	Mark	HATELEY
11	Brian	LAUDRUP

Subs

12	*Duncan*	*FERGUSON (*81)*
13	Ally	MAXWELL (gk)
14	Steven	PRESSLEY

FALKIRK

1	Tony	PARKS
2	David	WEIR
3	Jamie	McGOWAN – *Booked*
4	Neil	OLIVER
5	Joe	McLAUGHLIN – *Booked*
6	Scott	McKENZIE
7	Eddie	MAY
8	Steve	FULTON – *Booked*
9	Richard	CADETTE
10	*Nicky*	*HENDERSON (*67) – Bkd*
11	Colin	McDONALD – *Booked*

12	*Colin*	*CRAMB (*67) – Booked*
13	Billy	LAMONT (gk)
14	John	McSTAY

Match Facts

• This was Falkirk's first win at Ibrox since 1927!

• Brian Laudrup scored his first-ever competitive goal for Rangers.

• The last time Rangers lost three games in a row at home was in August-September 1971.

Score Sheet

R. CADETTE 28 min – 0-1

B. LAUDRUP 64 min – 1-1

R. CADETTE 76 min – 1-2

Referee:
Mr. J. Timmons (Kilwinning)

Coca-Cola Cup Third Round

An Unwanted Treble Whammy

After crashing out of Europe, there had been defiant noises from Ibrox over achieving the Treble to make up for that crushing disappointment. This third home defeat in a week put paid to those hopes too, and sparked off a string of *'Rangers in Crisis'* stories in the tabloid press.

A breathtaking point-blank save from Tony Parks from sub Duncan Ferguson in the closing stages of this match more or less summed up Rangers' night. A string of chances were squandered, although Falkirk could also lay claim to being unduly wasteful in front of goal. More importantly, they defended stoutly in the face of a tremendous Light Blue onslaught in the second half, with Brian Laudrup's form, so mysteriously erratic, back in majestic full flight again. Nevertheless, despite the improved creative display, the defence again failed to inspire any confidence whatsoever. The signs were there from the word go. In just the third minute, Goram saved spectacularly from Colin McDonald and the tone was set. The Bairns were prepared to attack at any opportunity, and Eddie May could have opened the scoring before Richard Cadette actually did in 28 minutes. The goal was a disaster for Dave McPherson. He lost possession in the middle of his own half and had to watch as McDonald glided into the box and provided a perfect cross for Cadette to impressively side-foot the ball in. As Rangers visibly got more edgy, Jim Jefferies' men had chances to add to their lead, most particularly when Goram again foiled Eddie May. There were gilt-edged chances for the home side too, though, but the panic from the crowd was beginning to filter through to the players and both Hateley and Durie wasted openings they would have tucked away under normal circumstances.

After Rangers had survived a late scare in the first half, when a McDonald strike was ruled offside, they resumed with more purpose. The opportunities started to come thick and fast, and it was no surprise when the siege finally resulted in a goal that came from Brian Laudrup. The Dane had shown some mesmerising skills, and finally got the effort he deserved when he played a neat one-two with Ian Durrant and fired a shot which took a slight deflection and nestled beyond Parks. If that seemed the cue for Rangers to perform a salvage mission, Falkirk obviously had not read the script. Twelve minutes later, they were back in the lead!

Ex-Celtic man Steve Fulton threaded a beautiful ball through for Cadette to run on to and the little striker finished splendidly to send the visiting support into euphoria. Panic set in again, and Cadette could have completed a hat-trick, before that frantic finish which saw Duncan Ferguson almost retrieve things.

After the match, a dejected Walter Smith identified accurately where the team's major problem was. *"Right now, there's not a lot that encourages me. When you're going through a spell like this, you're always likely to give goals away."* It was a famous victory for Falkirk, but yet another night Rangers fans would want to forget.

	Home	Away	Total
Coca-Cola attendances	40,697	4,665	45,362

Rangers
Hearts

(0) 3
(0) 0

Sunday 11th September 1994, Ibrox   Attendance: 41,041

RANGERS

1	Andy	GORAM
2	Stuart	McCALL
3	David	ROBERTSON
4	Richard	GOUGH
5	Dave	McPHERSON (*46)
6	Craig	MOORE
7	Neil	MURRAY
8	Ian	FERGUSON
9	Ian	DURRANT
10	Mark	HATELEY
11	Brian	LAUDRUP (†77)

Subs

12	Gordon	DURIE (*46)
13	Ally	MAXWELL (gk)
14	Duncan	FERGUSON (†77)

HEARTS

1	Henry	SMITH
2	Gary	LOCKE (* 79)
3	Tosh	McKINLAY – *Booked*
4	Craig	LEVEIN
5	Neil	BERRY
6	Alan	McLAREN
7	John	COLQUHOUN
8	Scott	LEITCH
9	Maurice	JOHNSTON
10	John	MILLAR
11	John	ROBERTSON (†79)

12	Allan	JOHNSTON (†79)
13	Gary	O'CONNOR (gk)
14	Graeme	HOGG (*79)

Match Facts

- Hogg's appearance as a sub for Hearts meant he and Levein appeared on the same side for the first time since being sent-off for fighting with each other in a pre-season friendly at Raith Rovers. • Mark Hateley's goals made him equal top scorer in the Premier League – in all competitions – with Richard Cadette of Falkirk.

Score Sheet

M. HATELEY 59 min pen – 1-0
M. HATELEY 71 min – 2-0
G. DURIE 76 min – 3-0

Referee:
Mr. J. McCluskey (Stewarton)

Bell's Premier Division

		P	W	D	L	W	D	L	F	A	Pts
1	Celtic	4	1	0	0	2	1	0	7	3	10
2	**RANGERS**	**4**	**2**	**0**	**1**	**1**	**0**	**0**	**7**	**3**	**9**
3	Hibernian	4	1	2	0	1	0	0	8	2	8
4	Falkirk	4	1	1	0	0	2	0	6	5	6
5	Aberdeen	4	1	1	0	0	1	1	8	7	5

The *'Crisis'* Is Quelled

Rangers may not have turned on their Sunday best, but they did enough to overcome a poor Hearts outfit and expel any lingering seeds of doubt which may have remained in the players' minds after the recent poor run. It was an important win, not merely for the team's confidence, but also in view of the fact that the game was beamed live to an ITV audience throughout Scotland. More failure would have resulted in inevitable criticism.

Inspiration behind what eventually emerged as a convincing three points was Brian Laudrup. The Dane produced a sensational display, which saw him create all three of the Light Blues goals. However, Basile Boli was absent because of an injury, after being welcomed back into the fold following his alleged outbursts against the club in the French press.

'*A game of two halves*' would not be an entirely accurate description of the first live television fixture of the season, but Rangers' level of performance was certainly two or three times improved after the interval, the wariness of the last handful of matches filtering away to be replaced by the swagger which the fans were so used to seeing. Before the break, Laudrup had set up a couple of opportunities, but these were frittering away by David Robertson and Neil Murray. In contrast, all Hearts had to offer was a John Colquhoun attempt to cash in on a short Richard Gough back-header. But he failed to better the ever-alert Andy Goram. If they needed encouragement, though, Rangers' nervousness was mirrored by the supporters, whose silence in the initial 45 minutes meant that the usual Fortress Ibrox was a bit less intimidating than normal.

There could be no denying the first goal settled Rangers, and after that it was all more or less plain sailing. A beautiful Laudrup piece of vision sent Mark Hateley clear, and Henry Smith's despairing tackle on the big English striker inside the penalty box was a clear spot-kick. Indeed, most in the stadium felt the veteran 'keeper deserved a red card for his sins, and were surprised when he was not even awarded a yellow. There were no complaints, though, when Mark dusted himself down to convert a pressure-breaking opener. Twelve minutes later, the relief was even more tangible when Laudrup and McCall combined and the winger sent in a cross which Hateley managed to turn into the net – despite the attentions of John Millar – with the sole of his boot. Another five minutes on, the three points were signed, sealed and delivered as Laudrup supplied Robertson and his cross, while missed by a hat-trick seeking Hateley, was gleefully sent goalwards by substitute Gordon Durie, who had appeared after half-time for the injured Dave McPherson.

After the match, two-goal hero Hateley admitted that it was a welcome result, which had come at exactly the right time. *"It feels like a ton weight has been lifted off us. We got back to the traditional Rangers way, creating lots of chances. Long may it continue!"* Few would have argued with that!

	Home	Away	Total
Attendances	130,257	15,030	145,287

Falkirk
Rangers

(0) 0
(1) 2

BELL'S

Match Nine

Saturday 17th September 1994, Brockville

Attendance: 12,500

FALKIRK

1	Billy	LAMONT
2	David	WEIR – *Sent Off*
3	*Neil*	*OLIVER* (*37)
4	John	CLARK
5	Joe	McLAUGHLIN
6	Scott	McKENZIE
7	Eddie	MAY
8	Steve	FULTON – *Sent Off*
9	Richard	CADETTE – *Booked*
10	Brian	RICE
11	*Colin*	*McDONALD* (†75)

Subs

12	*Jamie*	*McGOWAN* (*37)
13		TRIALISt (gk)
14	*Frank*	*McAVENNIE* (†75)

RANGERS

1	Andy	GORAM
2	Stuart	McCALL – *Booked*
3	David	ROBERTSON
4	Richard	GOUGH – *Booked*
5	Craig	MOORE – *Booked*
6	Basile	BOLI
7	Gordon	DURIE
8	Ian	FERGUSON – *Booked*
9	Ian	DURRANT
10	Mark	HATELEY
11	Brian	LAUDRUP – *Booked*

12	Duncan	FERGUSON
13	Ally	MAXWELL (gk)
14	Gary	STEVENS

Match Facts

• Falkirk had two players sent off in a game for the second Saturday in a row, after Tony Parks and Colin Cramb saw red against Killie the week before.

• Brian Laudrup scored his second goal in Scottish football – the other was against the Bairns too!

Score Sheet

B. BOLI 7 min – 0-1

B. LAUDRUP 80 min – 0-2

Referee:
Mr. M. Pocock (Aberdeen)

Bell's Premier Division

		P	W	D	L	W	D	L	F	A	Pts
1	**RANGERS**	5	2	0	1	2	0	0	9	3	12
2	Celtic	5	1	1	0	2	1	0	8	4	11
3	Hibernian	5	1	2	0	1	0	9	3	9
4	Aberdeen	5	1	2	0	0	1	1	9	8	6
5	Motherwell	5	0	2	0	1	1	1	5	5	6

Basile Is Back With A Bang

Rangers returned to the top of the Premier Division in a match in which Basile Boli, making his first appearance since the controversy over his alleged comments in French football magazines, instantly appeased the fans. The extrovert defender set Rangers up for a comfortable win with his first competitive goal for the club after only seven minutes, and while Walter Smith's men were hardly on easy street after that, there never seemed any doubt as to the eventual destination of the points.

Falkirk gave a decent account of themselves in the first half, but by the end were a mere shadow of the outfit which had caused such a sensation at Ibrox in the Coca-Cola Cup only a couple of weeks previously. Indeed, they finished in some disarray, with David Weir sent off for a professional foul on Gordon Durie, then Steve Fulton red-carded for taking his own form of retribution on the Rangers attacker. Defender Neil Oliver ended up in hospital with a serious jaw injury, too, on an afternoon when everything which could go wrong for the Bairns did.

To suggest that the result was only down to the home side's misfortunes, though, would be doing them a disservice. Rangers turned in one of their Chris Eubank-style performances, where they did enough to win, without ever operating on full throttle. The first goal was a tribute to Boli's perseverance and commitment. His charge into the penalty box was like that of a raging bull, and he seemed to go through Falkirk debutant John Clark, rather than round him, before dispatching a low shot past 'keeper Billy Lamont, deputising for the suspended Tony Parks.

Oliver's injury came in 31 minutes, just after he had directed a well-placed header towards Andy Goram's top corner, which the 'keeper did well to save. Rangers raced upfield and Mark Hateley fired in a low shot at the 'keeper, which he parried. As the ball rebounded out, Ian Ferguson and Oliver collided, and it was worst luck for the English stopper that he was on end of a fairly coarse challenge which ended his interest in the match. The visitors came close to adding a second when the soon-to-be-dismissed David Weir flicked a Durie cross against his own post in 53 minutes. The goal which dispelled any final doubts as to the outcome came from the free-kick Weir conceded when committing the foul that earned his sending-off in 80 minutes. 'Keeper Lamont seemed slightly unsighted as Laudrup flighted in a super free-kick which confirmed the three points.

Afterwards, Boli, who had received a healthy reception on his return, was understandably full of the joys again after his apparent displeasure over his move when back in France. *"It has been a very difficult spell for me, and it hasn't been easy settling in beside Richard Gough,"* he admitted. *"The goal pleased me no end, and I was delighted how the fans reacted to it, and me, afterwards."* Walter Smith was understandably a more relaxed man after his recent problems, and enthused, *"Richard and Basile can now go on and become a great partnership for Rangers."*

After all the talk of crisis, Rangers were back on top of the Premier Division – and without hitting anything close to their best form!

	Home	Away	Total
Attendances	130,257	27,530	157,787

Aberdeen **(1) 2**
Rangers **(1) 2**

Saturday 24th September 1994, Pittodrie   Attendance: 21,000

ABERDEEN

1	Michael	WATT
2	Stewart	McKIMMIE – *Booked*
3	Colin	WOODTHORPE
4	Brian	GRANT
5	Brian	IRVINE
6	Stephen	WRIGHT
7	Eoin	JESS
8	Gary	SMITH – *Bkd/Sent Off*
9	Scott	BOOTH – *Booked*
10	*Billy*	*DODDS (*86)*
11	*Ray*	*McKINNON (†77)*

Subs

12	*Peter*	*HETHERSTON (†77)*
13	Derek	STILLIE (gk)
14	*Joe*	*MILLER (*86)*

RANGERS

1	Andy	GORAM
2	Craig	MOORE
3	David	ROBERTSON – *Booked*
4	Richard	GOUGH
5	Dave	McPHERSON
6	Basile	BOLI – *Booked*
7	Neil	MURRAY – *Booked*
8	*Stuart*	*McCALL (*84)*
9	Gordon	DURIE – *Booked*
10	Mark	HATELEY
11	Brian	LAUDRUP

12	*Ian*	*DURRANT (*84)*
13	Ally	MAXWELL (gk)
14	Ally	McCOIST

Match Facts

- Craig Moore scored his first-ever goal for the club.

- Gary Smith became the fourth player sent-off against Rangers in the season, following Rab Shannon's red-card in the opening league game against Motherwell and Falkirk's David Weir and Steve Fulton the week before.

Score Sheet

S. BOOTH 13 min – 1-0
M. HATELEY 42 min – 1-1
C. MOORE 71 min – 1-2
B. DODDS 81 min pen – 2-2

Referee:
Mr. L. Mottram (Forth)

Bell's Premier Division

		P	W	D	L	W	D	L	F	A	Pts
1	Celtic	6	2	1	0	2	1	0	10	4	14
2	**RANGERS**	6	2	0	1	2	1	0	11	5	13
3	Hibernian	6	1	2	0	1	1	1	9	5	9
4	Aberdeen	6	1	3	0	0	1	1	11	10	7
5	Motherwell	6	0	2	0	1	2	1	7	7	7

Uproar In The Granite City

A day of incredible controversy in Aberdeen saw Rangers lose their position at the summit of the Premier Division, as they let a 10-man Dons come back from 2-1 down to snatch a late equaliser from the spot. It was a hotly disputed penalty, but hardly the only moment of contention in a game provocatively refereed by Scotland's World Cup official, Les Mottram. There were seven bookings and a second yellow card, and hence dismissal, for Aberdeen's Gary Smith as card-happy Mottram officiated in a fashion which enraged both the home side and the visitors. Both teams certainly had reason to be annoyed.

However, apart from the plethora of bookings, the real trouble started when the Forth man awarded an indirect free-kick to Rangers deep in the penalty box right on time, when Michael Watt picked up the ball from what appeared a passback. The Granite City men were incensed, claiming Gordon Durie had had the last touch. Within seconds, Rangers were the team feeling aggrieved as, after a deflected Brian Laudrup shot, the ball headed goalwards, only for Mottram to unbelievably insist that he had blown for time up in the seconds between the free-kick being awarded, and the scramble which followed. The furore continued long into the tunnel, with Gordon Durie sufficiently raising the ref's ire to be reported to the SFA and earn a technical sending-off. Events boiled over afterwards as Mark Hateley was involved in an incident with an Aberdeen supporter in the car park after the game. There had been no hint of the controversy which was to ensue when Scott Booth gave Aberdeen the lead after just 15 minutes. This was to be yet another afternoon, though, when Brian Laudrup was to stamp his authority on proceedings, and it was the Danish wing king who inspired the Light Blues comeback. He tied Smith in knots on the left after some neat work from Stuart McCall and Neil Murray, before planting a cross right onto the forehead of Hateley. It was the sort of chance the *'Hammer of the Dons'* just does not miss – and he didn't. That goal seemed to affect the Reds' confidence somewhat, and when Smith received his red card, following a foolish elbowed challenge on Durie after earlier being booked for fouling Laudrup, only one winner seemed a possibility. When Aussie Craig Moore brilliantly side-footed home following some more wonderful Laudrup skill on the left which befuddled Brian Irvine, those thoughts appeared confirmed. With nine minutes to go, however, the hand of Mottram took control again. Firstly Aberdeen were awarded a free-kick in mysterious circumstances, as Stuart McCall had appeared to win the ball cleanly from Eoin Jess. From that free-kick, Moore was adjudged to have fouled Irvine, and Mottram pointed to the spot.

In an absolutely electric Pittodrie atmosphere, Billy Dodds kept his cool to convert the golden opportunity, and save two points, which ensured the Dons did not fall a huge nine behind Rangers at this early stage of the season.

A contemplative Walter Smith said afterwards, "When the opposition is down to ten men, it's amazing how often they rally."

	Home	Away	Total
Attendances		48,530	178,787

Rangers
Dundee United

(1) 2
(0) 0

Saturday 1st October 1994, Ibrox   Attendance: 43,030

RANGERS

1	Andy	GORAM
2	Craig	MOORE
3	David	ROBERTSON
4	Richard	GOUGH
5	Dave	McPHERSON
6	Basile	BOLI
7	Stuart	McCALL
8	Charlie	MILLER (*69)
9	Alexei	MIKHAILITCHENKO (†69)
10	Mark	HATELEY
11	Brian	LAUDRUP

Subs

12	Neil	MURRAY (†69)
13	Ally	MAXWELL (gk)
14	Ally	McCOIST (*69)

DUNDEE UNITED

1	Alan	MAIN (*30)
2	Gary	BOLLAN – Booked
3	Maurice	MALPAS
4	Jim	McINALLY
5	Gordan	PETRIC
6	Brian	WELSH
7	Dave	BOWMAN (†65)
8	Billy	McKINLAY – Booked
9	Andy	McLAREN (**57)
10	Craig	BREWSTER
11	Christian	DAILLY

12	Jerren	NIXON (**57)
13	Henrik	JORGENSEN (gk) (*30)
14	Grant	JOHNSON (†65)

Match Facts

- Charlie Miller and Alexei Mikhailitchenko made their first starts of the season.

Score Sheet

M. HATELEY 25 min. – 1-0

B. LAUDRUP 87 min – 2-0

Referee:
Mr. J. McGilvray (Edinburgh)

Bell's Premier Division

		P	W	D	L	W	D	L	F	A	Pts
1	**RANGERS**	7	3	0	1	2	1	0	13	5	16
2	Celtic	7	2	1	0	2	2	0	11	5	15
3	Hibernian	7	2	2	0	1	1	1	12	5	12
4	Falkirk	7	2	1	1	0	2	2	8	9	9
5	Motherwell	7	0	3	0	1	2	1	8	8	8

Laudrup's Late Clincher

Rangers met up with Dundee United for the first time since their disappointing 1-0 defeat in the previous season's Scottish Cup Final, which had denied them a record-breaking double Treble. Heavily favoured to overturn that loss, particularly in view of the fact United had been playing a European tie in Slovakia just two days before, Walter Smith's men proceeded to back up the bookies' confidence with a performance which was more than enough for the visitors.

Yet, it was an odd game, for despite the obvious superiority of the Light Blues, they only managed to sew the three points up three minutes from the end when Brian Laudrup crashed a super shot high into the net after leaving Gordan Petric for dead. Between that, and their opening goal in 25 minutes, they had to endure Jerren Nixon smashing a shot off the crossbar and Craig Brewster finding the stands when the goal seemed an easier target.

The side had taken the lead with a goal which owed itself to youth AND experience. Charlie Miller, an 18-year-old from Castlemilk, making his first appearance of the season, was the provider and Mark Hateley the chief executioner. It was a strike which baffled Brian Welsh and Gary Bollan, who ended up on their backsides after a piece of Hateley wizardry.

It was also a goal which did no favours for United 'keeper Alan Main either. He had twisted an ankle stopping a shot from Stuart McCall early on and within five minutes of conceding the opener, Ivan Golac considered him not fit enough to continue and replaced him with sub Henrik Jorgensen.

Bollan's nightmare continued when, in 56 minutes, he conceded a penalty which was earned by flying Dane Brian Laudrup. A late challenge brought him down, and the scene seemed set for big Mark to score his second. However, Jorgensen guessed correctly, dived to his right and saved the effort. Bollan, who had been booked earlier, appeared lucky not to get a second booking and a red card.

After spurning a string of chances, and watching United twice come close, it was no surprise that the home fans got slightly restless. Laudrup's strike put an end to their anxieties.

As well as a welcome three points, there were sightings again of two old favourites for the Ibrox faithful. Alexei Mikhailitchenko, whose last game had been against United in the Scottish Cup Final, finally returned after injury, while Ally McCoist, missing since the opening League game of the season, also put in an appearance as a sub for the last 21 minutes.

Walter Smith summed up the afternoon perfectly when he commented, *"We created enough chances to win a few games, but contrived to miss them and that let United in. We were a bit jittery after that – but we thoroughly deserved to win."*

	Home	Away	Total
Attendances	173,287	48,530	221,817

Hibernian
Rangers

(0) 2
(1) 1

Saturday 8th October 1994, Easter Road   Attendance: 12,118

HIBERNIAN

1	Jim	LEIGHTON
2	Willie	MILLER
3	Graeme	LOVE
4	*David*	FARRELL *(*60)*
5	Steven	TWEED
6	Gordon	HUNTER
7	Kevin	HARPER
8	Brian	HAMILTON
9	Gareth	EVANS
10	*Darren*	JACKSON *(†46)*
11	Michael	O'NEILL

Subs

12	*Mickey*	WEIR *(*60)*
13	Jason	GARDINER (gk)
14	*Mark*	McGRAW *(†46)*

RANGERS

1	Andy	GORAM
2	Craig	MOORE – *Booked*
3	David	ROBERTSON
4	*Richard*	GOUGH *(*29)*
5	*Dave*	McPHERSON *(†46)*
6	Basile	BOLI – *Booked/Sent Off*
7	Stuart	McCALL
8	Pieter	HUISTRA
9	Charlie	MILLER
10	Mark	HATELEY
11	Brian	LAUDRUP

12	*Neil*	MURRAY *(*29)*
13	Colin	SCOTT (gk)
14	*Ally*	McCOIST *(†46)*

Match Facts

• Hateley moved back into defence for only the second time, after operating there once before, at Kilmarnock at the end of 93-94.

• Basile Boli became the first Rangers player sent-off in the League season and since Ian Ferguson, against Dundee United, on December 11th, 1993.

Score Sheet

B. BOLI 10 min – 0-1

G. HUNTER 46 min – 1-1

K. HARPER 81 min – 2-1

Referee:
Mr. S. Roy (Aberdeen)

Bell's Premier Division

		P	W	D	L	W	D	L	F	A	Pts
1	**RANGERS**	**8**	**3**	**0**	**1**	**2**	**1**	**1**	**14**	**7**	**16**
2	Celtic	8	2	2	0	2	2	0	11	5	16
3	Hibernian	8	3	2	0	1	1	1	14	6	15
4	Motherwell	8	1	3	0	1	2	1	13	11	11
5	Hearts	8	2	0	1	1	1	3	9	11	10

Caught Short In Defence

Rangers lost three defenders and, subsequently, three points, in a torrid match at Easter Road. However, while Richard Gough and Dave McPherson's problems were not of their own making – injury ending their match prematurely – Basile Boli foolishly got himself sent off for a second bookable offence five minutes from time.

Perhaps thankfully for the Frenchman, by that stage the damage had been done and the Light Blues were already trailing. Boli's red card ensured there would be no grandstand finish from Walter Smith's men and the usual late fightback which would normally have been expected in the circumstances never materialised.

Perversely, the afternoon had started happily for Basile. After only ten minutes he fired them into the lead, with a bullet header from Brian Laudrup's corner. And although Hibs looked sprightly too, Rangers, with Pieter Huistra making a first appearance of the campaign in preference to Alexei Mikhailitchenko – who was on international duty with Ukraine – and young Charlie Miller retaining his place, knocked the ball about well and were good value for their lead.

It was in 29 minutes that things started to go wrong. Richard Gough had been toiling from just about the off, and although the limping captain signalled he'd like to continue, commonsense won the day and Neil Murray came on for him. By half-time, the rearguard was reduced by one more, as McPherson failed to reappear on the resumption of the game after the interval.

As notable a contribution second sub Ally McCoist has made to the Ibrox cause over the years was, it was perfectly obvious to manager Smith that he was no replacement defender, so Mark Hateley was moved back with Super Ally taking his place up front alongside Miller.

Disappointingly, within a minute of the restart Big Mark demonstrated he still had a lot to learn about his new position when needlessly fouling Gareth Evans on the edge of the box. From Michael O'Neill's perfectly flighted free-kick, Gordon Hunter stole in at the back post to equalise.

The Hi-bees' young striker Kevin Harper began to make his mark on the game as his colleagues rose in confidence, and although Rangers created a couple of chances, it was Alex Miller's side who looked the more likely. And, indeed, Harper it was who headed the winner in 81 minutes from an O'Neill corner which Andy Goram – for once in his explosive season – looked less than comfortable at.

If Rangers had reason to curse Harper then, they were even less impressed four minutes later when he was upended by Boli, while darting forward, to give ref Sandy Roy no option but flash his red card. Craig Moore was Rangers' other booking for a foul on Evans.

Afterwards, Walter Smith reflected, *"It was a good start for us, but we lost our grip on the game. After playing so well in recent matches, it turned out to be a disappointing day."*

	Home	Away	Total
Attendances	173,287	60,648	233,935

Rangers **(0) 2**
Kilmarnock **(0) 0**

Saturday 15th October 1994, Ibrox · · · · · · · · · · Attendance: 44,099

RANGERS

1	Andy	GORAM
2	Craig	MOORE
3	David	ROBERTSON – *Booked*
4	Stuart	McCALL
5	Dave	McPHERSON
6	Steven	PRESSLEY – *Booked*
7	Neil	MURRAY
8	Pieter	HUISTRA
9	Charlie	MILLER
10	Mark	HATELEY
11	Brian	LAUDRUP

Subs

12	Lee	ROBERTSON
13	Colin	SCOTT (gk)
14	Scott	WILSON

KILMARNOCK

1	Bobby	GEDDES
2	Angus	MacPHERSON
3	Tom	BLACK
4	Robert	REILLY
5	Neil	WHITWORTH – *Booked*
6	Andy	MILLEN
7	Ally	MITCHELL
8	John	HENRY
9	*Bobby*	*WILLIAMSON (*81) Bkd*
10	Tom	BROWN
11	Shaun	McSKIMMING

12	*Colin*	*McKEE (*81)*
13	Colin	MELDRUM (gk)
14	James	LAUCHLAN

Match Facts

● Charlie Miller scored his first-ever goal for the first team.

● David Robertson collected his first of the campaign and his first since April 16, when he netted against Raith Rovers.

Score Sheet

C. MILLER 76 min – 1-0
D. ROBERTSON 87 min – 2-0

Referee:
Mr. G. Clyde (Bearsden)

Bell's Premier Division

		P	W	D	L	W	D	L	F	A	Pts
1	**RANGERS**	9	4	0	1	2	1	1	16	7	19
2	Hibernian	9	3	2	0	1	2	1	14	6	16
3	Celtic	9	2	2	0	2	2	1	11	6	16
4	Motherwell	9	1	3	0	2	2	1	16	12	14
5	Hearts	9	3	0	1	1	1	3	10	11	13

Charlie Says How's That?

With as many star names missing as actually made it on to the pitch, Rangers still proved too good for a spirited, but limited, Kilmarnock side. However, the collection of another three priceless points was, in the main, forgettable, and only Charlie Miller will look back at this game with any great fondness, as he notched his first first-team goal.

With Gough, Boli, McCoist, Mikhailitchenko and Steven all absent, Walter Smith fielded very much an under-strength side, with Steven Pressley, out of favour since submitting a transfer request, recalled and Pieter Huistra given another chance following his first start of the campaign at Hibs the previous week.

The story of the 90 minutes was of few chances created, and many of the openings which did arrive were by default rather than design. Dave McPherson's miskick in the first half, which left Tom Brown with a splendid opportunity, was typical. Thankfully for the Light Blues, the little striker's shot was blocked by Big Mac, making up for his error.

Killie did have the ball in the net four minutes after the restart, when Shaun McSkimming fired past Goram, but referee Clyde had spotted a handball by Bobby Williamson in setting up the chance and disallowed the effort, much to the Scotland 'keeper's relief. The former Rangers striker was booked for his misdemeanour, to be joined by Pressley for a foul on Brown, Robertson for a foul on Mitchell and Killie's Whitworth after a shocker on Brian Laudrup.

That scrape should have prompted Rangers to step up the pace, but it took them another 27 minutes to finally break the deadlock, just as their Ayrshire visitors seemed to be heading towards a point. A cross from Stuart McCall predictably found the head of Mark Hateley, and his header flew across to young Miller, who demonstrated his finishing ability with a cool strike.

The second goal, just three minutes from time, was a real case of deja vu from the opening league game of the season against Alex McLeish's Motherwell. Brian Laudrup got things moving on the right and started a diagonal run across the pitch, brushing past defenders seemingly at will. He delivered a perfect ball for the on-rushing David Robertson, and his clinching shot was just as impressive as Duncan Ferguson's had been on that initial Saturday of the campaign.

There was no doubt Kilmarnock had reason to feel a little hard done by, possibly not to pick up a point and certainly at the scoreline, which suggested a more emphatic win than it had actually been. As Alex Totten lamented afterwards, *"We deserved to take something, as every player did his bit."*

Stuart McCall, unsurprisingly, saw things slightly differently, and hailed hero Miller as a star of the future. *"The goal is important because it will do his confidence the world of good, thought that's one thing he doesn't lack. We reckon he could take over from Coisty on and off the pitch!"*

	Home	Away	Total
Attendances	17,386	60,648	278,034

Motherwell
Rangers

(1) 2
(0) 1

Match 14

MOTHERWELL

1	Stephen	WOODS
2	Rab	SHANNON
3	Rob	McKINNON
4	John	PHILLIBEN
5	Brian	MARTIN
6	Chris	McCART
7	Paul	LAMBERT
8	Jamie	DOLAN – *Booked*
9	Tommy	COYNE – *Booked*
10	Dougie	ARNOTT
11	*Billy*	*DAVIES (*87) – Booked*

Subs

12	*Andy*	*RODDIE (*87)*
13	Scott	HOWIE (gk)
14	Steve	KIRK

RANGERS

1	Andy	GORAM
2	Craig	MOORE – *Sent Off*
3	David	ROBERTSON – *Booked*
4	Stuart	McCALL
5	Dave	McPHERSON
6	Basile	BOLI – *Booked*
7	*Neil*	*MURRAY (*76)*
8	Pieter	HUISTRA
9	Charlie	MILLER
10	Mark	HATELEY
11	Brian	LAUDRUP

12	Fraser	WISHART
13	Colin	SCOTT (gk)
14	*David*	*HAGEN (*76)*

Match Facts

- David Hagen's first appearance of the season.

- John Philliben scored an own goal against Rangers for the third time.

- Dougie Arnott scored a brace against Rangers for the third time, after two in a 3-0 win in 1991 and both in a 2-1 victory at Ibrox in 1993-94.

Score Sheet

D. ARNOTT 12 min – 1-0

D. ARNOTT 50 min – 2-0

J. PHILLIBEN 82 min og – 2-1

Referee:
Mr. J. O'Hare (Glenboig)

Bell's Premier Division

		P	W	D	L	W	D	L	F	A	Pts
1	**RANGERS**	10	4	0	1	2	1	2	17	9	19
2	Hibernian	10	3	2	0	1	3	1	14	6	18
3	Motherwell	10	2	3	0	2	2	1	18	13	17
4	Celtic	10	2	2	1	2	2	1	11	8	16
5	Hearts	10	4	0	1	1	1	3	12	11	16

Gers Arnott Looking Good

The warning signs Motherwell had posted in the opening league fixture of the season at Ibrox were not heeded, as Rangers slumped to a disappointing defeat. Although it was a severely understrength team manager Smith fielded, the Steelmen were worth their victory for a display of attacking football which stretched the Gers' reargard.

For a second consecutive away game, following Basile Boli's red card at Falkirk, Rangers found themselves reduced to ten men, when Craig Moore was ordered off for what referee O'Hare deemed a professional foul on Dougie Arnott. However, while the 2-1 defeat at Brockville could not be directly attributed to Boli's dismissal, the Aussie defender's sending-off had more of an impact on this game, coming after only 36 minutes.

Even by then, though, the Light Blues had fallen one behind, to the first of two strikes from Arnott, in the 12th minute. A measured pass from Jamie Dolan found Tommy Coyne, and his cross- cum-pass deceived Boli and Dave McPherson, for the little striker to fire comfortably past Andy Goram.

It was Arnott who was central to Moore's early departure as well. Again it was Coyne who was involved, with a head-flick which sent the Motherwell front man clear. As he bore down on goal, Moore clearly tripped him, and as the Glenboig official considered the youngster the last defender, an early bath was inevitable. Indeed, Moore appeared to accept his fate as soon as he'd made his fateful tackle.

Five minutes after the break, Arnott looked to have put the game beyond Rangers when he added a second. Lambert and Davies combined well from a corner, and when the former sent in a fine cross, the little striker glanced his header in.

It was only really after this that Rangers began to pose a threat, and they looked to have given themselves a chance of saving the game eight minutes from time when Brian Laudrup, who had been their most potent force going forward, made a dash down the right and fired in a cross which was deflected past Stephen Woods by John Philliben.

That was on 82 minutes, but it came too late for Rangers to retrieve even a point from a match in which there was very little they could reflect positively on. Basile Boli was given a torrid time by Arnott, while it was Dave McPherson – the defender Smith had tried to offload to Hearts two days earlier – who had been their most steady performer at the back.

As well as Moore's sending-off, referee O'Hare saw fit to book five others, although Coyne, Davies and Boli earned their yellow cards for nothing were than dissent. Dolan, for persistent fouling, and Robertson, for a foul on the troublesome Arnott, were the other offenders.

A philosophical Walter Smith said afterwards, *"I'm disappointed we lost. The injury situation is drastic, but whatever we have lacked this season, it isn't spirit."*

	Home	Away	Total
Attendances	217,386	71,808	289,194

Celtic
Rangers

(1) 1
(2) 3

Sunday 30th October 1994, Hampden   Attendance: 32,171

CELTIC

1	Gordon	MARSHALL
2	*Barry*	*SMITH (*46)*
3	Tom	BOYD
4	Mark	McNALLY
5	Brian	O'NEIL
6	Phil	O'DONNELL
7	*Paul*	*BYRNE (†60)*
8	Paul	McSTAY
9	Simon	DONNELLY
10	Andy	WALKER
11	John	COLLINS

Subs

12	*Charlie*	*NICHOLAS (†60)*
13	Pat	BONNER (gk)
14	*Willie*	*FALCONER (*46)*

RANGERS

1	Andy	GORAM
2	Fraser	WISHART
3	David	ROBERTSON – *Booked*
4	Stuart	McCALL
5	Alan	McLAREN – *Booked*
6	Basile	BOLI
7	Pieter	HUISTRA
8	Neil	MURRAY
9	*Charlie*	*MILLER (*86)*
10	Mark	HATELEY – *Booked*
11	*Brian*	*LAUDRUP (†88)*

12	*David*	*HAGEN (*86)*
13	Colin	SCOTT (gk)
14	*Ally*	*McCOIST (†88)*

Match Facts

• Rangers created a little piece of history. In the two Old Firm matches previously played on an October 30, Celtic had won them both!

• Brian Laudrup was presented with the Bell's Premier Player of the Month trophy prior to kick-off – from Celtic boss Tommy Burns.

Score Sheet

M. HATELEY 25 min – 0-1
P. BYRNE 39 min – 1-1
M. HATELEY 42 min – 1-2
B. LAUDRUP 65 min – 1-3

Referee:
Mr. W. Crombie (Edinburgh)

Bell's Premier Division

		P	W	D	L	W	D	L	F	A	Pts
1	**RANGERS**	11	4	0	1	3	1	2	20	10	22
2	Hibernian	11	4	2	0	1	3	1	16	7	20
3	Motherwell	11	3	3	0	2	2	1	21	15	20
4	Celtic	11	2	2	2	2	2	1	12	11	16
5	Falkirk	11	2	2	1	2	2	2	15	15	16

Gers Get Their Revenge

A performance undeniably Rangers' finest since the season started was more than enough to provide ample revenge for their 2-0 loss to Celtic at Ibrox in August. There were no failures in a patchwork Light Blue side for the 234th League meeting of football's oldest rivals, but Brian Laudrup stole the show with a stunning display of skill which confirmed that, when on song, there was no-one in Scottish football who could hold a candle to him. And yet, pre kick-off, even the most optimistic of the Bears could have been forgiven for approaching the fixture with trepidation. Tommy Burns' side had been buoyed by reaching their first final for four years in midweek with a Coca-Cola semi win over Aberdeen, while Rangers entered the match with a makeshift defence, which included Fraser Wishart making a first start of the season, and debutant Alan McLaren facing a baptism of fire. From the first minute though, when Mark Hateley forced a goal-line clearance from Mark McNally, there was to be no doubting which side had the greater appetite for the task in hand. Rangers had a penalty claim refused when Smith fouled Hateley and chances went a-begging for big Mark again, and more particularly Neil Murray, who should have fired the visitors into the lead from an inch-perfect Laudrup cross, before they actually did make their mark in 25 minutes. Old Firm debutant, Charlie Miller dispossessed Tom Boyd and fed a lovely ball through the inside right channel, which Hateley latched on to and beat Gordon Marshall with a first-time effort. Despite Rangers' undoubted dominance, Celtic made a game of it, but it was still a surprise when they equalised 14 minutes later. There was an element of luck about the goal, as the live TV pictures seemed to confirm that Tom Boyd's cross was a complete miskick, but even the most churlish of Gers fans would have to concede that Paul Byrne placed his low left-foot shot very well into Andy Goram's right-hand corner. Rangers did not deserve to go in at the interval merely on level terms and the lead they were worth arrived three minute before the break, when David Robertson did excellently on the left to power in a cross which Hateley, who had nipped in ahead of Mark McNally, powered home.

The second half didn't really match the first in terms of quality, as Rangers – with McLaren making a glorious debut, defensive partner Basile Boli having his finest game for the club simply by concentrating on defending and Wishart impressive at right-back – looked watertight at the back. Celtic did have the ball in the net once, when Andy Walker converted at close-range from a corner, but referee Bill Crombie, who had a fine game, ruled that Willie Falconer had fouled Goram in setting up the opportunity. Whether it was a correct decision or not was irrelevant, as Laudrup was causing havoc on the flanks and looked capable of winning the game at will. His clinching goal had come minutes before and was a classic, as he raced on to a Hateley flick-on, beat Brian O'Neil for pace and rounded Marshall before making a difficult chance look easy by slotting home.

Walter Smith warned afterwards though, *"We haven't yet shown the consistency to go on and win the championship. We've lost too many games already."*

	Home	Away	Total
Attendances	217,386	103,979	321,365

Rangers
Partick Thistle

(0) 3
(0) 0

Saturday, November 5th 1994, Ibrox.

Att.: 43,696

RANGERS

1	Andy	GORAM
2	Fraser	WISHART (*42)
3	David	ROBERTSON
4	Stuart	McCALL
5	Alan	McLAREN
6	Basile	BOLI
7	Pieter	HUISTRA
8	Neil	MURRAY
9	Charlie	MILLER
10	Mark	HATELEY
11	Brian	LAUDRUP

Subs

12	Ian	DURRANT (*42)
13	Colin	SCOTT (gk)
14	Ally	McCOIST

PARTICK THISTLE

1	Craig	NELSON
2	Kevin	McKEE (79)
3	Steve	PITTMAN
4	Gregg	WATSON
5	Willie	JAMIESON
6	Alan	DINNIE
7	Rod	McDONALD (71)
8	Albert	CRAIG
9	Andy	GIBSON
10	Ian	CAMERON
11	Derek	McWILLIAMS

12	Isaac	ENGLISH (71)
13	Mark	CAIRNS (gk)
14	Chic	CHARNLEY (79)

Match Facts

- A home debut for Alan McLaren.

Score Sheet

B. LAUDRUP 49 min – 1-0
C. MILLER 59 min – 2-0
M. HATELEY 86 min – 3-0

Referee:
J. Rowbotham (Kirkcaldy)

Bell's Premier Division

		P	W	D	L	W	D	L	F	A	Pts
1	**RANGERS**	**12**	**5**	**0**	**1**	**3**	**1**	**2**	**23**	**10**	**25**
2	Motherwell	12	3	3	0	3	2	1	23	16	23
3	Hibernian	12	4	2	0	1	4	1	16	7	21
4	Falkirk	12	3	2	1	2	2	2	17	16	19
5	Celtic	12	2	2	2	2	3	1	14	13	17

More Fireworks From Laudrup

A damp squib of a first half from Rangers was followed by a sparkling second as rocket–assisted Brian Laudrup ensured the collection of another three points from struggling Thistle. A goal from him and others from Charlie Miller and Mark Hateley – his 11th of the season – were the counters that mattered in a lop-sided clash.

The opening period hinted at the supremacy Walter Smith's men would enjoy, without actually ever delivering it. Not for the first time in the campaign, the main danger to the opposition came from the right flank – but, for once, it was not Danish sensation Laudrup who provided it. Rejuvenated Fraser Wishart, buoyed by his unexpected call to arms for the previous week's Old Firm clash, continued his blistering form with some splendid surges up the flank. The former Motherwell, St Mirren and Falkirk man contributed three worthwhile efforts, which Thistle 'keeper Craig Nelson, a Scotland B cap, denied, before Wishart had the misfortune to pull a hamstring and was forced to depart after 42 minutes. The stop-gap received a great ovation from the stands, but that was overshadowed by the reception granted to the man who replaced him – returning loan Ranger Ian Durrant!

It was four minutes after the break when the home side finally made the breakthrough, albeit with a goal which owed a little to the slippery conditions. A super Miller pass sent Laudrup in the clear and as he bore down on Nelson, the 'keeper was unfortunate enough to lose his footing, presenting the number 11 with the easiest of chances. From a narrow angle, he converted most impressively.

The points were made safe after an hour, when Miller rammed home the clincher. Again Laudrup was involved, his pass releasing David Robertson, whose cross was headed out from Gregg Watson to find the young Castlemilk prospect 18 yards out and with enough room to fire in a deflected shot. Brian's second assist arrived a mere four minutes from the end, when Rangers got the third goal their domination deserved and put a more accurate reflection on the scoreline.

He utterly befuddled the Thistle defence on the bye–line, leaving them in knots before flighting over the sort of cross which Hateley just does not miss. He didn't!.

The Thistle fans could point to a couple of chances which might have seen their heroes make more of a show of things, most notably when Derek McWilliams headed over a Rod McDonald cross in 31 minutes, which, if more accurately placed, would have given them the lead. The Jags also had the opportunity to equalise when Andy Gibson found himself with the goal at his mercy at close range just after Rangers' opener, but the otherwise redundant Andy Goram did what he is paid to and blocked. After the match, talk centred around Ian Durrant, fresh from his traumatic experience at Everton, and whether he could use his Ibrox lifeline as a chance to kick start his career at the club he loves.

"My head was at Everton, but my heart will always be at Ibrox," confirmed Durranty. "The reception the fans gave me today will live with me for the rest of my life."

	Home	Away	Total
Attendances	261,082	103,979	365,061

Hearts
Rangers

Wednesday November 9th 1994, Tynecastle   Att: 12,347

.HEARTS			RANGERS		
1	Henry	SMITH	1	Andy	GORAM
2	Steve	FRAIL *Booked*	2	Craig	MOORE *Booked*
3	John	MILLAR	3	David	ROBERTSON *Booked*
4	Gary	MACKAY	4	Stuart	McCALL
5	Neil	BERRY	5	Alan	McLAREN
6	Dave	McPHERSON	6	Basile	BOLI
7	John	COLQUHOUN *Booked*	7	Pieter	HUISTRA *Booked*
8	Jim	BETT *Booked*	*8*	*Neil*	*MURRAY (70)*
9	John	ROBERTSON *Booked*	9	Ian	DURRANT
10	Scott	LEITCH	10	Mark	HATELEY
11	Allan	JOHNSTON	11	Brian	LAUDRUP
Subs					
12	George	WRIGHT *(unused)*	12	David	HAGEN
13	Gary	O'CONNOR (gk)	13	Colin	SCOTT
14	Kevin	THOMAS *(unused)*	*14*	*Ally*	*McCOIST (70)*

Match Facts

• Mark Hateley's penalty was, incredibly, his 11th goal in his last seven games against Hearts. • The Tynecastle side had Craig Levein and Graeme Hogg, sitting out because of suspension – the first fixtures of the ten-match ban they were handed by the SFA for fighting with each other in a friendly at Raith Rovers

Score Sheet

M. HATELEY pen. 49 – 0-1
J. COLQUHOUN 67 min – 1-1

Referee:
Mr. H. Dallas (Bonkle)

Bell's Premier Division

		P	W	D	L	W	D	L	F	A	Pts.
1	**RANGERS**	**13**	**5**	**0**	**1**	**3**	**2**	**2**	**24**	**11**	**26**
2	Motherwell	13	3	4	0	3	2	1	24	17	24
3	Hibernian	13	4	2	0	1	5	1	16	7	22
4	Falkirk	13	3	3	1	2	2	2	20	19	20
5	Celtic	13	2	3	2	2	3	1	14	13	18

Goram Saves The Day

A sensational save by Andy Goram from a John Robertson drive towards the end of a wet and windy 90 minutes in Edinburgh ensured Rangers made the journey back across the central belt with one point. It was the hardly their best performance of the season, and there could not have been too many complaints from the Ibrox camp if Hearts had just nicked a win. However. a draw was probably just about the fairest outcome.

The Wednesday fixture – brought forward from the weekend to allow national coach Craig Brown ample preparation for Scotland's European Championship clash with Russia – was a big night for new signing Alan McLaren, Only two weeks previously, he had still been a Hearts player, yet he returned to his old home and turned in a showing which suggested the million–pounds–plus Rangers shelled out to get his signature was money well spent. On the plus side for the Jam Tarts, their recruit from Walter Smith, Dave McPherson, also demonstrated he would be a value–for–money signing.

Indeed, it was Big Mac who caused one or two scares for the Light Blues in the opening 45 minutes. Yet another rejigged side, which saw Craig Moore and Ian Durrant reclaim starting berths at the expense of Fraser Wishart and Charlie Miller, saw a number of chances created against them.

McPherson fired in a header and a volley which went closer to the target than the Light Blue rearguard would have hoped. In contrast, Rangers' attacking limitations were exposed by the fact that their most threatening effort came via Jambo defender Neil Berry, who almost smashed the ball home for an own goal after a fierce Brian Laudrup cross.

However, despite their shortcomings, it was Rangers who seized the lead shortly after the interval. Steve Frail clearly pushed Mark Hateley as he attempted to meet a Laudrup cross, and referee Hugh Dallas from Bonkle, for once on a night when he made some inexplicable decisions, called it correct and pointed to the spot. Hateley himself took the penalty and gave veteran 'keeper Henry Smith little chance.

Frail redeemed himself after 67 minutes, when he was instrumental in bringing his men back into the game. From his wide–right role, he delivered a telling cross which Goram could only half–clear. John Robertson, as usual, was lurking about looking for any scraps, but in fact the ball found John Colquhoun, who sent a low shot into the corner of the net.

There were other chances after that, the majority from the home men, but it was Robertson's late effort which came closest to deciding the winner. From close-range, his drive looked netbound, until Goram miraculously scrambled it around the post. Robbo was left shaking his head in disbelief!

With nearest rivals Motherwell and Hibs failing to pick up wins in their midweek fixtures, the two dropped points were in no way disastrous. Manager Smith summed things up afterwards, when he commented. "Nothing lost – nothing gained." Typically, though, he added, "I'm disappointed we let Hearts back into the game."

	Home	Away	Total
League Attendances	261,082	116,326	377,408

Rangers **(1) 1**
Falkirk **(0) 1**

Saturday, November 19th 1994, Ibrox   Att: 44,018

RANGERS

1	Andy	GORAM
2	Craig	MOORE *Booked*
3	David	ROBERTSON
4	Stuart	McCALL
5	Alan	McLAREN
6	Basile	BOLI
7	Pieter	HUISTRA *Booked*
8	Charlie	MILLER (*75)
9	Ally	McCOIST
10	Mark	HATELEY
11	Brian	LAUDRUP

Subs

12	Ian	DURRANT (*75)
13	Colin	SCOTT (gk)
14	Gordon	DURIE

FALKIRK

1	John	BURRIDGE
2	David	WEIR
3	Jamie	McGOWAN
4	Neil	OLIVER
5	Joe	McLAUGHLIN
6	Scott	MacKENZIE
7	Eddie	MAY *Booked*
8	John	CLARK
9	Steve	FULTON
10	Nicky	HENDERSON
11	Colin	McDONALD

12	Brian	RICE
GK	Willie	LAMONT
14	Colin	CRAMB

Match Facts

• Henderson's goal at Ibrox was the first conceded in 429 minutes at Ibrox – since Richard Cadette notched Falkirk's second in their Coca-Cola Cup win back in August!

Score Sheet

M. HATELEY 7 min – 1-0
N. HENDERSON 55 min – 1-1

Referee:

Mr. Thow (Prestwick)

Bell's Premier Division

		P	W	D	L	W	D	L	F	A	Pts
1	**RANGERS**	14	5	1	1	3	2	2	25	12	27
2	Motherwell	14	3	4	0	3	3	1	26	19	25
3	Hibernian	14	4	3	0	1	5	1	18	9	23
4	Falkirk	14	3	3	1	2	3	2	21	20	21
5	Celtic	14	2	3	2	2	4	1	14	13	19

Bairns Prove Troublesome Again

Falkirk's Bairns had already showed their mischievous side at Ibrox earlier in the season, when two Richard Cadette goals eliminated Rangers from the Coca-Cola Cup. Cadette has since departed to Millwall, but the visitors proved no less awkward, and despite a first-half as impressive as the Light Blues had produced all season, Jim Jefferies' men weathered the storm to claim a point.

There could be no denying, however, that the outcome was largely influenced by some indifferent finishing from Rangers, with Ally McCoist, back in the starting line-up, still to return to full potency. That, allied with a mixture of competent and fortunate goalkeeping from the remarkable veteran John Burridge, was sufficient to cause Rangers to drop rare League points at home. Only Celtic had left anything other than empty-handed previously. And yet it had all started so promisingly. There had already been a couple of chances before Mark Hateley scored what looked like the first of many in the seventh minute. And a cracking strike it was too. Pieter Huistra started the ball rolling, with a splendid pass to the big English striker. He sent in an inviting cross, from which McCoist couldn't quite control and sent deflected back to Hateley. From around the edge of the box, big Mark sent in a magnificent curling shot which had extrovert 'Budgie' beaten all ends up.

The early goal set up a half of concerted Rangers' pressure, during which Hateley, McCoist, Robertson and McCall all came agonisingly close – but not close enough! After the break, the pattern continued, with Super Ally, now with an MBE to his name, even closer to his elusive 300th goal for the club with a shot which rattled the junction of the post and the bar.

However, the narrowness of that one-goal lead was brought home to roost after 55 minutes, when Falkirk, completely against the run of the play, equalised. Nicky Henderson, who a year before had been plying his trade with lowly Cowdenbeath, was the executioner and Andy Goram was left fuming. The visiting striker showed commendable skill in turning and firing home from eight yards after a Jamie McGowan free-kick had bobbled around inside the penalty box, but the Rangers defence – and the 'keeper in particular – were convinced the scorer had been offside, and protested vigorously. Not surprisingly, the leveller spurred the visitors, who enjoyed their best period of the match after it. But the best chance for claiming all three points still fell to Rangers – a fair reflection on their superiority over the 90 minutes. Brian Laudrup did everything right as, clean through on the right, he rounded Burridge, and took aim at an empty goal. Unaccountably, though, by his own awesome standards, he failed to hit the target, and located the side-netting instead.

Not surprisingly, Walter Smith was less than pleased at the dropping of two points, especially because in his view – and most of the observers – "In terms of football, the first half-hour was the best we've played all season." The Falkirk goal had not amused him though. "Definitely offside," was his succinct description.

On a more pleasing note, sub Gordon Durie finally returned to the side after his latest injury problems, while Ally McCoist fresh from a midweek jaunt to Buckingham Palace to pick up his honour, got a valuable 72 minutes. "I was pleased to get the game, but my legs turned to rubber later on," he said.

	Home	Away	Total
Attendances	305,100	116,326	421,426

Rangers
Aberdeen

(0) 1
(0) 0

Saturday November 27th 1994, Ibrox   Att: 45,072

RANGERS

1	Andy	GORAM
2	Fraser	WISHART
3	David	ROBERTSON
4	Stuart	McCALL
5	Alan	McLAREN
6	Basile	BOLI *Booked*
7	Pieter	HUISTRA
8	Charlie	MILLER
9	Ally	McCOIST
10	*Mark*	*HATELEY (*63)*
11	Brian	LAUDRUP

Subs

12	Neil	MURRAY
13	Colin	SCOTT *(gk)*
14	*Gordon*	*DURIE (*63)*

ABERDEEN

1	Theo	SNELDERS
2	*Stewart*	*McKIMMIE (*73)*
3	Colin	WOODTHORPE
4	Paul	KANE
5	John	INGLIS *Booked*
6	Stephen	WRIGHT
7	Gary	SMITH
8	Brian	GRANT *Booked*
9	Scott	THOMSON *Booked*
10	Billy	DODDS
11	*Eoin*	*JESS (79)*

12	*Peter*	*HETHERSTON (79)*
13	Michael	WATT *(gk)*
14	*Steve*	*GLASS (*73)*

Match Facts

• Ally McCoist scored his 299th goal for the club then claimed it was his 300th!

• Another win for Rangers over the Dons at Ibrox meant that Willie Miller had still not recorded a victory against the Light Blues in Glasgow as manager – in nine attempts.

• The Sunday Coca-Cola Cup Final between Raith Rovers and Celtic at Ibrox meant this match had to be played on a Friday.

Score Sheet

A. McCOIST 55min – 1-0

Referee:
Mr. J. McGilvray (Edinburgh)

Bell's Premier Division

		P	W	D	L	W	D	L	F	A	Pts
1	**RANGERS**	15	6	1	1	3	2	2	26	12	30
2	Motherwell	15	4	4	0	3	3	1	29	20	28
3	Hibernian	15	4	3	0	1	5	1	18	9	23
4	Falkirk	15	3	3	2	2	3	2	22	23	21
5	Celtic	14	2	3	2	2	4	1	14	13	19

Ally's Back!

There have been precious few seasons during his stint at Ibrox that Ally McCoist has taken until November to open his scoring account. However, for the second campaign running, injury ensured this was the case in 1994-95 – and an important effort it was too. His 55th minute goal was enough to clinch the points in a poor Ibrox tussle with Aberdeen. In previous years, fixtures with men from the Granite City had been looked back on as real highlights on the calendar, but a combination of indifferent Rangers form and Aberdeen's low confidence, on the strength of a string of shocking reverses, saw this one evolve as an endurance test of a match – but one which the Light Blues comfortably survived.

Their only real rocky spell came in the closing stages of the first half, when Aberdeen had three genuine chances of opening the scoring in just three minutes. Eoin Jess fired a left-foot half volley past the post, a sloppy McLaren passback was blasted straight on to Scott Thomson's head by Andy Goram, but fortunately found safety, then Colin Woodthorpe squandered an opening when shooting wide, after a Jess cross had caused problems. Rangers' contribution in an attacking sense had been more widespread before the break, although most of it came through Brian Laudrup, who started out on the left and tied Stewart McKimmie, then Stephen Wright, in knots.

Pieter Huistra, enjoying a splendid run of form, started the winning move with a precise ball fed through the middle to Laudrup. An exquisite piece of Danish magic saw him flick it directly into McCoist's path, and it was just the sort of invitation he was after to record his 299th – or was it 300th?! – goal for the club.

Just one minute later, Huistra almost got the goal his first-team rebirth would have warranted, when Snelders raced out of goal to tackle Mark Hateley, and from 40-odd yards, the Dutchman bulleted a tremendous shot on to the crossbar. Goal of the season had it gone in – without a doubt! It was a costly challenge from the Dons' keeper because Hateley limped off with ankle problems seven minutes later – an injury which kept him out for weeks. But it never threatened the outcome of the match, and although Aberdeen, as might have been expected, upped the pace a little, their midfield of Kane, Grant and Thomson lacked the necessary guile to break down the Rangers reaguard and it seemed to sum up their problems when Kane got involved in a full-scale slanging match with Willie Miller on the touchlines. Huistra came close to putting a more realistic slant on the scoreline with another effort which cannoned off the bar in the dying seconds, but it was not to be and the massive Friday night crowd went home happy with what they'd witnessed.

Explaining the dispute over his tally of goals afterwards, McCoist explained, "Ian Ferguson has admitted a shot of his FIVE years ago against Celtic at Parkhead hadn't crossed the line before I touched it.

"I'll be getting in touch with the League to let them know all about this. And if you think I'm giving up a goal against Celtic, you must be mad!"

	Home	Away	Total
Attendances	350,172	116,326	466,498

Dundee United (0) 0
Rangers (1) 3

Sunday December 4th 1994, Tannadice   Att: 10,692

DUNDEE UNITED			**RANGERS**		
1	Kelham	O'HANLON	1	Andy	GORAM
2	Alex	CLELAND (*59)	2	Stuart	McCALL
3	Maurice	MALPAS	3	David	ROBERTSON
4	David	HANNAH Booked	4	Richard	GOUGH
5	Gary	BOLLAN	5	Alan	McLAREN
6	Brian	WELSH Booked	6	Basile	BOLI
7	David	BOWMAN	7	Pieter	HUISTRA
8	Billy	McKINLAY	8	Charlie	MILLER
9	Christian	DAILLY	9	Ally	McCOIST (*37)
10	Craig	BREWSTER	10	Gordon	DURIE
11	Grant	JOHNSON Booked	11	Brian	LAUDRUP

Subs

12	Andy	McLAREN	12.	Ian	DURRANT (*37)
13	Henrik	JORGENSEN (gk)	13	Colin	SCOTT (gk)
14	Robbie	WINTERS (*59)	14	Neil	MURRAY

Match Facts

- Richard Gough made his return after a six game absence due to an operation on a persistent toe injury.

Score Sheet

B. LAUDRUP 17 min – 0-1

P. HUISTRA 52 min – 0-2

I. DURRANT 56 min – 0-3

Referee:
Mr. J. McCluskey (Stewarton)

Bell's Premier Division

		P	W	D	L	W	D	L	F	A	Pts
1	**RANGERS**	16	6	1	1	4	2	2	29	12	33
2	Motherwell	16	4	4	0	3	4	1	31	22	29
3	Hibernian	16	4	4	0	1	6	1	21	12	25
4	Falkirk	16	3	3	2	2	4	2	23	24	22
5	Celtic	16	2	4	2	2	5	1	17	16	21

"Golac Talks A Lot Of …"

To the tune of the Village People and Pet Shop Boys' "Go West", the Rangers fans entered into a prolonged rendition of "Golac Talks A Lot Of S****" on a chilly Sunday on Tayside. It was the perfect response to the outspoken Terrors' manager's pre-match assertion that he expected his side to win by about four clear goals – and one that was matched by the players. For a live TV audience on ITV, Rangers yet again put on their Sunday best to eventually demoralise and humiliate the side who had cost them the Treble the season before.

Needless to say, the primary difference between the two outfits was, once again, Brian Laudrup. The Dane got a memorable fans' party underway with a classic strike in the 18th minute, then proceeded to tease and torment United with his wiles and guiles on the flank. The modest Laudrup described his wonder strike afterwards as 'lucky', but it was far from the fluke he suggested. Ally McCoist, looking as sharp as he'd done since coming back into the side, supplied Gordon Durie with a simple pass, and he managed to float a super chip almost straight to Brian's feet. From a seemingly impossible position, he sold Alex Cleland and Scotland international Billy McKinlay an outrageous dummy, and created space for himself, before flighting a breathtaking shot into the top corner.

A quickfire double not long after the break made sure of the points – and put a smile on the faces of two players whose Ibrox futures had been shrouded in doubt. Pieter Huistra claimed the second with a piece of skill which would not have looked out of place from his more illustrious Scandinavian team-mate. An Ian Durrant cross from the right found the Dutch master's head, and although the ball ricocheted off Brian Welsh, Blue Pieter kept his head to control it and dispatch a high shot past Kelham O'Hanlon. Substitute Durrant, back in the thick of things after his Everton scare, added another in 56 minutes – and what a beauty it was. Laudrup again stole the show, taking on three defenders on the left, before slotting a perfect pass inside Maurice Malpas for the on-rushing Ian to easily convert. After that, it was exhibition time for the side and a singalong session for the support, with the cruel but amusing ditty 'Could You Go A Coca-Cola Paul McStay?' – reference to his penalty miss in the Cup Final a week earlier – sharing top billing with the aforementioned Golac taunt.

The perfect flowing football delivered for most of the game was marred, however, by another two injury scares. McCoist, desperately requiring a run of games to attain full match fitness, lasted only 36 minutes when a hamstring scare saw him replaced by Durrant. The returning Richard Gough also spent time on the sidelines after a head collision with Welsh and Alan McLaren, but was able to continue despite confessing, "I can't remember a thing about the second half."

Walter Smith, while obviously concerned about the fitness two of his major influential figures, was a happy man nonetheless. "In terms of the football we played and in showing a competitive streak, that's the best performance of the season." Few who'd stayed at home in their armchairs would have disputed that.

	Home	Away	Total
Attendances	350,172	127,018	477,190

Kilmarnock
Rangers

(0) 1
(1) 2

Saturday December 10th 1994, Rugby Park   Att: 17,283

		KILMARNOCK				RANGERS
1	Dragoje	LEKOVIC		1	Andy	GORAM *Booked*
2	Gus	MacPHERSON		2	Stuart	McCALL
3	Tom	BLACK		3	David	ROBERTSON
4	Mark	REILLY		4	Richard	GOUGH
5	Neil	WHITWORTH		5	Alan	McLAREN *Booked*
6	Derek	ANDERSON		6	Neil	MURRAY
7	Ally	MITCHELL		7	Pieter	HUISTRA
8	*Mark*	*SKILLING (*60)*		8	*Charlie*	*MILLER (*75)*
9	Colin	McKEE		9	Gordon	DURIE
10	*Robert*	*CONNOR Booked (71)*		10	Ian	DURRANT
11	Steve	MASKREY		11	Brian	LAUDRUP *Booked*

Subs

12	John	HENDRY *(*60)*		12	Fraser	WISHART
13	Colin	MELDRUM *(gk)*		13	Billy	THOMSON *(gk)*
14	*Robert*	*WILLIAMSON (71)*		14	*Ian*	*FERGUSON (*75)*

Match Facts

• Alan McLaren scored his first ever goal for the club.

Score Sheet

A. McLAREN 6 min – 0-1

B. LAUDRUP 62 min – 0-2

C. McKEE 77 min – 1-2

Referee:
Mr. J. O'Hare (Glenboig)

Bell's Premier Division

		P	W	D	L	W	D	L	F	A	Pts
1	**RANGERS**	**17**	**6**	**1**	**1**	**5**	**2**	**2**	**31**	**13**	**36**
2	Motherwell	17	4	4	1	3	4	1	31	23	29
3	Hibernian	17	4	5	0	1	6	1	23	14	26
4	Falkirk	17	3	3	2	2	5	2	25	26	23
5	Celtic	16	2	4	2	2	5	1	17	16	21

Great Dane Sparkles in the Rain

As the Scottish winter set in, Brian Laudrup demonstrated he was a man for all seasons yet again with a tremendous performance which saw the safe garnering of another important three points.

With closest rivals Motherwell falling to an unlikely 1-0 reverse at home to Aberdeen, this was a crucial win indeed, and opened up a welcome seven point gap at the top of the Premier. Laudrup aside, Rangers had Gus Hollas to be grateful for, the Killie groundsman who had defied the lashing rain to get the pitch playable. Fixtures had fallen ten-a-penny north of the border, and the Tennents Scottish Cup was completely washed out, while other top-flight clashes at Celtic and Partick Thistle were postponed.

It was to both sides' credit that they attempted to play football in the unrelenting rain, and perhaps no surprise in the circumstances that the more-talented Rangers won the day. They got off to a perfect start, and that, as much as anything, probably helped settle the issue.

After only six minutes, a Laudrup cross caused panic in the Rugby Park defence and Tom Black needlessly conceded a corner. The flag-kick, from the Dane of course, arrived at the feet of Ian Durrant, and his low drive looked a goal all the way – until young Charlie Miller inadvertently got in its way on the goalline! There was no permananent damage done, though, as it fell for Alan McLaren to rattle in.

The rest of the opening period was an end-to-end affair, with Laudrup having the best chance of adding to the scoresheet, but finding Yugoslav 'keeper Lekovic the equal of his on-target shot. Nevertheless, he was not to be denied, and managed to get a second in 62 minutes.

Alan McLaren was the scorer turned provider, with a long ball which totally deceived the home backlot. It left Laudrup with a clear run in on goal, even though he was in his own half, and he stuck to his task manfully, running into the wind and rain, to evade a despairing tackle and round Lekovic, then slot the ball into the empty net. Two minutes later, a carbon copy run saw his effort finish just wide.

Kilmarnock's never-say-die approach was rewarded 13 minutes from the end, as their capture from Manchester United, Colin McKee, hauled them back into proceedings. His shot from 22 yards didn't look the most threatening, but took a deflection off Ally Mitchell which was sufficient to carry it home.

On a slippery surface, bookings were inevitable, and Goram, McLaren and Connor all fell foul of whistler Jim O'Hare. Unusually, so did Brian Laudrup, for once committing a foul rather than being sinned against.

Happiest man after the match was Alan McLaren, after his rare goal, which he laughably described as a "blockbuster"! He added, "At the second goal, I was just trying to clear my lines, but you can describe it as an accurate 60-yard pass if you like!"

Kilmarnock manager Alex Totten, meanwhile, was convinced that he had just witnessed the confirmation of the season's champions. "I can see Rangers winning the League for the forseeable future," he stressed. "They keep buying and because of that I don't see anyone around who can match them at present."

	Home	Away	Total.
Attendances	350,172	144,301	494,433

Rangers (2) 2
Hibernian (0) 0

Monday December 26th 1994, Ibrox   Att: 44,892

RANGERS

1	Colin	SCOTT
2	Stuart	McCALL
3	David	ROBERTSON
4	Richard	GOUGH
5	Alan	McLAREN
6	Basile	BOLI
7	Pieter	HUISTRA
8	Charlie	MILLER
9	Gordon	DURIE *Booked*
10	*Mark*	*HATELEY (*73) Booked*
11	Brian	LAUDRUP

Subs

12	*Craig*	*MOORE (*73)*
13	Billy	THOMSON *(gk)*
14	Ian	FERGUSON

HIBERNIAN

1	Jim	LEIGHTON
2	*Willie*	*MILLER (+25)*
3	Pat	McGINLAY *Booked*
4	Brian	HAMILTON
5	Steven	TWEED
6	Gordon	HUNTER *Booked*
7	*Kevin*	*HARPER (*70)*
8	Gareth	EVANS
9	Keith	WRIGHT
10	Darren	JACKSON
11	Michael	O'NEILL *Booked*

12	*Billy*	*FINDLAY (+25)*
13	Chris	REID *(gk)*
14	*Kevin*	*McALLISTER (*70)*

Match Facts

• Colin Scott, making his seventh League appearance for the club, *finally* appeared in a winning side!

• Richard Gough scored his goal of the season and his first in the League since the away win at Partick Thistle on March 29 earlier in the year.

Score Sheet

M. HATELEY 15 min – 1-0
R. GOUGH 18 min – 2-0

Referee:
Mr. E Martindale (Newlands)

Bell's Premier Division

		P	W	D	L	W	D	L	F	A	Pts
1	**RANGERS**	18	7	1	1	5	2	2	33	13	39
2	Motherwell	18	4	4	1	4	4	1	32	23	32
3	Hibernian	18	4	5	0	1	6	2	23	16	26
4	Falkirk	18	3	3	3	2	5	2	25	27	23
5	Celtic	17	2	4	2	2	6	1	17	16	22

Boxing Day Massacre KOs Hibs' Challenge

This was a match the visitors simply had to win if they had any realistic hopes of continuing their challenge for the League. A victory would have seen them a manageable seven points behind the Light Blues – as it was, they were outplayed and over-run as Rangers recorded the most one-sided 2-0 win anyone is ever likely to see.

Mark Hateley said as much after the game. Easter Road boss Alex Miller winced, "If their nearest rivals can't beat them, it looks to me as if nobody can stop them. Of course, there's a long way to go, but that's us 13 points behind them now."

And yet, before the fixture, Hibs could have made a decent claim that they could expect something out of the game. Prior to this holiday dust-up, they had only lost one league match, the best record in the Top 10, but a record of 11 draws had undermined their hopes of a long-overdue title flag for Edinburgh.

From the very start, though, there was only going to be one winner. Rangers were quite simply brilliant in a superb 45 minutes which was the best the Ibrox faithful had seen in a long, long time.

A quarter of an hour in, and the first goal was recorded on the festive electronic scoreboards. Pieter Huistra, enjoying a new lease of life, supplied an incisive pass for comeback man Hateley, fit again after an ankle injury, to blast past Scotland's most capped 'keeper Jim Leighton.

If the veteran number one could do nothing about that opener, the second was one of the weakest goals he has conceded in his entire career. To be fair, though, his was only the last in a line of mistakes which, to maintain the Yuletide theme, at times resembled a pantomime.

First of the Christmas turkeys was Willie Miller, who conceded a thoroughly needless corner. Central defender Gordon Hunter then clumsily sliced the Laudrup cross high into the air, from where Richard Gough cashed in with a poor-looking header, which somehow beat it beyond Leighton.

The mystery after that was just how Hibs managed to keep the scoreline at two. Laudrup hit the underside of the bar, Gordon Durie had a fine header just tipped over, Steven Tweed nodded just past his own post and David Robertson was unfortunate to see a shot whizz just past the post.

After the break, Hibs' one real threatening moment came when Basile Boli apparently used a hand to flick the ball clear when challenged by Keith Wright. It did look a clear penalty, but referee Eric Martindale somehow managed to miss the apparent offence, and the sizeable crowd breathed a sigh of relief again.

The rampant Huistra became increasingly effective, and he was at the heart of many of the impressive moves, including two of the better chances on offer in the second half, firstly when he set up Robertson to fire in a cross which Durie almost scored from, then again when he provided another opening for the left-back.

As usual, the man who seemed least impressed by what had been a super show was Walter Smith, who in his usual under-stated fashion, commented, "For the first hour we played very well, but I thought the heavy pitch took its toll on the teams. We created a lot of chances, but should have scored more." He must have been the only man in the stadium who would not have accepted that sort of performance and scoreline *every* week!

	Home	Away	Total
Attendances	395,064	144,301	539,365

Motherwell

Rangers

(0) 1

(1) 2

Saturday December 31st 1995, Fir Park   Att: 11,269

MOTHERWELL

1	Steve	WOODS
2	Rab	SHANNON
3	Rob	McKINNON
4	John	PHILLIBEN (83)
5	Miodrag	KRIVOKAPIC Booked
6	Chris	McCART
7	Paul	LAMBERT
8	Shaun	McSKIMMING Booked
9	Tommy	COYNE
10	Dougie	ARNOTT (*45)
11	Billy	DAVIES

Subs

12	Paul	McGRILLEN (*45) Booked
13	Scott	HOWIE (gk)
14	Steve	KIRK (83)

RANGERS

1	Colin	SCOTT
2	Stuart	McCALL Booked
3	David	ROBERTSON
4	Richard	GOUGH
5	Alan	McLAREN
6	Basile	BOLI
7	Pieter	HUISTRA
8	Charlie	MILLER Booked
9	Gordon	DURIE Booked
10	Craig	MOORE (*62)
11	Brian	LAUDRUP

12	Ian	FERGUSON (*62)
13	Billy	THOMSON (gk)
14	Ian	DURRANT

Match Facts

• Captain Richard Gough joined an elite band of players by playing his 300th game for the club.

• This was Rangers' fifth consecutive win – their best run of the campaign.

Score Sheet

S. McCALL 43 min – 0-1

P. McGRILLEN 64 min – 1-1

B. LAUDRUP 66 min – 1-2

G. DURIE 89 min – 1-3

Referee:

Mr. H. Williamson (Renfrew)

Bell's Premier Division

		P	W	D	L	W	D	L	F	A	Pts
1	**RANGERS**	19	7	1	1	6	2	2	36	14	42
2	Motherwell	19	4	4	2	4	4	1	33	26	32
3	Hibernian	19	5	5	0	1	6	2	27	16	29
4	Celtic	18	3	4	2	2	6	1	19	16	25
5	Falkirk	19	3	3	3	2	5	3	25	29	23

Fir Park Party Time

Rangers set themselves up nicely for the Hogmanay celebrations with a comfortable win over their closest title challengers at Fir Park. Motherwell had already accounted for the Light Blues in Lanarkshire earlier in the season, but there was to be no repeat of that performance as Walter Smith's men kept a firm grip on proceedings. After a convincing defeat, Alex McLeish, whose side were left lagging ten points behind the champions, joked, "I think we need a snooker now!" However, manager Smith was at pains not to concede anything. "I can't remember having a three-game gap between ourselves and the opposition at this point of the season. But I think it is premature to suggest that the gap is significant, because there is still a lot of football to be played."

The goal which sent Rangers on their way came courtesy of Stuart McCall, who hit the target for the first time since the Coca-Cola Cup tie in Arbroath back in August. The strike came just before half-time, as Pieter Huistra's attempt at a shot found its way across goal, and McCall was in the right place to stroke the ball beyond Steve Woods. The game opened out after this, and Rangers had to survive a suspicious equaliser in 64 minutes , when Paul McGrillen slotted home from a Shaun McSkimming pass, despite looking as though he may have been offside. But the Light Blues quickly resumed their control. Indeed, they offered the perfect response, scoring just two minutes later to almost immediately reclaim their advantage.

The counter was yet another from Brian Laudrup's box of magic tricks. He sent in a quite marvellous curling effort which struck the inside of the post, rebounded off the luckless Woods, before nestling in the back of the net.

Victory was sealed just one minute from time, with a more than welcome goal for Gordon Durie. The striker whose superb scoring form had contributed so much to the 1993-94 championship campaign collected only his second of a suspension and injury blighted season. Pieter Huistra, again in tremendous form despite the spectre of his move to Japan looming, sent the former Tottenham striker clear, and Durie comfortably rounded Woods before converting. It was his reward for the power of running he'd gone through.

As well as the three points, Rangers also had the boost of Craig Moore making his first start since getting back to full fitness after his Achilles and calf problems, while Ian Ferguson was given his first half-hour, following his hernia, as a second-half substitute.

And there was some welcome adulation for the departing Huistra, who heard his name chanted by the fans throughout the game. Never the most popular of players with the support at Ibrox, his attitude and excellent display with such a large pay day on the cards were testimony to his professionalism as a top-grade footballer.

	Home	Away	Total
Attendances	395,064	155,570	550,634

Rangers
Celtic

(1) 1
(0) 1

Wednesday January 4th 1995, Ibrox   Att: 45,794

RANGERS

1	Colin	SCOTT
2	Stuart	McCALL
3	David	ROBERTSON
4	Richard	GOUGH
5	Alan	McLAREN
6	Basile	BOLI
7	Pieter	HUISTRA
8	Ian	FERGUSON (*82)
9	Gordon	DURIE
10	Charlie	MILLER (46)
11	Brian	LAUDRUP

Subs

12	John	BROWN (*82)
13	Billy	THOMSON (gk)
14	Ian	DURRANT (46)

CELTIC

1	Pat	BONNER
2	Tom	BOYD
3	Stuart	GRAY
4	Brian	O'NEIL *Booked*
5	Mike	GALLOWAY *Booked*
6	Phil	O'DONNELL
7	Paul	BYRNE (*87)
8	Paul	McSTAY
9	Brian	McLAUGHLIN
10	Andy	WALKER
11	John	COLLINS

12	Chris	HAY (*87)
13	Gordon	MARSHALL (gk)
14	Charlie	NICHOLAS

Match Facts

- This was the first time since the 1987-88 season, when Celtic last won the League, that Rangers had failed to win the New Year derby.

- The match attracted the biggest crowd of the season in Scotland.

Score Sheet

I. FERGUSON 38 min – 1-0
P. BYRNE 59 min – 1-1

Referee:
Mr. J. McCluskey (Stewarton)

Bell's Premier Division

		P	W	D	L	W	D	L	F	A	Pts
1	**RANGERS**	20	7	2	1	6	2	2	37	15	43
2	Motherwell	19	4	4	2	4	4	1	33	26	32
3	Hibernian	19	5	5	0	1	6	2	27	16	29
4	Celtic	19	3	4	2	2	7	1	20	17	26
5	Falkirk	19	3	3	3	2	5	3	25	29	23

Celtic's Bhoys Do A Men's Job

The New Year derby moved away from its traditional January 1 date due to the demands of Sky Television, but thankfully this caused no dilution of the passion the fixture evokes. For 45 minutes, if not totally at ease, the Light Blues looked the more likely of the two teams and this was mirrored in the half-time 1-0 scoreline. After the break, though, their city rivals regained their appetite, and controlled much of the play, and whilst creating little, Tommy Burns' youngsters put enough effort in to eke out an equaliser. Rangers' second-half display, in contrast, was decidedly poor, but Walter Smith put that down to that number of still relatively new faces in his line-up. "We're changing the team around," he explained. "We're still struggling for consistency, and I hope it comes soon."

But even the gaffer had a smile on his face after 38 minutes, when comeback man Ian Ferguson, recently recovered from a hernia, fired Rangers into the lead. As Celtic tried to clear their lines, Stuart McCall lofted a high ball into the match, which Charlie Miller attempted to fire towards goal. Young Celt Stuart Gray, son of former Scotland international Eddie, tried to clear with his more natural left foot, instead of his right which would have been easier, and only succeeded in diverting the ball into Fergie's path. From close range, he had little difficulty in drilling it jubilantly into the net. Despite Rangers' ascendancy, it was only their second really good chance of the half. Brian Laudrup had earlier driven past the post, after a Gordon Durie pass had deflected off Brian O'Neil straight to the Dane.

Fourteen minutes into the second period, the equaliser came. Although Celtic had hardly offered an onslaught towards Colin Scott, they had served warning of their intentions, with a Phil O'Donnell header zipping just over, after an impressive passing move, and the same player being thwarted whilst steadying himself for shooting by a despairing David Robertson tackle. Their goal came from a familiar source. Irishman Paul Byrne had scored in the Hampden dust-up in November, and converted once more with a well-taken volley from a flighted cross field pass from John Collins. That was to be the end of the scoring, but not the action. Although the visitors kept possession well, it was Rangers who made the better chances, with Durie managing to shoot against Bonner when bearing down on goal, then providing a first touch which suggested he was wearing clogs, on rounding the keeper. The ball ended up heading for the Copland Road stand rather than towards the goal. A Bonner double save from Laudrup and sub Durrant concluded the action. And so the 313th Old Firm match ended in deadlock, an outcome which pleased the away contingent, after their recent dismal run, far more than Rangers.

There were one or two smiles in the ground for the Teddy Bears, though, as Paul McStay was baited mercilessly over his penalty miss which allowed Raith Rovers to lift the Coca Cola Cup at Ibrox. Sometimes, Celtic's misfortunes are more important than Rangers' successes!

	Home	Away	Total
Attendances	440,858	155,570	596,428

Partick Thistle
Rangers

(0) 1
(0) 1

Saturday, January 7th 1995, Firhill   Att: 19,351

PARTICK THISTLE

1	Nicky	WALKER
2	Alan	DINNIE
3	Steve	PITTMAN
4	Gregg	WATSON
5	Steve	WELSH
6	Tommy	TURNER
7	Rod	McDONALD
8	Albert	CRAIG
9	*Derek*	*McWILLIAMS (*89)*
10	Chic	CHARNLEY
11	Alex	TAYLOR

Subs

12	*Ian*	*CAMERON (*89)*
13	Mark	CAIRNS *(gk)*
14	Bobby	LAW

RANGERS

1	*Andy*	*GORAM (*28)*
2	Craig	MOORE
3	David	ROBERTSON *Booked*
4	Stuart	McCALL
5	Alan	McLAREN *Booked*
6	John	BROWN
7	Pieter	HUISTRA
8	Ian	FERGUSON
9	Ian	DURRANT
10	Brian	McGINTY
11	Neil	MURRAY

12	Fraser	WISHART
13	*Collin*	*SCOTT (gk) (*28)*
14	Scott	WILSON

Match Facts

- Brian McGinty became the first young Ranger to make his league debut in the season.

Score Sheet

D. ROBERTSON 80 min. 0-1

A. TAYLOR 83 min. 1-1

Referee:
Mr. L. Mottram (Forth)

Bell's Premier Division

		P	W	D	L	W	D	L	Pts
1	**RANGERS**	21	7	2	1	6	3	2	44
2	Hibernian	20	6	5	0	1	6	2	32
3	Motherwell	19	4	4	2	4	4	1	32
4	Celtic	20	3	5	2	2	7	1	27
5	Falkirk	20	3	3	3	2	6	3	24

Taylor Needles Patchwork Gers

A late goal by Thistle's Alex Taylor saw an under-strength Rangers outfit lurch to their second successive draw in a dull, dull encounter at Firhill. The Light Blues, without Laudrup, Gough, Hateley and McCoist, looked exactly what they were – a patchwork team lacking in cohesion.

The whole length of the table separated the sides, but a neutral would have been hard-pushed to guess which side was which on the basis of the fare on offer. Thistle played their usual huffing and puffing style game, but even then it looked to have done them no good as David Robertson fired a late goal which seemed certain to settle the issue. It was perhaps only fair, and predictable, that the lead did not last more than four minutes. Alex Taylor came to the strugglers' rescue, and a point apiece was all the sides could settle for.

Perhaps the only person this match was memorable for was youngster Brian McGinty, who made his full-team debut due to injuries to Hateley and Charlie Miller, and Brian Laudrup's enforced absence on international duty. To be fair to the youngster, he tried hard, but he did squander one splendid opportunity, when he was alert enough to pick up on a slack Craig backpass. His effort found the net, but disappointingly, it was the side-netting.

Andy Goram will not forget proceedings either, but 'memorable' probably wouldn't fit his description of the 90 minutes. Yet another injury – to the same calf which suffered with Scotland in Greece, but in a different place – curtailed his involvement to just 28 minutes, and Colin Scott reassumed his position in goal.

It was a simple pass back, of all things, which caused the national number one problems, and it was perhaps indicative of the quality of the clash that this was the only incident of note in the entire first half.

There were chances after the interval, but these were few and far between. McGinty's aside, Partick forged the best opening until the scoring, when Alan Dinnie fed off Chic Charnley, before forcing Scott into an assured save.

The goal which broke the tedium came when Robertson exchanged passes with Ian Ferguson in 80 minutes, then marched on to drill a right-footer in past Nicky Walker from the edge of the box.

Thistle's response was not immediate, but quick enough. It looked as though Scott should have done better with a Steve Pittman cross than divert it towards Rod McDonald. The skilful Scouser intelligently centred the ball to Taylor and he balsted the ball into the roof of the net.

After a 90 minutes which really defied analysis, manager Walter Smith saw enough inaction to comment, "It was scrappy stuff with few opportunities from either side, but I was disappointed that we lost a goal so soon after getting one. We were missing a few players, but I won't use that as an excuse. We should have done better than we did." John Lambie's assertion that if Thistle "kept producing performances like that, we'll get out of this spot" seemed well wide off the mark.

Truly a game to write off.

	Home	Away	Total
Attendances	440,858	174,921	615,778

Falkirk
Rangers

(0) 2
(1) 3

Saturday January 14th 1994, Brockville   Att: 13,495

FALKIRK

1	Tony	PARKS
2	John	CLARK
3	Jamie	McGOWAN
4	Neil	OLIVER
5	John	HUGHES
6	Brian	RICE *Booked*
7	Eddie	MAY *Booked*
8.	*Nicky*	*HAY (*61)*
9	Colin	McDONALD
10	Steve	FULTON *Booked*
11	Scott	McKENZIE

Subs

12	Jamie	PATERSON (*61)
13	*Willie*	*LAMONT (gk)*
14	*Graeme*	*HAMILTON*

RANGERS

1	Ally	MAXWELL
2	*Craig*	*MOORE (46)*
3	David	ROBERTSON *Booked*
4	Stuart	McCALL
5	Alan	McLAREN *Booked*
6	John	BROWN *Booked*
7	Pieter	HUISTRA *Booked*
8	Ian	FERGUSON *Booked*
9	Charlie	MILLER
10	Neil	MURRAY
11	*Ian*	*DURRANT (*75).*

12	*Trevor*	*STEVEN (*75).*
13	Colin	SCOTT (gk)
14	Fraser	WISHART (46) *Booked*

Match Facts

• Falkirk's dismal run of never having beaten Rangers in the Premier League – or indeed in any league fixture for 24 years – continued.

• Pieter Huistra played his 15th consecutive game for the club, and his last. This was his longest unbroken spell in the starting line-up in all his time at Rangers!

Score Sheet

P. HUISTRA pen 45 min – 0-1

C. McDONALD 72 min – 1-1

E. MAY 73 min – 2-1

P. HUISTRA 82 min – 2-2

S. McCALL 90 min – 2-3

Referee:
Mr. J. McGilvray (Edinburgh)

Bell's Premier Division

		P	W	D	L	W	D	L	F	A	Pts
1	**RANGERS**	**22**	**7**	**2**	**1**	**7**	**3**	**2**	**41**	**18**	**47**
2	Hibernian	21	6	5	0	1	7	2	29	17	33
3	Motherwell	22	4	5	3	4	4	1	34	28	33
4	Celtic	22	4	6	2	2	7	1	24	20	31
5	Hearts	21	6	2	2	2	2	7	28	30	28

Huistra Signs Off With A Flourish

Pieter Huistra's last game for the club became a personal triumph, as he laid the foundations for a win which looked extremely unlikely after 80 minutes. The Dutch winger, preparing for a new career in Japan's J-League, scored Rangers' first, then grabbed a dramatic equaliser which changed the course of the game. Captain Stuart McCall then scored a superb last-minute winner to secure all three points.

It was an emotional day for Piet, and he was given a rousing reception from the legions at the end, not only for his contribution to an exciting afternoon at Brockville, but over a rollercoaster four and a half years in Scotland. "I would like to thank the supporters very much for all the backing they have given me in all my time at Rangers. It has been a pleasure to play with the club and I will always follow their progress," he stressed.

It was right on half-time that Huistra opened the scoring from the penalty spot, after John Hughes had brought down Charlie Miller in the box. Tony Parks got a hand to his well-placed effort, but could not prevent it heading into his right-hand corner. A Rangers lead at the interval was pretty much just, as although Falkirk had had chances, the Light Blues had actually got the ball into the net when Ian Durrant turned in a Neil Murray shot – but the linesman's flag was up for offside.

As the second half meandered to a lazy finish, Rangers looked to be coasting to a win, until a crazy couple of minutes turned their world upside down. The Bairns' equaliser, in the 72nd minute, arrived when a lengthy Parks clearance caught sub Fraser Wishart and Alan McLaren unaware and Colin McDonald nipped in to blast the ball past Ally Maxwell. Just one minute later, the home side, after an insipid display, incredibly took the lead. Maxwell made a superb save to deny Scott MacKenzie's fine shot, but the ball shot up to permit little Eddie May to bullet it in with his head.

After such a shock double blow, Rangers could have been forgiven for folding, but Huistra had other ideas. With just eight minutes left on the clock, he took a cross from the right, skipped inside then fired an inch-perfect left foot drive into the net. An ideal way to say 'sayonara' indeed.

There was still time to land the killer blow, and that was precisely what happened right on the bell. Miller bore down on goal from the left and delivered a telling shot which Parks did well to get in the way of. Unfortunately for him, the ball landed perfectly for Stuart McCall to push into an open goal.

This late winner so irritated Bairns' captain Hughes that he contrived to get himself technically sent off in the tunnel after proceedings had officially ended. He felt there were shades of offside to the winner, and launched a vitriolic attack on the linesman to the extent he was called to ref Crombie's office and red-carded. He was in good company. There were nine other bookings.

Rangers had operated with no first-choice forwards, and that, more than anything else, put a smile on Walter Smith's face. "To score three goals without your recognised strikeforce is a major bonus and I'm delighted."

	Home	Away	Total
Attendances	440,858	188,416	629,274

Rangers
Hearts

(0) 1
(0) 0

Saturday January 21st 1995, Ibrox   Att: 44,231

RANGERS

1	Ally	MAXWELL
2	Stuart	McCALL
3	John	BROWN *Booked*
4	Richard	GOUGH
5	Alan	McLAREN
6	Basile	BOLI
7	Trevor	STEVEN *(*88)*
8	Ian	FERGUSON *(*24)*
9	Charlie	MILLER
10	Neil	MURRAY
11	Brian	LAUDRUP

Subs

12	Ian	DURRANT *(*24)*
13	Colin	SCOTT *(gk)*
14	Craig	MOORE *(*88)*

HEARTS

1	Craig	NELSON
2	Steve	FRAIL
3	Colin	MILLER
4	Craig	LEVEIN
5	Willie	JAMIESON *(60)*
6	Dave	McPHERSON
7	Brian	HAMILTON
8	Jim	BETT
9	John	COLQUHOUN *(*69)*
10	John	MILLAR
11	David	HAGEN

12	John	ROBERTSON *(60)*
13	Henry	SMITH
14	Gary	MACKAY *(*69)*

Match Facts

- Dave McPherson and David Hagen made their first appearances at Ibrox since their transfer from Rangers.

- Hearts' defeat extended their sequence without a win agianst Rangers to 18 matches – the last victory coming in August 1991 when they triumphed 1-0.

Score Sheet

C. MILLER 1 min – 1-0

Referee:
Mr. W. Young (Clarkston)

Bell's Premier Division

		P	W	D	L	W	D	L	F	A	Pts
1	**RANGERS**	23	8	2	1	7	3	2	42	18	50
2	Hibernian	23	7	5	0	1	7	3	33	21	36
3	Motherwell	23	4	5	3	4	4	3	35	36	33
4	Celtic	23	4	6	2	2	8	1	24	20	32
5	Hearts	23	7	2	2	2	2	8	30	31	31

Good Start – Shame About The Rest

"Given the cicumstances, it's been more about results than performances recently," mumbled Walter Smith afterwards. Countered Hearts gaffer, Tommy McLean, "The second half turned into a complete bore. Two teams absolutely cancelling each other out." Those two after-match comments said it all about an encounter which proved so tiresome, even the floodlights wanted to give up on it at the start of the second half. The goal came after just 80 seconds. Brian Laudrup, the one saving grace, in all the inaction, made one of his trademark waltzes through an opposing defence, before offering Miller the perfect chance to sidefoot his third strike of the season. It was Laudrup's first performance since his Arabian excursion with Denmark, who he'd captained to Inter-Continental Cup glory, and although weather conditions were strikingly different to what he had experienced in the desert, with howling winds and swirling rain the order of the day, his skill stood out like a beacon on the drabbest of Glasgow afternoons.

While Charlie Miller proved Rangers' saviour with the winning goal, it was his Hearts' namesakes John Millar and ex-Ger Colin Miller who offered the best resistance the Tynecastle side could muster. The latter fired in a super free-kick which tested Ally Maxwell, while John managed to direct two headers towards Andy Goram's deputy which kept him warm, if nothing else. That was the extent of the Edinburgh challenge. In fairness, Rangers had little to enthuse about in an attacking sense either, although Laudrup did his best to raise everyone's spirits as he continued to beat defenders at will, even if it was to no real positive effect.

One plus for Rangers was the return of Trevor Steven, who started his first competitive match since the last game of the previous League season, a 0-0 draw with Dundee. The Englishman lasted well in heavy conditions, but could not quite complete the 90 minutes and received a well-earned breather when he was substituted by Craig Moore just before time.

On the debit side, though, was a knock for Ian Ferguson, operating again as a stand-in striker, which caused him to depart after only 25 minutes. A goin injury was the diagnosis. Tommy McLean's analysis of the proceedings was baffling. "Half-time came too soon for us because we had been dominating the game and didn't deserve to lose. The delay at half-time beause of the floodlight failure hurt us," he rasped. With a view of the match like that, one would have thought the lights had been out for the entire 90 minutes.

In the end, despite the weather and performance, Rangers could not complain. Winning, after all is the name of the game, and that had been achieved with a minimum of fuss again. Hibs remained 14 points behind, with 13 games left and the Light Blues could boast of a goal difference advantage of 12 over the Easter Road men. The odd bad showing would be tolerated with statistics like that.

	Home	Away	Total
Attendances	485,089	188,416	673,505

Rangers
Dundee United

(1) 1
(1) 1

Saturday February 4th 1995, Ibrox

Att: 44,197

RANGERS

1	Ally	MAXWELL
2	Craig	MOORE
3	David	ROBERTSON
4	Richard	GOUGH
5	Basile	BOLI
6	Stuart	McCALL *Booked*
7	Trevor	STEVEN
8	Charlie	MILLER *(*88) Booked*
9	Gordon	DURIE *(78)*
10	Mark	HATELEY
11	Brian	LAUDRUP

Subs

12	John	BROWN *(*88)*
13	Colin	SCOTT *(gk)*
14	Ally	McCOIST *(78)*

DUNDEE UNITED

1	Kelham	O'HANLON
2	Jim	McINALLY
3	Maurice	MALPAS *Booked*
4	David	HANNAH
5	Gordan	PETRIC
6	Christian	DAILLY *Booked*
7	David	BOWMAN
8	Billy	McKINLAY
9		SERGIO *(*70)*
10	Craig	BREWSTER
11	Jerren	NIXON *(*81)*

12	Robbie	WINTERS *(*70)*
13	Henrik	JORGENSEN *(gk)*
14	David	CRAIG *(*81)*

Match Facts

• David Robertson scored his third goal of the season, equalling his best league total since joining the club in 1991.

• Rangers' most recent signings Alex Cleeland and Gary Bollan both missed out on debuts against their previous club.

Score Sheet

J. NIXON 22 min. 0-1
D. ROBERTSON 28 min. 1-1

Referee:
Mr. H. Dallas (Bonkle)

Bell's Premier Division

		P	W	D	L	W	D	L	F	A	Pts
1	**RANGERS**	24	8	3	1	7	3	2	43	19	51
2	Hibernian	24	7	5	1	1	7	3	34	23	36
3	Motherwell	24	5	5	3	4	4	3	36	36	36
4	Celtic	24	4	6	2	2	8	2	24	21	32
5	Hearts	24	7	2	2	2	2	9	30	33	31

Penalty Posers Cost Gers The Points

Two penalty claims rejected by referee Hugh Dallas, both involving full-back David Robertson, dominated the pub chat after an intriguing game against Dundee United. It was a shame that the controversies both involved the marauding left-back, because they overshadowed his all-round contribution, not to mention a super goal which proved invaluable as Rangers extended their lead at the top of the table to 15 points.

The first scrape came in the first half, when Robbo raced clear on to a Charlie Miller pass, only to find himself upended by Sergio. The offence was clearly inside the box, but the official was not convinced and gave the Tannadice import the benefit of the doubt.

Late in the game, Robertson was again fouled in the penalty area, this time by sub Robbie Winters, and once more Dallas rejected the Light Blue claims. Not surprisingly, his stubborness provoked justified uproar in the stands.

The normally reticent Walter Smith afterwards offered an opinion which suggested he felt the ref was bonkers, rather than from Bonkle, near Wishaw. "The Dundee United manager said when they came to Ibrox last season that they never got any decisions here. He must realise after today's game that this is not the case. He said then in any other ground in Scotland they would have had a penalty. After today, we can say that in any other ground in Scotland, we might have had two!"

Ivan Golac, typically, took the opposite view. "I don't think David Robertson will dive as well in the swimming pool as he did in the box," he smirked. "I thought the referee was absolutely tremendous."

As the debate raged, the goals which *were* scored seemed largely forgotten. United's Trinidad international Jerren Nixon gave the visitors an unlikely lead after 22 minutes. A Maurice Malpas cross was flicked on by David Hannah and left Nixon with an easy header past Ally Maxwell, deputising for Andy Goram.

But their lead lasted only six minutes as Robertson took a hand in proceedings. He latched on to the end of Laudrup's pass after Trevor Steven weaved across the pitch to set up the scoring opportunity. His precision finish left Kelham O'Hanlon with no chance as it eked through the gap between him and his near post.

There were other chances in a clash which really ebbed and flowed and produced enough entertainment to keep the purists happy. International Billy McKinlay produced an excellent 30 yard effort which just scraped the bar, while at the other end, Stuart McCall caused a few moments of anxiety for the Irish goalie, who also had to look smart at the feet of Mark Hateley.

The one disappointing note, spot-kick fury aside, was the failed comeback of seemingly jinxed Ally McCoist. An innocuous collison with O'Hanlon, after a mere 12 minutes in action, resulted in ankle ligament damage and another lengthy lay-off. It was his first game back after a spell on the sidelines after hamstring problems.

	Home	Away	Total
Attendances	529,286	188,416	716,899

Hamilton Accies   (0) 1
Rangers   (2) 3

Monday February 8th 1995, Firhill   Att: 18,379

HAMILTON

1	Allan	FERGUSON
2	Steven	RENICKS
3	Chris	HILLCOAT
4	Sean	McENTEGART *Booked*
5	Ian	McCALL
6	Martin	McINTOSH
7	Gary	CLARK
8	Raymond	McSTAY (*46)
9.	Paul	CHALMERS
10	Peter	DUFFIELD
11.	John	McQUADE (*63)

RANGERS

1	Ally	MAXWELL
2	Craig	MOORE *Booked*
3	David	ROBERTSON
4	Richard	GOUGH
5	Basile	BOLI *Booked*
6	Stuart	McCALL
7	Trevor	STEVEN
8	Charlie	MILLER
9	Gordon	DURIE (*75) *Booked*
10	Mark	HATELEY
11	Brian	LAUDRUP

Subs

12	Crawford	BAPTIE (63)
13	David	CORMACK (gk)
14	David	LORIMER (46)

12	John	BROWN (*75)
13	Colin	SCOTT (gk)
14	Ian	DURRANT

Match Facts

• Hamilton enjoyed their biggest home crowd – albeit at Firhill – 42 years. No fewer than four of the Rangers team made their Scottish Cup debuts – Boli, Moore, Miller, and Laudrup.

Score Sheet

T. STEVEN 19 min – 0-1

B. BOLI 24 min – 0-2

B. LAUDRUP 57 min – 0-3

D. LORIMER 66 min – 1-3

Referee:
Mr. W. Crombie (Edinburgh)

Tennents Scottish Cup Third Round

Third Time Lucky For Gers

Much of the pre-match publicity for this clash centred around Accies' sensational 1-0 Cup win over Rangers in 1987, and the possibility of a repeat. From the very start it did not look likely, and so it proved on a muddy pitch at Partick Thistle's Firhill, the Lanarkshire side's temporary home.

After two previous postponements, the Monday clash proved third time lucky for the Light Blues, who were in command from the moment Trevor Steven notched his first of the season in 19 minutes.

The goal was a sweet one. The former Marseille star made good use of some impressive build-up play from Stuart McCall and Gordon Durie to turn intelligently in the box to and strike a cute left-foot shot into Allan Ferguson's left-hand corner.

When Basile Boli made it two just five minutes later, the tie was all but won. Aussie Craig Moore delivered a tempting ball into the stride of Rangers' other former Marseille hero, and the big Frenchman confidently charged forward to dispatch the ball into the net. Unfortunately, as impressive as the effort was, his subsequent charge towards the fans behind the Firhill goal failed to strike a chord with ref Bill Crombie, who promptly booked him for his over-elaborate celebrations.

On a pitch which, in places, was a quagmire, both sides put in an admirable work-rate to make the game an entertaining spectacle for the large crowd, and although Rangers could have added to their lead before the break through McCall and Durie, the First Division side, bossed by former Ibrox star Iain Munro, looked a tidy enough outfit in their own right.

Two minutes after the break Charlie Miller missed yet another chance to make it three when he kicked the ground rather than the ball with the goal at his mercy, but the inevitable was only delayed until the 59th minute.

The youngster atoned for his miss with a super flick from a Maxwell clearance which Brian Laudrup collected and converted, after rounding Ferguson. It was a strike which delighted the sizeable Teddy Bear legions, not to mention the Danish contingent in the press box who had made the journey over from Scandinavia especially to monitor their national captain.

Only the churlish would have denied Accies their consolation in 66 minutes, when sub David Lorimer, on for Raymond McStay – brother of Celtic's Paul – volleyed past Maxwell from close range.

That consolation may have proved more significant had Richard Gough not scrambled away a header from ex-Ger Ian McCall, but there was still time after that for Mark Hateley and Laudrup to fritter away reasonable openings, which simply underlined Rangers' superiority.

Walter Smith praised his men for comfortably overcoming a potentially tricky hurdle. "It was a professional performance, especially in the first half." Iain Munro, on the other hand, felt his men had contributed to their own downfall, but would not dispute Rangers' right to proceed to a fourth round tie at Tynecastle against Hearts. "We shot ourselves in the foot and it's hard to come back against a team like Rangers when you do that."

	Home	Away	Total.
Cup attendances		18,379	18,379

Aberdeen
Rangers

(0) 2
(0) 0

Sunday February 12th 1995, Pittodrie   Att: 20,000

ABERDEEN

1	Theo	SNELDERS
2	Stewart	McKIMMIE (* 46)
3	Stephen	WRIGHT
4	Paul	KANE
5	John	INGLIS *Booked*
6	Gary	SMITH
7	Eoin	JESS
8	Duncan	SHEARER
9	Joe	MILLER
10	Billy	DODDS
11	Ray	McKINNON

Subs

12	Peter	HETHERSTON
13	Michael	WATT
14	Stephen	GLASS (*46).

RANGERS

1	Ally	MAXWELL
2	Craig	MOORE *Booked*
3	David	ROBERTSON *Booked*
4	Richard	GOUGH
5	Basile	BOLI
6	Gary	BOLLAN (61)
7	Alex	CLELAND
8	Stuart	McCALL
9	Charlie	MILLER (*75) *Booked*
10	Mark	HATELEY
11	Brian	LAUDRUP *Booked*

12	Ian	DURRANT (*75)
13	Billy	THOMSON (gk)
14	Gordon	DURIE (61)

Match Facts

• Rangers' dismal record at Pittodrie continued, where they have won only six times since the formation of the Premier League in 1975.

• Alex Cleland and Gary Bollan became the 29th and 30th players to feature in the first team for Rangers the season.

Score Sheet

B. DODDS pen. 57 min – 1-0
D. SHEARER 87 min – 2-0

Referee:
Mr. J McCluskey (Stewarton)

Bell's Premier Division

		P	W	D	L	W	D	L	F	A	Pts
1	**RANGERS**	9	4	0	1	2	1	1	16	7	19
2	Hibernian	9	3	2	0	1	2	1	14	6	16
3	Celtic	9	2	2	0	2	2	1	11	6	16
4	Motherwell	9	1	3	0	2	2	1	16	12	14
5	Hearts	9	3	0	1	1	1	3	10	11	13

More Controversy At Pittodrie

Rangers' second visit to Aberdeen on League duty ended in as controversial fashion as the first, with the game decided on referee Jim McCluskey's decision to award the home side a penalty, whilst denying the Light Blues two claims.

In the end, Billy Dodds converted from the spot and a late goal from Duncan Shearer clinched the three points for the Granite City men. Manager Walter Smith had warned his players beforehand about the danger the struggling Dons would pose under the new stewardship of Roy Aitken, follwing Willie Miller's dismissal. How right he proved.

The first half was an even affair with chances at both ends, although Rangers could probably claim to have held the upper hand. As usual, Brian Laudrup was prominent, and he was involved in two of his men's brighter opportunities, when he crossed for debutant Gary Bollan to head just past, then latched on to a Robertson pass which beat the offside trap, but delayed a bit too long and eventually managed to hit Mark Hateley, rather than the target, with his shot. There were other chances, too, for the Light Blues' second debut boy, Alex Cleland, Richard Gough and Charlie Miller in a refreshingly open game.

The Granite City men could point to worthy attempts by Duncan Shearer, who was well thwarted by Ally Maxwell at close range, Eoin Jess, also denied by Maxi and Billy Dodds, who squandered the most gilt-edged of openings with a shocking header when clear, as testimony of their attacking threat.

Aitken, the former Celtic star, who needed no motivation to fire his players up for a clash with Rangers, sent his men out in the second half with even more purpose. But it was the Light Blues who came closest to breaking the deadlock with a penalty claim which looked to have more than a bit of merit. Stephen Wright tripped Charlie Miller in the box, but ref McCluskey was adamant there had been no offence and waved play on.

If that outraged the vociferous away support, it was nothing on what occurred two minutes later when Gough was short with a header, Maxwell came to collect and Shearer raced in to fall theatrically at his feet. There was definitely contact – but enough to warrant a penalty? McCluskey thought so and Dodds placed the ball to the 'keeper's left.

Rangers' chance to retrieve the game was lost in the 68th and 69th minutes. Firstly, sub Gordon Durie was penalised for a foul on Theo Snelders as a Gough header floated goalwards, then McCluskey again denied them what looked as good a penalty as John Inglis appeared to shove Laudrup off the ball.

The suspicion it was just not to be Rangers' day was confirmed three minutes from time when Aberdeen notched their clincher, again partly due to a mistake. A Gough pass caught McCall unawares and he was robbed by Shearer on the edge of the box, from where he showed his finishing poise by calmly despatching the ball past Maxwell.

Walter Smith told the press afterwards, "We did not get a break anywhere. But we cannot complain about the overall result. I felt the game was fairly even until their penalty, which turned it against us."

	Home	Away	Total
League Attendances	529,286	208,416	737,702

Hearts   (2) 4
Rangers   (0) 2

Monday February 20th 1995, Tynecastle   Att: 12,375

HEARTS

1	Craig	NELSON
2	Steve	FRAIL
3	*Colin*	*MILLER (*70)*
4	Craig	LEVEIN
5	Jim	BETT *Booked*
6	Dave	McPHERSON
7	Brian	HAMILTON
8	Gary	MACKAY
9	*John*	*ROBERTSON (*81)*
10	John	MILLAR
11	David	HAGEN

Subs

12	*John*	*COLQUHOUN (70)*
13	Henry	SMITH *(gk)*
14	*Kevin*	*THOMAS (*81)*

RANGERS

1	Ally	MAXWELL
2	Craig	MOORE
3	*David*	*ROBERTSON (*81)*
4	Richard	GOUGH *Booked*
5	Stuart	McCALL
6	*Alex*	*CLELAND (+86)*
7	Trevor	STEVEN
8	Alan	McLAREN
9	Charlie	MILLER
10	Gordon	DURIE *Booked*
11	Brian	LAUDRUP

12	*John*	*BROWN (+86)*
13	Billy	THOMSON *(gk)*
14	*Ian*	*DURRANT (*81)*

Match Facts

- A punter from Paisley was waiting on a correct score from this game to pick up £22,000 from a 50p stake bet for four correct scores. His prediction? 2-2, unfortunately for him!

- This was Hearts' first win in 18 attempts against Rangers.

Score Sheet

C MILLER 23 min 1-0

D McPHERSON 45 min 2-0

B. LAUDRUP 46 min – 2-1

G. DURIE 56 min – 2-2

J. ROBERTSON 58 min – 3-2

K. THOMAS 87 min – 4-2

Referee:
Mr. W. Young (Glasgow)

Tennents Scottish Cup Fourth Round

Suicide After Coming Back From The Dead

Rangers' disastrous season in the cup competitions came to an appropriate end as they lost out in a sensational match in Edinburgh. It was no consolation to the Light Blue hordes that their exit provided a compelling spectacle live on Sky Sports.

For the second game running, there was a degree of controversy surrounding the defeat. Yet again, there was a plausible penalty claim turned down, when Colin Miller appeared to clearly handle a Brian Laudrup cross in the box. But, just as ref Dallas had been unimpressed at Pittodrie, official Willie Young of Clarkston waved away the claims and the side was left to wonder what might have been.

The contentious decision came shortly after Hearts' second, which was also the subject of some dispute. A frantic Richard Gough sliced clearance was picked up by Ally Maxwell, and inexplicably Mr Young awarded a free-kick. From this award, Rangers proceeded to concede a corner which was to cost them dearly. Jim Bett flighted a perfect ball in, which Craig Moore unaccountably headed towards his own goal. Dave McPherson was in ideal position to nod past Ally Maxwell.

Rangers had already been in trouble, falling 1-0 down when another former Ibrox star, Colin Miller, blasted a 25-yard free-kick just beyond Maxwell on 23 minutes. This effort, too, owed a lot to defensive frailty, as Charlie Miller, in the defensive wall, clearly jumped over the ball as it sped toward goal. It eventually went in off Maxi's far right post.

From this desperate half-time deficit, Rangers fought back magnificently, before throwing the match away.

Within one minute of the re-start, they were back in contention as Brian Laudrup touched a Gordon Durie header over the line. It had been a splendid move as Durie fed Miller, before receiving his cross and providing the crucial header.

Ten minutes later, few would have bet on Hearts' eventual win, as Durie equalised. A typically brilliant mazy Laudrup run fed Alex Cleland and his superb ball was nodded in at close range by Durie.

The momentum was short-lived – around one and a half minutes to be exact. A Miller header fell to Bett, whose shot was only parried by Maxwell and fell invitingly to John Robertson, who converted from an acute angle.

As Rangers pressed forward, the chances came thick and fast, but it was their desire to save the game which was to cost them the fourth and decisive goal. McPherson, relishing a battle against the club which rejected him, went off a blistering run after a one-two with sub Kevin Thomas, made it into the box then delayed sensibly before cutting the ball back for the youngster to score the clincher.

Stuart McCall summed up the mood in the camp perfectly afterwards. "We blew it. It's as simple as that," he rapped. "Losing two soft goals in the first half was a nightmare. I don't think Colin Miller hit the free-kick that well, but he got it through and squeezed it in off the post. And the next one was a little bit dodgy."

	Home	Away	Total
Cup attendances	-	30,754	30,754

Rangers   (0) 3
Kilmarnock   (0) 0

Saturday February 25th 1995, Ibrox   Att: 44,859

RANGERS

1	Ally	MAXWELL
2	Stuart	McCALL
3	David	ROBERTSON (*46)
4	Richard	GOUGH
5	Alan	McLAREN
6	Basile	BOLI Booked
7	Trevor	STEVEN (85)
8	Alex	CLELAND
9	Charlie	MILLER
10	Gordon	DURIE
11	Brian	LAUDRUP

12	John	BROWN (*46)
13	Colin	SCOTT (gk)
14	Ian	DURRANT (85)

KILMARNOCK

1	Dragoje	LEKOVIC
2	Gus	MacPHERSON
3	Tom	BLACK
4	Mark	REILLY Booked
5	Neil	WHITWORTH Bkd
6	Derek	ANDERSON
7	Ally	MITCHELL
8	John	HENDRY (71)
9	Colin	McKEE
10	Robert	CONNOR Booked
11	Steve	MASKREY (*76)

12	Ray	MONTGOMERIE (71)
13	Colin	MELDRUM (gk)
14	Mark	ROBERTS (*76)

Match Facts

- Brian Laudrup and Ian Durrant became the third and fourth players to score penalties for Rangers in the season, after Mark Hateley and Pieter Huistra.

Score Sheet

G. DURIE 64 min – 1-0

B. LAUDRUP pen. 68 min – 2-0

I. DURRANT 88 pen – 3-0

Referee:
Mr. A. Huett (Edinburgh)

Bell's Premier Division

		P	W	D	L	W	D	L	F	A	Pts
1	**RANGERS**	26	9	3	1	7	3	3	46	21	54
2	Motherwell	25	5	5	3	5	4	3	38	36	39
3	Hibernian	26	7	5	1	1	8	4	36	36	37
4	Celtic	26	4	7	2	2	9	2	27	24	34
5	Hearts	26	7	4	2	2	2	9	33	36	33

In For The Killie

Another three points were acquired on the march to the title, but yet again the manner of the victory was unconvincing. For the first 45 painful minutes, Rangers were more or less dominated by a Kilmarnock side battling to save their Premier skins. The Ayrshire side squandered a number of chances which could have had the match sewn up by half-time. Their failure to convert any of these opportunities proved their undoing as a more purposeful Light Blues emerged after the interval to cut the upstarts down to size. Surprisingly, given the abuse that he had to suffer throughout proceedings, it was Gordon Durie who relieved the frustration. After an afternoon in which his casual approach was enraging the support even more than usual, he managed to placate the legions with a welcome 64th minute opener.

Charlie Miller provided the ammo with a splendid through ball, and Juke Box comfortably shook off his marker before comfortably rattling a left-foot past Lekovic. Rangers gained in confidence with that one goal advantage to their name, and began to look more like champions. The second arrived via the penalty spot, and after the controversies of the previous matches, there could be absolutely no disputing this one. Killie defender Derek Anderson produced the sort of challenge that had endeared John Brown to the support over the years on the Bomber himself, and there could be no denying that referee Huett's decision to award a spot-kick was the correct one. Brian Laudrup, who was having yet another of those games where he seemed to do what he want, easily slotted home.

The third was also from the penalty-spot – but from a different source. Ian Durrant had been on the pitch for a mere four minutes when he easily made it three after Charlie Miller had been fouled by Ray Montgomerie. Again the only dispute which surrounded this kick was over who would take it. Stuart McCall seemed keen, but it was Durrant who did the business.

So it finished 3-0, which was perhaps unfair on the Rugby Park men, who had given as good an account in the first half as they'd done in recent memory at Ibrox. Unfortunately for them, their superiority was not really translated into a glut of openings and their best effort saw Ally Maxwell save a Colin McKee 25-yarder.

Typically, in a match where there was precious little real controversy, somebody managed to find something to get worked up about. That somebody was Killie's Alex Totten, who felt that the opening goal should have been disallowed. "Neil Whitworth was on the ground injured in the Rangers penalty area at the time. The game should have been stopped." Walter Smith's comments were close to the point, as usual. "I wasn't happy with the way we played in the first half," he moaned. He could afford to be happy about the outcome, however. With Hibs slipping up at Falkirk, Rangers extended their lead at the top of the table to 15 points, with just ten matches remaining. Motherwell took over in second after their 1-0 win at Aberdeen.

	Home	Away	Total
Attendances	574,145	208,416	782,561

Hibernian
Rangers

(0) 1
(0) 1

Saturday March 4th 1995, Easter Road   Att: 12,059

		HIBERNIAN			**RANGERS**
1	Jim	LEIGHTON *Booked*	1	Ally	MAXWELL
2	Willie	MILLER	2	Craig	MOORE *(*62) Bk'd*
3	Graham	MITCHELL	3	Gary	BOLLAN
4	David	FARRELL *Booked*	4	Richard	GOUGH *Booked*
5	Steven	TWEED	5	Alan	McLAREN
6	Gordon	HUNTER	6	Basile	BOLI
7	Kevin	McALLISTER *(*73)*	7	Trevor	STEVEN
8	Joe	TORTOLANO	8	Neil	MURRAY *(*83)*
9	Keith	WRIGHT	9	Gordon	DURIE
10	Darren	JACKSON	10	Stuart	McCALL *Booked*
11	Michael	O'NEILL	11	John	BROWN

Subs

12	Mark	McGRAW *(*73)*	14	Ian	FERGUSON *(*62)*
13	Chris	REID (gk)	13	Billy	THOMSON (gk)
14	Chris	JACKSON	12	Ian	DURRANT *(*83)*

Match Facts

• Craig Moore picked up his *eighth* booking of the season. This was the last match at Easter Road as it was known, with demolition work beginning the day after.

Score Sheet

S. McCALL 58 min – 0-1
K. WRIGHT 76 min – 1-1

Referee:
Mr. R. Tait (Kilbride)

Bell's Premier Division

		P	W	D	L	W	D	L	F	A	Pts
1	**RANGERS**	27	9	3	1	7	4	3	47	22	55
2	Motherwell	25	5	5	3	5	4	3	38	36	39
3	Hibernian	27	7	6	1	1	8	4	37	27	38
4	Celtic	26	4	7	2	2	9	2	27	24	34
5	Hearts	26	7	4	2	2	2	9	33	36	33

Gers Wright Hard Done By

Rangers fielded a side almost unrecognisable from Walter Smith's preferred first-choice XI, but still managed to outplay their closest title rivals for much of the match before Keith Wright took a hand in proceedings.

The team really was startling. Apart from the expected absences like Goram, Hateley and McCoist, there was no Laudrup either, which caused John Brown to operate in an unfamiliar left-wing role. The suspension of Charlie Miller also saw Trevor Steven in the extraordinary role, for him at least, of striker! Alan McLaren even made it into midfield . . . .

Nevertheless, Rangers demonstrated why they are streets ahead of the competition in Scotland by reacting positively to all the upheaval.

The signs were good from early on, and Gordon Durie was the first to threaten with a shot which hit the post on only eight minutes. This set the pattern for the opening 45 minutes, with Rangers dominating the play and Hibs only really looking lively on the break.

The week previously, John Brown had said he would gladly sell confectionary if it meant he had a job at Ibrox for life. Playing left-wing was possibly the next most obscure thing, but Bomber showed he had all the talents required when he sent in a cross which Stuart McCall almost managed to shoot past Jim Leighton from.

Therefore it was no surprise when it was McCall himself who opened the scoring 13 minutes after the interval. As was becoming a habit with Rangers goals, the opposition managed to find something to complain about. Hibs believed that Gordon Durie fouled Graham Mitchell on the start of his run which was to provide the ammunition, and the challenge was a contentious one. Nevertheless Juke Box weaved his way into the goal area and found McCall, whose shot was more than enough to break the stalemate.

The former Everton man obviously relished the opportunity to show that not all Rangers' goals have to come through Laudrup and Hateley, as he continued to trouble Leighton. A superb 25-yard effort, after some great build-up work from Brown and Murray, was his next attempt.

That close shave for Hibs was to prove crucial for them as they equalised with 14 minutes left. Willie Miller noticed Keith Wright wandering about unmarked and posted the ideal ball for him to head home.

And two dropped points could have become three in the dying seconds, when yet another cross highlighted uncertainty in the defence. Jackson found Joe Tortolano and Maxwell had to pounce to prevent the ball going in.

With the team Rangers had out, a draw would probably have been acceptable at the start of the game, but their overall superiority meant the result was looked on with some disappointment. As scorer McCall emphasised, "Normally when we come to Hibs we can expect it to be a bit backs-to-the-wall, with them turning on the pressure. But today was different. We gave away a silly goal."

Guess what? Alex Miller saw it differently. "I think we deserved a point," was his judgement.

	Home	Away	Total
League Attendances	574,145	220,475	794,620

Rangers (1) 2
Falkirk (1) 2

Saturday March 11th 1995, Ibrox   Att: 43,359

RANGERS

1	Ally	MAXWELL
2	Stuart	McCALL
3	Gary	BOLLAN *(*76)*
4	Richard	GOUGH
5	Alan	McLAREN
6	Basile	BOLI
7	Ian	DURRANT
8	Ian	FERGUSON
9	Gordon	DURIE
10	John	BROWN *Booked*
11	Brian	LAUDRUP

Subs

12	Neil	MURRAY
13	Billy	THOMSON *(gk)*
14	Alexie	MIKHAILITCHENKO *(*76)*

FALKIRK

1	Tony	PARKS
2	Graeme	HAMILTON *Booked/Sentoff*
3	Jamie	McGOWAN
4	John	HUGHES
5	Joe	McLAUGHLIN *Booked*
6	John	CLARK
7	Stevie	KIRK
8	Brian	RICE *(*58)*
9	Colin	McDONALD *(89)*
10	Maurice	JOHNSTON
11	Scott	MacKENZIE

12	Tommy	McQUEEN *(*58)*
13	Billy	LAMONT *(gk)*
14	Nicky	HENDERSON *(89)*

Match Facts

- Brian Laudrup's dad Finn saw his son 'live' with Rangers for the fourth time – and Rangers still could not win! The previous game werer aginst AEK at home, and live on Danish TV against Celtic at New Year and in the Cup against Hearts.

- John Brown scored his first goal of an injury troubled season.

Score Sheet

C. McDONALD 26 min – 0-1
B. LAUDRUP pen. 45 – 1-1
C. McDONALD 55 min – 1-2
J. BROWN 65 min – 2-2

Referee:
Mr. L. Mottram (Forth)

Bell's Premier Division

1	**RANGERS**	28	9	4	1	7	4	3	49	24	56
2	Motherwell	26	5	6	3	5	4	3	44	38	40
3	Hibernian	27	7	6	1	1	8	4	37	27	38
4	Celtic	26	5	7	2	2	9	2	29	24	37
5	Hearts	26	7	4	2	2	2	9	33	36	33

Mo The Merrier As Bairns Claim A Point

It was Sod's law, really, that Mo Johnston, on his Falkirk debut, would come up trumps on his old stamping ground. His signing for Rangers years previously had been a two-fingered salute at former employers Celtic, and here he turned up again with a raspberry for another previous partner.

Johnston made both goals as Falkirk, following their Coca-Cola Cup win earlier in the season, produced yet another creditable Ibrox performance which saw the Light Blues collect just one point in what was becoming a stagger to the title.

As big an impact as Scotland's 'enfant terrible' made, though, there could be no overshadowing the awesome contribution Brian Laudrup made to the match. Superlatives were not enough to describe his dazzling display.

Astonishingly, his virtuoso performance was rewarded only with a penalty goal just before half-time, after Ian Durrant had been upended by John Clark. And that was an equaliser too, as the Brockville side had taken a shock lead in 26 minutes when Mo, after some good work from Graeme Hamilton, fired in a shot which found its way to Colin McDonald, whose first-time finish landed in the bottom corner of the net.

Hamilton, unfortunately for him, was involved in less pleasing circumstances later on when his second booking in the 71st minute, for a foul on the rampant Laudrup, earned him a red card.

That Falkirk had even taken the lead was a reflection on the profligacy shown by the Rangers strikeforce, who missed chance after chance. Gordon Durie had a shot saved by Tony Parks, as did Alan McLaren, then Durie missed another easy header.

The pattern continued after the break, with Basile Boli finding the net but having his effort disallowed, Ian Ferguson squandering another golden opportunity and then the great man Laudrup himself being foiled by the in-form keeper.

Falkirk weren't so wasteful, and took the lead again after Johnston got the better of Alan McLaren, a former team-mate at Hearts, and crossed for McDonald to score his second.

So Rangers were left to chase the game again, and it was left to Laudrup to conjure up the inspiration which saved a point. The Dane accepted a short corner and flighted in a lovely ball which John Brown powered home with his head.

A winner could have come, but the song remained the same, with chances being missed left right and centre and Ferguson, and more particularly Durie, still the main culprits. It was not all frustration, though, as Alexei Mikhailitchenko emerged to the biggest cheer of the day as a sub for Gary Bollan, for only his second sighting of the season. Not even the Ukrainian star could find the finish which would have deprived Mo his gloating in the tabloids the next day.

Walter Smith was again left fed-up after a game which did nothing to suggest consistency was any closer. "That's twice now we have dictated most of the game and come away with a point. However we are still creating a lot of chances and in terms of movement and passing, it's as well as we have done for a long while."

With the Scottish Cup meaning there were no other Premier games, Rangers moved 16 points clear.

	Home	Away	Total
Attendances	617,504	220,475	837,979

121

Hearts **(2) 2**
Rangers **(1) 1**

Saturday March 18th 1995, Tynecastle   Att: 9806

HEARTS			RANGERS		
1	Craig	NELSON	1	Ally	MAXWELL
2	Steve	FRAIL	2	Alex	CLELAND *Booked*
3	Scott	LEITCH	*3*	*Gary*	*BOLLAN (*75) Booked*
4	Neil	BERRY	4	Richard	GOUGH
5	Willie	JAMIESON *Booked*	5	Alan	McLAREN
6	Dave	McPHERSON	6	Basile	BOLI
7	Gary	MACKAY	*7*	*Trevor*	*STEVEN (19)*
8	Jim	BETT	8	Ian	FERGUSON
9	*John*	*ROBERTSON (*66)*	9	Gordon	DURIE
10	John	MILLAR	10	Stuart	McCALL *Booked*
11	*David*	*HAGEN (*62)*	11	Brian	LAUDRUP

Subs

12	*Allan*	*JOHNSTON (*62)*	12	*Ian*	*DURRANT (19)*
13	Henry	SMITH *(gk)*	13	Billy	THOMSON *(gk)*
14	*John*	*COLQUHOUN (*66)*	14	*Neil*	*MURRAY (*75)*

Match Facts

- Gary Bollan's unhappy start to his career with Rangers continued with him yet to notch a win in four appearances.

- Hearts, managed by ex-Gers Tommy McLean and Tommy Forsyth, fielded three others formerly at Ibrox– Dave McPherson, David Hagen and Jim Bett.

Score Sheet

J. ROBERTSON 9 min – 1-0

J. MILLAR 30 min – 2-0

B. LAUDRUP 44 min – 2-1

Referee:
Mr. H. Williamson (Renfrew)

Bell's Premier Division

		P	W	D	L	W	D	L	F	A	Pts
1	**RANGERS**	29	9	4	1	7	4	4	50	26	56
2	Motherwell	28	6	6	3	5	5	3	42	39	44
3	Hibernian	28	7	6	1	1	9	4	37	27	39
4	Celtic	27	5	7	2	2	9	2	29	24	37
5	Hearts	27	8	4	2	2	2	9	35	37	36

Hearts Bett-er Poor Rangers

Rangers' magnificent run against Hearts had ended in the Scottish Cup, and the Edinburgh men repeated the medicine again. And once more, after the exploits of Colin Miller and Dave McPherson in that Cup tie, it was a former Ibrox man who was to pay a pivotal role in the outcome.

When Jim Bett signed for Tommy McLean midway through the season, most sceptics predicted a short stay under a manager not noted for his encouragement of silky football. However, Bett enjoyed the sort of new lease of life Davie Cooper received under McLean at Motherwell, and Brian Laudrup apart, was the most influential man on the pitch.

Strangely, he played no major part in either of Hearts' two goals. The first, after nine minutes, was a result of some tricky play by old-timers Gary Mackay and John Robertson, and a poor effort from goalkeeper Ally Maxwell.

Mackay threaded an impressive ball into the box which Robertson, who had timed his run to perfection, finished off sweetly. But there was no denying that Maxi's attempt to stop could have been more convincing.

Half an hour in, and Hearts were two up. McPherson again proved a nuisance, as he robbed Stuart McCall and went on a loping run, only to feed yet another ex-Light Blue, David Hagen. He fired over a terrific cross, which John Millar bulleted in to leave Maxwell somewhat bemused.

Not for the first time, the responsibility of dragging Rangers back into proceedings fell on the shoulders of Brian Laudrup. And he responded magnificently with a goal just before the break which was the equal of anything he had produced previously in his landmark season.

Neil Berry was the latest mortal to suffer, as the Dane left him for dead, reached the corner of the penalty box and engineered a bend on his shot which Craig Nelson was not capable of matching.

Hearts were worth their first-half lead, but Rangers made a real fight of it in the second half, with Laudrup on centre-stage as ever. He delivered two dangerous free-kicks which caused alarm in the home defence, before causing panic with another dart into the box before McPherson could eventually avert the danger. Gordon Durie, it was though, who fashioned the best opportunity to equalise when he made space for himself to blast in a low show which went goalwards with venom, but unfortunately hit a post.

Hearts held on, however, with Bett influential in keeping a few heads around him calm.

There was more to feel glum about than just defeat, as well, with Trevor Steven limping off early with thigh problems, and Stuart McCall, Gary Bollan and Alex Cleland, for a shocking tackle on Robertson, all booked. Cleland, in fact, was lucky not to get a red for a challenge which saw the Scotland international depart the action.

Lamented Walter Smith, "I felt we paid for a very slack opening spell. We didn't compete the way we should, and our opponents put more into the opening spell."

So disappointment was the order of the day, rather than panic, despite Motherwell's 2-1 win over Dundee United which cut the gap at the top of the table to a mere 12 points.

	Home	Away.	Total
Attendances	617,504	230,281	847,758

Dundee United
Rangers

(0) 0
(2) 2

Saturday April 1st 1995, Tannadice   Att: 11,500

DUNDEE UNITED

1	Kelham	O'HANLON
2	Jim	McINALLY
3	Maurice	MALPAS *Booked*
4	David	HANNAH
5	Gordan	PETRIC *Booked*
6	Brian	WELSH
7	David	BOWMAN *Booked*
8	Billy	McKINLAY
9	Andy	McLAREN
10	Craig	BREWSTER (66)
11	Mark	PERRY (*79)

Subs

12		SERGIO (*66)
13	Henrik	JORGENSEN *(gk)*
14	Christian	DAILLY (*79)

RANGERS

1	Billy	THOMSON
2	Alex	CLELAND *Booked*
3	John	BROWN
4	Richard	GOUGH
5	Alan	McLAREN
6	*Basile*	*BOLI (*58)*
7	Stuart	McCALL *Booked*
8	Charlie	MILLER
9	*Gordon*	*DURIE (+75) Booked*
10	Ian	DURRANT
11	Brian	LAUDRUP

12	Alexei	MIKHAILITCHENKO (+75)
13	Ally	MAXWELL *(gk)*
14	Gary	BOLLAN (*58)

Match Facts

- Billy Thomson became the 31st player to appear on League business for Rangers – an average of a new player *every* game.

- Rangers featured four ex-United players – Gough, Thomson, Bollan and Cleland.

Score Sheet

G. DURIE 10 sec – 0-1
A. McLAREN 8 min – 0-2

Referee:
Mr. S. Roy (Aberdeen)

Bell's Premier Division

		P	W	D	L	W	D	L	F	A	Pts
1	**RANGERS**	30	9	4	1	8	4	4	52	26	59
2	Motherwell	30	6	6	3	5	6	4	43	42	45
3	Hibernian	30	8	6	1	1	10	4	41	29	43
4	Celtic	29	5	8	2	3	9	2	31	25	41
5	Hearts	30	6	3	5	3	8	5	39	42	38

Gers Make A Fool Of Kirky

An April Fool's day clash with Dundee United left the joke on the Tangerines' new boss Billy Kirkwood, who departed the Ibrox coaching staff for the Tannadice hot-seat during the week. Indeed, it only took ten seconds for Rangers to deliver the punchline. Incredibly, that was as long as took for Gordon Durie to open the scoring, and from there on in, it was more or less plain sailing.

No United player had touched the ball as the Light Blues went one up. And when Alan McLaren added a second after eight minutes, more than one terracing prankster was suggesting that a couple of the home men had still to see any action.

The first really was quite extraordinary. Direct from the kick-off, the ball was moved back to Alan McLaren, who sent a long ball forward for Durie to chase. Brian Welsh tried in vain to keep up with Juke-Box, but was out of luck as the striker kept his nerve to lob Kelham O'Hanlon and score the fastest Premier goal of the season. If that start was a stunner, United were rocking again when McLaren hit the second. A needless Andy McLaren foul was punished by Alan McLaren from 35 yards out, with a free-kick of awesome power. As Walter Smith reflected afterwards, "He has never wanted to take free-kicks before – and we have been encouraging him to do so. It showed what a great striker of the ball he is."

Needless to say, after the recent ropey results and such a purposeful start, Rangers were more than content to hang on to what they had and concentrate on picking up the three points with the minimum of fuss. Who could blame them? With Hibs drawing at Partick Thistle and Motherwell and Celtic cancelling each other out at Hampden, the outcome ensured Rangers were a mere two wins away from their seventh consecutive title.

However, there were other talking points in an interesting tussle. Rangers had most of the other chances to score, with Ian Durrant coming closest on a couple of occasions. And there was a chance for debutant Billy Thomson, making his first competitive appearance in goal at the tender age of 37, to shine as he defied Sergio and Gordan Petric with super saves, as well as producing one stunning stop from Billy McKinlay. That 21st minute save proved a crucial moment, for if the Scotland star had scored, there would have been plenty of time left for United to get back into the game. As it proved, though, it was not to be.

As usual, though, there were more injury problems for Walter Smith to worry about, as he watched Basile Boli (back) and Gordon Durie (hamstring) depart the action early. And Stuart McCall, who had missed Scotland's midweek draw in Russia due to his persistent Achilles problem, picked up a knee knock into the bargain.

Nevertheless, there were more smiles on the bus back to Glasgow than frowns – particularly from Thomson, who performed well in his first Premier game for TWO years!

"I always thought my chance would come again," he said. "If I had thought my days were over I'd have packed it in." With the possibility of a championship clinching party on the horizon, he was forgiven for being glad he didn't.

	Home	Away	Total
Attendances	617,504	241,781	859,285

Rangers
Aberdeen

(2) 3
(2) 2

Saturday, April 8th 1995, Ibrox

Att: 44,460

RANGERS

1	Billy	THOMSON
2	Alex	CLELAND
3	John	BROWN
4	Richard	GOUGH
5	Alan	McLAREN
6	*Basile*	*BOLI (13)*
7	Trevor	STEVEN
8	Charlie	MILLER *Booked*
9	Ian	DURRANT
10	Mark	HATELEY
11	*Brian*	*LAUDRUP (*76)*

Subs

12	*Neil*	*MURRAY (13)*
13	Ally	MAXWELL (gk)
14	*Alexei*	*MIKHAILITCHENKO (*76)*

ABERDEEN

1	Michael	WATT
2	Stewart	McKIMMIE
3	Stephen	WRIGHT
4	Paul	KANE *Booked*
5	John	INGLIS
6	Gary	SMITH *Booked*
7	Peter	HETHERSTON
8	Duncan	SHEARER
9	Joe	MILLER
10	Billy	DODDS *Booked*
11	*Brian*	*GRANT (*56)*

12	Brian	IRVINE
13	Derek	STILLIE (gk)
14	*Eoin*	*JESS (*56)*

Match Facts

• Neil Murray scored his first ever Premier League goal for the club – despite Cup efforts before, including a strike in the 1993 Scottish Cup final Mark Hateley ended his longest run without scoring for the club – four months.

Score Sheet

I. DURRANT 20 min – 1-0

N. MURRAY 24 min – 2-0

B. DODDS 32 min – 2-1

D. SHEARER 45 min – 2-2

M. HATELEY 52 min – 3-2

Referee:
Mr. H. Williamson (Renfrew)

Bell's Premier Division

		P	W	D	L	W	D	L	F	A	Pts
1	**RANGERS**	31	10	4	1	8	4	4	55	28	62
2	Motherwell	31	6	6	4	5	6	4	44	44	45
3	Hibernian	30	8	6	1	1	10	4	41	29	43
4	Celtic	29	5	8	2	3	9	2	31	25	41
5	Falkirk	31	7	3	5	3	8	5	42	43	41

Champion Day As Dons Look Doomed

Back in 1991, Rangers clinched their third consecutive championship with a 2-0 win over their closest challengers, Aberdeen, on the final day of the season.

Four years later, it was again the Dons who provided the opposition as Rangers all but sealed another flag. But the circumstances could not have been more different. Their 3-2 win left the once proud Granite City club marooned at the bottom of the Premier Division, four points adrift, and in very real danger of relegation for the first time in their history after a pathetic run of results.

Not that anyone at Ibrox was complaining. Although it was still arithmetically possible for Celtic to even things up at the top of the table, it would be the most improbable comeback in the history of football and so this win ensured a championship party against Hibs the following Sunday was very much on the agenda.

Bafflingly, however, after two of their better performances during the season against Rangers at their Pittodrie home, the visitors again put up a sterling fight and contributed to one of the best games seen at Ibrox during the season.

The Light Blues, on occasion, played some exhilarating stuff. The lead they deserved arrived in the 20th minute when Ian Durrant, in only because of injury to the likes of Ian Ferguson and Stuart McCall, was in the right place to take advantage of Michael Watt's vain parry from a Brian Laudrup shot after some super skill from Charlie Miller. It was no coincidence that there was more skilful football on offer with a rejuvenated Durrant pulling the strings.

Just four minutes later, the lead was two, with Laudrup again involved. Freed by a clever flick from Mark Hateley, he wrongfooted the Dons defence to set up Neil Murray to convert a simple move. Murray had only been on the park for 11 minutes, replacing Basile Boli who looked to have dislocated his shoulder.

Strangely, this was the spur which Aberdeen required. And, while a rout had looked on the cards, it was actually at the other end another goal came. Joe Miller and Duncan Shearer combined on the left to allow Billy Dodds to notch a simple goal at the far post. Amazingly, right on the stroke of half-time, Aberdeen drew level, and again it was Miller and Shearer who proved integral parts of the move. The little winger offered an enticing cutback for the Scotland striker and he showed the sort of clinical finishing which had been missing from the Dons attack for much of the campaign. With a thriller of a second period set-up, the fans were not disappointed, and even more pleasingly for the home legions, it was Rangers who proved to just have the edge. Just seven minutes after the break recent signing Alex Cleland made one of his first positive contributions for the club – after a string of poor games and some reckless tackles – by crossing for Hateley to score for the first time in 1995 after his injury problems. Both sides came close after this, but there were no further goals and Rangers had got the three points they required to sew up their seventh consecutive title.

After the game, a relieved Richard Gough admitted the League had been collected without any great consistency and perhaps not in the style which the season-ticket holders expect. But he still claimed it was a worthy triumph. "It's been a transitional year when we have used an awful lot of players. We have been without so many key players for long spells and that has meant we have often had to grind out results."

	Home	Away	Total
Attendances	661,964	241,781	903,775

Rangers
Hibernian

(1) 3
(1) 1

Sunday April 16th 1995, Ibrox   Att: 44,193

RANGERS

1	Billy	THOMSON
2	Alex	CLELAND
3	John	BROWN (*29)
4	Richard	GOUGH
5	Alan	McLAREN
6	Ian	DURRANT
7	Trevor	STEVEN
8	Charlie	MILLER
9	Gordon	DURIE (+46)
10	Mark	HATELEY
11	Brian	LAUDRUP

Subs

12	Neil	MURRAY (*29)
13	Ally	MAXWELL (gk)
14	Alexei	MIKHAILITCHENKO (+46)

HIBERNIAN

1	Jim	LEIGHTON
2	Willie	MILLER
3	Graham	MITCHELL
4	Pat	McGINLAY
5	Steven	TWEED
6	Andy	MILLEN
7	Gareth	EVANS (*66)
8	David	FARRELL
9	Keith	WRIGHT (+81)
10	Darren	JACKSON
11	Michael	O'NEILL

12	Kevin	McALLISTER (*66)
13	Chris	REID (gk)
14	Joe	TORTOLANO (+81)

Match Facts

• Alexei Mikhailitchenko became the 18th player to score on League duty for Rangers during the season.

Score Sheet

G. DURIE 24 min – 1-0

M. O'NEILL 39 min – 1-1

I. DURRANT 85 min – 2-1

MIKHAILITCHENKO 87 min – 3-1

Referee:
Mr. W. Young (Clarkston)

Bell's Premier Division

		P	W	D	L	W	D	L	F	A	Pts
1	RANGERS	32	11	4	1	8	4	4	58	29	65
2	Motherwell	32	6	6	4	5	6	5	44	47	45
3	Falkirk	32	8	3	5	3	8	5	45	43	44
4	Hibernian	31	8	6	1	1	10	5	42	32	43
5	Kilmarnock	32	8	3	4	3	6	8	39	43	42

The Magnificent Seven

It's Sky TV who call their live football show on the Sabbath "Super Sunday", but that's exactly what it proved to be for Scottish Television, who captured Rangers' championship party for viewers on a glory day at Ibrox.

The title clinched the Saturday before, arithmetically confirmed with Celtic's defeat at Pittodrie the previous day, was celebrated with gusto by a full house who saw the undisputed kings of Scottish football turn in one of their best displays of the season. The encounter was a treat for the 44,000 plus who were at Ibrox, as well as the telly fans.

And yet, it looked at one point that the brilliance of Jim Leighton was going to deny Walter Smith's men the champagne show they so desperately wanted to deliver for their supporters. He produced an inspirational showing which demonstrated fully why he is ranked only behind Andy Goram by Scots boss Craig Brown. Nevertheless, there was nothing he could do about Gordon Durie's 24th minute strike which put the Gers in front. The ex-Hibee blasted a header past Jim after Mark Hateley had touched on a Laudrup cross.

Alex Miller's men responded with an equaliser which did not go down at all well with the home legions. Rangers were vehement that play should have been stopped as Alex Cleland was treated by physio Gordon Allison, but it only came to a halt when Alan McLaren fouled Darren Jackson. Darren Jackson moved the free-kick to Michael O'Neill and the Northern Ireland international fired a superb 25-yard rocket past Billy Thomson.

This lull muted Rangers for a period in the second half, but they eventually got back into gear and Leighton was required again to be at his best to deny efforts from Alexei Mikhailitchenko and Richard Gough. But, as the pressure increased and increased, there was nothing he could do to prevent the eventual inevitability of a Rangers second.

And there was nobody more fitting to score it than Ian Durrant, who earlier in the season had looked to be on his way to Everton. Back in the team and back on form, he conducted a brilliant one-two with Charlie Miller he collected a super goal on 85 minutes to send Ibrox into rhapsody.

And when Mikhailitchenko collected the third two minutes later, following yet another magical Laudrup run, a perfect day was sealed.

Walter Smith could not hide his pride after another memorable day in the Rangers revolution. "There were a lot of awkward moments to handle this season, but it's a credit to the players here that they handled things so well. The football we played in November and December was as good as anything since I came here. We had a run of injuries from January which affected our performances, but we managed to hold onto the lead we built up."

And, of course, there were special plaudits for the man who had done so much to put a smile on the Scottish game throughout the season – Brian Laudrup. "We don't see players quite as often as him now. Even opponents admire him greatly. He'd conducted himself extremely well on and off the park."

	Home	Away	Total
Attendances	706,157	241,781	947,938

Kilmarnock
Rangers

(0) 0
(1) 1

Thursday April 20th 1995, Rugby Park   Att: 16,086

KILMARNOCK

1	Dragoje	LEKOVIC
2	Gus	MacPHERSON
3	Tom	BLACK
4	Mark	SKILLING
5	Neil	WHITWORTH *Booked*
6	Derek	ANDERSON *Booked*
7	Ally	MITCHELL
8	Billy	FINDLAY
9	Paul	WRIGHT
10	Robert	CONNOR *Booked*
11	*Steve*	*MASKREY (*75)*

Subs

12	*Tom*	*BROWN (*75)*
13	Bobby	GEDDES *(gk)*
14	Mark	REILLY

RANGERS

1	Ally	MAXWELL
2	Craig	MOORE
3	Gary	BOLLAN
4	Richard	GOUGH
5	Alan	McLAREN
6	Neil	MURRAY
7	Alex	CLELAND
8	*Ian*	*FERGUSON (* 77)*
9	Ian	DURRANT
10	Alexei	MIKHAILITCHENKO
11	Brian	LAUDRUP

12	Brian	REID
13	Neil	INGLIS *(gk)*
14	*Lee*	*ROBERTSON (*77)*

Match Facts

• This was Rangers' first match of the season on a Thursday, meaning that they had played on every day of the week to satisfy the TV cameras.

•Gordon Durie and Ally McCoist, both out injured, paid their way into the ground and watched the match with the rest of the Light Blue fans. The pair returned from a day at Ayr races to find no tickets had been left for them.

Score Sheet

MIKHAILITCHENKO 38 min – 0-1

Referee:
Mr. H. Williamson (Renfrew)

Bell's Premier Division

		P	W	D	L	W	D	L	F	A	Pts
1	**RANGERS**	**33**	**11**	**4**	**1**	**9**	**4**	**4**	**59**	**29**	**68**
2	Motherwell	33	7	6	4	5	6	5	46	48	48
3	Falkirk	33	8	3	5	4	8	5	44	43	47
4	Hibernian	32	8	6	2	1	10	5	42	34	43
5	Kilmarnock	33	8	3	5	3	6	8	39	44	42

Miko Makes His Mark

If there was one player seemingly certain to leave Ibrox at the end of the season, virtually every journalist north of the border would have had you believe that it was Alexei Mikhailitchenko – and not without good reason.

The Ukrainian, never the most consistent of individuals during his career at Rangers, had had his most frustrating season to date, with a succession of injuries limiting his appearances to a mere handful.

However, after opening his scoring account for the season in the title party against Hibs, Miko continued where he had left off in a largely non-eventful 1-0 win under Sky's TV cameras at Rugby Park. And, although the pictures beamed to the nation were of a less than inspiring spectacle, his match-winning effort was a real classic.

The move stemmed from the right, where Craig Moore found Brian Laudrup with an inch perfect pass. The Dane appeared to have a better-than-evens chance of scoring himself, but swept across a majestic ball which left Miko to pass the ball away from Dragoje Lekovic, from an acute angle, with his left foot. An Aussie to a Dane to a Ukranian, deceiving a Yugoslav. Who says Scottish football ain't cosmopolitan?!

That apart, it was not a fixture to write home about. Killie were fairly poor, although they had their moments, witr reinstated keeper Ally Maxwell struggling with high balls most of the evening. One such moment came early on, in the 17th minute, when he contrived to collide with Ally Mitchell in an incident which saw the home fans and players on the look-out for a penalty. They were to receive no joy from referee Hugh Williamson of Renfrew.

They came even closer when Steve Maskrey was presented an opening after some unselfish and impressive work from former 'Ger Gus MacPherson and recent signing Paul Wright, but the best Maskrey could do was to hit the post.

But it was the champions who offered the better work. Alex Cleland came close to scoring his first goal for the club since his signing from Dundee United, but was thwarted at the last gasp by Lekovic saving at his feet, after he had been sent clear by Ian Durrant. And Durrant himself, like Mikhailitchenko enjoying a new lease of life, came even closer. Converted to a striker for the night, he latched on to a pass from the scorer to beat the 'keeper but found the woodwork in the shape of the crossbar in his way.

Asked after the match whether Mikhailitchenko would be staying or departing in the summer at the end of his contract, Walter Smith was playing his cards close to his chest, confirming suspicions that it was to be his last season at the club. But the gaffer did concede. "He's only played a few games after his injury problems, but he's certainly doing well. That's two goals in a few days and he's taken them both well. He's making up for lost time!"

Counterpart Alex Totten had less to smile about, and he was concise and to the point in his analysis. "After three wins, I'm disappointed. Our passing was poor and let us down. We can do much better."

	Home	Away	Total
Attendances	706,157	257,867	964,024

Rangers
Motherwell

(0) 0
(1) 2

Saturday April 30th 1995, Ibrox

Att: 43,756

RANGERS

1	Billy	THOMSON
2	Alex	CLELAND
3	Alexei	MIKHAILITCHENKO *Booked*
4	Richard	GOUGH
5	Alan	McLAREN
6	Basile	BOLI
7	Trevor	STEVEN
8	Ian	FERGUSON
9	Ian	DURRANT
10	Mark	HATELEY *Booked*
11	Brian	LAUDRUP

Subs

12	Neil	MURRAY
13	Neil	INGLIS *(gk)*
14	Craig	MOORE

MOTHERWELL

1	Stephen	WOODS
2	Eddie	MAY
3	Rab	McKINNON *Booked*
4	John	PHILLIBEN
5	Brian	MARTIN
6	Shaun	McSKIMMING *Booked*
7	Paul	LAMBERT
8	Jamie	DOLAN *Booked*
9	Tommy	COYNE *Booked*
10	Dougie	ARNOTT *(*76)*
11	Billy	DAVIES

12	Andy	RODDIE
13	Scott	HOWIE *(gk)*
14	Alex	BURNS *(*76)*

Match Facts

• Rangers and Motherwell fans undertook a walk between Fir Park and Ibrox before the game to raise money for the Davie Cooper Appeal.

• The attendance of 43,756 took Rangers' total league crowds for the season over the million mark.

Score Sheet

D. ARNOTT 12 min – 0-1

S. McSKIMMING 80 min 0-2

Referee:
Mr. W. Crombie (Edinburgh)

Bell's Premier Division

		P	W	D	L	W	D	L	F	A	Pts
1	**RANGERS**	34	11	4	2	9	4	4	59	31	68
2	Motherwell	34	7	6	4	6	6	5	48	48	51
3	Falkirk	34	8	3	6	4	8	5	48	45	47
4	Hibernian	33	8	6	2	2	10	5	43	34	46
5	Celtic	32	5	8	3	4	9	3	33	29	44

A Kick In The Bolis

Rangers' form in previous seasons once the League title had been won had been poor, but there was optimism 1994-95 would finish on a high after the wins against Hibs and Kilmarnock. Sadly, the fans were to be disappointed again, with a sub-standard performance against Motherwell resulting in a deserved defeat.

Even more disconcerting was a dreadful display display from Basile Boli, who was supposed to be putting on a showcase performance for the watching contingent from his next potential employers, Fenerbahce of Turkey. All Baz succeeded in doing was convince Turkish supremo Ali Sen he would be wasting his money. Said Sen afterwards, "I was interested in the Boli of yesterday, not the Boli of today. Unfortunately, yesterdays mean nothing in football."

Perhaps the fact that the title was won, while Motherwell were still chasing a potentially lucrative European place, was a factor in the match. Nevertheless, it did not excuse Rangers' poverty of play.

They had the first real chance when Boli fired in an effort which did little to trouble Woods in the ninth minute, but before long the champs were behind.

Just one minute after Dougie Arnott had blasted over from a Tommy Coyne cutback, the pair combined again with a more devastating result. A cross from Shaun McSkimming was headed across goal by the Republic of Ireland international, and Arnott, a thorn in the side of Rangers over the years, did the needful.

Indeed, Arnott could have increased the Lanarkshire side's advantage just before the interval when he was sent clear by Coyne yet again, but it was Richard Gough – demonstrating to Boli the art of defending – who saved the day with a last gasp tackle.

Trevor Steven had Rangers' best chance of pulling one back, but his chip shot right on the interval went narrowly past.

Rangers re-started with a bit more purpose, and could have got the equaliser almost immediately. Keeper Stephen Woods totally missed a through ball from Steven, under pressure from Alex Cleland, and the former Dundee United player looked odds on to score. But Brian Martin, who was later to hear manager Alex McLeish describe his showing as "awesome", was on hand to block on the line , which just about summed up Rangers' day.

Another chance went abegging in the 59th minute when Ian Durrant nodded over a cross from Brian Laudrup – strangely quiet by his own standards – and there was a feeling of resignation when Boli, far more effective going forward than at the back, hit a post in 68 minutes.

That feeling was proved correct just ten minutes from time as Motherwell sealed only the second home league defeat of the season with a super 25 yard strike from McSkimming, which even the home fans would grudgingly have admitted was a worthy one to confirm their three points.

As Walter Smith agreed, this was one to forget. "We had more pressure in the second half, but it's disappointing because we don't like to lose at any time. There was nothing for me to take from this game."

	Home	Away	Total
Attendances	749,913	257,867	1,007,780

133

Celtic
Rangers

(0) 3
(0) 0

Sunday May 7th 1995, Hampden

Att: 31,025

CELTIC

1	Pat	BONNER
2	Tom	BOYD
3	Tosh	McKINLAY
4	Rudi	VATA
5	Brian	O'NEIL *Booked*
6	Peter	GRANT
7	Brian	McLAUGHLIN
8	Paul	McSTAY
9	*Pierre*	*Van HOOYDONK (76)*
10	*Simon*	*DONNELLY (*67)*
11	John	COLLINS

Subs

12	*Phil*	*O'DONNELL (76)*
13	Gordon	MARSHALL *(gk)*
14	*Willie*	*FALCONER (*67)*

RANGERS

1	Billy	THOMSON *sent off*
2	Craig	MOORE
3	Alex	CLELAND
4	Basile	BOLI
5	Alan	McLAREN
6	*John*	*BROWN (26) Booked*
7	Trevor	STEVEN
8	*Ian*	*FERGUSON (*72)*
9	Ian	DURRANT
10	Mark	HATELEY
11	*Brian*	*LAUDRUP (*84)*

12	*Alexei*	*MIKHAILITCHENKO (*72)*
13	*Ally*	*MAXWELL (gk) (*84)*
14	*Neil*	*MURRAY (*26)*

Match Facts

- The goals came from an unlikely combination of nationalities; a Dutchman, an Autralian and an Albanian.

- The 7000 or so empty seats was the biggest shortfall on capacity for an Old Firm game in years.

Score Sheet

P. VAN HOOYDONK 50 min – 1-0
C. MOORE OG 62 min – 2-0
R. VATA 83 min – 3-0

Referee:
Mr. L. Mottram (Forth)

Bell's Premier Division

		P	W	D	L	W	D	L	F	A	Pts
1	**RANGERS**	35	11	4	2	9	4	5	59	34	68
2	Motherwell	35	8	6	4	6	6	5	50	48	54
3	Hibernian	34	9	6	2	2	10	5	46	35	49
4	Falkirk	35	8	3	6	4	9	5	48	45	48
5	Celtic	34	5	8	4	4	9	3	37	32	47

Old Firm Fiasco

If ever there was a meaningless Old Firm match, this was it. Celtic marking time until the Scottish Cup Final, Rangers winding down after claiming the championship. Even so, there were few in the 4000 strong contingent of Bears at the National Stadium prepared to console themselves with this fact as they watched their side comprehensively beaten in a shocker of a match.

Sky yet again opted to show the derby as part of their Scottish football deal, and what their viewers must have made of the first 45 minutes is unthinkable. The first half, not to put too fine a point on it, was appalling. From a Rangers perspective the second half was worse – but at least something happened to keep the armchair viewer awake.

Perhaps a sign of what was to come came arrived after only 26 minutes, when John Brown, captain for the day, uncharacteristically had to leave the battle zone early, injured, to be replaced by Neil Murray. It was a rare moment of activity in that opening period, as chances were limited to Celtic's Simon Donnelly, who saw his shot saved by Billy Thomson, and Ian Durrant, who surprisingly opted for a safe cutback to Mark Hateley after finding himself in the clear.

Those in blue would have settled for a repeat of those torpid 45 minutes had they know what lay in store.

Five minutes after the break, Dutchman Pierre Van Hooydonk, making his Old Firm debut for Celtic, opened the scoring with a smart drive to capitalise on good work from winger Brian McLaughlin. Just 12 minutes later, Craig Moore – who despite a regular slot throughout the season had yet to savour the Old Firm atmosphere – contrived to divert a Donnelly cross past Thomson after some impressive footwork had deceived Alan McLaren. Then, to rub salt into the already gaping wounds, Rudi Vata fired in a free-kick, which left Thomson looking none too clever, with seven minutes left, to confirm the champions' biggest defeat of the campaign.

That would have been enough for even the hardiest of followers. But just one minute later, Thomson's unhappy afternoon had the seal put on it, as he was red-carded for taking the legs away from McLaughlin, who had led Rangers a merry dance since half-time. This prompted the ignominious substitution of Footballer of the Year Brian Laudrup, who received his award at a ceremony in Glasgow later in the day, for Ally Maxwell, purely to prevent any further damage being done.

On a day when Gascoigne-mania reached a frenzy in the west of Scotland, with rumours suggesting that he had already signed, this was a result which injected a bit of reality back into proceedings. About the one saving grace for Rangers was, as far as it could be for a clash with their bitterest rivals, it was totally irrelevant. But it still left a nasty taste in the mouth. At least the fans could walk away with their heads held high after filling their allocation, unlike the missing thousands of Celtic supporters.

"It was a disappointing performance from us. Celtic were the better team and deserved to win. At no stage did we really put any pressure on them," was the realistic appraisal of Walter Smith.

	Home	Away	Total
Attendances	749,913	288,892	1,038,805

Rangers
Partick Thistle

(1) 1
(0) 1

Saturday May 13th 1995, Ibrox

Att: 45,280

RANGERS

1	Ally	MAXWELL *(+79)*
2	Neil	CALDWELL
3	Alex	CLELAND
4	Craig	MOORE
5	Alan	McLAREN
6	Alexei	MIKHAILITCHENKO
7	Trevor	STEVEN
8	Gordon	DURIE *(*52)*
9.	Ian	DURRANT
10.	Mark	HATELEY
11	Brian	LAUDRUP

Subs

12	Ian	NICOLSON
13	Andy	GORAM *(+79)*
14	Paul	McKNIGHT *(*52)*

PARTICK THISTLE

1	Nicky	WALKER
2	Callum	MILNE *(*74)*
3	Alan	DINNIE
4	Gregg	WATSON
5	Grant	TIERNEY
6	Steve	WELSH
7	Rod	McDONALD
8	Tom	SMITH *(+62)*
9	Wayne	FOSTER
10	Ian	CAMERON
11	Alex	TAYLOR

12	Roddy	GRANT *(*74)*
13	Mark	CAIRNS *(gk)*
14	Stuart	AYTON *(+62)*

Match Facts

• Caldwell and McKnight's appearances meant that Rangers had used a total of 33 players on League duty. No champions had ever reached a total of 30 before.

• 45,280 was the biggest League crowd at Ibrox outwith the two Old Firm matches.

Score Sheet

C. MOORE 45 min – 1-0

A. TAYLOR 87 min – 1-1

Referee:

Mr. H. Williamson (Renfrew)

Bell's Premier Division

		P	W	D	L	W	D	L	F	A	Pts
1	**RANGERS**	36	11	5	2	9	4	5	60	35	69
2	Motherwell	36	8	6	4	6	6	6	50	50	54
3	Hibernian	36	9	7	2	3	10	5	49	37	53
4	Celtic	36	6	8	4	5	10	3	39	33	51
5	Falkirk	36	8	3	7	4	9	5	48	47	48

Low Key End To A Low Key Season

Can a season which ended with Rangers as champions again be termed low-key? Sadly, it can, and the side went out with a whimper rather than a bang, which had been the story for much of the previous nine months.

The final scoreline was not impressive, and neither was the performance, although it still should have been good enough to claim the points. However, Mark Hateley apart, nobody in blue seemed unduly concerned with proceedings, and to a man they all looked relieved when the match and the season was brought to halt by ref Hugh Williamson close to quarter to five.

Perhaps an indicator on just how seriously Rangers took things was emphasised in their team selection, which saw Neil Caldwell, shortly to be freed, making his first-ever first, team appearance and 18-year-olds Iain Nicolson and Paul McNight on the bench. Admittedly, the injury crisis at the club had worsened, but it was hard to imagine any of the trio being anywhere close to the action had three points been required for the title. It's perhaps just as well nothing was at stake, because Thistle more than matched Rangers in the first half, and had two exceptional chances to take the lead before the champions finally got their act together.

Opportunity one came when Alex Taylor posted notice of his potency with a 16-yard strike which rebounded from the woodwork in the 20th minute. And just a few minutes later, Alex Cleland was the hero for the Light Blues with a marvellous last gasp tackle which thwarted the lively Rod McDonald fashioning a chance for himself. The danger signals heeded, Rangers began to impose themselves slightly more and it was right on half-time that they finally got the goal the large crowd had been waiting for. Ian Durrant, captain for the day, sent in a corner which Craig Moore delivered past Scotland squad keeper Nicky Walker. It was the Aussie's second goal of the season, or third if you count his mishap in the Old Firm clash a week previously. The champions' best period followed immediately after the interval, when numerous chances were spurned. Durrant and Alexei Mikhailitchenko were the most blatant culprits, but even Brian Laudrup, confirmed as Players' Player of the Year to add to the press award, got in on the act. He watched in disbelief as he fired over the bar in 70 minutes, and sank to his knees. In the circumstances, it surprised no-one when Thistle got their equaliser. Taylor, after his brush with the woodwork earlier on, fired past substitute Andy Goram from around 18 yards with just three minutes left. While that hardly raised spirits, if nothing else, it was heartening to see Goram back in goal again, appearing as he did as late substitute for Ally Maxwell.

After such a soporific match, it was no surprise that the talk all centred on the possible arrival of Paul Gascoigne, rather than the general inaction on the field. Said Mark Hateley, "The players would be delighted to see Paul here – he's very talented. It's time we did something in Europe again. Two or three new high profile players would be good."

After a season in which Rangers slogged but rarely sparkled, there were few at Ibrox who would have disputed those sentiments.

	Home	Away	Total
Attendances	795,193	288,892	1,084,085

Rangers (0) 2
St Johnstone (0) 0

Tuesday April 18th 1995, BP Youth Cup Final, Hampden

RANGERS

1	Michael	RAE
2	Greg	SHIELDS
3	Roddy	KERR
4	Scott	WILSON
5	Andrew	GALLOWAY
6	Iain	NICOLSON
7	Brian	McGINTY
8	Barry	FERGUSON
9	Paul	McKNIGHT *(*87)*
10	Paul	McSHANE *Booked*
11	Steven	BOYACK *Booked*

Subs

	Lee	DAIR (*87)
	Ross	MATHESON

It's often said that Rangers owe their success in Scotland thanks to their spending power. And it's an unarguable fact that expensively acquired players of the quality of Brian Laudrup, Mark Hateley and Paul Gascoigne do give them a head-start in the Premier.

However, perhaps the most ominous aspect of the continued success is not the prospect of more of these big name stars arriving from the continent, but the fact that Rangers also have the best *young* players in Scotland. This was proved again last season as the club lifted the BP Youth Cup, the premier competition for youths in the country, for the third time in a row! St Johnstone were the victims in a final which proved entertaining, after a slow start, at the National Stadium. Although the lads from Perth put in a solid enough display, there could be no disputing the young Gers their victory.

Goal heroes were Brian McGinty, who made a first-team appearance at Partick Thistle during the season, and Paul McShane, both in the second half.

McGinty's came first, when he was allowed time in the box and fired in a shot which was blocked by the Saints' defence. However, the loose ball fell perfectly for him and he was able to make his second attempt count by blasting past Saints 'keeper.

The second came ten minutes from time, and was a reward for McShane's endeavours through the evening. He came close to scoring more than once, particularly in the 51st minute, when he cannoned a header off the crossbar. But the one which did come was a peach. After receiving a tempting ball from Steven Boyack from the right hand side of the field, he sent a breathtaking volley past the bewildered Robertson.

There had been opportunities before the interval, and Paul McKnight was the man who most of them fell to. The young attacker came close on three occasions, but especially so just on the half-time whistle, with a shot which inched just wide of the keeper's right hand post.

Coach John McGregor was not surprisingly pleased with his young charges. "St Johnstone did cause us a few problems in the first half, and I was not happy with the way the team played. But they picked up their ideas in the second half, doing really well."

Score Sheet

B. McGINTY 47 min – 1-0

P. McSHANE 80 min – 2-0

138

1994-95 Records

Attendance by Number

Home			Away		
4/1/95	Celtic	45,794	30/10/94	Celtic	32,171
27/8/94	Celtic	45,466	7/5/95	Celtic	31,025
13/5/95	Partick Thistle	45,280	24/9/94	Aberdeen	21,000
25/11/94	Aberdeen	45,072	12/2/95	Aberdeen	20,000
26/12/94	Hibs	44,892	7/1/95	Partick Thistle	19,351
25/2/95	Kilmarnock	44,859	10/12/94	Kilmarnock	17,283
8/4/95	Aberdeen	44,460	20/4/95	Kilmarnock	16,086
21/1/95	Hearts	44,231	20/8/94	Partick Thistle	15,030
4/2/95	Dundee United	44,197	14/1/95	Falkirk	13,495
16/4/95	Hibs	44,193	17/9/94	Falkirk	12,500
15/10/94	Kilmarnock	44,099	9/11/94	Hearts	12,347
19/11/94	Falkirk	44,018	8/10/94	Hibs	12,118
13/8/94	Motherwell	43,750	4/3/95	Hibs	12,059
5/11/94	Partick Thistle	43,696	31/12/94	Motherwell	11,500
30/4/95	Motherwell	43,576	1/4/95	Dundee United	11,500
11/3/95	Falkirk	43,359	22/10/94	Motherwell	11,160
1/10/94	Dundee United	43,030	4/12/94	Dundee United	10,692
11/9/94	Hearts	41,041	18/3/95	Hearts	9,806

European Cup

Home			Away		
24/8/94	AEK Athens	44,789	10/8/94	AEK Athens	30,000

Coco-Cola Cup

Home			Away		
31/8/94	Falkirk	40,697	17/8/94	Arbroath	4,665

Scottish Cup

Home			Away		
5/2/95	Hamilton Accies	18,379	20/2/95	Hearts	12,375

RANGERS' APPEARANCES 1994-95

Players		Lge	Coca	Scot C	Euro	Total
Brian	LAUDRUP	33	1	2	2	38
Stuart	McCALL	30	2	2	2	36
Basile	BOLI	28	1	1	1	31
Richard	GOUGH	25	2	2	2	31
Mark	HATELEY	23	2	1	2	28
David	ROBERTSON	23	1	2	2	28
Alan	McLAREN	24	0	2	0	26
Craig	MOORE	19 (2)	2	2	0	23 (2)
Charlie	MILLER	21	0	2	0	23
Gordon	DURIE	16 (4)	1	2	2	21 (4)
Andy	GORAM	18 (1)	1	0	2	21 (1)
Ian	DURRANT	16 (10)	2	0 (1)	0 (2)	18 (13)
Ian	FERGUSON	13 (3)	2	0	2	17 (3)
Neil	MURRAY	14 (6)	0 (1)	1	0	15 (7)
Pieter	HUISTRA	15	0	0	0	15
Ally	MAXWELL	10 (1)	1	2	0	13 (1)
Trevor	STEVEN	10 (1)	0	2	0	12 (1)
Dave	McPHERSON	9	2	0	1	12
John	BROWN	10 (3)	1	0 (2)	0	11 (5)
Alex	CLELAND	10	0	1	0	11
Gary	BOLLAN	5 (1)	0	0	0	5 (1)
Billy	THOMSON	5	0	0	0	5
Alexei	MIKHAILITCHENKO	4 (5)	0	0	0	4 (5)
Ally	McCOIST	4 (5)	0	0	0	4 (5)
Duncan	FERGUSON	1 (3)	1 (1)	0	1	3 (4)
Colin	SCOTT	3 (1)	0	0	0	3 (1)
Fraser	WISHART	3 (1)	0	0	0	3 (1)
Steven	PRESSLEY	2	0	0	1	3
Neil	CALDWELL	1	0	0	0	1
Brian	McGINTY	1	0	0	0	1
Gary	STEVENS	0	0	0	1	1
David	HAGEN	0 (2)	0	0	0	0 (2)
Paul	McKNIGHT	0 (1)	0	0	0	0 (1)
Lee	ROBERTSON	0 (1)	0	0	0	0 (1)

BOOKINGS

Basile	BOLI	v Partick Thistle	away	20/8/94
		v AEK Athens	home	24/8/94
		v Aberdeen	away	24/9/94
		v Hibs	away	1-10-94*
		v Motherwell	away	22/10/94
		v Aberdeen	home	25/11/94
		v Hamilton A	away	6/2/95
		v Kilmarnock	home	25/2/95
Gary	BOLLAN	v Hearts	away	18/3/95
John	BROWN	v Falkirk	away	14/1/95
		v Hearts	home	21/1/95
		v Falkirk	home	11/3/95
		v Celtic	away	7/5/95
Alex	CLELAND	v Hearts	away	18/3/95
		v Dundee United	away	1/4/95
Gordon	DURIE	v Aberdeen	away	24/9/94
		v Hibs	home	26/12/94
		v Motherwell	away	31/12/94
		v Hamilton A	away	6/2/95
		v Hearts	away	20/2/95
		v Dundee United	away	1/4/95
Ian	FERGUSON	v AEK Athens	home	24/8/94
		v Celtic	home	27/8/94
		v Falkirk	home	31/8/94
		v Falkirk	away	17/9/94
		v Falkirk	away	14/1/95
Andy	GORAM	v Kilmarnock	away	10/12/94
Richard	GOUGH	v Motherwell	home	13/8/94
		v Falkirk	away	17/9/94
		v Hearts	away	20/2/95
		v Hibs	away	4/3/95
Mark	HATELEY	v AEK Athens	away	10/8/94
		v Celtic	away	30/10/94
		v Hibs	home	26/12/94
		v Motherwell	home	30/4/95
Pieter	HUISTRA	v Hearts	away	9/11/94
		v Falkirk	home	19/11/94
		v Falkirk	away	14/1/95
Brian	LAUDRUP	v Falkirk	away	17/9/94
		v Kilmarnock	away	12/10/94
		v Aberdeen	away	12/2/95

Stuart	McCALL	v Motherwell	home	13/8/94
		v Falkirk	away	17/9/94
		v Motherwell	away	31/12/94
		v Dundee United	home	4/2/95
		v Hibs	away	4/3/95
		v Dundee United	home	1/4/95
		v Hearts	away	18/3/95
Alan	McLAREN	v Celtic	away	30/10/94
		v Kilmarnock	away	10/12/94
		v Partick Thistle	away	7/1/95
		v Falkirk	away	14/1/95
Alexei	MIKHAILITCHENKO	v Motherwell	home	30/4/95
Charlie	MILLER	v Motherwell	away	31/12/94
		v Dundee United	home	4/2/95
		v Aberdeen	away	12/2/95
		v Aberdeen	home	8/4/95
Craig	MOORE	v Falkirk	home	31/8/94
		v Falkirk	away	17/9/94
		v Hibs	away	8/10/94
		v Hearts	away	9/11/94
		v Falkirk	home	19/11/94
		v Hamilton A	away	6/2/95
		v Aberdeen	away	12/2/95
		v Hibs	away	4/3/95
Neil	MURRAY	v Aberdeen	home	24/9/94
Steven	PRESSLEY	v AEK Athens	away	10/8/94
		v Kilmarnock	home	15/10/94
David	ROBERTSON	v AEK Athens	away	10/8/94
		v Aberdeen	home	24/9/94
		v Kilmarnock	home	15/10/94
		v Motherwell	away	22/10/94
		v Celtic	away	30/10/94
		v Hearts	away	9/11/94
		v Partick Thistle	away	8/1/95
		v Falkirk	away	14/1/95
		v Aberdeen	away	12/2/95
Fraser	WISHART	v Falkirk	away	14/1/95

* denotes two bookings and sending-off

DISMISSALS

Basile BOLI	v	Hibs	away	1/10/94
		(for two bookings)		
Gordon DURIE	v	Aberdeen	away	24/9/94
		(technical dismissal in tunnel after game)		
Craig MOORE	v	Motherwell	away	22/10/94
		(for a professional foul on Dougie Arnott)		
Billy THOMSON	v	Celtic	away	7/5/95
		(for a professional foul on Brian McLaughlin)		

SUSPENSIONS

Gordon DURIE from	v	Dundee United	1 game	1/10/94
Basile BOLI from	v	Kilmarnock	1 game	15/10/94
Craig MOORE from	v	Celtic	1 game	30/10/94
Craig MOORE from	v	Aberdeen	2 games	25/11/94
Basile BOLI from	v	Kilmarnock	1 game	10/12/94
Gordon DURIE from	v	Falkirk	2 games	14/1/95
David ROBERTSON from	v	Hearts	1 game	21/1/95
Alan McLAREN from	v	Dundee United	3 games	4/2/95
Charlie MILLER from	v	Hibs	3 games	4/3/95
Craig MOORE from	v	Hearts	3 games	18/3/95

PENALTIES

Mark HATELEY	v	Hearts	11/9/94	Scored
Mark HATELEY	v	Dundee Utd	1/10/94	Missed (saved)
Mark HATELEY	v	Hearts	9/11/94	Scored
Pieter HUISTRA	v	Falkirk	14/1/95	Scored
Brian LAUDRUP	v	Kilmarnock	25/2/95	Scored
Ian DURRANT	v	Kilmarnock	25/2/95	Scored
Brian LAUDRUP	v	Falkirk	11/3/95	Scored

RANGERS' SCORERS 1994-95

Players		League				
		League	CC	Scot	Euro	Total
Mark	HATELEY	13	2	0	0	15
Brian	LAUDRUP	10	1	2	0	13
Gordon	DURIE	5	0	1	0	6
Stuart	McCALL	3	1	0	0	4
Ian	DURRANT	4	0	0	0	4
Duncan	FERGUSON	1	3	0	0	4
Basile	BOLI	2	0	1	0	3
David	ROBERTSON	3	0	0	0	3

Charlie	MILLER	3	0	0	0	3
Pieter	HUISTRA	3	0	0	0	3
Alan	McLAREN	2	0	0	0	2
Craig	MOORE	2	0	0	0	2
Alexei	MIKHAILITCHENKO	2	0	0	0	2
Richard	GOUGH	1	0	0	0	1
Ian	FERGUSON	1	0	0	0	1
Neil	MURRAY	1	0	0	0	1
Trevor	STEVEN	0	0	1	0	1
John	BROWN	1	0	0	0	1
Ally	McCOIST	1	0	0	0	1

REFEREES SEASON 1994-95

Because of the condensed nature of Scottish football, certain referees tend to make as much of a name for themselves as players. The list below identifies the officials' match by match allocation of Rangers' fixtures – and should help settle a few pub arguments as to which of the whistlers really does have it in for the club!

HUGH WILLIAMSON (Renfrew)
27-8-94	v Celtic (h)	L	0-2
31-12-94	v Motherwell (a)	L	3-1
18-3-95	v Hearts (a)	L	1-2
8-4-95	v Aberdeen (h)	L	3-2
20-4-95	v Kilmarnock (a)	L	1-0
13-5-95	v Partick Thistle (h)	L	1-1

LES MOTTRAM (Forth)
24-9-94	v Aberdeen (a)	L	2-2
7-1-95	v Partick Thistle (a)	L	1-1
11-3-95	v Falkirk (h)	L	2-2
7-5-95	v Celtic (a)	L	0-3

JIM McCLUSKEY (Stewarton)
11-9-94	v Hearts (h)	L	3-0
4-12-94	v Dundee United (a)	L	3-0
4-1-95	v Celtic (h)	L	1-1
12-2-95	v Aberdeen (a)	L	0-2

JIM McGILVRAY (Edinburgh)
1-10-94	v Dundee United (h)	L	2-0
25-11-94	v Aberdeen (h)	L	1-0
14-1-95	v Falkirk (a)	L	3-2

BILL CROMBIE (Edinburgh)
30-10-94	v Celtic (a)	L	3-1
6-2-95	v Hamilton Accies (a)	SC	3-1
29-4-95	v Motherwell (h)	L	0-2

WILLIE YOUNG (Clarkston)

21-1-95	v Hearts (h)	L	1-0
20-2-95	v Hearts (a)	SC	2-4
16-4-95	v Hibs (h)	L	3-1

BOBBY TAIT (East Kilbride)

20-8-94	v Partick Thistle (a)	L	2-0
4-3-95	v Hibs (a)	L	1-1

SANDY ROY (Aberdeen)

8-10-94	v Hibs (a)	L	1-2
1-4-95	v Dundee United (a)	L	2-0

JIM O'HARE (Motherwell)

22-10-94	v Motherwell (a)	L	1-2
10-12-94	v Kilmarnock (a)	L	2-1

HUGH DALLAS (Bonkle)

9-11-94	v Hearts (a)	L	1-1
4-2-95	v Dundee United (h)	L	1-1

ANDREW WADDELL (Edinburgh)

13-8-94	v Motherwell (h)	L	2-1

SCOTT DOUGAL (Burnside)

17-8-94	v Arbroath (a)	CC	6-1

JOE TIMMONS (Kilwinning)

31-8-94	v Falkirk (h)	CC	1-2

MIKE POCOCK (Aberdeen)

17-9-94	v Falkirk (a)	L	2-0

GEORGE CLYDE (Bearsden)

15-10-94	v Kilmarnock (h)	L	2-0

JOHN ROWBOTHAM (Kirkcaldy)

5-11-94	v Partick Thistle (h)	L	3-0

LOUIS THOW (Prestwick)

19-11-94	v Falkirk (h)	L	1-1

ERIC MARTINDALE (Newlands)

26-12-94	v Hibs (h)	L	2-0

ALISTAIR HUETT (Edinburgh)

25-2-95	v Kilmarnock (h)	L	3-0

RESERVE LEAGUE TABLES 1994-95

Premier Reserve League

		P	W	D	L	F	A	Pts
1	Celtic	36	21	10	5	76	28	73
2	Motherwell	36	16	12	8	56	42	60
3	Dundee United	36	18	5	13	55	53	59
4	Partick Thistle	36	15	9	12	59	49	54
5	Hearts	36	13	11	12	43	47	50
6	Hibernian	36	11	11	14	39	49	44
7	Aberdeen	36	10	12	14	39	44	42
8	RANGERS	36	10	10	16	40	49	40
9	Kilmarnock	36	11	5	20	45	63	38
10	Falkirk	36	9	7	20	46	74	34

Reserve League West

		P	W	D	L	F	A	Pts
1	RANGERS	28	20	5	3	66	25	65
2	St Mirren	28	18	6	4	66	29	60
3	Clydebank	28	17	5	6	50	34	56
4	Hamilton	28	15	2	11	52	34	47
5	Airdrie	28	13	6	9	43	48	45
6	Stirling	28	13	4	11	46	37	43
7	Stranraer	28	11	5	12	43	46	38
8	Clyde	28	11	4	13	51	38	37
9	Queen's Park	28	10	6	12	36	44	36
10	QOS	28	9	5	14	33	43	32
11	Ayr United	28	8	7	13	34	45	31
12	Dumbarton	28	9	4	15	45	59	31
13	Morton	28	7	9	12	31	42	30
14	Albion Rov	28	6	4	18	33	70	22
15	Stenhousemuir	28	4	6	18	22	57	18

Scottish Youth League

		P	W	D	L	F	A	Pts
1	Celtic	24	19	1	4	80	23	58
2	Aberdeen	24	17	4	3	72	25	55
3	RANGERS	24	15	7	2	82	20	52
4	Dundee United	24	16	4	4	70	17	52

5	St Johnstone	24	12	8	4	49	22	44
6	Hearts	24	11	2	11	71	26	35
7	Dundee	24	10	4	10	56	46	34
8	Partick Th	24	7	8	9	36	40	29
9	Cowdenbeath	24	8	5	11	33	69	29
10	Morton	24	5	4	15	30	54	19
11	QOS	24	5	2	17	24	65	17
12	Berwick	24	3	5	16	24	88	14
13	Alloa	24	0	2	22	10	14	22

A hectic season for Rangers on the reserve front, which saw a total of 77 different players used in the three leagues. No less than 68 players appeared in the Reserve League West, 56 in the second team while a mere 35 turned out in the Youth League. Late season fixture congestion caused Rangers to consider their participation in the Reserve League West, the traditional home of the third team. The unappealing thought of seeing Terry Butcher try to squeeze into a shirt in 1995-96, as was the case last season, obviously swayed the management; Rangers will not compete. Friendlies will make up for the fixtures the club loses.

OTHER PREMIER MILESTONES
Rangers' Hat-Trick Heroes In The Premier Division

			Venue	Score	Date	Goals
GORDON DALZIEL						
	v	Dundee	(h)	4-0	8-5-82	3 goals
MARK FALCO						
	v	Morton	(h)	7-0	26-9-87	3 goals
ROBERT FLECK						
	v	Clydebank	(h)	4-0	13-9-86	3 goals
	v	Falkirk	(a)	5-1	18-10-86	3 goals
	v	Clydebank	(h)	5-0	10-1-87	3 goals
MARK HATELEY						
	v	St Johnstone	(h)	6-0	10-8-91	3 goals
	v	Airdrie	(h)	5-0	29-2-92	3 goals
DEREK JOHNSTONE						
	v	Ayr United	(a)	5-0	26-11-77	3 goals
	v	Hearts	(h)	5-3	16-12-78	4 goals
JOHN MacDONALD						
	v	Kilmarnock	(a)	8-1	20-9-80	3 goals

ALLY McCOIST

	v	Morton	(h)	3-0	20-4-85	3 goals
	v	Dundee	(h)	5-0	4-1-86	3 goals
	v	Hibs (h)		3-1	1-3-86	3 goals
	v	St Mirren	(a)	3-1	14-2-87	3 goals
	v	Hearts	(h)	3-0	25-4-87	3 goals
	v	Falkirk	(h)	4-0	22-8-87	3 goals
	v	Dunfermline	(h)	4-0	12-9-87	3 goals
	v	Morton	(h)	7-0	26-9-87	3 goals
	v	Morton	(h)	4-0	9-1-88	3 goals
	v	Falkirk	(h)	4-1	7-4-92	3 goals
	v	Motherwell	(a)	4-1	2-9-93	3 goals
	v	Falkirk	(h)	4-0	3-10-93	4 goals
	v	Motherwell	(h)	4-2	31-10-93	3 goals

BOBBY RUSSELL

	v	Hearts	(h)	4-0	28-4-79	3 goals

Players Scoring in Every Match Against One Side in a Premier Season

1	Gordon Smith	v	Motherwell in 1977-78	5 goals
2	Derek Johnstone	v	St Mirren in 1977-78	4 goals
3	Ally McCoist	v	Dundee United in 1985-86	4 goals
	(all Rangers goals against United that season)			
4	Ally McCoist	v	Dunfermline in 1987-88	6 goals
5	Ally McCoist	v	Hibs in 1991-92	6 goals
6	Ally McCoist	v	Dundee in 1992-93	6 goals
7	Mark Hateley	v	Hearts in 1993-94	6 goals

Clubs Who Have Failed To Score Against Rangers in One Premier Season (in Chronological Order)

1	Dundee United	1977-78
2	Motherwell	1987-88
3	Hibs	1988-89
4	Hibs	1990-91
5	St Mirren	1990-91
6	Airdrie	1991-92
7	Hibs	1993-94

Rangers have never gone through a series of four Premier games against an individual club in one season without a goal.

Most Goals Scored by Rangers Against Individual Clubs in One Season

1	17 goals	v	Morton	1987-88
2	16 goals	v	Clydebank	1986-87
3	14 goals	v	St Johnstone	1975-76
	14 goals	v	Motherwell	1977-78
	14 goals	v	St Johnstone	1991-92
	14 goals	v	Dunfermline	1991-92
7	13 goals	v	Ayr United	1977-78
	13 goals	v	Kilmarnock	1980-81
	13 goals	v	St Johnstone	1983-84
	13 goals	v	Dunfermline	1987-88
	13 goals	v	Falkirk	1987-88
	13 goals	v	Airdrie	1991-92
	13 goals	v	Falkirk	1992-93
	13 goals	v	Motherwell	1992-93

Most Goals Conceded by Rangers Against Individual Clubs in One Season

1	11 goals	v	Aberdeen	1977-78
2	10 goals	v	Aberdeen	1981-82
3	9 goals	v	Aberdeen	1979-80
	9 goals	v	St Mirren	1979-80
	9 goals	v	Dundee United	1980-81
	9 goals	v	Celtic	1982-83
	9 goals	v	Aberdeen	1984-85
	9 goals	v	Hearts	1985-86
9	8 goals	v	Celtic	1978-79
	8 goals	v	Dundee United	1982-83

Rangers' Top Ten Home Wins in The Premier

1	7-0	v	Morton	26-9-87
2	6-0	v	St Johnstone	10-8-91
3	5-0	v	Kilmarnock	18-9-82
	5-0	v	Dundee	4-1-86
	5-0	v	Clydebank	10-1-87
	5-0	v	Morton	9-1-88
	5-0	v	St Mirren	13-10-90
	5-0	v	Airdrie	29-2-92
	5-0	v	Falkirk	9-2-93
10	5-1	v	Ayr United	16-4-77
	5-1	v	Celtic	27-8-88
	5-1	v	Partick Thistle	5-2-94

Rangers' Top Ten Away Wins in The Premier

1	8-1	v	Kilmarnock	20-9-80
2	5-0	v	Ayr United	26-11-77
	5-0	v	Morton	12-2-83
	5-0	v	Falkirk	7-5-88
	5-0	v	Dunfermline	9-11-91
6	5-1	v	St Johnstone	15-11-75
	5-1	v	Falkirk	18-10-86
	5-1	v	St Johnstone	7-10-92
9	4-0	v	Kilmarnock	13-11-76
	4-0	v	Partick Thistle	27-8-77
	4-0	v	Dundee	17-3-87
	4-0	v	Dunfermline	28-10-87
	4-0	v	Airdrie	5-10-91
	4-0	v	Dundee United	26-9-92
	4-0	v	Motherwell	23-2-93
	4-0	v	St Johnstone	18-12-93

Rangers' Ten Biggest Defeats in The Premier

1	1-5	v	Aberdeen	(a)	19-1-85
2	0-4	v	Aberdeen	(a)	24-12-77
	0-4	v	Aberdeen	(a)	15-5-82
4	1-4	v	St Mirren	(a)	7-5-80
	1-4	v	Dundee United	(h)	18-3-81
6	0-3	v	Ayr United	(a)	11-10-75
	0-3	v	Aberdeen	(h)	4-3-78
	0-3	v	Dundee United	(a)	9-12-78
	0-3	v	Motherwell	(a)	3-1-83
	0-3	v	St Mirren	(a)	29-10-83
	0-3	v	Celtic	(a)	2-4-84
	0-3	v	Aberdeen	(h)	28-9-85
	0-3	v	Hearts	(a)	16-11-85
	0-3	v	Aberdeen	(h)	13-5-89
	0-3	v	Celtic	(a)	24-3-91
	0-3	v	Motherwell	(a)	4-5-91
	0-3	v	Dundee United	(h)	11-12-93
	0-3	v	Partick Thistle	(a)	4-5-93

Rangers' Complete Performance in The Premier

		P	W	D	L	F	A	%Success
1	Hamilton	8	8	0	0	17	2	100
2	St Johnstone	24	21	3	0	70	14	93.8
3	Dunfermline	16	14	2	0	41	6	93.8
4	Falkirk	20	17	3	0	56	15	92.5
5	Clydebank	12	10	1	1	32	6	87.5
6	Dumbarton	4	3	1	0	9	4	87.5
7	Ayr United	12	8	3	1	28	10	79.2
8	Morton	28	18	8	2	65	15	78.5
9	Airdrie	16	9	7	0	31	8	78.1
10	Motherwell	64	48	3	13	121	53	77.3
11	Raith Rovers	4	2	2	0	9	4	75
12	St Mirren	60	36	11	3	103	48	70.8
13	Kilmarnock	24	15	4	5	45	12	70.8
14	Hearts	64	35	16	13	117	68	67.2
15	Hibs	76	38	25	13	104	53	66.4
16	Dundee United	80	45	25	15	107	70	65.6
17	Dundee	54	28	13	11	97	55	63.9
18	Celtic	80	26	24	30	104	110	51.25
19	Aberdeen	80	24	22	34	72	101	43.8

Premier Division 1994-95 Final Table

	P	W	D	L	F	A	Pts
RANGERS	**36**	**20**	**9**	**7**	**60**	**35**	**69**
Motherwell	36	14	12	10	50	50	54
Hibernian	36	12	17	7	49	37	53
Celtic	36	11	18	7	39	33	51
Falkirk	36	12	12	12	48	47	48
Heats	36	12	7	17	44	51	43
Kilmarnock	36	12	10	15	40	48	43
Partick Thistle	36	11	13	13	40	50	43
Aberdeen	36	10	11	15	43	46	41
Dundee United	36	9	9	18	40	56	36

The Season's Memorable Quotes About Rangers By Rangers

"Rangers are good enough to win the European Champions League." **Basile Boli**, on signing, prior to the preliminary round exit to AEK Athens.

"We're going through a period which will be remembered for a long time by Rangers fans and that's why I really want to achieve ten in a row. That's another four seasons and I'm confident I have that left in me." **Richard Gough** on the eve of the season.

"We should be looking to win *every* home game by 4-0 or 5-0, because we have better players." **Richard Gough** in an optimistic frame of mind.

"I don't think he'll have any problems settling into Scottish football." **Trevor Steven** on Basile Boli. Within a month, Boli's Rangers career was in the balance after comments attributed to him in the French press.

"Rangers are a club with ambition. Their directors and manager have great ambitions, but the supporters don't live up to these ambitions. The supporters are not big time. If they are going to boo every good team which comes to Ibrox for friendlies, then teams might stop coming." Manchester United manager **Alex Ferguson's** explosive comments on the Rangers support during the Ibrox international tournament. Not surprisingly, Fergie is not flavour of the month in Glasgow.

"Time is running out for a lot of us in the Rangers team. You wonder how many more chances we'll get in the European Cup." **Richard Gough** in less optimistic mood.

"One of our fans could have been killed. The behaviour of the Greeks was absolutely and utterly irresponsible." **Alistair Hood** on THAT tie in Athens.

"Every club needs a support who can create a bit of hostility and be an influence. We encountered that kind of thing against the Greeks and I hope it will be the same with our fans." **Walter Smith** before the Athens home tie.

"We can have no great complaints. AEK were the better team and deserved to win over two legs." **Walter Smith**, to his credit, takes it on the chin after the Euro exit.

"It's long enough to get the sack." **Walter Smith** faces up to reality on the terms of his four year contract after the AEK game.

"We've been overtaken by countries that didn't merit a mention a few years ago." **David Murray** after the same match.

"Backing, not barracking, is what is needed." **Ally McCoist's** reminder after August's 2-0 Old Firm defeat.

"You can't go about winning an important game by having a laugh in the dressing room half-an-hour before kick-off." One of the infamous comments attributed to **Basile Boli** in the French press, referring to the AEK fiasco, which was subsequently claimed to be a misquote.

"People are trying to put the knives in because of these three games." An irritated **Andy Goram** mouths off following home losses to AEK, Celtic and Falkirk.

"I hope to be here so long they have to kick me out!" back-in-favour **Andy Goram** on signing a four-year contract.

"What offended me was the alleged criticism that our European preparation was a joke and criticism of team-mates. But there's been shown there is no foundation for it." **Walter Smith** limits the damage after Boli's blasts.

"I believe we are going to find it more and more difficult. There is no way I can see – unless we win the European Cup itself – that the champions of Scotland will gain automatic entry to the League set-up." Euro failings hit home to **Walter Smith**.

"I wouldn't say it's a relief to get out of Scotland, but it's a new challenge." **Duncan Ferguson** on his loan move to Everton.

"It beats playing in the Rangers reserves, that's for sure," **Ian Durrant** on HIS loan move to Goodison. A month later, Durranty was playing a very different tune!

"He'll be worth 50 points a season." The value of Brian Laudrup isn't lost on **David Robertson**.

"I would rather sell something else than Rangers. I'd sell other things. The loves of my life are the metal business and Rangers." Owner **David Murray** gets his priorities right.

"Now that I have time to reflect on the move, I have to say that I made a big mistake leaving Ibrox when I did," A self-analytical **Mark Walters** reflects on his transfer to Liverpool.

"With a pinch of salt." **Alan McLaren**, on being asked what his reaction was to Hearts initially saying his dream move to Ibrox was off.

"A lot was made of that fact that the fans didn't like me, but I think that was exaggerated." The Ibrox legions get the thumps-up from departing **Dave McPherson**.

"This is absolutely no reflection on his ability and fitness, but we've got Vinny Samways, who is a similar type of player. I only ever wanted Ian on loan to have a look at him." **Mike Walker** displays the sort of logic which earned him the bullet at Everton.

"Ian (Durrant) would be a far better player in a decent football side – and Everton don't come into that category judging by what I saw of them. They look like relegation material." **John Brown** explains Durrant's inability to get a regular game at Goodison.

"Even in training, we can't get the ball off him. The only way is to a rugby tackle. He's a gentleman. He has no right being at Rangers!" **Andy Goram** expresses his admiration for Brian Laudrup.

"None of us is in the position to pick the Scotland team other than Craig Brown. But Alan has all the qualities that will make him a first-class captain." **Walter Smith** predicts the national captaincy for Alan McLaren.

"I went to Duisburg and QPR on trial spells earlier this season. And they made me realise just what a big operation I'm involved in. Both clubs are firmly in Rangers' shadow and leaving here would be a real sickener." **Pieter Huistra** reiterates his determination to stay at Ibrox.

"There's no doubt I was overshadowed at Ibrox by Richard Gough. But Phil Neal wants me to be a leader at Coventry, and I think I'll rise to the challenge and responsibility." **Steven Pressley** stresses the reasoning behind his decision to leave Glasgow.

"I'm going to be early for this one. I can be late for the likes of Ian Durrant – but not The Queen." **Super Ally MBE** prepares for his Buckingham Palace meeting with Her Majesty.

"Imagine someone bringing the Judge into our pub!" **A Linlithgow drinker** on spotting Ally McCoist in his local boozer – oblivious to the fact that he was speaking to Gordon Durie!

"I've scored 219 league goals and to break Mr (Bob) McPhail's record would mean more than any other honour. It really is the achievement I would like to have against my name, for I don't think it will be broken." **Ally McCoist** lays bare his greatest ambition.

"All right, big man!" Linguistically challenged **Basile Boli** tells TV interviewer Jim White the extent of the Scottish he has picked up during his stay in Glasgow.

"I don't like to be smug, but I think it turned out that way." **David Murray** recalls telling Graeme Souness that leaving Ibrox for Anfield would be the biggest mistake of his life.

"That's another thing I don't recall! I'll need to look at the video to find out." **Richard Gough** suffers memory loss, following a head-knock against Dundee United, and is told of an argument he had with referee Jim McCluskey.

"He's a lovely big lad, but I believe it's important for Duncan to get out of Scotland. He's something of a marked man there." Everton boss **Joe Royle** on Big Dunc – who else?

"Rangers paid £2 million for Brian Laudrup. How can Duncan be worth double?" Dundee United captain **Maurice Malpas** talks some sense on Fergie's move.

"Leaving Rangers was a wrench at the time, but now I have to say it was the best decision I ever made." Words of comfort for the departing Dunc from Chelsea's **John Spencer**.

"In Italy, with AC Milan and Fiorentina, I felt like a bird in a cage. With Rangers, Walter Smith has told me I can go where I want – left, right and centre. It's bringing the best out of me and I love it." **Brian Laudrup** explains to the doubters how he can get more of a thrill out of playing against Partick than Parma.

"I respect other religions, and I have the advantage of being foreign. The chairman said, "We noticed you have crossed yourself going on to the pitch. It would be better to do it in the dressing room." I replied that I could not change my habits. I always cross myself before a match." **Basile Boli** refuses to bow to certain Ibrox sensitivities.

"I'm becoming a player like any other in a championship that isn't highly rated. Even if that didn't live up to my hopes, I haven't regretted my decision." **Baz** again, on his slightly less than auspicious start to his Rangers career.

"He's better than I ever was. I'm sure of that. He has a right foot for a start." Tragic Rangers legend **Davie Cooper** heaps praise on Laudrup.

"He's a real nutcase – in the nicest possible way." Duncan Ferguson again comes in for analysis, this time from **Gary Stevens**.

"I don't think Duncan is as bad as he's been painted. He couldn't be!" **Joe Royle** on everyone's favourite topic of discussion.

"It was a terrible experience, although fortunately he didn't get me with his spitting." **Charlie Miller** comes to terms with man–marking in international football, after his Under-21 debut against Greece.

"I haven't seen a better 'keeper in the world. Take the highest priced 'keeper and Andy matches him." Scotland boss **Andy Goram** speaks frankly on Andy Goram.

"It's a lot better playing in front of a full house at Ibrox than a handful of people at Stenhousemuir in the Reserve League Cup." **Billy Thomson** looking forward to his competitive debut.

"Even if you slip a ball and chain on him, he'd still beat people." Hibs' **Darren Jackson** comes up with a novel way to stop Brian Laudrup.

"Football is full of ups and downs, but the ups have easily outweighed the downs I don't leave with any grudges or bitterness." **Pieter Huistra's** acceptance that his Rangers career is over and that a new life beckons in Japan.

"He would need to change before he's going to do well at any club, never mind Rangers." **Walter Smith**, after selling Duncam Ferguson, offers some timely advice.

"The Dundee United manager said when they came to Ibrox last season that they never got any decisions here. He must realise after today's game that this is not the case. He said then that in any other ground in Scotland they would have had penalty. After today, we can say that in any other ground in Scotland we would have had two." **Walter Smith** takes a pop at Ivan Golac and referee High Dallas after a 1-1 Ibrox draw with Dundee United on February 4.

"I don't think Davie Robertson will dive as well in the swimming pool as he did in the box. I thought the referee was tremendous." **Ivan Golac** responds.

"If Rangers came back in for me – which is unlikely – I would jump at it." **Pieter Huistra** 'enjoying life' in Japan.

"At 25, I could play badly for a couple of weeks and no-one would make much o it. At 33, a couple of bad games and Richard Gough is ready for the scrapheap." The captain reflects on growing old.

Player by Player

GARY BOLLAN

Date of birth: 24th March 1973, Dundee

Like Neil Murray, he first came to the fore with the Scottish Under-16 side which reached the World Cup Final against Saudi Arabia at Hampden. Bollan, however, made the breakthrough to first-team football quicker than his team-mate, who was concentrating on accountancy.

A native of Dundee, Bollan signed for Dundee United and first appeared on the scene in the 1990-91 season, when he made a couple of league appearances. They should have been the prelude to him staking a claim for a regular place at Tannadice, but like so many of the outstanding young players under Jim McLean, his appearances were sporadic and he seemed to be failing to realise his potential when Rangers stepped in with their shock signing.

Bollan can point to his Scottish Cup medal of 1993-94, when he was an unused sub as United beat Rangers 1-0, as proof of his progress, and has gone on record as saying he will not be happy coming to Ibrox just to exist as a squad player. But that is precisely what he would have appeared to have been signed as.

His natural position, he claims, is building from defence on the left-hand side, which would seem to make him a left-back in layman's terms. However, if there is one outfield position at Ibrox which seems as safe as houses, it's David Robertson's slot, and it just does not seem reasonable to expect Bollan to oust the former Aberdeen star from the number three shirt. His natural left-footedness could make him a candidate for midfield, where Alexei Mikhailitchenko's injury problems and general erratic form made it difficult for Walter Smith to get any sort of consistency of selection in recent seasons. But, even accounting for his age, it is hard to see how a fringe Dundee United player can be turned into a first-choice Rangers flanker.

And so, it is hard to come to any other conclusion but that Bollan has been signed as a squad player, and there can be no disputing that he can be very useful in this sphere. He can play at the back and in the middle of the pitch, he is left-footed, seemingly a rarity in Scottish football these days, he is young, but most importantly, he is Scottish, which could be a real asset if Rangers can get into the Champions League.

However, Bollan is perhaps not a character to rule out as a first-team regular, if his determination is anything to go by. At the time of his signing, he was in the process of taking Dundee United to court over what he saw as the unfair length of his contract. Anyone who is prepared to go to those extremes is obviously a resolute character, and just as Scottish football was shocked when Walter Smith unveiled Bollan and Alex Cleland at an Ibrox press conference, maybe there will be another shock in store again as Gary goes on to become a fixture in the first-team.

INTERNATIONAL HONOURS

Scotland Under-21: 14 caps. Debut v. Denmark 1992.

HONOURS IN THE SCOTTISH GAME

League: (0)
Scottish Cup: 1993-1994 with Dundee United (1)
League Cup: (0)
Total: 1

LEAGUE RECORD

		Apps	Goals
1990-91	Dundee United	2	-
1991-92	Dundee United	10	1
1992-93	Dundee United	15	3
1993-94	Dundee United	12	-
1994-95	Dundee United	7	-
1994-95	Rangers	6	-
	Total	52	4

VALUATION

Potential, certainly, and his versatility is a bonus. His experience with Dundee United and Scotland Under-21s, despite his comparative youth, mark him out as a player useful to most squads in Scotland.

Estimated value: £300,000

asile BOLI

Date of Birth: 2nd January 1967, Adjame, Ivory Coast

's very difficult to imagine that in years to come, the name Basile Boli will be remembered with any great affection by the Ibrox hordes. And yet, when his capture was announced by manager Walter Smith on July 5, 1994, there was not a oice of dissent heard from fans or press alike. The £2.7 million signing from Marseille was widely believed to be the type of individual who could steer Rangers n to the sort of success they craved in the European Cup. After all, he had the edigree; Boli scored the winner in the 1993 Champions Cup in the French club's -0 triumph over Milan.

So what went wrong and caused his departure from Rangers? A quicker xplanation would be forthcoming if the question was "what went right?" Boli's ell at Ibrox was largely inglorious.

Perhaps an indicator of what was to follow arrived almost immediately he signed. he news emerged within days that Boli would be missing from the opening uropean Cup match with AEK Athens due to suspension. Rangers, of course, lost

2-0 and the realisation that they could be out of the continent's premier competition before the man they'd signed to help them win it had even played was dawning.

The home leg was even worse, when Boli did feature. Picked at right-back, he looked unhappy and performed woefully. Rangers lost 1-0 and were dispensed yet again as also-rans. But that was small beer compared to the storm which was shortly to blow up. Unwisely, Boli gave an interview back home in France, in which he criticised the club, the city of Glasgow, his team-mates and most damningly, the tactics in the Greek debacle. His Ibrox career looked over before it had started, but Walter Smith did about all he could in the circumstances and claimed his expensive hard man had been misquoted. It seemed an implausible story to swallow even then, and as the season progressed, it became increasingly evident that misquoted or otherwise, Boli's heart was not really in the Rangers' cause. There was a sending-off at Hibs, a row over crossing himself at the start of matches – never very popular at Ibrox – but overall, a string of sub-standard displays where he looked a run-of-the-mill defender, and certainly not the £2.7 million superstar he had been hyped up to be.

So where was the problem? It could probably be attributed to both the player, and to a lesser extent, the Scottish League. That Boli is, or at least, *was* a class act is beyond dispute. No player wins European Cup medals and becomes an integral part of an international side as splendidly blessed as the French outfit of 1990-92 was without having something to offer. So was it down to attitude, or simply a diminishing in pace and ability due to a long-term knee injury? Essentially both.

Once Rangers were out of the European Cup, there must have been very little enthusiasm, from a man who'd done it all, at the prospect of regular jousts with the poor domestic opposition. Even the fans are getting tired of that fare. However, his failure to build up any sort of relationship with Richard Gough suggested that, possibly, his best days were behind him. Only time, and how he fares on the continent, will tell.

If there is a lesson to be learned from Basile Boli, it must be that if Rangers are to spend big on European stars, they would be wiser to invest in skilful individuals, a la Laudrup, whom Scotland cannot produce, as opposed to physical stoppers with attitude problems, whom the country has a production line of.

INTERNATIONAL HONOURS
French international

HONOURS IN THE SCOTTISH GAME
League: 1994-95 (1)
Scottish Cup: 0
League Cup: 0
Total: 1

LEAGUE RECORD

	Apps	Goals
1994-95	28	2
Total	28	2

VALUATION

Boli still has a name, but does he have the game? Last season with Rangers did nothing to enhance his reputation, and there have to be doubts about his long term durability fitness wise. No longer the man he was with Marseille, Boli's best days look behind him. He is not worth the £2.7 million Rangers paid.

Estimated value: £1,500,000

John BROWN

Date of Birth: 26th January 1962, Stirling

Although he may be closer to the end of his career than the start, there is no diminishing in the affinity the fans have for John Brown. Make no mistake, ''Bomber'' is one of them, and don't they know it.

Signed in January 1988, from Dundee, he has since gone on, against all the odds, to become one of the most popular players at the club in recent memory, a testament to his "never say die" approach to the game.

Brown first began to catch the eye with Hamilton, but it was at Dens in the mid-eighties that he really began to make a name for himself. Dundee had a gifted team then, with men like Tommy Coyne, Keith Wright, Rab Shannon and Tosh McKinlay key players, but none has gone on to enjoy the sort of honour strewn career that their flame-haired team-mate has. Used as a left-back occasionally, a centre-half now and again, it was as a midfielder that Bomber was most effective for the Dark Blues. He was certainly a thorn in the side of his boyhood heroes, Rangers. A hat-trick in a League game and a strike which eliminated Rangers from the Scottish Cup of 1984-85 provided ample proof.

His signing from Dens, as he suffered a rocky period with the Tayside men, came after a move to Hearts had fallen through following the questioning of his medical record by the Tynecastle side. It was their loss. He made his debut in a 5-0 romp over Morton, and managed to record his first goal for the club in a 3-1 win at Falkirk just a couple of matches later.

However, it is not as a scorer that Brown became invaluable for Rangers. The utility man gradually evolved as a central defender of the highest order, with indomitable spirit to boot. Sure, there have been occasions when he has been required to slot in at left-back or in midfield, but it is as a stopper that he has proved his worth time and again.

His finest season came in 1992-93, Rangers' last European campaign of any note, when Bomber, along with many other Ibrox stars, performed heroically. His lion-hearted showings in defence brought him to the notice of many outside Scotland for the first time and prompted a number of tributes. "In many ways, outstanding," Howard Wilkinson was left to reflect after his Leeds side had been eliminated from the European Cup after the Battle of Britain.

His willingness to play on through the pain barrier has also endeared him to the

161

fans. In the legendary championship decider of 1991 against Aberdeen, he opted to play despite injury problems, and helped steer a shopworn Rangers to the title. His reward? Missing much of the start of the next season as he recovered from an operation.

Strangely, for a player who has achieved so much with Scotland's biggest club, the closest he has ever come to international recognition have been a couple of call-ups to squads in the 1992-93 season. But there have been no caps; a shocking oversight.

John Brown has gone on record as saying he would gladly sell confectionary to remain at Ibrox. That won't be necessary, as a coaching role, assisting John McGregor, has been agreed for a man whose life revolves around Rangers.

And you can bet your life that when his spell at Ibrox does eventually end – John Brown will be seen at the ground, week-in, week-out, anyway – as a supporter, cheering the new breed on to more success.

INTERNATIONAL HONOURS
None

HONOURS IN THE SCOTTISH GAME
League: 1988-89, 1989-90, 1990-91, 1991-92, 1992-93, 1993-94 (6)
Scottish Cup: 1991-92, 1992-93 (2)
League Cup: 1988-89, 1990-91, 1992-93 (3)
Total: 11

LEAGUE RECORD

		Apps	Goals
1979-80	Hamilton	19	0
1980-81	Hamilton	38	6
1981-82	Hamilton	28	5
1982-83	Hamilton	9	0
1983-84	Hamilton	39	0
1984-85	Dundee	34	7
1985-86	Dundee	29	11
1986-87	Dundee	31	10
1987-88	Dundee	20	3
1987-88	Rangers	9	2
1988-89	Rangers	29	1
1989-90	Rangers	27	1
1990-91	Rangers	27	1
1991-92	Rangers	25	4
1992-93	Rangers	39	4
1993-94	Rangers	24	0
1994-95	Rangers	13	1
Total		440	56

VALUATION

His new coaching role means he won't be sold. But players of his age and stature have fetched six figure fees in the past.

Estimated value: £150,000

Alex CLELAND

Date of Birth: 10th December 1970, Glasgow

To say that the arrival of Alex Cleland and Gary Bollan from Dundee United in February of last season was greeted with a lukewarm response from the fans would be an understatement.

With names like Dennis Bergkamp, David Platt and Gary McAllister among those regularly linked with Rangers through the course of 1994-95, the pair from Tannadice were not most supporters' ideas of the calibre of pro the club should be interested in.

However, that is not to say that Cleland and Bollan cannot make a significant contribution, and of the two, the former would appear to have the better chance of proving himself in the biggest arena in Scottish football. Perhaps he is the ideal example of what is sometimes termed a 'modern-day footballer'. Cleland can play in a variety of positions with aplomb and that is what makes him an ideal man to have around the place, and a player highly rated by many Scottish managers. It is no coincidence that Dundee United chairman Jim McLean, formerly his boss on Tayside, was privately raging, at the sale of someone he had brought through the ranks, by then United boss Ivan Golac.

At 24, too, his best years are in front of him. Cleland came to the fore with the Tangerines, with whom he made his League debut as a teenager. A full-back initially, he has since demonstrated his ability to play on both the right and in the centre, and even, if absolutely necessary, on the left too. Midfield holds no fears for the Glaswegian either and, if Rangers ever get round to regularly playing the sweeper system Walter Smith seems so keen to employ, it is not hard to imagine Cleland, Stephen Wright and Craig Moore vying for the position as the right-sided component in a five-man defence. Indeed, the fact that that he has already worn numbers two, six, seven and eight in his short time at Ibrox perhaps best demonstrates his versatility, as well as emphasising the likelihood that he will be moved around the pitch as and when manager Smith requires.

On the career front, Cleland's move to Glasgow may be the kickstart he needs. Like many of the youngsters who burst to prominence with Dundee United, his early potential, when he looked a dead cert for full Scotland honours, seemed not to have been fulfilled completely. A player who was a mainstay of the Scotland Under-21 side which made it to the European Championship semi-finals a few years back has watched Alan McLaren, Scott Booth and Duncan Ferguson from the

163

same team become key members of the full squad. That should be an aim of his too, now, because there will be no higher profile venue for him to demonstrate his skills than Ibrox.

Nevertheless, he already has a Scottish Cup Winner's medal to his credit, following United's 1-0 win over Rangers in the 1994 final, and it should be the first of a few if things go according to plan at Ibrox.

But for those who believe in fate, perhaps the best omen for Cleland's future with the Light Blues came almost exactly seven years prior to his signing on. That was when Graeme Souness shelled out £350,000 for another under-rated, no frills utility man from the City of Discovery. Few were cheering around Govan way that day, but their opinions were quick to change. The player's name? John Brown. If Alex Cleland can make even half the impact that 'Bomber' has made, his status is assured.

INTERNATIONAL HONOURS

11 Scotland Under-21 caps. Debut v. France 1990.

HONOURS IN THE SCOTTISH GAME

League: 0
Scottish Cup: 1993-94 with Dundee United (1).
League Cup: 0.
Total: 1.

LEAGUE RECORD

		Apps	Goals
1987-88	Dundee United	1	0
1988-89	Dundee United	9	0
1989-90	Dundee United	15	0
1990-91	Dundee United	20	2
1991-92	Dundee United	31	4
1992-93	Dundee United	24	-
1993-94	Dundee United	33	1
1994-95	Dundee United	18	1
1994-95	Rangers	10	0
	Total	161	8

VALUATION

Players like Cleland go up in value simply from having spent time at Ibrox. So whereas normally he might be expected to fetch around £450,000, expect him to go for more than that if is ever to leave.

Estimated value: £650,000

Gordon Durie

Gordon DURIE

Date of Birth: 6th December 1965, Paisley

Signed in the run-in to the 1993-94 league season from Tottenham, Gordon Durie proved a worthwhile acquisition as he ended the campaign as the Light Blues' second top scorer, with 12 Premier Division goals from only 23 starts. At £1.2 million, he represented good value for a player who had cost the London side £1 million more when they captured him from Chelsea in August 1991 – their then record signing.

There was no doubting Walter Smith's delight at his contribution, but the move proved mutually beneficial, as the Paisley-born star earned his first major medal in the game – after only picking up a Zenith Data Systems Cup badge and a Second Division championship gong at Stamford Bridge. That was a real monkey off his back, as international team-mates Ian Durrant and Ally McCoist had amused themselves by teasing Durie about his lack of success after he'd joined the Ibrox family. "You could safely say I've taken a bit of stick about that," he admitted at the time. The young Durie initially came to prominence at East Fife, where his strong running as much as his goal prowess persuaded Hibs to swoop for him. It was at Easter Road that he really made his mark on the Scottish game, although he had nothing tangible to show for his successful spell there. A runner's up medal for the League Cup, after a particularly convincing 3-0 defeat from Aberdeen in the 1985-86 season, was as good as it got. It was a Hi-bees' side of promise, though, as alongside him in the 13 that day was another man to become an Old Firm star of the future – John Collins, now of Celtic.

English clubs began to sniff around, and it wasn't long before Chelsea took Gordon south. It was in West London that he enjoyed the best period of his career, certainly in terms of goalscoring, in a team that, for a while, also included a soon-to-be Ger, Nigel Spackman. In contrast, his spell at Tottenham was less enjoyable, with a 'cheating' charge, although eventually dismissed, hanging over him for a while, a poor goals record and a very public bust-up with manager Ossie Ardiles over a substitution he did not agree with.

Internationally, Durie's experiences at club level have been repeated, as he's suffered the highs and lows. His 27 caps to date have been enough to earn a silver medal from the SFA in their Hall of Fame scheme, but do not tell the entire story. Amongst his four goals were vital strikes against San Marino and Switzerland in Scotland's unlikely qualification for the 1992 European Championship – but there have also been real disasters, including a horror performance against Egypt in 1990, a ludicrous penalty conceded against Romania in that same European campaign, and a wayward shooting display against Italy in the last World Cup qualifying section at Ibrox, when suffering from double vision. Of late, Durie has not featured consistently in Craig Brown's plans, because of his irregular appearances in Walter Smith's starting XI.

Nevertheless, a fit Durie remains a boon to the Light Blues, certainly at domestic level. His immediate success in finding the net on arrival proved that, while better players will be required if the ultimate goal of success in Europe is to be finally attained, he will be a useful man to have around in the coming seasons.

INTERNATIONAL HONOURS

Scotland international: 27 caps, 4 goals. Debut v. Bulgaria. 1988.
Under-21: Four caps. Debut v West Germany 1987.

HONOURS IN THE SCOTTISH GAME

League Championship: 1993-94 with Rangers, 199-/95 (2)
Total: 2

LEAGUE RECORD

		Apps	Goals
1981-82	East Fife	13	1
1982-83	East Fife	25	2
1983-84	East Fife	34	16
1984-85	East Fife	9	7
1984-85	Hibs	22	8
1985-86	Hibs	25	6
1985-86	Chelsea	1	-
1986-87	Chelsea	25	5
1987-88	Chelsea	26	12
1988-89	Chelsea	32	17
1989-90	Chelsea	15	5
1990-91	Chelsea	24	12
1991-92	Tottenham Hotspur	31	7
1992-93	Tottenham Hotspur	17	3
1993-94	Tottenham Hotspur	10	1
1993-94	Rangers	24	12
1994-95	Rangers	20	5
	Total	353	119

VALUATION

Rangers very rarely have to accept a loss on players they have bought, but it would be hard to see someone matching the £1.2 million they spent on Durie, given his advancing years. However, a man of his experience could still fetch around £800,000 down south.

Estimated value: £800,000

Ian DURRANT

Date of Birth: 29th October 1966, Glasgow

Ray Wilkins considered him at least as good as Paul Gascoigne as a youngster. Possibly he would have gone on to be even better. But one afternoon in 1988 forever changed Ian Durrant's career and football fans will never know just what levels the wee Glaswegian may have reached.

And, whilst admittedly time dulls the memory, it does not seem overly outrageous to suggest that Durrant could have become one of the all-time greats at Ibrox. As a youngster, he was quite simply brilliant, and displayed the sort of passing ability that most players can only dream of. As it is, he will go down as one of the most popular players ever to grace the colours of the club, and that in itself is testimony to the courage and determination of an individual whose career looked over prematurely.

The wild tackle by Aberdeen's Neil Simpson and the two-year lay-off it caused have been well-documented. The fact that an out-of-court settlement was reached for compensation was proof enough of its recklessness. So perhaps it is doing Durrant a disservice to dwell on what might have been, and concentrate on what has been achieved, for his feats are still well beyond what most players will ever manage.

Since he came back into the first-team, he has picked up five Scotland caps, almost half of his total of 11, and won four League championship medals with Rangers, one League Cup – including scoring in the final against Hibs – and two Scottish Cups, not to mention playing a significant role in the club's best European campaign for over 20 years, when he collected significant goals against Lyngby and Marseille. It's not a bad CV by anyone's standards.

It is only really in the last couple of seasons that things have gone wrong again for Durranty, and only the management can explain exactly why. Their willingness to send him on loan to Everton suggested they would happily part with him if the price was right. Almost immediately he arrived at Goodison, though, questions were being asked about the little man's fitness, and they, more than anything else, perhaps hold the key to his failure to completely re-establish himself at Ibrox.

There is no disputing that a fit Durrant, in the right frame of mind, is an asset that no price can be put on. He has the vision required at European level, and as a Scotsman, would presumably become an integral part of a successful Rangers side at that level. And he has also proved his liking for the big stage at Cup Final level, with several valuable contributions over the years. The problem is that Cup Finals only come, at the maximum, every twice a year, and in the last couple of campaigns, European Cup ties have been thin on the ground. So Durrant has been asked to perform at Premier level, where there is precious little time on the ball, and therefore he appears not the necessity that tacklers like Stuart McCall and Ian Ferguson are.

And it seems he just does not have the fitness required for that standard of football, week-in, week-out. If the pace of the game was similar to that in France or Italy, he could probably survive; possibly even flourish. It is Durrant's misfortune that he is being asked to play in an alien way to his natural style because the Scottish league cannot be tailored to his skilful talents.

Whatever the reason behind his continuing problems, his popularity will never diminish at Ibrox. He is a rarity there these days – a fan in a jersey, who has shown courage against overwhelming odds to reclaim his status, and become the hero of the support once again.

LEAGUE RECORD

		Apps	Goals
1984-85	Rangers	5	-
1985-86	Rangers	30	2
1986-87	Rangers	39	4
1987-88	Rangers	40	10
1988-89	Rangers	8	2
1989-90	Rangers	-	-
1990-91	Rangers	4	1
1991-92	Rangers	13	-
1992-93	Rangers	30	3
1993-94	Rangers	23	-
1994-95	Rangers	26	4
	Total	218	26

INTERNATIONAL RECORD

Scotland: 11 caps, 0 goals. Debut v. Holland 1988.
Under-21: Four caps. Debut v West Germany 1987.

HONOURS IN THE SCOTTISH GAME

League Championship: 1986-87, 1991-92, 1992-93, 1993-94 1994-95 (5)
Scottish Cup: 1991-92, 1992-93 (2)
League Cup: 1986-87, 1987-88, 1993-94 (3)
Total: 10

VALUATION

His apparent inability to last a full season would place doubts against him. But if the going rate for a midfielder like Vinny Samways is over £2 million, Durrant, with his experience and acknowledged ability, should at least fetch that.

Estimated value: £2,000,000

Ian FERGUSON

Date of Birth: 15th March 1967, Stirling

Since the Souness revolution, there have been imports from as diverse locations as Israel, Ukraine, England and Denmark at Ibrox, and few could deny the contribution these foreigners have made to the continuing success of the club. One drawback, however, has been the diminishing number of Glaswegians in the Rangers first-team – but they are not yet a dying breed. Ian Ferguson has been a reassuring constant in an ever-changing era.

From the Mount Vernon area of Glasgow, Fergie makes no bones where his allegiances lie – and no apologies for it. It is an attitude which has undoubtedly helped the support warm to him after a couple of injury-hit seasons early in his Ibrox career. Indifferent form saw him attract a few boos, but few would now deny his worth to the club. When he first burst on to the scene with Clyde in the 1985-86 season, Fergie was already earmarked as a star in the making. Clyde have provided a few players with their first chance in professional football – among them Pat Nevin and Steve Archibald. Certainly Alex Smith at St Mirren was impressed enough, and took the promising Starlet to Paisley in 1986.

It was to be a move the Buddies were to be grateful they made many times over at the tail end of the 1986-87 season, when it seemed like the whole of Renfrewshire was at Hampden to see them beat Dundee United, jaded by their efforts in making the UEFA Cup Final, 1-0 in the Scottish Cup showpiece. After a dull 90 minutes, it was youngster Ferguson, then only 20, who crashed home the winner for the Buddies' first major silverware in 37 years.

Naturally, Scotland's bigger guns were waiting in the wings, and it was only nine months later that Rangers handed over £1,000,000 to secure his signature – the first seven figure fee agreed by two clubs north of the border.

Fergie's Ibrox career has not been the most consistent, but when not hampered by injury under Souness and on regaining his full fitness under Walter Smith, he has come into his own. His liking for the big time has been highlighted time and again, particularly in his first full season – 1988-89 – when his goal in the superb 3-2 win over Aberdeen helped clinch the Skol Cup. Long-range shooting has become his forte, and there are few individuals in Scottish football who pack a harder shot.

Yet, for all his success, there have been low spots, most notably in 1993-94, when the temperamental Ferguson was red-carded for spitting on Gordan Petric, then of Dundee United – an offence extremely rare in the Scottish game. Previous culprits like Victor Ferreyra of United and St Mirren's Chic Charnley had been booted out of their clubs for the same misdemeanour, and despite the fact the Yugoslavian had clearly elbowed Fergie, the furore was massive, probably more so because of the team he played for. Outspoken TV commentator Gerry McNee even called for the player to be kicked out of the club for good, such was the shame he had brought on

170

such a fine institution! As usual, Walter Smith's commonsense prevailed, and the punishment was kept within the walls at Ibrox, although the SFA hammered the errant midfielder with a lengthy match ban. Smith warned that no Rangers player would ever be allowed to commit the same offence again – a clear ultimatum to Fergie to toe the line. It worked. After 'doing his time', he was soon back to his best, charging forward and winning balls in the centre of the park.

The only other blight on Ferguson's career has been his lamentable international record, which has frustrated successive managers Andy Roxburgh and Craig Brown. A debut against Italy back in 1988 was only the prelude to a string of squad withdrawals for a variety of injuries, and although Graeme Souness' thoughts on international football were widely known, disappointingly the bad luck has continued under Walter Smith. Maybe Ian will eventually the chance to demonstrate he is the perfect foil for Gary McAllister in midfield.

INTERNATIONAL HONOURS
Scotland: Eight caps, 0 goals. Debut v. Italy 1989.
Under-21: Six caps. Debut v. West Germany 1987.

HONOURS IN THE SCOTTISH GAME
League Championship: 1988-89, 1989-90, 1991-92, 1992-93, 1993-94, 1994-95 (6)
Scottish Cup: 1986-87 (with St Mirren), 1992-93 (with Rangers) (2)
League Cup: 1988-89, 1990-91, 1992-93, 1993-94 (4)
Total: 12

LEAGUE RECORD

		Apps	Goals
1984-85	Clyde	2	-
1985-86	Clyde	19	4
1986-87	Clyde	5	-
1986-87	St Mirren	35	4
1987-88	St Mirren	22	6
1988-89	Rangers	30	6
1989-90	Rangers	24	-
1990-91	Rangers	11	1
1991-92	Rangers	16	1
1992-93	Rangers	30	4
1993-94	Rangers	35	5
1994-95	Rangers	16	1
	Total	245	32

VALUATION
Injuries have disrupted the career, but there can be no arguing over the vital role Ferguson fills when in top shape. A player of his skill and steel would expect to fetch around £1.9 million.

Estimated value: £1,900,000

Andy GORAM

Date of Birth: 13th April 1964, Bury

When Walter Smith placed Andy Goram on the transfer list at the end of the 1993-94 season, the reporters who had heard the shock news at first thought the Rangers gaffer was playing a joke on them. Smith's terse voice soon dispelled any thoughts of a prank. It was certainly no joke for Goram.

After a string of injury problems, most of them surrounding a suspect knee, Smith's patience had run out on Goram's cavalier attitude towards training and his more thorough approach to his social life. The warning was clear – shape up or ship out. After all, this was a man who had confessed he'd likely be a heavy drinking labourer if it wasn't for the love of a good woman.

The start to the season Goram enjoyed speaks louder than any words ever could about his desire to save his career. Quite simply, he was sensational. Had it not been for Goram, the European exit to AEK Athens could have been that bit more embarrasing. The sheer quality of his performances should not have taken anyone by surprise, although after his weight problems and turbulent off-field activities – his second wife filed for divorce, and was then re-united with him, last year – doubts existed about his commitment. The worries were worthless though, as Andy demonstrated just why he is one of the continent's top 'keepers, or in Craig Brown's opinion, the best.

The garden has not always been rosy for Goram, however, and his path to the top has, at times, been a rocky one. Boundary Park, Oldham, is not the sort of haunt which springs to mind as a hotbed of English soccer, but it was there that he learned his trade under Joe Royle, now Duncan Ferguson's boss at Everton. A Scotland debut, when the Tartan Army sang, "You're not English anymore," was the fruit of his labours there. A £300,000 transfer to Hibs ensued, as Goram set about his campaign to win a regular international place. That arrived, but still there were no honours at club level and it was his hopes on that front, coupled with Walter Smith's need for Scots for the European challenge, which saw him travel down the M8 from Edinburgh to Glasgow in June 1991 for a cool £1 million.

Even then, things did not go especially smoothly, as Rangers' traditional up and down start to a season was even poorer than normal, and they suffered some unlikely League defeats before a Goram error caused a League Cup semi loss to his previous club, Hibs, at Hampden. It was even more galling for Goram, the man who craved silverware, as he had to watch his former team-mates beat Dunfermline in the final and get their hands on the cup.

However, success was not long in coming by way of a League title and a championship. In 1992-93, he produced form few south of the border would have thought capable from a Scot, as he was a key figure in the Treble winning line-up. It was his displays in Europe which really caught the eye, particularly away from home, where he was inspirational against Leeds and Marseille. Player and footballer of the year honours followed. Injury caught up with him at the tail end of 1993-94, and it was probably significant that Rangers' League-winning points tally at the end of the season was notably lower than in previous seasons. Goram managed only eight matches.

Now, the future for Andy Goram looks good, if he can maintain his attitude, fitness and desire. After looking as though he was heading for the exit door, he seems set to be a fixture at Ibrox for a long time yet.

INTERNATIONAL HONOURS

Scotland. 33 caps, 0 goals. Debut 1986 v. East Germany.
Under-21: One cap v. Eire 1987.

HONOURS IN THE SCOTTISH GAME

League Championship: 1991-92, 1992-93, 1994-95 (3)
Scottish Cup: 1991-92, 1992-93 (2)
League Cup: 1992-93 (1)
Total: 6.

LEAGUE RECORD

		Apps	Goals
1981-82	Oldham	3	-
1982-83	Oldham	38	-
1983-84	Oldham	22	-
1984-85	Oldham	41	-
1985-86	Oldham	41	-
1986-87	Oldham	41	-
1987-88	Oldham	9	-
1987-88	Hibs	33	1
1988-89	Hibs	36	-
1989-90	Hibs	34	-
1990-91	Hibs	35	-
1991-92	Rangers	44	-
1992-93	Rangers	34	-
1993-94	Rangers	8	-
1994-95	Rangers	19	0
	Total	438	1

VALUATION

Goalkeepers traditionally go for less than outfield players, but Andy Goram is one of the top men in his position in Europe. Prospective buyers would probably be asked to splash out around £2 million if they wanted to try to prise him from Ibrox.

Estimated value: £2,000,000

Richard GOUGH

Date of Birth: 5th April 1962, Stockholm

When the flak was flying after Rangers' Scottish Cup loss to Dundee United at the end of 1993-94, then again after their defeats to AEK, Celtic and Falkirk last term, Richard Gough's name was the one frequently mentioned by fans as a possible reason behind it. It is a measure of the stature of one of the club's all-time great captains that he rebounded to have another superb season at the heart of the defence, helping break newcomer Alan McLaren into the Rangers way of doing things.

There is no denying Gough went through a rocky patch whilst the team were struggling, but only a fool would have written have him off. During a career which started back at Dundee United in the early eighties, the Swedish-born, South African-raised Scotland international has been recognised as one of the most durable and reliable men in the game.

Disappointingly, one of the doubters was former national boss Andy Roxburgh, who expressed reservations about the legitimacy of Gough's injuries on international duty, an accusation which was to be one of many disputes between the pair, and caused Richard to retire from the Scotland scene after the disastrous 5-0 collapse in Portugal in 1993. It was all the more disturbing for the national side, as Gough had been inspirational in Scotland's European Championship Finals appearance in 1992 and named in the team of the tournament on its completion. Nevertheless, his achievements at club level are phenomenal. He came within one match, the Scottish Cup Final of 1993-94, of captaining the club to an unprecedented Double Treble, and that, possibly more than any other reward, would have been a fitting tribute to one of the most trophy-laden skippers in Ibrox history.

It was Graeme Souness who signed him from Tottenham just after the start of the 1987-88 campaign, over a year after he had initially inquired about Gough. Spurs' fans' continuing complaints that the club has not had a central defender to match him since his departure are proof enough of his impact there in such a short time. The only blemish was a shock Cup Final loss in 1986-87 to Coventry, but the silverware began to flown on his return north of the border.

After dotting the i's and crossing the t's on his contract on October 2, 1987 it was only 23 days later that he was in the middle of a successful Skol Cup final showdown with Aberdeen, which Rangers won on penalties after a 3-3 draw. That was just the start of it, as his personal honours list demonstrates!

However, there have been disappointments too, including a brief and unsuccessful spell in the 1990 World Cup Finals, when injury counted him out after only 45 minutes of the defeat against Costa Rica, and successive early exits in Europe, an area he is particularly keen to do well in, having made the European Cup semi-finals with Dundee United as a youngster, and confessing afterwards that he believed that sort of experience came along every season.

It is his stated ambition to lead Rangers to those record-busting 10 titles in a row, and if the rest of the squad can match his determination, few would bet against him achieving that. It would be a fitting end to a glittering career for a dominating centre-half who got the ball rolling with a Championship medal in his first full term at Tannadice, and hopes to wind things up in the same manner.

Gough will be remembered in years to come as a commanding defender with the ability to score at vital times. Let's hope he is also known as the man who led the club to that tenth title!

INTERNATIONAL HONOURS

Scotland: 61 caps, 6 goals. Debut 1983 v. Switzerland.

Under-21: Five caps. Debut 1983 - v. East Germany.

HONOURS IN THE SCOTTISH GAME

League Championship: 1981-82 (with Dundee United), 1988-89, 1989-90, 1990-91, 1991-92, 1992-93, 1993-94, 1994-95 (8).

Scottish Cup: 1991-92, 1992-93 (2).

League Cup: 1987-88, 1988-89, 1990-91, 1992-93, 1993-94. (5).

Total: 15.

LEAGUE RECORD

		Apps	Goals
1980-81	Dundee United	4	-
1981-82	Dundee United	30	1
1982-83	Dundee United	34	8
1983-84	Dundee United	33	3
1984-85	Dundee United	33	6
1985-86	Dundee United	31	5
1986-87	Tottenham Hotspur	40	2
1987-88	Tottenham Hotspur	9	-
1987-88	Rangers	31	5
1988-89	Rangers	35	4
1989-90	Rangers	26	-
1990-91	Rangers	26	-
1991-92	Rangers	33	2
1992-93	Rangers	25	2
1993-94	Rangers	37	3
1994-95	Rangers	28	2
	Total	455	43

VALUATION

Richard will almost certainly stay at Rangers until the end of his playing days, having signed a long-term contract last year. If the unthinkable was to happen and he left, his age should mean he'd go for around £500,000.

Estimated value: £500,000

Mark HATELEY

Date of Birth: 7th November 1961, Wallesey

Five years after Mark Hateley arrived at Ibrox, it says everything about his contribution to the club in that time that his departure now seems unthinkable. After an unsteady start, when he was hardly flavour of the month with the fans, he has consistently produced the sort of form which explains why he can number the likes of continent big guns Monaco and more especially AC Milan amongst his former clubs. A big and bustling centre forward who first came to prominence at Coventry City, he earned his first England caps with Portsmouth before becoming a cult at Milan – where he was known as 'Atilla' – then taking the short hop to France. However, it has been at Ibrox that he has produced his best and most consistent form and he has to be considered one of Graeme Souness' top signings for the club. The highlights during his spell in Glasgow have been numerous:

- A brace in the all-important championship decider against Aberdeen in 1991.
- Goals in successive Scottish Cup Finals against Airdrie then the Dons again.
- An out-of-this-world strike in the wonderful 2-1 Battle of Britain win against Leeds at Elland Road.
- 112 goals, in all competitions, in just over five years and the Premier Division's top scorer in 1993-94 and Player of the Year honours.
- A mind boggling partnership with Ally McCoist, which yielded the fantastic tally of 108 League goals in the career-best 1991-92 and 1992-93 campaigns.

In contrast, the lows have been few and far between. Red cards against Celtic, in a torrid Scottish Cup game in 1991, and Bruges in the Champions League – which saw him suspended for Rangers' crucial last two games – were obvious blips. And his persistent and mystifying absence from English squads under Graham Taylor, when in the best form of his career, hurt him deeply. At least he was in good company – Chris Waddle and Peter Beardsley were others who the former English manager chose to ignore.

While the last two seasons have seen the Coisty-Hateley partnership come to a halt, because of the former's injury problems, there is no sign of Big Mark slowing up. Injury interrupted last season, but by the end of the campaign he was restored to the first team and, indeed, looking like the only player with the correct appetite as Rangers played out their fixtures.

His importance off the pitch should not be under-stated either. He was instrumental in persuading Brian Laudrup to come to the club, knowing full well how different the atmosphere was to the pressure pot that is Italy, and if there was no Laudrup at Ibrox, who's to say if Gazza would have come on board? A thinker, Hateley has made no secret he considers the club one of the greatest in Europe and would like to further his education in football in Glasgow once his playing days are over. With Oleg Salenko in place for the new season, pundits will be speculating those days may come sooner than we would all like, but those who've charted his career know better. Only a fool would suggest the indestructible Mark Hateley is on his way out as a first-team player.

Indeed, to prolong his playing career, don't bet against a move to defence – although he had an unhappy time at the back against Hibs last season – and then, who knows? He's on record as saying he'd love to manage Rangers and if he shows the same dedication to achieving that as he has the rest of his career, few would bet against him achieving it.

INTERNATIONAL HONOURS

England: 32 caps, 9 goals. Debut v. USSR 1984.

Under-21: 10 caps. Debut v. Poland 1982.

HONOURS IN THE SCOTTISH GAME

League Championship: 1990-91, 1991-92, 1992-93,1993-94, 1994-95 (5)

Scottish Cup: 1991-92, 1992-93 (2)

League Cup: 1990-91, 1992-93, 1993-94 (3)

Total: 10

LEAGUE RECORD

		Apps	Goals
1978-79	Coventry	1	-
1979-80	Coventry	4	-
1980-81	Coventry	19	3
1981-82	Coventry	34	13
1982-83	Coventry	35	9
1983-84	Portsmouth	38	22
1984-85	AC Milan	21	7
1985-86	AC Milan	22	8
1986-87	AC Milan	23	2
	Monaco record n/a		
1990-91	Rangers	33	10
1991-92	Rangers	30	21
1992-93	Rangers	37	19
1993-94	Rangers	42	22
1994-95	Rangers	23	13
	Total	362	149

VALUATION

Age would obviously play a major role in determining Hateley's worth, but a fee of £1,500,00 would hardly seem outrageous in the current market place.

◊ **Estimated value: £1,500,000**

Brian LAUDRUP

Date of Birth: 22nd February 1969, Vienna

If Jurgen Klinsmann was the steal of the 1994-95 English season at £2 million for Spurs, then Brian Laudrup's arrival at Ibrox for £2.3 million was a bit of business at least its equal. It's not often that a player almost single-handedly wins his side the championship, but that was more or less the case with the Dane last season.

That is not to do any of the other Ibrox stars a disservice. Yes, there were fine performances from the likes of Alan McLaren, David Robertson and Andy Goram. But the one man who consistently ensured Rangers won matches, as opposed to not losing them, was Laudrup. Not surprisingly he was the football writers' and players' player of the year. The joke went thus: "What's the difference between a black cab and Brian Laudrup? A black cab only carries five passengers." And while that is stretching a point, Laudrup arrived on the Scottish football scene in a way which made his previous indifferent form in Italy and Germany all the more puzzling. Week-in, week-out, his free role on either wing baffled full-backs, despite opposing managers' attempts to stifle his freeflowing skills. It prompted more than one commentator to claim at the end of the season that he was on a different planet to everyone else in the Scottish game!

The easy answers to why Laudrup has succeeded in Scotland is that he's playing weaker sides and able to make full advantage of his speed and ball skills. But his form is not that simple to explain, because he proved, even when struggling in Italy, that on the international stage he could make a monkey of the very best.

Possibly the real reason Laudrup has excelled with Rangers is a credit to Walter Smith. When he and David Murray were contemplating purchasing him from Fiorentina, Smith did a bit of research on the sort of character the Dane was, and realised he would be well suited to the type of environment he find in Scotland. Whilst Rangers fans worship the man they now accord "We're not worthy" bows to, they realise that he has a private life as well and respect that, a luxury he never had in Italy. Of course, Scotland's similarity to Denmark, as well as its relative proximity, helped as well and Laudrup's off-field happiness has probably contributed to him playing the best football of his career.

It was a career which started with Brondby, the Danish club involved in the controversy of John Jensen's transfer to Arsenal which ultimately saw George Graham sacked. A move to Bayer Uerdingen in Germany followed, but after just one season, he moved on to Bayern Munich.

The biggest club side in Germany should have been the ideal place for Brian to showcase his talents, but injuries persistently interrupted his progress and it was to be in a Danish shirt that he began to realise the potential which has always been in him. Brought in to make up the numbers in the European Championship finals in Sweden in 1992, after Yugoslavia dissolved into civil war, the Scandinavians shocked the world by going all the way to the final and then beating favourites

Germany 2-0. Laudrup was outstanding and captured the imagination of scouts throughout Europe, including those of Fiorentina, which was to be his next destination. Florence did not prove a happy hunting ground. As the team struggled, Laudrup and German Stefan Effenberg were made the scapegoats for relegation and the heat turned up off the pitch, as they were roundly abused by the club's idiot element. At one stage, Laudrup decided his family had had enough, whisked them backed to the relative safety of Denmark and vowed to leave. A loan deal to Milan was arranged for the 1993-94 season, but with six foreigners on the books, places were at a premium and Fabio Capello was unwilling to risk one of them on the unpredictable genius of Laudrup. When he did get his chance, the restraints were put on and a player who should have been destroying defences with his talents invariably ended up in defensive positions himself.

And so to the summer of 1994. One of Europe's best footballers is again looking for a new club, yet he has acquired a reputation of never staying very long anywhere and has still to produce the goods for a season with anyone. Rangers step in and to the surprise of all his close friends, family and associates, Laudrup says "yes". That in itself is again a tribute to Smith, for as Brian has himself explained, "I realised that if the move to Rangers did not come off, it would have been very difficult for my career. But it is the best move I have ever made."

Mark Hateley proved a key element too, chatting to the uncertain Dane and reassuring him that Scotland was not the soccer backwater many believed it to be.

Laudrup's assertion that this has been his best move would be a difficult sentiment for the manager to dispute too. As the club craves European success, he looks the one player at his disposal who can carry Rangers to the pinnacle of the continental game as the side which did so well in the Champions League ages and moves on. He has proved himself the best player in the Premier Division for around 20 years, and is one of a rare breed who genuinely is worth paying to go and see.

In the season that Davie Cooper died, it is perhaps the best tribute possible to the Dane to say he has been taken to the fans' hearts in the same way that Coop was, despite his short stay at the club to date. If a history of the club is penned in 50 years time, it seems fair to suggest that Laudrup, however long his tenure as the King of Ibrox, will be in there as one of the club's all-time great players.

INTERNATIONAL HONOURS

Danish international

HONOURS IN THE SCOTTISH GAME

League Championship: 1994-95 (1)

VALUATION

As transfer fees rocket out of control in England, Laudrup's value of just over £2 million is beginning to resemble the deal of the century. Surely worth at least four times that in the current inflated market.

Estimated value: £8,000,000

Stuart McCALL

Date of Birth: 10th June 1964, Leeds

It is perhaps fitting that Stuart McCall was born in Leeds, given that he seems to have modelled his style of play on that great Elland Road Scot of the seventies Billy Bremner. A tenacious tackler and a real 90 minute man, McCall has exemplified the superb will to win which has ensured Rangers have continued their domination of the domestic game in Scotland in recent seasons.

Signed for what now seems a bargain £1.2 million from Everton, he has, by nature of his Scottish heritage, become a valued member of the national side in recent seasons and will be long-remembered for a crucial goal against Sweden in the 1990 World Cup Finals.

However, his unparalleled success of late is a far cry from the humble beginnings of his career, which kicked off at Bradford City, his hometown team, despite his red herring of a birthplace. It didn't take long for the little man with the red hair to become a big star there, and it was at Valley Parade that he received his first international recognition – for England Under 21s! Thankfully, for both Scotland and Rangers, he did not play for the young English, although he was perilously close as an unused substitute.

It was also at Bradford that he endured his worst memory in football; the fire disaster which plunged British soccer into mourning in 1985. McCall played in the fateful game against Bristol City. A move to a big club was inevitable, and it duly arrived with a transfer to Everton. However, McCall strangely failed to really establish himself at Goodison, and it is worth remembering that his finest moment there – two goals in their 3-2 1989 FA Cup Final defeat against Liverpool – was achieved as a substitute.

The departure of Trevor Steven for his multi-million deal to Marseille in August 1991 paved the way for McCall's arrival at Ibrox and he quickly established himself as a fixture in the team, wearing the number eight shirt. Since then he has proved himself the perfect workhorse in midfield, as well as his accomplished wide midfielder, and on occasion, a competent right back. Indeed, his willingness to play anywhere at Ibrox has resulted in him wearing every outfield shirt at Ibrox bar one – the number 11 currently occupied by Brian Laudrup. Career highlights with Rangers have been many and varied, but a goal against Aberdeen in the 1992-93 Skol Cup final was a crucial one and paved the way for an eventual 2-1 success.

The future? How long he can maintain the tremendous workrate which makes him an automatic choice for Walter Smith's team remains to be seen, but it is something he has given thought to himself. "Obviously the amount of running I have to do means I am not going to play in midfield for ever," he has said. "So I have thought about other positions, and I must admit I fancy having a crack at playing at the back eventually. Keeping fit and maintaining your enthusiasm is the key to playing as long as you can and that's certainly my aim. I want to stay at Rangers as long as possible, because everywhere else would be downhill from here." Few would bet against this determined little man making as big a success of defending as he has his midfield role during his time at Rangers.

INTERNATIONAL HONOURS

Scotland: 30 caps, one goal. Debut v. Argentina, 1990.
Scotland Under-21: Two caps. Debut v. England 1988.

HONOURS IN THE SCOTTISH GAME

League Championship: 1991-92, 1992-93, 1993-94, 1994-95 (4)
Scottish Cup: 1991-92, 1992-93 (2)
League Cup: 1993-94 (1)
Total: 7

LEAGUE RECORD

		Apps	Goals
1982-83	Bradford City	28	4
1983-84	Bradford City	46	5
1984-85	Bradford City	46	8
1985-86	Bradford City	38	4
1986-87	Bradford City	36	7
1987-88	Bradford City	36	7
1988-89	Everton	33	0
1989-90	Everton	37	3
1990-91	Everton	33	3
1991-92	Rangers	36	1
1992-93	Rangers	36	5
1993-94	Rangers	34	3
1994-95	Rangers	30	3
	Total	469	53

VALUATION

The year are dragging on for Stuart, but he still remains a big influence on the side. An attractive target for clubs looking for an older head in a young midfield.

Estimated value: £1,000,000

Ally McCOIST

Date of Birth: 24th September 1962, Bellshill

Only a spate of injuries in the last couple of seasons has prevented Ally McCoist smashing his way into the record books ahead of Bob McPhail as the club's top league scorer ever. However, statistics alone do not do justice to a player who has become a scoring phenomenon at Ibrox.

Signed by current PR man and then manager John Greig on June 9, 1983, for £175,000 from Sunderland, Ally is one of those rare individuals who turned down Ibrox once, before getting another opportunity to join the fold. On leaving St Johnstone a couple of seasons previously, the youngster had opted to try his luck down south with the Wearside club and declined Greig's advances. Both club and player have had good reason to be grateful for his change of mind shortly after.

Where do you start with McCoist? On a personal level, he has twice lifted the Golden Boot, awarded to European football's top marksman in his domestic league. Those honours arrived in 1991-92 and 1992-93, when the prolific Ally was truly on fire. In the two seasons, he scored 68 times in a total of just 72 appearances – a rate bordering on the unbelievable in the modern era.

He has been the international side's most reliable striker of recent times, and although his record of 15 goals in 46 games does not come close to his club statistics, it is more than acceptable for a national team who have always struggled up front, despite the number of quality players they have had at their disposal over the years. Again, that would also be much improved if his career had not stalled because of injury, an unfortunate run which started with a broken leg in the national team's 5-0 debacle in Lisbon in 1993. However, even since then Ally has risen to grab the headlines on occasion, most memorably when he scored a sensational overhead winner in the 1993-94 League Cup final against Hibs, after coming on as a substitute, and prompting one team-mate to allege that the "sun truly did shine out of his backside!"

Obviously the key to McCoist's enduring popularity is not just his acknowledged ability, but the personality he brings into football as well. Even the most churlish of supporters of other clubs would have to recognise him as a genuine character in a generally stale Scottish scene at present, and as somebody who lives life to the full. A career in broadcasting as an 'expert' seems assured for such a talkative star when he hangs up his boots, and there is no doubt he will make as successful pundit as he has a striker.

McCoist deserves his status as the pin-up boy too. There have been real rocky spells for him at Ibrox, most particularly when he was on the receiving end of some vitriolic abuse in the early days of his Rangers career, when the team was serving up some dreadful fare, and then in a spell where Graeme Souness decided that he did not like the idea of one of his star players being bigger than the club, or more pointedly him, and decreed that lengthy spells as a substitute would dim his shining light. As things stood, though, Ally earned himself a new nickname, 'The Judge', a result of all the time he spent on the bench, and returned more purposeful than ever under Walter Smith.

At the tail end of 1994, McCoist's contribution to Scottish football and Rangers was recognised as he picked up an MBE at Buckingham Palace. Typically, he was in at Ibrox early the next day, greeting the rest of the squad on their arrival, with his newly-awarded gong pinned to his lapel. It seems safe to say that history will look kindly on Coisty. His scoring feats alone dictate that he will be remembered as one of the club's greatest ever marksmen. And if anyone should ever debate his status, the man himself will probably be knocking about for a few years yet to quickly put things right!

INTERNATIONAL HONOURS

Scotland: 46 caps, 15 goals. Debut 1986 v. Holland.
Under-21: One cap, v. Belgium 1984.

HONOURS IN THE SCOTTISH GAME

League Championship: 1986-87, 1988-89, 1989-90, 1990-91, 1991-92, 1992-93, 1993-94 (7)
Scottish Cup: 1991-92 (1)
League Cup: 1983-84, 1985-85, 1986-87, 1987-88, 1988-89, 1990-91, 1992-93, 1993-94 (8)
Total: 16

LEAGUE RECORD

		Apps	Goals
1978-79	St Johnstone	4	-
1979-80	St Johnstone	15	-
1980-81	St Johnstone	38	22
1981-82	Sunderland	28	2
1982-83	Sunderland	28	6
1983-84	Rangers	30	9
1984-85	Rangers	25	12
1985-86	Rangers	33	24
1986-87	Rangers	44	33
1987-88	Rangers	40	31
1988-89	Rangers	19	9
1989-90	Rangers	34	14
1990-91	Rangers	26	11
1991-92	Rangers	38	34
1992-93	Rangers	34	34
1993-94	Rangers	21	7
1994-95	Rangers	9	1
	Total	466	249

VALUATION

Yet another Ger who looks unlikely to leave the club, McCoist would now be a bit a risk anyway in the transfer market, after a disappointing fitness record in recent easons. If the unthinkable was to happen, around £600,000 would probably find its ay into the coffers. John Aldridge has proved that good strikers know how to ore goals, whatever their age.

Estimated value: £600,000

Alan McLAREN

Date of Birth: 4th January 1971, Edinburgh

Like the Mounties, Rangers always get their man! That was certainly the case with Alan McLaren, who arrived at Ibrox on October 25 1994, after a protracted and confusing transfer deal. The eventual agreement saw Hearts take Dave McPherson back and a large sum of money, believed to be about £1.2 million, in exchange for the Scotland international.

Rumours had abounded over McLaren's move to Ibrox for an age; since McPherson re-signed for the club in June 1992, in fact. There were more than a few raised eyebrows at the press conference that day when it was McPherson who was presented, rather than his younger Hearts colleague.

There were never any doubts, however, about McLaren's pedigree to play for Rangers. A debutant with the Tynecastle side at the age of 17, he had captained the club before he had even moved out of his teens and had then Gorgie-boss Alex MacDonald proclaiming, "He'll be the captain of Scotland." That prediction looked plausible at the time – McLaren's performances for the national team in the last couple of seasons have made it inevitable.

And there is an easy explanation for his success – he does the things a defender is required to do simply and well. McLaren is a good tackler, a good organiser and an adequate passer, and above all, a confident player. That, more than anything, has explained his success at international level, where he has comfortably coped with superstars like Dennis Bergkamp, Jari Litmanen and most memorably Roberto Baggio. One or two worries have been expressed, naturally enough, but the two most common seem over-anxiety on behalf of the critics to find faults for the sake of it, rather than legitimate shortcomings. Accusations of future weight problems appear to be derived from a fat face rather than any real lack of pace on the pitch, while the opinion that he is a better marker than defender, and so hardly required for Rangers' domestic season, was quickly proved a nonsense last term.

As well as a future Scotland captain, McLaren will surely skipper Rangers as well. The ease with which he slid into the side after his move, with potentially torrid clashes against Celtic and Hearts in his first three matches, demonstrated that he understands just what playing at Ibrox is all about. Since the very early days of his career, he has consistently progressed as expected – of the Under-21 side which reached the European Championship semi-finals, for example, he is the one player who has gone on to become indispensable for the national team, where others like Eoin Jess, Scott Booth and Phil O'Donnell have flattered to deceive. So bestowing the captaincy on him before it happens does not appear to be the rashest of predictions.

INTERNATIONAL HONOURS

Scotland: 24 caps, no goals. Debut v. USA 1992.
Under-21: 11 caps. Debut v. France 1989.

HONOURS IN THE SCOTTISH GAME

League Championship: 1994-5 (1)
Scottish Cup: 0
League Cup: 0
Total: 1

LEAGUE RECORD

		Apps	Goals
1987-88	Hearts	1	-
1988-89	Hearts	12	1
1989-90	Hearts	27	1
1990-91	Hearts	23	1
1991-92	Hearts	38	1
1992-93	Hearts	34	-
1993-94	Hearts	37	1
1994-95	Hearts	24	2
	Total	196	7

VALUATION

McLaren is undoubtedly a genuine and blossoming talent. There are very few sides in Britain who would not be boosted by his presence, and in view of recent deals involving the likes of John Scales and Phil Babb, he would be a snip at around £3 million.

Estimated value: £3,000,000

Alexei MIKHAILITCHENKO

Date of Birth: 30th March 1963, Kiev, Ukraine

At one stage last season, it looked as if Alexei Mikhailitchenko would almost certainly leave Rangers before the present campaign started. Persistent, frustrating injury problems left him on the sidelines for much of 1994-95 and it was widely felt that with his contract expiring in the summer and a new visa required from the Department of Employment, Miko's number was up at Ibrox. However, goals in successive games, against Hibs and Kilmarnock (Rangers' last two wins of the season) were enough to help swing Walter Smith's opinion and earn the Ukrainian another 12 months in Glasgow.

When Miko arrived in Scotland in July 1991, from Sampdoria, expectation was high. He had come to the attention whilst playing against the club for Dynamo Kiev in Europe a few years before and, indeed, had been responsible for scoring the goal which gave the then Soviet champs a one goal win on their own turf. But, like Oleg Kuznetsov before him, he has failed to live up to the lofty billing which preceded him. Whilst the former's failure was down to desperate luck with injuries, Alexei has rather let himself down with erratic displays and a tendency to wander in and out of games. On his day he is devastating, as has been seen in a couple of Old Firm games and one superb Scottish Cup tie against Motherwell in the 1991-92 season.

But too often there has been an unwillingness to impose himself on matches, with the result that he can become an anonymous, and sometimes dispirited looking figure on the pitch. Someone who has played for Kiev and Sampdoria and captained the Commonwealth of Independent States in the European Championship finals of 1992 should have no trouble in standing out like a beacon, rather in the way Laudrup has, in the Premier Division mediocrity. Not even the biggest Mikhailitchenko fan could claim that has happened.

There are no answers from the man himself, as he refuses to conduct interviews in English, despite an apparent ability to speak the language well enough to make himself understood in the dressing room. And therein possibly lies a clue; Mikhailitchenko only ever seems to do what *he* fancies, and there are just some days he cannot be bothered with football. Amid these negatives, though, there is the indisputable skill, a wonderful left foot and a decent scoring record for the club from midfield. So he's far from a flop; everyone has just wanted a little more. The prospect of him teaming up in the centre of the pitch with Gascoigne is an intriguing one. In one of the few interviews he has given in Scotland – conducted in his native tongue of course – he identified the more skilful operators in the Premier, like John Collins and Eoin Jess, as individuals he would pay to watch. Miko obviously has very definite ideas on how football should be played, and Gazza fits in with these. The charismatic Geordie may just be the catalyst the enigmatic Ukrainian needs to get some fire in his belly and show us all what he is really capable of. At 31, approaching 32, he is no spring chicken, but if the speed may have ebbed a bit since his peak, the ability hasn't and it would be fitting if he repaid Walter Smith's faith in awarding him another year's contract with his best campaign yet for Rangers. For a man who looked set to leave the club on a free transfer not so long ago, it would be a fitting swansong.

INTERNATIONAL HONOURS
Full international for Soviet Union, Commonwealth of Independent States and Ukraine.

HONOURS IN THE SCOTTISH GAME
League : 1991-92, 1992-93, 1993-94 (3).
League Cup : 1992-93, 1993-94 (2)
Scottish Cup: 1991-92. (1)
Total: 6

LEAGUE RECORD

		Apps	Goals
1991-92	Rangers	27	10
1992-93	Rangers	29	5
1993-94	Rangers	34	5
1994-95	Rangers	9	2
	Total	99	22

186

VALUATION

Miko still has much to offer, particularly on the continent, where the slower pace of the game would undoubtedly be to his benefit.

Estimated value: £800,000

Charlie MILLER

Date of Birth: 18th March 1976, Glasgow

One of the most frequent accusations levelled at Rangers is that they do not rear their own youngsters. Certainly, over the years, there has more than a hint of truth to that. Any youngsters who have been tried for not been good enough to make the grade, like John Morrow or David Hagen, given up what they see as a fruitless task in trying to claim a regular first-team place, a la Steven Pressley or John Spencer, or hung about without ever fully imposing themselves, rather in the way Neil Murray has remained a fringe player.

Last season, things changed ever so slightly. Two young men, who had appeared briefly prior to 1994-95, emerged as fully fledged members of the first-team squad. Craig Moore enjoyed a steady campaign, and generally acquitted himself well against some of the League's top strikers. Charlie Miller, on the other hand, was a sensation. He had made his debut against Aberdeen in 1993-94 and had been popularly tipped as a potential star of the future by those in the know. By Christmas 1994, when Miller had played a dozen matches in the first team, influential figures in the game were raving about the Glasgow-born teenager.

Said Scotland Under-21 coach Tommy Craig, "What I like about Charlie is his confidence. He's already come into the team and shown he feels right at home on that stage. "And the reason he has the confidence is his footballing awareness. It's something that cannot be coached into young players. Miller is one of the lucky ones though. He was born with it."

By the end of the season, a full call-up was on the cards. Craig Brown was talking glowingly about Miller and the likelihood of him playing for the national team within the next 12 months. It might have happened already, had suspension and injury not taken their toll. Miller is a modern day player; adaptable, skilful and with great brain. Not necessarily the fastest player in the world, he makes up for that with his vision. He sees openings where others don't.

Craig hit it on the head when he praised his maturity. A typical gallus Glasgow lad is the stereotypical description of the lad from Castlemilk, a down to earth housing estate on the south side of the city. But anyone who has seen him at home inside the confines of Ibrox knows it is true, and it perhaps explains why he has looked so at home in the first team. Next season will be a big test for him. Other young players have burst on to the scene in Scotland in recent seasons and failed to make a sustained impact. Eoin Jess and Gary Smith at Aberdeen spring readily to mind. Others like Simon Donnelly, at Celtic, have almost sunk without trace after a blistering start. It seems unlikely that will be the case with Miller. But the next 12 months will be another vital stage in his development, if he is to go on to become the player many believe he is capable of being.

More goals would help. In a Rangers team which does not rely on any individual to score, it is not imperative that Miller hits the target from his role in midfield, tucked in behind the front two. But he is capable of more. Inquiries from the press will escalate too, and having so far been kept away from the media in the same way Ryan Giggs was protected initially at Manchester United, it will be interesting to see how he copes with this facet of the game too. Most observers agree he will probably take it in his stride.

INTERNATIONAL HONOURS
Scotland Under-21: Two caps. Debut v. Greece 1994.

HONOURS IN THE SCOTTISH GAME
League Championship: 1994-95 (1)
Scottish Cup: 0
League Cup: 0
Total: 1

LEAGUE RECORD

		Apps	Goals
1993-94	Rangers	3	0
1994-95	Rangers	21	3
	Total	24	3

VALUATION
Unlimited potential. But he is already a big star in the Scottish game so a monster fee would be justified.

Estimated value: £2,500,000

Craig MOORE

Date of Birth: 12th December 1975, Canterbury, Australia

When Rangers endured such a disappointing series of results at the end of their 1993-94 championship season, then lost the opportunity of a historic second successive Treble by falling to Dundee United in the Scottish Cup Final, the vultures had a field day. The team was too old; the defence, in particular, was ageing by the day. As tends to be the case, Walter Smith did not respond to these criticisms with the stream of words which might be expected from other managers. In Smith's book, actions speak louder than words, but his decision to field Moore i the first team for most of the 1994-95 campaign indicated that he too had noticed the doubters' observations were correct.

Moore's arrival at Ibrox is a fairy-tale. As a boy in Australia, he wrote to top

British clubs, asking for trials. Paying his own way over, he attempted to make the grade at both Arsenal, and Rangers. At Ibrox, manager Smith has said before that there's only ever a one-in-a-hundred chance that a lad who comes asking for trials will make the grade. Moore was that long-shot chance. He instantly impressed in Glasgow, whereas in the English capital, he felt more ill-at-ease. In fact, the young Antipodean believed some of the big names at the Gunners felt he was a threat to them, and so needed no persuasion when a contract from the Light Blues was on offer. Perhaps he has just been in the right place at the right time to make such an impact on the first-team at a tender age. With Gary Stevens' career at the club drawing to a close, and young blood required, Moore made his debut against Dundee United on April 5, 1994, then at the start of the most recent campaign, really began to establish himself. He admitted that the club's European exit almost certainly helped him, with his Australian credentials meaning he would have played little or, more likely, no part in any Champions League run Rangers might have enjoyed. But with no need to field a settled team with Europe in mind, he was given his opportunity – and seized it.

That, perhaps more than any good fortune Moore has had, is probably the secret of his success. While in past years, other youngsters at the club have been offered openings, few have taken advantage of them to the extent that Moore has. Despite the limited number of natural right full-backs at the club for much of the season, he would not have played so many games if he was not good enough.

What his long-term future holds is unclear. On ability, the early stages of his career suggest he has it in him to hold down a place at Ibrox for many years. However, his decision to stick with Australia, come what may, could well work against him. It looks certain to deprive him of any top-class European action at any rate. Nevertheless, the arrival of Craig Moore as a genuine first-team squad member last season was one of the big plus points for Rangers.

INTERNATIONAL HONOURS

Australian Under-21 international.

HONOURS IN THE SCOTTISH GAME

League Championship: 1994-95 (1)
Scottish Cup: 0
League Cup: 0
Total: 1

LEAGUE RECORD

		Apps	Goals
1993-94	Rangers	1	0
1994-95	Rangers	21	2
	Total	22	2

VALUATION

His Australian background will obviously be a hindrance to him as regards playing
European football for British sides, but there is no doubt that his ability and
potential make him an attractive target. At present, a fee of £800,000 – based on
Steven Pressley's sale to Coventry – would seem fair.

Estimated value: £800,000

Neil MURRAY

Date of Birth: 21st February 1973, Bellshill

Rangers' Champions League run of 1992-93 had many benefits for the club,
including a higher profile on the continent, large financial rewards and a new-found
respect within the United Kingdom. Amongst all that, the emergence of Neil
Murray went largely unnoticed.

Murray is not a player who will ever grab the limelight at Ibrox. As well as
operating in fairly unglamorous roles within the side, usually at right-back or as a
'worker' in midfield, the youngster is quiet, well-spoken and, although always
polite with the media, does not go out of his way to court publicity. A qualified
accountant, he seems to accept that there is more to life than football, an outlook
which perhaps does not make him one of the bigger crowd favourites at Ibrox.

There can be no doubting his usefulness, though. Good with either foot, and
possessing a sound football brain, he can slot into most positions in defence or
midfield effectively. Lack of pace, perhaps, makes him just that little bit short when
it comes to claiming a regular place, but more often than not, Murray will be
involved. There can be no denying that the management at Ibrox consider him an
asset – when Hearts made noises about taking him to Tynecastle as part of the Dave
McPherson deal, they may not have refused, but made it perfectly clear that he was
not someone who had been offered to them. Murray was their selection, not
Rangers', and no-one seemed too distraught when the deal broke down because of
the youngster's correct request for financial guarantees. At the time it was a stance
which annoyed some fans, who felt he and McPherson were holding the club to
ransom and preventing McLaren's signing, but he was soon forgiven as he
continued to produce his usual stable performances.

Possibly Murray's level-headedness is his greatest attribute, although it
sometimes seems to prevent him being more forceful on the pitch. His calmness
was best demonstrated when he was gearing up for Rangers' crunch match with
CSKA Moscow in the Champions League in 1992-93, when he candidly admitted,
"I think I've come to terms with the fact that, even though I'm still young in
football terms, this run might be the pinnacle of my career." There was another

highlight later that season when he started the Cup Final against Aberdeen, and shocked everyone by scoring the opening goal in the 2-1 triumph. Neil would be the first to concede that his scoring record has been, in general, disappointing since he became a first-team squad regular but he caught everyone on the hop that day. He wasn't even included on the bookies' fixed odds coupons.

What does the future hold for Neil Murray? An Under-21 international, he would command a generous fee if he left, but despite the Hearts move, Rangers do not appear in any great rush to lose him. He appears to be a squad player, a man who will fill the role that Scott Nisbet did for many seasons, as the first-choice second choice! That should mean around 30 games a season, a clutch of medals and financial security. On the other hand, he may do a John Spencer and seek a move to prove himself elsewhere. One thing is certain, with his accountancy degree there is no danger of him ending up a penniless ex-pro somewhere!

INTERNATIONAL HONOURS
Scotland Under-21: 10 caps. Debut v. Portugal 1993.

HONOURS IN THE SCOTTISH GAME
League Championship: 1992-93, 1993-94, 1994-95 (3)
Scottish Cup: 1992-93 (1)
League Cup: 0
Total: 4

LEAGUE RECORD

		Apps	Goals
1992-93	Rangers	16	-
1993-94	Rangers	22	-
1994-95	Rangers	20	1
	Total	58	1

VALUATION
Rangers could expect to pick up around £500,000 for Murray if previous deals for Gary McSwegan and John Spencer are anything to go by.

Estimated value: £500,000

David ROBERTSON

Date of Birth: 17th October 1968, Aberdeen

Since bursting on to the scene with Aberdeen in the mid-eighties, David Robertson has undoubtedly been the most consistent left-back in Scotland. A pacy and direct defender, he causes opposition reaguards much trouble, a quality which has seen detractors accuse him of neglecting his own defensive duties. However that's an opinion which cuts no ice with Walter Smith, who has seen the 26-year-old

Aberdonian emerge as the only first-team player with virtually no competition for his place. The one mystery which surrounds Robbo is the comparatively few Scotland caps he has to his name at this stage in his career. Despite his outstanding displays at home and in Europe, he has suffered because of the link-up between Celtic's Tom Boyd and John Collins with club and country on the left flank, which has seen Boyd come through as a regular member of Craig Brown's sides.

From the moment Robertson made his League debut as a sub with Aberdeen against Hamilton on August 16th in the 1986-87 season, there was no looking back. He made 34 appearances in the Premier that season, establishing himself as the Dons' regular number three. In 1988-89, David really endeared himself to Rangers fans as he was involved in a shocking mix-up with Granite City 'keeper Theo Snelders as the two sides collided in a superb Skol Cup Final at Hampden. A poor Robertson throw-in had the Dutch 'keeper in total confusion, and Ally McCoist – who else? – nipped in to open the scoring. Rangers were to win that match, but there were to be more happy occasions at the national stadium for Robertson, not all of them in a Light Blue top. The very next season, Aberdeen, under the guidance of Alex Smith, returned to Hampden to face Rangers in the clubs' third successive League Cup Final showdown. This time, he had the last laugh, as two Paul Mason goals took the Cup north for his first medal in professional football. More glory was to come at the national stadium that season, as Aberdeen also lifted the Scottish Cup, after a thrilling penalty shoot-out with Celtic, which saw Brian Irvine fire the winner in a 9-8 success. David successfully converted his spot-kick.

Perhaps one of the most important matches in Robertson's career came the following season, as Aberdeen, determined to prove their Cup successes the previous season were no fluke, arrived at Ibrox for the League decider, which, as every Teddy Bear knows, was Mark Hateley's finest hour. Who knows what David Robertson might have decided to do had the Dons won the title? As it was, he made up his mind to leave at the end of his contract and Walter Smith, eager to start accumulating Scots because of the Euro restrictions, signed him for a fee which the League tribunal was to set at £930,000.

Since arriving at Ibrox, it has been one success after another for the quiet-man of the club. There have been few setbacks, although a red card in the opening minute of the Scottish Cup semi at Hampden against Celtic in the 1991-92 season was a real low-point. To make matters worse, the dismissal was earned for a foul on his close friend from their Aberdeen days, Joe Miller. No real damage was done though, as the Light Blues marched on to win the match and the trophy, with their left-back firmly in place for the final with Airdrie. The next, Treble-winning, season, emphasised Robertson's increasing importance through his sterling display at home and in the club's glorious Champions League run. It's only really in the past couple of seasons that his international career has taken off, despite a debut in 1992 prior to the European Championship finals, in a warm-up against Northern Ireland. An outstanding display in a low-key B game with Wales at Wrexham at the start of 1994 was enough to warrant regular selection in new manager Brown's squads, and although a first-team place has yet to be claimed, the signs are that he will be handed one before too long.

LEAGUE RECORD

		Apps	Goals
1986-87	Aberdeen	34	-
1987-88	Aberdeen	23	-
1988-89	Aberdeen	23	-
1989-90	Aberdeen	20	1
1990-91	Aberdeen	35	1
1991-92	Rangers	42	1
1992-93	Rangers	39	3
1993-94	Rangers	32	1
	Total	248	7

INTERNATIONAL HONOURS

Scotland: Three caps, 0 goals. Debut v. Northern Ireland 1992.
Scotland Under-21: Seven caps. Debut v Eire 1987.

HONOURS IN THE SCOTTISH GAME

League: 1991-92, 1992-93, 1993-94 1994-95 all with Rangers (4)
League Cup: 1989-90 with Aberdeen, 1992-93, 1993-94 with Rangers (3)
Scottish Cup: 1989-90 with Aberdeen, 1991-92, 1992-93 with Rangers (3)
Total: 10

VALUATION

With his peak years to come, and the experience he has already gathered, there seems no reason why Robertson could not command a fee of around £2 million on the transfer market.

Estimated value: £2,000,000

Trevor STEVEN

Date of Birth: 21st September 1963, Berwick

In retrospect, maybe Rangers should not have sold Trevor Steven to Marseille at the start of the 1991-92 campaign. The fee, around the £5 million mark, was too good to be turned down at the time. But there can be no dispute that since his return, a year later, Steven has failed to consistently produce the form he is capable of. Injuries have played their part and that is a shame, because, especially during his first spell at Ibrox, he displayed all the poise, vision and passing ability which made him such a force for Everton and England in the mid to late eighties.

It is worth noting, too, that his phasing out of the international side has coincided with these up and down times. Admittedly, England have some super up and coming young players. And yes, it is hard for a player in Scotland to prove their worth to the international manager down south (although Paul Gascoigne could go a long way to changing Terry Venables' mind). But if Steven had been fit and at the top of his game, it is hard to imagine that someone with so much adaptability could have not been used somewhere in the fold. It was at Goodison that the young Steven first came to the fore, having moved there from Burnley. In Howard Kendall's all-conquering side of the time, he won FA Cup and League gongs, as well as a European Cup-Winners' Cup medal in 1985. Alongside Gary Stevens, who he was to team up with again at Ibrox, he formed a formidable partnership on the right flank of the pitch, the full-back providing the strength and the power, the midfielder the guile and the finesse. Steven also chipped in with his fair share of goals too, including one in that memorable 3-1 win over Rapid Vienna in Rotterdam – Andy Gray, a former Ger, was also on the mark that night .

When the time came to quit Merseyside, a player of such obvious talent attracted the attention of a number of clubs, but it was Rangers who won the day, with Stevens – who Steven was close to and had co-penned a book with – possibly helping influence the decision after a successful first campaign in the Light Blues' colours. Steven was an instant success, displaying an all too rare ability to put his foot on the ball and spray passes around in the hurly burly of the Premier Division. A successful first season was capped by him scoring the goal, at Dundee United, which saw Rangers collect the Premier Division championship.

The move to France came by way of his own super form, and a high standing in the game, which saw the likes of Graeme Souness and Kenny Dalglish publicly sing his praises. The French side were more than happy with the sensational form o' Chris Waddle following his, at the time, unbelievable £4.5 million transfer from Tottenham. He had carried them to the final of the European Cup, which they lost, on penalties, to Red Star Belgrade, and were on the lookout for a Brit who could take them that one step further. Steven fitted the bill.

His move, for the mind boggling fee, was not a great success. Steven spent a lot of time on the bench, and could not help to be looked on less favourably by the fans than the likes of Waddle, whose dazzling skills were worshipped. After a season in which he only really hit the headlines after the disaster of numerous deaths when a stand collapsed at a Cup match involving Marseille, it was no surprise when Rangers were linked with his return move, and even less so when he actually signed on again. For th' £2 million plus fee they splashed out then, it can hardly be said that Steven has justified the outlay. Injuries have regularly afflicted him and at one point last season, just as he was about to return to the first team, he did admit he wondered if his time was up. That sort of thinking is premature, but with the arrival of Gazza, there is plent' for Steven, an undeniably classy performer on his day, to prove.

INTERNATIONAL HONOURS

England international: 36 caps, four goals. Debut v. Northern Ireland 1985.
England Under-21: Two caps. Debut v. Finland 1985.

HONOURS IN THE SCOTTISH GAME

League: 1989-90, 1990-91, 1992-93, 1993-94. (4)
Scottish Cup: 0
League Cup: 1990-91, 1992-93, 1993-94 (3)
Total: 7

LEAGUE RECORD

		Apps	Goals
1980-81	Burnley	1	0
1981-82	Burnley	36	3
1982-83	Burnley	39	8
1983-84	Everton	27	1
1984-85	Everton	40	12
1985-86	Everton	41	9
1986-87	Everton	41	14
1987-88	Everton	36	6
1988-89	Everton	29	6
1989-90	Rangers	34	3
1990-91	Rangers	19	2
1991-92	Rangers	2	1
1991-92	Marseille	27	3
1992-93	Rangers	24	5
1993-94	Rangers	32	4
1994-95	Rangers	11	0
	Total	439	77

VALUATION

Despite his advancing years, Trevor, if fit, would be able to do a job in the
Premiership in the same manner Ray Wilkins did at QPR.

Estimated value: £1,000,000

They Played Their Part

Duncan FERGUSON

Date of Birth: 27th December 1971, Stirling

Two pages in a pocket annual hardly seems to do justice to a man who has
generated a mountain of newsprint in his career already! A book would probably
be fitting – but that will undoubtedly come in the future. Any author certainly won't
be short of material. Quite simply Big Dunc is the sort of controversial character

who wouldn't have been out of place in the heady days of sixties football north of the border, when tales of misdemeanour from Rangers legends Jim Baxter and Willie Henderson and Celtic's Jimmy Johnstone were ten-a-penny.

Sadly, in the last couple of years, it has been Fergie's off-field antics which have prompted the media interest, rather than his exploits on the pitch, and eventually caused his transfer from Ibrox to Everton. Perhaps the erratic behaviour is to be expected when you are the most expensive footballer in Britain, as he was during the 1993-94 season. Rangers had shelled out £3.75 million, with the promise of more to come to Dundee United, for his precocious talents. Unfortunately, it has to be admitted that he has invited most of the negative publicity, with various court cases for violence-related charges dominating the newspapers.

There can be no doubting, though, that away from all the controversy, there lies a supremely talented player, who perhaps needs his wayward talent channelled in a more positive direction. Everton, on the evidence of his FA Cup exploits, may be the place to do that. The monster fee Rangers were prepared to pay was more than they had wanted, but on potential, appeared justified. Despite an average scoring ratio at United, Fergie showed that he was one of the hottest young talents in Britain. He was a rarity in the domestic game – a highly skilled, BIG forward, good in equal measure on the ground or in the air. Under the oppressive reign of Jim McLean he found it hard to feel comfortable, however, and he had various brushes with the Tannadice taskmaster, including walkouts and public slanging matches. A runner's-up medal from United's Cup Final loss to Motherwell in 1992 and Scotland representation were his rewards from that spell.

After a saga which seemed to last all summer long, on the eve of the 1993-94 term Fergie finally signed on at Ibrox, the move he claimed he had always wanted. Leeds had emerged as favourites early on, but when Rangers began to make noises, it was clear that there would be only one destination for the big man – despite McLean's claims he would never sell to another Scottish club. As it was, he didn't because it was new manager Ivan Golac who saw the deal through!

Duncan showed great promise on occasion, but it was perfectly clear he could not operate in the same team as Mark Hateley at the highest level. The home defeat by AEK Athens proved that. The few highs Fergie enjoyed in Glasgow were tarnished. After an injury-blighted debut season, his first goal against Raith Rovers was forgotten about as he earned a police charge and a record 12 game ban from the SFA for a headbutting offence on John McStay. He was subsequently sentenced to three months in jail. When the club let him go on loan to Merseyside, the insistence of manager Walter Smith that the move was for three months only seemed legitimate enough. Under Mike Walker, his form, though solid enough, suggested that Everton would be happy to stick to that agreement too. It was only when Joe Royle took charge that the big man took off and two goals in his opening four games, including a derby strike against Liverpool, made their mind up. And, as it became obvious that the player was flourishing out of the Scottish goldfish bowl, and that Everton were prepared to throw massive amounts of money in Rangers' direction – £4.26 million all told – then a transfer became inevitable.

These last two years have, unquestionably, merely been opening chapters in the Duncan Ferguson story. There will be many more to come, and they will probably be just as colourful. What is beyond doubt, though, is that there are thousands of Teddy Bears throughout the world who are willing him to sort himself out and prove himself to be the 'great' he has the talent to be. It's a pity he could not do it at Ibrox, but he still carries the good feelings of the support.

INTERNATIONAL HONOURS

Scotland international: Five caps, no goals. Debut v. USA 1992.
Under-21 record: Seven caps. Debut v. Denmark 1992.

HONOURS IN THE SCOTTISH GAME

League Championship: 1993-94 (1)
Scottish Cup: 0
League Cup: 0
Total: 1

LEAGUE RECORD

		Apps	Goals
1990-91	Dundee United	9	1
1991-92	Dundee United	38	15
1992-93	Dundee United	30	12
1993-94	Rangers	10	1
1994-95	Rangers	4	1
1994-95	Everton	23	7
	Total	114	37

VALUATION

The way he turned Everton's season round last terms suggests that the millions shelled out for him were worthwhile. A more dedicated attitude to the game – a la Alan Shearer – could see him become one of the greatest players produced by Scotland.

Estimated value: £4,500,000

Pieter HUISTRA

Date of Birth: 18th January 1967, Goenga, Holland

If ever there was a perfect swansong to a Rangers career, it came on January 14 last season, at Brockville. Pieter Huistra, shortly to depart to a new career in Japan, rapped his last game for the club which helped seal a 3-2 victory over Falkirk. He left to the chants of "There's Only One Pieter Huistra" to ensure some happy memories of his time at Ibrox.

The uncharitable might say that if he had performed as well as he did that day, he might still be with Rangers, but even that seems unlikely. As valuable a player as Pieter Huistra was during his four and a half year residency, the UEFA restrictions meant he would only rarely appear in European games, and with the club so geared to making an impact on the continent, they effectively sealed his fate. That is not to say he was never anything less than an effective player. Erratic, certainly, but on his day a real asset. His arrival, from Twente Enschede, was fairly low key by Rangers' standards, but he demonstrated during the 1990-91 season that there was no reason to question his ability. He scored four times and set up countless others, as he more than justified the £300,000 fee.

The one doubt, which persisted throughout his stay, was his durability and this was to cost him a couple of Cup Final performances, as Walter Smith opted for a more physical approach. All's well that ends well, though, and Piet left Scotland with a full set of domestic medals, after appearing in the League Cup wins of 1990-91 and 1993-94 and the Scottish Cup triumph in 1992-93. However, it was in Europe that he probably enjoyed his finest moment in the colours, with a vital strike in the Champions League run of 1992-93, against Bruges. Trailing to a goal from the Belgians, the Dutchman took the opportunity to put one over on his close neighbours with a superb equaliser which ensured that the momentum which so nearly carried Gers to the Champions Cup Final was maintained.

However, from the tail end of the 1993-94 season, it became apparent that he would be surplus to requirements, as Walter Smith sought to add Scots to the squad. Trials with Duisburg in Germany and QPR in London came to nothing, probably to Huistra's relief, as, with Rangers eliminated from Europe early, he came back into the League side for his longest run of starts since joining the club – 15 – and played superbly. It was during this period that his £500,000 transfer to Sanfrecce Hiroshima was arranged, a mutually beneficial move which allowed Rangers to make a profit on the player and Huistra to make himself financially secure for the rest of his life.

How will Huistra be remembered? Probably as a skilful winger, not quite a Rangers great, but one who put more into the club than he took out and who developed a great affinity for its traditions. At the time of his departure, he reflected, "I couldn't believe the number of fans they have all over the world. I would like to thank them very much for all the support they have given me in my time at Rangers. It has been a pleasure to play with the club and I will always follow their progress."

It's a safe bet that there will be many Rangers fans looking out for results in the J-League over the next couple of years to find out how one of their former heroes is faring.

INTERNATIONAL HONOURS
Dutch international.

HONOURS IN THE SCOTTISH GAME

League Cup: 1990-91, 1993-94 (2)
Scottish Cup: 1992-93 (1)
League Championship: 1990-91, 1991-92, 1992-93, 1993-94, 1994-95 (5)
Total:

LEAGUE RECORD

		Apps	Goals
1990-91	Rangers	27	4
1991-92	Rangers	32	5
1992-93	Rangers	30	4
1993-94	Rangers	21	6
1994-95	Rangers	15	3
	Total	125	22

VALUATION

Huistra's move to Japan was under exceptional circumstances. But he did improve in Scotland, and would probably have rated just under a million had he stayed in Britain.

Estimated value: £900,000

Ally MAXWELL

Date of Birth: 16th February 1965, Hamilton

Andy Goram's ex-deputy is a fine goalkeeper in his own right, as his personal honours haul demonstrates. Not many players pick up every major piece of silverware in the game, and poor ones certainly don't. Dundee United have purchased a competent keeper for a relatively cheap fee, £150,000, in the current market. Maxi's misfortune was that he was competing for a place with arguably Scotland's best-ever number one, and there seemed to be absolutely no chance of dislodging him from the first team. However, his spell at Ibrox was a fruitful one, and should stand him in good stead in the future.

Rangers picked up Maxwell for £300,000 from Motherwell, after a period of inactivity caused by events which would beggar belief in a Roy of the Rovers-style publication. The hero of Well's heroic Scottish Cup triumph in 1990-91, when they triumphed over Dundee United in a 4-3 Hampden thriller, he then found himself on the sidelines the very next season, after failing to agree terms with hard-line Fir Park boss Tommy McLean. Some reward for playing on in a major Cup Final with serious internal injuries, which required intensive hospital treatment for days afterwards, and which also caused him to miss the Lanarkshire club's lengthy celebrations! Maxwell's career was on hold and loan spells to Bolton and Liverpool promised much but did not deliver, and it was only when Rangers came in at the start of the 1992-93 season that he could happily concentrate on football again. By coincidence that was the campaign where Goram's injury problems really started, and Maxi got his first taste of action with the champions.

1993-94 was really his banner year, though, as Goram was counted out from the start and he went on to play in 32 of the League matches and pick up a League Cup medal for his role in the defeat of Hibs. Indeed, Ally might have expected to pick up a Scotland cap too that season, but one or two very public errors worked against him, especially in the Old Firm match of October 31st, when Celtic won 2-1 at Ibrox. By the end of the campaign, he might have been back in the running too, but his mix-up with Dave McPherson in the Scottish Cup Final, when his attempted clearance from Mac's passback hit Christian Dailly and set up Craig Brewster's winning goal, probably counted him out again too. In years to come, he will quite rightly not be looked back on as one of the major stars of this trophy-littered era, but his medals will be more than ample compensation for that. Ally Maxwell more than played his part in continuing the Rangers success story, and whatever he goes on to achieve in his career from here will probably pale into insignificance when compared to his life and times at Ibrox. He goes to Tannadice with everyone's good wishes.

HONOURS IN THE SCOTTISH GAME

League Championship: 1993-94. (1)
Scottish Cup: 1990-91 (with Motherwell) (1).
League Cup: 1993-94 (1).
Total: 3.

LEAGUE RECORD

		Apps	Goals
1983-84	Motherwell	4	-
1984-85	Motherwell	15	-
1985-86	Motherwell	4	-
1986-87	Motherwell	21	-
1987-88	Motherwell	1	-
1987-88	Clydebank (loan)	1	-
1988-89	Motherwell	17	-
1989-90	Motherwell	36	1
1990-91	Motherwell	36	1
1991-92	Motherwell	-	-
1991-92	Liverpool (loan)	-	-
1991-92	Bolton (loan)	3	-
1992-93	Rangers	10	-
1993-94	Rangers	32	-
1994-95	Rangers	11	-
	Total	191	2

VALUATION

Dundee United paid £150,000 for Maxwell – and who's going to argue with Billy Kirkwood?

Estimated value: £150,000

Dave McPHERSON

Date of Birth: 28th January, Paisley

A series of high profile blunders put paid to Dave McPherson's Rangers career last season – to the relief of many of the Ibrox faithful. But to dismiss the tall defender as not good enough for the club would be doing him a disservice, as his medal collection and his two spells in Light Blue testify.

McPherson first broke through as a teenager in the 1982-83 season and was immediately tipped as a great prospect for the future. Good in the air and comfortable in the ground, he looked set to be a fixture in the Rangers team for years. He was also good value for goals from the back, or in his occasional performances in midfield too, and notched no less than four in one UEFA Cup tie in an 8-0 win in Malta.

Even the arrival of Graeme Souness – the death knell for many players on the books at the time – failed to dislodge Dave from the team. In Souness' first season in charge, he formed an impressive backbone to defence with Terry Butcher, as the side romped to the club's first championship in nine seasons, conceding a miserly 23 goals, including 11 League clean sheets in a row. But if Big Mac thought he'd solidified his place at the club, he was wrong. Despite that title gong, and a Skol Cup medal to boot, disaster in the Scottish Cup was to prove his undoing.

A home tie against Hamilton was widely expected to give the club an easy passage into the fourth round, but, in one of the biggest upsets in the competition's history, a goal from unheralded Adrian Sprott, in front of a disbelieving Ibrox, sealed a humiliating 1-0 elimination. Souness blamed McPherson for the goal, and Dave was to learn – in the same way Terry Butcher and Graham Roberts later did – that the good work tended to be forgotten, if the gaffer held a grudge. In the close season that followed, he was dispatched to Hearts, in what was widely seen as a move prompted by his Hamilton faux pas.

But credit where credit's due, what could have been a shunt into the wilderness became nothing of the sort, as the determined defender showed his resolve. He became an inspiration for the perennially under-achieving Edinburgh side and indeed, went on to win 24 of his 27 caps whilst with the Jam Tarts. His form proved so good that just prior to the European Championship finals in 1992, where he played with Scotland, Walter Smith re-signed him for Rangers in a million pound deal. Two seasons of honours followed, including a key role in the glorious European run of 1992-93, when Rangers came within a whisker of a place in the

Champions Cup final. McPherson was a top performer in the comprehensive Battle of Britain triumph over Leeds. But despite a treble in his first campaign back, by the tail end of 1994-95 the fans were beginning to get on his back, after some below par performances. A catastrophic mix-up with Ally Maxwell, which allowed Dundee United's Craig Brewster to score the only goal of the Scottish Cup final and deny Rangers a second consecutive Treble, was a nail in his coffin.

When Rangers started last season so poorly, with McPherson alternating between right-back and centre-half, the critics had a field day. He was the scapegoat, and when it became clear that Alan McLaren from Hearts was a definite target, he seemed an obvious candidate to go in the other direction. So it proved, with £1.2 million and Slim, valued at £800,000, heading to Tynecastle. His second departure from the club, again under less than pleasing circumstances, should not obscure the fact that Dave McPherson was a good player for Rangers over a long period of time.

INTERNATIONAL HONOURS

Scotland: 27 caps, 0 goals. Debut v. USA 1992.
Scotland Under-21: 11 caps. Debut v. France 1989.

HONOURS IN THE SCOTTISH GAME

League: 1994-95 (1)
Scottish Cup: 0
League Cup: 0
Total: 1

LEAGUE RECORD

		Apps	Goals
1982-83	Rangers	18	1
1983-84	Rangers	36	2
1984-85	Rangers	31	0
1985-86	Rangers	34	5
1986-87	Rangers	42	7
1987-88	Rangers	44	4
1988-89	Hearts	32	4
1989-90	Hearts	35	4
1990-91	Hearts	34	2
1991-92	Hearts	44	2
1992-93	Rangers	34	2
1993-94	Rangers	28	1
1994-95	Rangers	9	0
1994-95	Hearts	23	2
	Total	444	36

VALUATION

Usually reliable, Mac thrives on confidence which he'll get at Hearts playing regularly in defence. Worth a dabble at £700,000.

Estimated value: £700,000

Scott NISBET

Date of Birth: 30th January 1968, Edinburgh

Nizzy's career was, of course, long over by last season. But as 1994-95 was his testimonial year, it seems only fitting that he is included in this appraisal of Rangers' stars. Certainly, the fans were still eager to pay tribute to one of the cult stars of recent years. A healthy crowd of 27,500 turned up for his testimonial to pay homage to a man whose very existence is still plagued by hip problems, acquired over the years through his whole-hearted commitment to the club.

And yet, in the early days, the very thought of the Edinburgh resident lasting even more than a couple of seasons at Ibrox seemed laughable. It would not be too unkind to Scott to say that his spell as a striker as a youngster in the infancy of Graeme Souness' reign was less than profitable. Quite simply, he did not have the speed or the guile to make it as a top class striker. And it's well documented that he did not see eye to eye with Souness, whose act of throwing a football yearbook at the youngster after he'd refused a move to Dundee and telling him to "find a club" has now gone down in Ibrox legend.

With the persistence which personified his time at Rangers, Nizzy re-emerged as a defender, and, surprisingly to those who'd witnessed him up front, a very good one to boot. Under Walter Smith, he became a squad regular, and at the start of 1991-92, a first-team stalwart, and, according to some, a candidate for Scotland. He started the first 16 League matches, scoring an impressive five goals before injury took a hand and he was never to enjoy such a prolonged run in the first team again.

However, there were sporadic appearances in 1992-93, the season when he scored the goal that he will forever be remembered for in Glasgow. An outrageous long distance shot cum cross was lobbed in against Bruges in a Champions League match of the utmost importance, and, after a bounce which had to be seen to be believed, nestled in the back of the Belgians' net. It was one of the most astonishing sights in Ibrox history. Sadly, the joy was shortlived, because later that month, he played his last game ever in the Light Blue, being forced to troop off early against Celtic. Ask the man himself what his proudest moment at Ibrox was, though, and there's no question it would be the Championship decider against Aberdeen in 1991, when he was just one of 13 bears who gave their all to ensure that the title stayed at home. When it became apparent that his career was over, moves were quickly put in place to honour the loyal servant, and on May 1st, 1995 a Rangers International Select, managed by his old adversary Graeme Souness, took on the first team, in front of an appreciative stadium. The differences had been patched up, with the abrasive ex-boss confessing that, on account of the player's performances after his departure from Ibrox, he would have been wrong to sell him. Nisbet himself was just touched by the response from the Rangers public. "It was very emotional for me," he admitted, "and it brought home just how much I've missed playing with the boys."

For the record, the first-team won 3-2 with goals from Alexei Mikhailitchenko, Mark Hateley and Ally McCoist. The International Select, boasting ex-greats like Ray Wilkins, Derek Ferguson and Terry Butcher, scored through Kevin Drinkell – and a penalty from the star of the show! It may not have matched his Bruges effort, but it was a fitting end to his time at Rangers.

INTERNATIONAL HONOURS
Scotland Under-21: Five caps. Debut v. Norway 1989.

HONOURS IN THE SCOTTISH GAME
League: 1990-91, 1991-92 (2)
Scottish Cup: 0
League Cup: 0
Total: 2

LEAGUE RECORD

	Apps	Total
1985-86	4 (1)	0
1986-87	0 (1)	0
1987-88	22 (3)	0
1988-89	5 (2)	1
1989-90	4 (3)	0
1990-91	15	0
1991-92	20	5
1992-93	10	0
Total	80 (10)	6

Steven PRESSLEY

Date of Birth: 11th October 1973, Elgin

Steven Pressley last season became the latest young Blue to decide to call it quits in his battle for first-team football, and head south to make his fortune. In recent years that's a trend that the likes of John Spencer, Gary McSwegan and Sandy Robertson have set, and the signs were that big 'Elvis' had the potential to match the success enjoyed by Spenny at Chelsea. However, it was not to be and Pressley is back in Scotland with Dundee United, alongside Robertson. However, perhaps the best tribute to his undoubted ability was that Premiership side Coventry were willing to splash out close on £700,000 for someone who was essentially still a reserve player and that they wanted him to replace World Cup sensation Phil Babb, who was on the move to Liverpool. Only time will tell if Rangers were correct to sell 'Elvis'. Some fans remained convinced he was a player already on the books who would have been a more sensible option in replacing big McPherson on the team, allowing the money which went to Hearts to have been spent elsewhere. More seemed to happy to collect a fee for an individual whose performances in many of his 1993-94 appearances were not of the quality they, or he, expected. Steven came to prominence in the most unfortunate of manners, when he came on as a sub on that momentous Champions League night against Marseille at Ibrox, and almost immediately got involved in a mix-up with Andy Goram which saw Rangers fall 2-0 behind. However, whilst many youngsters might have fallen to pieces after such a traumatic start, Pressley impressed everyone by regaining his composure and offering a worthwhile contribution in the now legendary fightback.

That season ended with perhaps the easiest medal anyone will ever gain at Ibrox – a two minute sub appearance against Aberdeen in the Scottish Cup Final at Parkhead clinching his gong! It was silverware he deserved, for his displays after that Champions League night had earned the nickname of 'Son of Gough' around Ibrox, not only for their similar looks, but the self-assuredness which the club captain had also demonstrated at a young age. Unfortunately, the sky-high standards required by Rangers meant that he was not going to go on to emulate the glittering Ibrox career of Gough.

INTERNATIONAL HONOURS
Scotland Under-21: 20 caps.

HONOURS IN THE SCOTTISH GAME
League Championship: 1993-94 (1)
Scottish Cup: 1993-94 (1)
League Cup: 0
Total: 2

LEAGUE RECORD

		Apps	Goals
1991-92	Rangers	1	-
1992-93	Rangers	8	-
1993-94	Rangers	23	1
1994-95	Rangers	2	-
	Total	34	1

VALUATION
Pressley has looked like having the makings of a good player for years – but it is time he started to deliver. Coventry paid a lot of money for him, but he did not show enough immediately to show he could justify their faith. United will want a quick return on their £750,000 investment.

Estimated value: £750,000

New Arrivals

Oleg SALENKO

On July 28 1995 Oleg Salenko became Rangers' fourth signing of the summer, moving in to Ibrox from Valencia for £2.5 million. The Russian striker, who hit a record five goals for his international side in a World Cup match with Cameroon, became Rangers' top choice after the protracted deal to capture Romanian Florin Raducioiu fell through. Said manager Walter Smith: "Archie Knox and I have had our eyes on Oleg since the summer. He's a different type of player from Raducioiu.He was more of a runner, but Oleg links with players more."

Gordan PETRIC

Date of Birth: Belgrade 30th July 1969

Gordan Petric's shock capture on July 26 means that no less than three of the Dundee United Scottish Cup winning squad of 1993-94 are now at Ibrox.
The Serbian defender, like Gary Bollan and Alex Cleland, tasted that bit of success and fancied more of it after a disastrous season with the Tangerines which ultimately saw them relegated. And yet, whilst there is no disputing his quality, his signing was a major surprise, because throughout a long, hot, sticky summer of transfer speculation, it had been Celtic's name which had been persistently linked with the 26-year-old. The Daily Record likened the deal to that which took the controversial Maurice Johnston to the club in 1989. And, aside from the obvious religious problems caused by Mo-Jo's transfer, there were certainly similarities in the swoop. It had seemed inevitable that Petric would go to Celtic, who required a quality, affordable centre-half. And there had been contact between the clubs, as United supremo Jim McLean was only too happy to admit. But, as news of the talks hit the press, McLean was incensed and suspected someone from Parkhead had leaked the projected move. Celtic denied this; but a bad atmosphere was created between the pair. It has subsequently been suggested that United then touted Petric to Rangers – having just signed ex-Ger Steven Pressley - in a bid to stick two fingers up to the Bhoys Whatever the circumstances, Rangers stepped in and the deal was signed, sealed and delivered in double quick time. Petric, certainly, was over the moon at his luck. *"I want to win medals and this is the place to do it. Then there is Europe and the prospect of the Champions League, which I find very exciting,"* he bubbled. Petric's success in the Scottish game poured cold water on the suggestion that his previous boss at Dundee United, Ivan Golac, was a joker who knew little about football. While the eccentric Serb did sign some dead wood in his time at Tannadice, there can be no disputing that his November 1993 capture from Partizan Belgrade, for £600,000 was a fantastic piece of business. After a

debut at Motherwell, Petric was ever present in the League side and his calm, cool but hard style of play was a significant factor in the club's successful battle against relegation and their unlikely but deserved Cup triumph over Rangers. The only blot on that super first campaign, in fact, came at Ibrox when he was involved in a somewhat unsavoury incident with Ian Ferguson. Television clearly showed that he used an elbow whilst challenging the Light Blues' midfielder and Fergie responded in hothead fashion by spitting back at him. The shenanigans were seen on Scotsport, Scottish TV's soccer programme, the following day and the upshot was that Fergie was banned by the SFA, amid calls from commentators for him to be kicked out of the club. No doubt the pair's differences will be patched up now! Last season was no great success story for Petric, but he had that in common with a number of Dundee United players. It seemed lack of motivation rather than lack of ability was the problem. And, for someone who made his debut at 19 for Yugoslavia at Wembley, a season in the First Division held little appeal. Rangers came in at just the right time. If Walter Smith goes ahead with his three central defender plan, expect Petric to play a pivotal role.

INTERNATIONAL HONOURS
Yugoslav international.

HONOURS IN THE SCOTTISH GAME
Scottish Cup: 1993-94 with Dundee United (1)

SCOTTISH LEAGUE RECORD

		Apps	Goals
1993-94	Dundee United	27	1
1994-95	Dundee United	33	2
	Total	60	3

VALUATION
Stylish, composed, with no previous fitness or disciplinary problems, Petric looks a snip at £1.5 million.

Estimated value: 1,500,000

Stephen WRIGHT

Date of Birth: 27th August 1971, Bellshill

If Stephen Wright proves as successful as Rangers' last capture from Aberdeen, David Robertson, there will be few complaints from the Ibrox faithful or the management team. Certainly, the signs are that Wright will prove a valuable acquisition. Already a Scotland cap, he has always looked the most likely of the Dons' talented youngsters to enjoy a genuinely successful career in the game. His arrival in June mirrored Robertson's transfer deal four years earlier, when again the clubs could not agree a fee. The Granite City club asked for a somewhat unrealistic £2.5 million, while Rangers were offering £800,000. A war of words also broke out in Aberdeen over his departure. Incredibly, the Pittodrie club did not even get round to offering the youngster new terms; confirmed vice-chairman Dennis Miller, "It is true terms were not discussed. We spoke to him twice, but at no time did he give us any encouragement." Wright himself, in typically understated fashion, only said he was 'surprised' at his failure to receive an offer. By the time you read this a fee will have been set; it seems unlikely to be anything less £1 million. However, transfer fee quibbles are not the only similarity between Wright and Robertson. As players, they are like two peas in a pod, with the obvious difference that Wright, aptly enough, operates on the right side of defence, while Robertson dominates the left. Very much in the mould of a modern full-back, Wright is quick, impressive going forward and adaptable enough to take a wide midfield role if required. Pleasingly, he is Scottish, which will undoubtedly do him a few favours, as Aussie Craig Moore is likely to be his most immediate rival for a first-team berth. Wright's experience at a higher level with Aberdeen, and general all-round ability should get him the nod. "I want to win things," he said on signing. "And Rangers is the sort of club where you will have the chance. I also hope this move helps me get back into the Scotland team. Playing for a club as big as this one can only enhance my chances." He is a fit player, as his appearance record with Aberdeen indicates, and he is also a rare breed for a Scottish defender in that he has an exemplary disciplinary record, so suspensions are likely to be minimal. Walter Smith deserves credit for Wright's signing; not the sort of name which will grab the headlines, but a player who will play a big part in securing future successes.

INTERNATIONAL HONOURS

Scotland: Two caps, 0 goals. Debut v. Germany 1993.
Under 21: 14 caps. Debut v. Bulgaria 1991.

LEAGUE RECORD

		Apps	Goals
1989-90	Aberdeen	1	0
1990-91	Aberdeen	17	1
1991-92	Aberdeen	23	0
1992-93	Aberdeen	36	0
1993-94	Aberdeen	36	0
1994-95	Aberdeen	32	1

VALUATION

The finished article, with years ahead of him, Wright should be one of the most sought-after players in the country.

Estimated value: £1,500,000

Davie COOPER

1956-95

In a season of such low vintage as 1994-95, it made the death of Rangers legend Davie Cooper, on March 23rd, so much harder for everyone associated with the club, and the whole of Scottish football to swallow.

The tragic and premature cutting down of one of the last great entertainers north of the border, due to a brain haemmorhage, sparked unprecedented scenes of mourning throughout the whole country.

It was precious little consolation that Cooper collapsed whilst passing on his God-given talents to youngsters at the filming of a Scottish Television series at Clyde's Broadwood Stadium.

For, if ever there was a man qualified to move into coaching and inject some rare quality into the uninspiring Scottish game, it was him. Sadly, we will never be able to confirm our suspicions that as a boss, he would have been one of the very best.

However, what is beyond dispute is that as a player, there were very few in the long history of Scottish soccer who could match the ability of the man known to all as 'Coop'.

It was at Clydebank where he first came to notice, as a young and exciting winger with a left foot which seemed to have the touch of Midas in it. Not surprisingly, he quickly came to the notice of bigger clubs, but it was always Rangers he wanted to play for and when Jock Wallace moved in with a bid in June 1977, after being impressed by the prospect in the previous season's League Cup, there was no hesitation from Coop.

"I must be the happiest guy in Scotland," he beamed on signing. "There's not another club I would have signed for at the moment."

And it was as much this affinity for the traditions and the stature of Rangers, as his supreme talent, which was to endear him so spectacularly to the masses.

He was an instant success. After a season of anti-climax in 1976-77, following the Treble of the year before, Rangers got back on the rails superbly with another triple crown in Cooper's first campaign, with the new boy an integral part of the glory. Gordon Smith and Derek Johnstone managed 45 goals between them in the league, with the new blue eyed boy of Ibrox laying on a hefty proportion of them. He even chipped in with six Premier counters of his own.

With Jock Wallace stepping down at the end of those glorious nine months, the club was about to embark on an era which would see them miss out on the championship flag until 1986-87. It was harsh on Cooper, who would have been at the peak of his powers at this stage, that he had to perform in a struggling team rather than a more potent force. Nevertheless, there were some glorious highlights to savour.

One of the most shown goals on Scottish TV, despite the appaling quality of the fil arrived in 1979. A Dryborough Cup final against Celtic was the occasion, and Cooper was in magician mode as he juggled with the ball on the edge of the box, flicked it ov defenders, twisted and turned then delivered a perfect finish from eight yards. There c have been rarely a better effort struck in an Old Firm match.

By 1980, Cooper had come to the attention of Scotland boss Jock Stein and it was i this year he made his Scotland debut against Peru. It took until 1984 for his internatio career to begin in earnest, but he went on to win 22 international caps, scoring six goa – a tally far lower than it should have been, possibly prompted by his own indifferenc to performing on that particular stage.

Incredibly, Rangers manager John Greig never seemed convinced on how best to utilise Coop's unique contributions, and this was never more amply demonstrated tha in the Scottish Cup final of 1981, when he took the decision to leave his winger out c the starting line-up against Dundee United. Greig almost got away with this too, as, in spite of a generally uninspiring display, Ian Redford squandered a last-minute penalty chance which would have given the club a trophy they had scarcely merited on the ba of their performance over 90 minutes.

Better to win the Cup with some flair, and in that case, who better to call on than Davie Cooper. Reinstated for a midweek replay, he was, quite simply, a revelation ar although the history books show that it was John MacDonald who recorded a brace ar goals in the 4-1 thrashing of Jim McLean's men, it was Coop who ran the show. He made it on to the scoresheet himself, but it was the level of creativity he provided, on evening when it was needed most, which had the fans and scribes slavering.

A liking for Cup finals against Dundee United had obviously developed, because l in the year, he scored again in a 2-1 success over the Taysiders in the League Cup showdown to earn the club a record 11th victory in the competition.

Rangers' serious decline began after that, but there was still the consolation of ano two League Cup medals for Coop, in 1983-84 against Celtic, when an Ally McCoist hat-trick sealed a 3-2 victory, then a year later when Iain Ferguson – later to feature ¥ an another explosive Cup Final day with Davie for Motherwell – collected the winne against perennial runners-up Dundee United.

In 1985, Cooper was to convert one of the most famous penalties in Scottish histo when his late spot-kick, after coming on as substitute, earned a draw against Wales i World Cup qualifier, which to all intents and purposes took the Tartan Army to Mex Typically, he showed amazing poise and nerve to fire the ball past Neville Southall a an entire nation watched with bated breath. However, the night was not to prove one celebration, as the high stakes and tension proved too much for boss Jock Stein, who died from a heart attack after the match. What should have been a period of jubilatio saw Scotland in mourning.

In his club colours, despite the odd magical display from their genius on the flank wasn't until 1986-87 that Rangers, now under the management of Graeme Souness, began their regeneration, and Cooper, not surprisingly, was reborn. The first trophy came again in the League Cup, when a late, late penalty from the man himself, denied Celtic in a tight 2-1 clash.

However, it was another League Championship medal which he deserved most after his efforts in the bleak years, and as stars like Terry Butcher, Graham Roberts and Chris Woods arrived, it was quickly apparent that Coop was now getting the sort of quality around him which would allow him to flourish.

That League Championship duly arrived on a memorable day in Aberdeen, and the second title gong he must have thought would elude him was safely in his keeping.

Yet another League Cup triumph came the next season, in one of the greatest games ever seen north of the border, when Rangers and Aberdeen drew 3-3 at Hampden. Cooper was to score a free-kick in that match which opposing keeper Jim Leighton – no slouch himself – was to describe as one of the best goals he ever conceded! It wasn't Coop's only scoring contribution of the afternoon either, as he was on the mark in the penalty shootout which eventually decided that the trophy would stay in Glasgow.

1988-89 brought yet more silverware, although by this stage, the player, now 33, was featuring less regularly in the first team. Indeed, he started only nine matches of the League season, but his 14 appearances as substitute were more than enough to secure his third and final League medal.

Ironically, a career at Rangers which had been so glorious ended on a sad note, as he played what was to be his final match for the club in the rather lacklustre defeat at the hands of Celtic in the Scottish Cup final.

It had been a special, special 12 years, which few players in the modern era can claim to have enjoyed the likes of. The club had showed their appreciation with a testimonial against Bordeaux in August 1988 which drew 43,000 appreciative fans and saw Rangers win 3-2. And the fans' devotion was clear as the tributes which were paid, when he left to join Motherwell in August of 1989, more than showed.

But a new career was dawning, and if anyone thought Coop had gone to Lanarkshire merely to play out his career, the man himself proved them wrong in the most emphatic of fashion, with football at Fir Park which was a revelation to the supporters who were more used to Tommy McLean's cautious approach, and a consistency which he'd rarely even produced at his home of Ibrox.

Scotland were interested again, and the fairytale was completed as he was recalled to the fold to play in the match against Norway which sealed qualification for Italy 1990, then made a final appearance against Egypt at Pittodrie just prior to the finals. Only injury was to rob him of a second crack at football's greatest event.

The crowning glory came on a sunny May day at Hampden in 1991, when Motherwell, who had not lifted a trophy for 39 years, overcame the hot favourites Dundee United 4-3 in a match which was a sensational advert for Scottish football. Old sparring partner Iain Ferguson was a scorer for Well, but it was Coop, an old head on old legs, who offered the inspiration for the unlikely win. Those old legs failed to last the pace of the whole 120 minutes, but the ovation he received from over 30,000 ecstatic Motherwell fans was to be one of his abiding memories of football. As much as he loved Rangers, Coop was later to admit the pleasure the win threw up for fans in one of the most deprived areas of Scotland, and the fact that he picked up a medal at the age of 35, meant the day numbered amongst the most satisfying of his career.

By 1993, his appearances were becoming more infrequent, and he again left in search of more regular games. This time he revisited Clydebank, and he was still playing week-in week-out for his first club at the time of his sudden death, although he had announced plans to retire at the end of the season.

Different people will remember him in different ways, but the genuine distress shown throughout the west of Scotland on the announcement of his death said everything about the high esteem he was held in. Even Celtic fans could acknowledge their respect for a legend.

Davie Cooper was, quite simply, one of the great Rangers.

COOPER'S RANGERS APPEARANCES

	Lge	LC	SC	E	O	Total
1977-78	35	8	5	4	6	58
1978-79	30	8	9	2	5	54
1979-80	30	4	6	6	11	57
1980-81	25	4	5	0	5	39
1981-82	30	11	5	1	11	58
1982-83	31	9	5	4	4	53
1983-84	34	10	3	4	20	71
1984-85	32	6	3	3	10	54
1985-86	32	4	1	2	7	46
1986-87	42	5	1	6	5	59
1987-88	33	4	3	3	9	52
1988-89	22	4	3	3	10	42
Total	376	77	49	38	103	643

INTERNATIONAL HONOURS

22 caps for Scotland, six goals. Debut v.Peru in 1980.
Six Under-21 caps. Debut v Czechoslovakia in 1977.

HONOURS IN THE SCOTTISH GAME

League Championship: 1977-78, 1986-87, 1988-89 (3)
Scottish Cup: 1978, 1979, 1981 with Rangers, 1991 with Motherwell (4)
League Cup: 1978, 1979, 1982, 1984, 1985, 1987, 1988 (7)
Total: 14

WHAT THEY SAID ABOUT DAVIE COOPER
A selection of tributes paid to the Rangers legend.

"He will be remembered forever by us all and Rangers will be honouring the service he gave to the club. As a genuine football supporter, the word 'class' is one that stands out when thinking of David Cooper." Rangers chairman **David Murray**.

"Although he had played away from the club for a number of years, he never *really* left and will always be a part of the club. As a person he is one of the best and had meant so much to myself and the rest of the players in the dressing room. The general feeling is that we've lost a brother more than anything." Former teammate and close friend, **Ally McCoist**.

"I'm sure the majority of people in the modern era would have had him in their all-time best Rangers team – he would certainly be in mine. Davie Cooper had a gift and he used it. Let's appreciate him for the good things he did." **Walter Smith.**

"Davie Cooper is one of the greatest players Scotland has ever produced." **Maurice Johnston.**

"The free-kick he hit past me in the Skol Cup Final eight years ago was probably the best goal to beat me." **Jim Leighton.**

"Working with Davie Cooper is the best learning experience I've ever had in football." Scotland cap **Rob McKinnon.**

"He was one of the most naturally gifted players Scotland have ever produced. Only Jim Baxter and Charlie Nicholas could really rival him when it came to natural skill and talent." Celtic manager **Tommy Burns.**

"Superstar is a word which is often used in football. But that is exactly what Davie was, although he would have been embarrassed to hear it." His last coach, Clydebank's **Brian Wright.**

"I'll never forget that penalty against Wales that got us to Mexico. Everyone knew of his talent, but he showed character and bottle that night after just coming on as a sub. It was one of the most important moments in our football history, but it didn't matter to Coop. He was so confident, but I couldn't even look." Former Scotland team-mate **Roy Aitken.**

"Davie was an inspiration to everyone over four outstanding seasons here – the highlight being his performance in the 1991 Scottish Cup Final, one of the great post-war finals." **Alex McLeish**, Motherwell boss.

Mark
Hateley

Rangers in the Premier Division
All-time Records

Club by Club
Player by Player
League, Cup, European

ABERDEEN

Ground: Pittodrie, Pittodrie Street, Aberdeen
Club colours: Red and white
Number of seasons in Premier Division: 20 (Champions 3 times)
Year of formation: 1903
Most capped player: Alex McLeish
No of caps: 77
Most league points in a season: 64 (Premier Division – season 1992-93) (44 games)
Most league goals scored by a player in a season: Benny Yorston, 1929-30
No of goals scored: 38
Record attendance: 45,061 v. Hearts 13-3-54
Record victory: 13-0 v. Peterhead 9-2-23
Record defeat: 0-8 v. Celtic 30-1-65

Rangers' Premier record against Aberdeen

Games played : 80	**Won :** 24
Drawn : 22	**Lost :** 34
Goals scored: 72	**Goals conceded:** 101
Clean sheets: 26	

Best seasonal performance: 1992-93. Won 3; Drawn 0; Lost 1; For 6; Against 2
Worst seasonal performance: 1981-82. Won 0; Drawn 0; Lost 1; For 2; Against 10

Clean sweeps (four wins): 0	**Whitewashed (four losses):** 0

Most goals scored in a season: 6 – 1976-77, 1992-93, 1994-95
Most goals conceded in a season: 10 – 1981-82
Least goals scored in a season: 1 – 1983-84
Least goals conceded in a season: 1 – 1989-90
Most goals shared between pair in season: 15 in 1977-78, Rangers 4, Aberdeen 11
Least goals shared between pair in season: 4 in 1989-90, Rangers 3, Aberdeen 1
Biggest home win: 3-1 on 22-10-77 and 29-8-92
Biggest home defeat : 0-3 on 4-3-78, 28-9-85 and 13-5-89
Biggest away win: 2-0 on 2-5-92
Biggest away defeat: 1-5 on 19-1-85

Rangers' top Premier scorers against Aberdeen

1. Ally McCoist 11
2. Mark Hateley 9
3. Derek Johnstone 7
4. Alex MacDonald 4
5. (tie) Gordon Smith and Robert Prytz 3

AIRDRIE

Ground: Broadwood Stadium, Cumbernauld
Club colours: White with red diamonds
Number of seasons in Premier Division: 4
Year of formation: 1878
Most capped player: Jimmy Crapnell
No of caps: 9
Most league points in a season: 60 (Division 2 – Season 1973-74)
Most league goals scored by a player in a season: Hugh Baird, 1954-55
No of goals scored: 53
Record attendance: 24,000 v. Hearts 8-3-52
Record victory: 15-1 v. Dundee Wanderers 1-12-1894
Record defeat: 11-1 v. Hibs 24-10-59

Rangers' Premier record against Airdrie

Games played: 16	**Won:** 9
Drawn: 7	**Lost:** 0
Goals scored: 31	**Goals conceded:** 8

Best seasonal performance: 1991-92. Won 3; Drawn 1; Lost 0; For 13; Against 0
Worst seasonal performance: 1980-81. Won 1; Drawn 3; Lost 0; For 4; Against 2

Clean sweeps: 0	**Whitewashed:** 0

Most goals scored in a season: 13 – 1991-92
Most goals conceded in a season: 3 – 1981-82 and 1992-93
Least goals scored in a season: 4 – 1980-81
Least goals conceded in a season: 0 – 1991-92
Most goals shared between pair in a season: 13 in 1991-92, Rangers 13, Airdrie 0
Least goals shared between pair in a season: 6 in 1980-81; Rangers 4, Airdrie 2
Biggest home win: 5-0 on 29-2-92
Biggest home defeat: not applicable
Biggest away win: 4-0 on 5-10-92
Biggest away defeat: not applicable

Rangers' top Premier scorers against Airdrie

1. Mark Hateley 6
2. Ally McCoist 5
3. John MacDonald 5
4. (tie) Jim Bett and John Brown 2

AYR UNITED

Ground: Somerset Park, Trylfield Place, Ayr
Club colours: White and black
Number of seasons in Premier: 3
Year of formation: 1910
Most capped player: Jim Nisbett
No of caps: 3
Most league points in a season: 61 (Second Division – season 1987-88)
Most league goals scored by a player in a season: Jimmy Smith (season 1927-28)
No of goals scored: 66
Record attendance: 25,225 v. Rangers 13-9-69
Record victory: 11-1 v. Dumbarton 13-8-52
Record defeat: 0-9 v. Rangers, Hearts and Third Lanark

Rangers' Premier record against Ayr United

Games played: 12	**Won:** 8
Drawn: 3	**Lost:** 1
Goals scored: 28	**Goals conceded:** 10

Clean sheets: 5
Best seasonal performance: 1977-78. Won 3; Drawn 1; Lost 0; For 13; Against 3
Worst seasonal performance: 1976-77. Won 2; Drawn 2; Lost 0; For 9; Against 3
Clean sweeps: 0   **Whitewashed:** 0
Most goals scored in a season: 13 – 1977-78
Most goals conceded in a season: 4 – 1975-76
Least goals scored in a season: 6 – 1975-76
Least goals conceded in a season: 3 – 1976-77 and 1977-78
Most goals shared between pair in a season: 16 – 1977-78; Rangers 6, Ayr 3
Least goals shared between pair in a season: 10 – 1975-76; Rangers 6, Ayr 4
Biggest home win: 5-1 on 16-4-77
Biggest home defeat: not applicable
Biggest away win: 5-0 on 26-11-77
Biggest away defeat: 0-3 on 11-10-75

Rangers' top Premier scorers against Ayr United

1. Derek Johnstone 9
2. Gordon Smith 4
3. (tie) Alex MacDonald and Derek Parlane 3

CELTIC

Ground: Celtic Park, 59 Kerrydale Street, Glasgow
Club colours: Green and white hoops
Number of seasons in Premier: 20 (Champions six times)
Year of formation: 1888
Most capped player: Paul McStay
No of caps: 72
Most League goals scored by a player in a season: Jimmy McGrory (season 1935-36)
No of goals scored: 50
Record attendance: 92,000 v. Rangers 1-1-38
Record victory: 11-0 v. Dundee 26-10-1895
Record defeat: 0-8 v. Motherwell 30-4-37

Rangers' Premier record against Celtic

Games played: 80.	**Won:** 26.
Drawn: 24.	**Lost:** 30
Goals scored: 104.	**Goals conceded:** 110
Clean sheets: 19	

Best seasonal performance: 1989-90. Won 3; Drawn 1; Lost 0; For 6; Against 1
Worst seasonal performance: 1982-83. Won 0; Drawn 1; Lost 3; For 5; Against 9
Clean sweeps: 0   **Whitewashed:** 0
Most goals scored in a season: 12 –1988-89
Most goals conceded in a season: 9 – 1982-83
Least goals scored in a season: 3 – 1979-80, 1983-84, 1984-85, 1987-88
Least goals conceded in a season: 1 – 1989-90
Most goals shared by pair in a season: 18 in 1988-89, Rangers 12, Celtic 6
Least goals shared between pair in a season: 6 in 1975-76, Rangers 4, Celtic 2
Biggest home win: 5-1 on 27-8-88
Biggest home defeat: 2-4 on 14-5-83
Biggest away win: 4-2 on 1-1-94
Biggest away defeat: 0-3 on 2-4-84, 24-3-91 and 7-5-95

Rangers' top Premier scorers against Celtic

1. Ally McCoist 15
2. Mark Hateley 8
3. Derek Johnstone 7
4. Mark Walters 6
5. Derek Parlane 5

CLYDEBANK

Ground: Kilbowie Park, Arran Place, Clydebank
Club colours: White, red and black
Number of seasons in Premier: 3
Year of formation: 1965
Most League points in a season: 58 (Division 1 – Season 1976-77)
Most League goals scored by a player in a season – Ken Eadie (Season 1990-91)
No. of goals scored – 29
Record attendance – 14,900 (v. Hibernian – 10-2-65)
Record victory – 8-1 v. Arbroath 3-1-77
Record defeat – 1-9 v. Gala Fairydean 15-9-65

Rangers' Premier record against Clydebank

Games played: 12 | **Won:** 10
Drawn: 1 | **Lost:** 1
Goals scored: 32 | **Goals conceded:** 6
Clean sheets: 8
Best seasonal performance: 1986-87. Won 4; Drawn 0; Lost 0; For 16; Against 1
Worst seasonal performance: 1985-86. Won 2; Drawn 1; Lost 1; For 6; Against 4
Clean sweeps: 2 (1977-78 and 1986-87)   **Whitewashed:** 0
Most goals scored in a season: 16 – 1986-87
Most goals conceded in a season: 4 – 1985-86
Least goals scored in a season: 6 – 1985-86
Least goals conceded in a season: 1 – 1977-78, 1986-87
Most goals shared between pair in a season: 17 in 1986-87, Rangers 16 Clydebank 1
Least goals shared between pair in a season: 10 in 1985-86; Rangers 6, Clydebank 4
Biggest home win: 5-0 on 10-1-87
Biggest home defeat: not applicable
Biggest away win: 4-1 on 15-11-86
Biggest away defeat: 1-2 on 12-4-86

Rangers' top Premier scorers against Clydebank

1. Ally McCoist 7
2. Robert Fleck 6
3. Derek Johnstone 5
4. Davie Cooper 3

DUMBARTON

Ground: Boghead Park, Miller Street, Dumbarton
Club colours: Gold and black
Number of seasons in Premier Division: 1 (1984-85)
Year of formation: 1872
Most capped player: J. Lindsay and J. McAulay
Number of caps: 8
Most league points in a season: 53 (First Division – Season 1986-87)
Most league goals scored by a player in a season: Kenneth Wilson (Season 1971-72)
No of goals scored: 38
Record attendance: 18,001 v. Raith Rovers 2-3-57
Record victory: 13-2 v. Kirkintilloch
Record defeat: 1-11 v. Ayr United and Albion Rovers

Rangers' Premier record against Dumbarton

Games played: 4	**Won:** 3	
Drawn: 1	**Lost:** 0	
Goals scored: 9	**Goals conceded:** 4	
Clean sheets: 1		

Biggest home win: 3-1 on 2-3-85
Biggest home defeat: not applicable
Biggest away win: 4-2 on 29-12-84

Rangers' top Premier scorers against Dumbarton

1. Ally McCoist 3
2. (tie) Ian Redford, Iain Ferguson, Davie Cooper, Davie Mitchell, Ted McMinn, Eric Ferguson 1

DUNDEE

Ground: Dens Park Stadium, Sandeman Street, Dundee
Club colours: Navy blue, red and white
Number of seasons in Premier: 13
Year of formation: 1893
Most capped player: Alex Hamilton
No of caps: 24
Most league goals scored by a player in a season: Alan Gilzean (season 1963-64)
No of goals scored: 52
Record attendance: 43,024 v. Rangers 1953
Record victory: 10-0 v. Fraserburgh 1931, v. Alloa 1947, v. Dunfermline 1947, v. Queen Of The South, 1962
Record defeat: 0-11 v. Celtic 26-10-1895

Rangers' Premier record against Dundee

Games played: 52	**Won:** 28
Drawn: 13	**Lost:** 11
Goals scored: 97	**Goals conceded:** 55
Clean sheets: 18	

Best seasonal performance: 1987-88. Won 4; Drawn 0; Lost 0; For 8; Against 3
Worst seasonal performance: 1985-86. Won 1; Drawn 0; Lost 3; For 8; Against 6

Clean sweeps: 1 (1987-88)	**Whitewashed:** 0

Most goals scored in a season: 12 – 1992-93
Most goals conceded in a season: 7 – 1983-84
Least goals scored in a season: 3 – 1982-83
Least goals conceded in a season: 2 – 1975-76, 1986-87, 1988-89
Most goals shared between pair in a season: 18 in 1992-93, Rangers 12, Dundee 6
Least goals shared between pair in a season: 8 in 1975-76, 1982-83 and 1993-94
Biggest home win: 5-0 on 4-1-86
Biggest home defeat: 1-3 on 23-3-85
Biggest away win: 4-0 on 17-2-87
Biggest away defeat: 1-3 on 24-11-79 and 14-4-82

Rangers' top Premier scorers against Dundee

1. Ally McCoist 27
2. Derek Johnstone 5
3. (tie) Davie Cooper, Robert Russell, Ian Redford, Iain Ferguson 4

DUNDEE UNITED

Ground: Tannadice Park, Tannadice Street, Dundee
Club colours: Tangerine and black
Number of seasons in Premier: 20 (Champions once)
Year of formation: 1923 (1909 as Dundee Hibs)
Most capped Player: Maurice Malpas
Number of caps: 55
Most League points in a season: 60 (Premier Division – 1986-87 season)
Most League goals scored by a player in a season: John Coyle (Season 1955-56)
No of goals scored: 41
Record attendance – 28,000 v. Barcelona 16-11-66
Record victory – 14-0 v. Nithsdale Wanderers 17-1-31
Record defeat – 1-12 v. Motherwell 23-1-54

Rangers' Premier record against Dundee United

Games played: 80	**Won:** 40
Drawn: 25	**Lost:** 15
Goals scored: 107	**Goals conceded:** 70

Clean sheets: 34
Best seasonal performance: 1977-78. Won 4; Drawn 0; Lost 0; For 7; Against 0
Worst seasonal performance: 1982-83. Won 1; Drawn 1; Lost 2; For 5; Against 8

Clean sweeps: 1 (1977-78)	**Whitewashed:** 0

Most goals scored in a season: 8 – 1980-81, 1992-93
Most goals conceded in a season: 9 – 1980-81
Most goals shared by a pair in a season: 17 in 1980-81, Rangers 8, Dundee United 9
Least goals shared by a pair in a season: 6 in 1975-76 (R5, DV1), 1984-85 (R3, DV3), 1987-88 (R3, DV3), 1988-89 (R4, DV2)
Biggest home win: 4-1 on 12-11-75
Biggest home defeat: 1-4 on 18-3-81
Biggest away win: 4-0 on 26-9-92
Biggest away defeat: 0-3 on 9-12-78

Rangers' top Premier scorers against Dundee United

1. Ally McCoist 23
2. Pieter Huistra 6
3. (tie) Derek Johnstone, Maurice Johnston 5
5. (tie) Davie Cooper, Colin Jackson 4

DUNFERMLINE ATHLETIC

Ground: East End Park, Halbeath Road, Dunfermline
Club colours: Black and white
Number of seasons in Premier Division: 4
Year of formation: 1885
Most capped player: Istvan Kozma (Hungary)
No of caps: 13 whilst with club
Most league points in a season: 65 (First Division – season 1993-94)
Most league goals scored by a player in a season: Bobby Skinner (season 1925-26)
No. of goals scored: 53
Record attendance: 27,816 v. Celtic 30-4-68
Record victory: 11-2 v. Stenhousemuir 27-9-30
Record defeat: 0-10 v. Dundee 22-3-47

Rangers' Premier record against Dunfermline

Games played: 16	**Won:** 14
Drawn: 2	**Lost:** 0
Goals scored: 41	**Goals conceded:** 6

Clean sheets: 11
Best seasonal performance: 1991-92. Won 4; Drawn 0; Lost 0; For 14; Against 2
Worst seasonal performance: 1989-90. Won 3; Drawn 1; Lost 0; For 7; Against
Clean sweeps: 2 (1990-91, 1991-92)   **Whitewashed:** 0
Biggest home win: 4-0 on 12-9-87 and 24-8-91
Biggest home defeat: not applicable
Biggest away win: 5-0 on 9-11-91
Biggest away defeat: not applicable

Rangers' top Premier scorers against Dunfermline

1. Ally McCoist 11
2. Mo Johnston 4
3. (tie) Gary Stevens , Mark Hateley, Dale Gordon 3

FALKIRK

Ground: Brockville Park, Hope Street, Falkirk
Club colours: Navy, red and white
Number of seasons in Premier: 5
Year of formation: 1876
Most capped player: Alex H. Parker
No. of caps: 14
Most league points in a season: 59 (Division 2 – Season 1935-36)
Most league goals scored by a player in a season: 59 (Division 2 Season 1935-36)
No. of goals scored in a season: 43
Record attendance: 23,100 v. Celtic 21-2-53
Record victory: 21-1 v. Laurieston 23-3-1893
Record defeat: 1-11 v. Airdrie 28-4-1951

Rangers' Premier record against Falkirk

Games played: 20	**Won:** 17
Drawn: 3	**Lost:** 0
Goals scored: 56	**Goals conceded:** 15
Clean sheets: 9	**Whitewashed:** 0

Clean sweeps: 3 – 1986-87, 1987-88, 1992-93
Most goals scored in a season: 13 – 1987-88, 1992-93
Most goals conceded in a season: 5 – 1994-95
Least goals scored in a season: 8 – 1994-95
Least goals conceded in a season: 1 – 1987-88
Most goals shared between pair in a season: 15 in 1992-93 Rangers 13, Falkirk 2
Least goals shared between pair in a season: 13 in 1991-92, Rangers 10, Falkirk 3, and in 1994-95, Rangers 8, Falkirk 5

Rangers' top Premier scorers against Falkirk

1. Ally McCoist 17
2. Mark Hateley 6
3. Robert Fleck 5
4. Pieter Huistra 4

HAMILTON ACCIES

Ground: Firhill Stadium, Firhill Road, Glasgow
Club colours: Red and white hoops
Number of seasons in Premier Division: 2
Year of formation: 1874
Most capped player: Colin Miller (Canada)
No of caps: 29
Most League points in a season: 57 (First Division – season 1991-92)
Most League goals scored by a player in a season: David Wilson (season 1936-37)
No. of goals scored: 34
Record attendance: 28,690 v. Hearts 3-3-37
Record victory: 10-2 v. Cowdenbeath 15-10-32
Record defeat: 1-11 v. Hibs 6-11-65

Rangers' Premier record against Hamilton

Games played: 8	**Won:** 8
Drawn: 0	**Lost:** 0
Goals scored: 17	**Goals conceded:** 2
Clean sheets: 6	

Most goals scored in a season: 9 – 1988-89
Most goals conceded in a season: 1 – 1986-87, 1988-89
Least goals scored in a season: 8 – 1986-87
Least goals conceded in a season: 1 – 1986-87, 1988-89
Most goals shared between pair in a season: 10 in 1988-89, Rangers 9, Hamilton 1
Least goals shared between pair in a season: 9 in 1986-87, Rangers 8, Hamilton 1
Biggest home win: 3-0 on 11-3-89
Biggest home defeat: not applicable
Biggest away win: 2-0 on 20-12-86 and 13-8-88
Biggest away defeat: not applicable

Rangers' top Premier scorers against Hamilton:

1. Ally McCoist 3
2. Ian Ferguson 2

HEARTS

Ground: Tynecastle Park, Gorgie Road, Edinburgh
Club colours: Maroon and white
Number of seasons in Premier Division: 16
Year of formation: 1874
Most capped player: Bobby Walker
No of caps: 29
Most League points in a season: 63 (Premier Division – Season 1991-92)
Most League goals scored by a player in a season: Barney Battles (season 1930-31)
No of goals scored: 44
Record attendance: 53,496 v. Rangers 13-2-32
Record victory: 18-0 v. Vale of Lothian 17-9-1887
Record defeat: 1-8 v. Vale of Leven 1883

Rangers Premier record against Hearts

Games played: 64	**Won:** 35
Drawn: 16	**Lost:** 13
Goals scored: 117	**Goals conceded:** 68
Clean sheets: 22	

Best seasonal performance: 1976-77. Won 4; Drawn 0; Lost 0; For 11; Against 5
Worst seasonal performance: 1985-85. Won 1; Drawn 0; Lost 3; For 4; Against 9
Clean sweeps: 1 (1976-77)   **Whitewashed:** 0
Most goals scored in a season: 12 – 1986-87
Most goals conceded in a season: 9 – 1985-86
Least goals scored in a season: 4 – 1985-86, 1989-90, 1991-92
Least goals conceded in a season: 2 – 1989-90, 1991-92
Most goals shared between pair in a season: 17 in 1978-79, Rangers 11, Hearts 6
Least goals shared between pair in a season: 6 in 1989-90 and 1991-92, both Rangers 4, Hearts 2
Biggest home win: 4-0 on four occasions
Biggest home defeat: 0-2 on 28-12-85
Biggest away win: 5-2 on 7-2-87
Biggest away defeat: 0-3 on 16-11-85

Rangers' top Premier scorers against Hearts

1. Ally McCoist 18
2. Mark Hateley 12
3. Derek Johnstone 8
4. (tie) Derek Parlane and own goals 5

HIBERNIAN

Ground: Easter Road Stadium, Albion Road, Edinburgh
Club colours: Green and white
Number of seasons in Premier: 19
Year of formation: 1875
Most capped player: Lawrie Reilly
No of caps: 38
Most League points in a season: 57 (First Division – season 1980-81)
Most League goals scored by a player in a season: Joe Baker (season 1959-60)
No of goals scored: 42
Record attendance: 65,860 v. Hearts 2-1-50
Record victory: 22-1 v. 42nd Highlanders 3-9-1881
Record defeat: 0-10 v. Rangers 24-12-1898

Rangers' Premier record against Hibernian

Games played: 76	**Won:** 38
Drawn: 25	**Lost:** 13
Goals scored: 104	**Goals conceded:** 53
Clean sheets: 38	

Best seasonal performance: 1991-92. Won 4; Drawn 0; Lost 0; For 12; Against 3
Worst seasonal performance: 1989-90. Won 1; Drawn 1; Lost 2; For 3; Against 3
Clean sweeps: 1 (1991-92)   **Whitewashed:** 0
Most goals scored in a season: 12 – 1991-92
Most goals conceded in a season: 5 – 1984-85 and 1985-86
Least goals scored in a season: 2 – 1977-78
Least goals conceded in a season: 0 – 1983-84, 1988-89 and 1990-91
Most goals shared between pair in a season: 15 in 1991-92, Rangers 12, Hibs 3
Least goals shared between pair in a season: 3 in 1983-84 and 1988-89, both
Rangers 3, Hibs 0
Biggest home win: 4-0 on 3-11-90
Biggest home defeat: 0-2 on 20-8-77
Biggest away win: 3-0 on 3-4-76 and 19-11-91
Biggest away defeat: 0-2 on 19-8-89

Rangers' top Premier scorers against Hibernian

1. Ally McCoist 17
2. (tie) Mark Hateley and Davie Cooper 8
4. Derek Johnstone 6
5. Derek Parlane 5

KILMARNOCK

Ground: Rugby Park, Rugby Road, Kilmarnock
Club colours: Blue and white
Number of seasons in Premier Division: 6
Year of formation: 1869
Most capped player: Joe Nibloe
No of caps: 3
Most League goals scored by a player in a season: Harry Cunningham (Season 1927-28) and Andy Kerr (Season 1960-61)
No. of goals scored: 34
Record attendance: 34,426 v. Rangers, August 1963
Record victory: 13-2 v. Saltcoats, Scottish Cup 12-9-1896
Record defeat: 0-8 v. Rangers and Hibernian

Rangers' Premier record against Kilmarnock

Games played: 24	**Won:** 15
Drawn: 4	**Lost:** 5
Goals scored: 45	**Goals conceded:** 12
Clean sheets: 14	

Best seasonal performance: 1994-95. Won 4; Drawn 0; Lost 0; For 8; Against 1
Worst seasonal performance: 1979-70. Won 2; Drawn 0; Lost 2; For 4; Against 4
Clean sweeps: 1 (1994-95)   **Whitewashed:** 0
Most goals scored in a season: 13 – 1980-81
Most goals conceded in a season: 4 – 1979-80
Least goals scored in a season: 4 – 1979-80
Least goals scored in a season: 1 – 1976-77, 1994-95
Most goals shared between pair in a season – 15 in 1980-81, Rangers 13, Killie 2
Least goals shared between pair in a season – 8 in 1976-77 (R 7, K1), 1979-80 (R 4, K 4) and 1982-83 (R 7, K 1)
Biggest home win: 5-0 on 18-9-82
Biggest home defeat: 1-2 on 4-8-93
Biggest away win: 8-1 on 20-9-80
Biggest away defeat: 1-2 on 29-9-79

Rangers' top Premier scorers against Kilmarnock

1. John MacDonald 8
2. Bobby Russell 4
3. (tie) Derek Parlane, Ian Redford 3

MORTON

:

Ground: Cappielow Park, Sinclair Street, Greenock
Club colours: Royal blue tartan
Number of seasons in Premier: 7
Year of formation: 1874
Most capped player: Jimmy Cowan
No of caps: 25
Most League points in a season: 69 (Division 2 – Season 1966-67)
Most League goals scored by a player in a season: Allan McGraw (Season 1963-64)
No of goals scored: 58
Record attendance: 23,500 v. Celtic 1922
Record victory: 11-0 v. Carfin Shamrock 13-11-1886
Record defeat: 1-10 v. Port Glasgow Athletic 5-5-1884

Rangers' Premier record against Morton

Games played: 28	**Won:** 16
Drawn: 8	**Lost** 2
Goals scored: 65	**Goals conceded:** 15
Clean sheets: 17	

Best seasonal performance: 1984-85 – Won 4; Drawn 0; Lost 0; For 10: Against 1
Worst seasonal performance: 1980-81 – Won 2; Drawn 1; Lost 1: For 8: Against 3
Clean sweeps: 1 (1984-85)   **Whitewashed:** 0
Most goals scored in a season: 17 – 1987-88
Most goals conceded in a season: 3 – 1978-79, 1979-80, 198081, 1987-88
Least goals scored in a season: 7 – 1979-80, 1981-82
Least goals conceded in a season: 1 – 1982-83, 1984-85
Most goals shared between pair in a season: 20 in 1987-88, Rangers 17, Morton 3
Least goals shared between pair in a season: 9 in 1981-82, Rangers 7, Morton 2, and in 1982-83, Rangers 8, Morton 1
Biggest home win: 7-0 on 26-9-87
Biggest home defeat: 0-1 on 29-11-80
Biggest away win: 5-0 on 12-2-83
Biggest away defeat: 2-3 on 9-4-88

Rangers' top Premier scorers against Morton

1. Ally McCoist 11
2. John MacDonald 10
3. Derek Johnstone 8
4. Ian Redford 5
5. Bobby Russell 4

MOTHERWELL

Ground: Fir Park, Firpark Street, Motherwell
Club colours: Claret and amber
Number of seasons in Premier: 16
Year of formation: 1886
Most capped player: George Stevenson
Number of caps: 12
Most League points in a season: 66 (Division One – Season 1931-32)
Most League goals scored in a season: William McFadyen (Season 1931-32)
No. of goals scored: 52
Record attendance: 35,632 v. Rangers 12-3-52
Record victory: 12-1 v. Dundee United 23-1-54
Record defeat: 0-8 v. Aberdeen 26-3-79

Rangers' Premier record against Motherwell:

Games played: 64	**Won:** 48
Drawn: 3	**Lost:** 13
Goals scored: 121	**Goals conceded:** 53
Clean sheets: 30	

Best seasonal performance: 1992-93. Won 4; Drawn 0; Lost 0; For 13; Against 3
Worst seasonal performance: 1994-95. Won 2; Drawn 0; Lost 2; For 6; Against 6
Clean sweeps: 4 (1977-78, 1987-88, 1991-92, 1992-93)
Whitewashed: 0
Most goals scored in a season: 14 – 1977-78
Most goals conceded in a season: 6 – 1994-95
Least goals scored in a season: 4 – 1986-87
Least goals conceded in a season: 0 – 1987-88
Most goals shared between pair in a season: 19 in 1977-78 (Rangers 14, Motherwell 5)
Least goals shared between pair in a season: 5 in 1986-87 (Rangers 4, Motherwell 1) and 1987-88 (Rangers 5, Motherwell 0)
Biggest home win: 4-0 on 6-11-82
Biggest home defeat: 0-2 on 29-4-95
Biggest away win: 4-0 on 23-2-93
Biggest away defeat: 3-0 on 3-1-83 and 4-5-91

Rangers' top Premier scorers against Motherwell

1. Ally McCoist 21
2. Derek Johnstone 12
3. Gordon Smith 9
4. John Brown 6
5. (tie) Mark Hateley and own goals 5

PARTICK THISTLE

Ground: Firhill Stadium, Firhill Road, Glasgow
Club colours: Red, yellow and black
Number of seasons in Premier: 9
Year of formation: 1876
Most capped player: Alan Rough
Number of caps: 53
Most League points in a season: 57 (First Division – Season 1991-92)
Most League goals scored by a player in a season: Alec Hair (Season 1926-27)
No. of goals scored: 41
Record attendance: 49,838 (v. Rangers 18-2-22)
Record victory: 16-0 v. Royal Albert 17-1-31
Record defeat: 0-10 v. Queen's Park 3-12-1881

Rangers' Premier record against Partick Thistle

Games played: 36	**Won:** 18
Drawn: 10	**Lost:** 8
Goals scored: 65	**Goals conceded:** 39

No of clean sheets: 10
Best seasonal performance: 1977-78. Won 3; Drawn 1; Lost 0; For 11; Against 5
Worst seasonal performance: 1979-80. Won 1; Drawn 1; Lost 2; For 6; Against 7
Clean sweeps: 0   **Whitewashed:** 0
Most goals scored in a season: 11 – 1977-78
Most goals conceded in a season: 7 – 1976-77, 1979-80
Least goals scored in a season: 3 – 1978-79
Least goals conceded in a season: 1 – 1978-79
Most goals shared between pair in a season: 16 in 1977-78. Rangers 11, Partick 5
Least goals shared between pair in a season: 4 in 1978-79, Rangers 3, Partick 1
Biggest home win: 4-0 on 16-8-80
Biggest home defeat: 0-2 on 31-10-81
Biggest away win: 4-0 on 27-8-77
Biggest away defeat: 0-3 on 4-5-83

Rangers' top Premier scorers against Partick

1. Derek Johnstone 8
2. Bobby Russell 5
3. Mark Hateley 4
4. (tie) Derek Parlane, Sandy Jardine, Gordon Smith, Billy Urquhart, Colin McAdam, Gary McSwegan 3

RAITH ROVERS

Ground: Stark's Park, Pratt Street, Kirkcaldy, Fife
Club colours: Navy blue and white
Number of seasons in Premier Division: 1
Year of formation: 1883
Most capped player: David Morris
No. of caps: 6
Most League points in a season: 65 (First Division – season 1992-93)
Most League goals scored by a player in a season: Norman Heywood (season 1937-38)
No. of goals scored: 42
Record attendance: 31,306 v. Hearts 7-2-53
Record victory: 10-1 v. Coldstream 13-2-54
Record defeat: 2-11 v. Morton 8-3-36

Rangers' Premier record against Raith Rovers

Games played: 4	**Won:** 2
Drawn: 2	**Lost:** 0
Goals scored: 9	**Goals conceded:** 4
Clean sheets: 1	

Biggest home win: 4-0 on 16-4-94
Biggest home defeat: not applicable
Biggest away win: 2-1 on 26-2-94
Biggest away defeat: not applicable

Rangers top Premier scorers against Raith Rovers

1. Mark Hateley 2
2. Ian Ferguson, Gordon Durie, David Robertson, Ally McCoist, Duncan Ferguson, Alexei Mikhailitchenko, own goal 1

ST. JOHNSTONE

Ground: McDiarmid Park, Crieff Road, Perth
Club colours: Blue and white
Number of seasons in Premier: 6
Year of formation: 1884
Most capped player: Sandy McLaren
No of caps: 5
Most League points in a season: 59 (Second Division – Season 1987-88)
Most League goals scored by a player in a season: Jimmy Benson (Season 1931-32)
No. of goals scored – 38
Record attendance – 29,972 (v. Dundee 10-2-51)
Record victory – 8-1 (v. Partick Thistle 16-8-69)
Record defeat – 0-12 (v. Cowdenbeath 21-1-28)

St Johnstone's Premier record against Rangers

Games played: 24	**Won:** 21
Drawn: 3	**Lost:** 0
Goals scored: 70	**Goals conceded:** 14
Clean sheets: 13	

Best seasonal performance: 1975-76. Won 4; Drawn 0; Lost 0; Goals scored 14; Goals conceded 1
Worst seasonal performance: 1990-91. Won 2; Drawn 2; Lost 0; Goals scored 8; Goals conceded 2

Clean sweeps: 4	**Whitewashed:** 0

Most goals scored in a season: 14 – 1975-76, 1991-92
Most goals conceded in a season: 4 – 1983-84, 1991-92
Least goals scored in a season: 8 – 1990-91
Least goals conceded in a season: 1 – 1975-76 and 1993-94
Most goals shared between pair in a season: 18 in 1991-92, Rangers 14, St Johnstone 4
Least goals shared between pair in a season: 10 in 1990-91, Rangers 8, St Johnstone 2
Biggest home win: 6-0 on 10-8-91
Biggest home defeat: not applicable
Biggest away win: 5-1 on 15-11-75 and 7-10-92
Biggest away defeat: not applicable

Rangers' top Premier scorers against St Johnstone

1. Mark Hateley 12
2. Ally McCoist 9
3. Derek Johnstone 4
4. (tie) Maurice Johnston and Sandy Clark 3

ST. MIRREN

Ground: St Mirren Park, Love Street, Paisley
Club colours: Black and white
Number of seasons in Premier: 15
Year of formation: 1877
Most capped players: Billy Thomson and Iain Munro
No of caps: 7
Most league points in a season: 62 (Division 2 – Season 1967-68)
Most league goals scored by a player in a season: Dunky Walker
No of goals scored: 45
Record attendance: 47,438
Record victory: 15-0 v. Glasgow University 30-1-60
Record defeat: 0-9 v. Rangers 4-12-1897

Rangers' Premier record against St Mirren

Games played: 60	**Won:** 36
Drawn: 13	**Lost:** 11
Goals scored: 103	**Goals conceded:** 48

Clean sheets: 28
Best seasonal performance: 1990-91 – Won 4; Drawn 0; Lost 0; For 10; Against 0
Worst seasonal performance: 1979-80 – Won 1; Drawn 0; Lost 3; For 6; Against 9
Clean sweeps: 2 – 1986-87 and 1990-91
Whitewashed: 0
Most goals scored in a season: 12 – 1987-88
Most goals conceded in a season: 9 – 1979-80
Least goals scored in a season: 3 – 1983-84, 1989-90
Least goals conceded in a season: 0 – 1990-91
Most goals shared between pair in a season: 15 in 1979-80, Rangers 6, St Mirren 9, in 1981-82 Rangers 11, St Mirren 4, and 1987-88, Rangers 12, St Mirren 3
Least goals shared between pair in a season: 4 in 1989-90, Rangers 3, St Mirren 1
Biggest home win: 5-0 on 13-10-90
Biggest home defeat: 1-2 on 5-1-80
Biggest away win: 3-0 on 23-4-88 and 15-12-90
Biggest away defeat: 1-4 on 7-5-80

Rangers' top Premier scorers against St Mirren

1. Ally McCoist 17
2. Derek Johnstone 9
3. (tie) Davie Cooper, Mark Walters 7
5. (tie) Jim Bett, John MacDonald 5

'Most league points in a season' records for all clubs refer only to the two points for a win system

235

Premier Division – The Players

Rangers have used a total of 147 players in the Premier Division since it started in 1975-76. The list which follows gives a brief resume of each player's career and a statistical breakdown of their Premier appearances.

ARMOUR David

Arrived in June 1974, but was never really anything more than a bit-part player in the successful mid-seventies sides. An inside forward.

	Apps	Goals
1976-77	0 (1)	0
1977-78	0	0
1978-79	0 (2)	0
Total	0 (3)	0

BARTRAM Jan

Skillful Danish left-back who looked to have a future at Ibrox, but made the mistake of publicly criticising Graeme Souness and his methods, and was soon back on the continent.

	Apps	Goals
1987-88	11	3
Total	11	3

BEATTIE Scott

A defender who looked to have a good career ahead of him after making a bit of a breakthrough in 85-86, but the campaign ended up as his Rangers swansong.

	Apps	Goals
1985-86	5	0
Total	5	0

BELL Dougie

Important squad player in Alex Ferguson's great Aberdeen side of the early eighties, but never quite hit the mark at Ibrox and was a victim of the Souness era.

	Apps	Goals
1985-86	20 (3)	0
1986-87	7 (5)	1
Total	27 (8)	1

BETT Jim

Skillful midfield playmaker, who joined the club from Lokeren and later enjoyed more success in Scotland with Aberdeen. Won 25 Scotland caps, but quit after a row with Andy Roxburgh.

	Apps	Goals
1980-81	34	4

1981-82	35	11
1982-83	35	6
Total	104	21

BLACK Kenny

Broke into the team in defence in the early eighties, but never established himself, partly due to disciplinary problems which were to resurface at Hearts, Portsmouth and Airdrie.

	Apps	Goals
1981-82	7 (1)	0
1982-83	11 (4)	1
Total	18 (5)	1

BOLI Basile

Hardman French international, signed from Marseille for £2.7 million, who criticised Walter Smith's tactics after defeat from AEK Athens and was subsequently a bit of a misfit.

	Apps	Goals
1994-95	28	2
Total	28	2

BOLLAN Gary

Arrived in a double deal which also took Alex Cleland to Ibrox, primarily as cover for defensive positions. Left-sided specialist with a good record at international level with the Under-21s.

	Apps	Goals
1994-95	5 (1)	0
Total	5 (1)	0

BOYD Gordon

Earmarked by Jock Wallace as a useful squad player, this July '74 signing was in the squad more often than he played!

	Apps	Goals
1975-76	1	0
Total	1	0

BROWN John

Bomber has become a legend at Rangers – but he only signed after a move to Hearts fell through on medical grounds. A whole-hearted defender.

	Apps	Goals
1987-88	9	2
1988-89	29	1
1989-90	24 (3)	1
1990-91	25 (2)	1

1991-92	18 (7)	4
1992-93	39	4
1993-94	24	0
1994-95	10 (3)	1
Total	178 (15)	14

BRUCE Andy

Reserve goalkeeper who did well to make any appearances during his time at the club, given the dominance Peter McCloy, Jim Stewart and Nicky Walker had over the position.

	Apps	Goals
1982-83	1	0
1983-84	0	0
1984-85	1	0
Total	2	0

BURNS Hugh

Picked up a League Cup medal at Ibrox, but was hindered by a tempestuous nature which flared up again last season when he walked out on Ayr. Also played for Hearts and Kilmarnock.

	Apps	Goals
1983-84	0 (5)	0
1984-85	11 (4)	0
1985-86	26 (2)	3
1986-87	3	0
Total	40 (11)	3

BUTCHER Terry

Graeme Souness' first big-name signing for Rangers, he captained the club to League and League Cup successes before leaving for Sunderland after a row with the boss.

	Apps	Goals
1986-87	43	3
1987-88	11	0
1988-89	34	2
1989-90	34	3
1990-91	5	0
Total	127	8

CALDWELL Neil

Defender who made his first appearance on the last day of the 1994-95 season against Partick Thistle, before being given a free transfer.

	Apps	Goals
1994-95	1	0
Total	1	

CLARK Robert

Replaced Derek Johnstone in a 2-1 defeat at Hearts then was never heard of again.

	Apps	Goals
1980-81	0 (1)	0
Total	0 (1)	0

CLARK Sandy

Traditional bustling centre-forward who made his name at Aidrie but signed from West Ham. Not a great success at Ibrox, but finished joint-top scorer in 1983-84.

	Apps	Goals
1982-83	10	4
1983-84	27 (3)	9*
1984-85	1	0
Total	38 (3)	13

CLELAND Alex

In May 1994, he was part of the Dundee United team which beat Rangers to win the Scottish Cup and prevent the Treble. A year later he was at Rangers, as his old club were relegated!

	Apps	Goals
1994-95	10	0
Total	10	0

COHEN Avi

Graeme Souness remembered this Israeli defender from Liverpool, where he once scored a championship winning goal for the Reds. Sadly his spell at Ibrox was less glorious.

	Apps	Goals
1987-88	4 (3)	0
Total	4 (3)	0

COOPER Davie

Fabulously skilled left-winger, who played 22 times for Scotland and scored the goal which took Scotland to the 1986 World Cup. Signed from Clydebank, later went to Motherwell and Bankies again, before a tragic and untimely death.

	Apps	Goals
1977-78	34 (1)	6
1978-79	26 (4)	5
1979-80	25 (5)	2

1980-81	17 (8)	3
1981-82	29 (1)	3
1982-83	26 (5)	5
1983-84	32 (2)	6
1984-85	32	5
1985-86	28 (4)	4
1986-87	42	8
1987-88	21 (12)	1
1988-89	9 (14)	1
Total	321 (56)	49

COOPER Neale

Pivotal part of the Aberdeen side which won the Cup-Winners' Cup, he arrived via Aston Villa and had a bright start, with a debut goal at Pittodrie. Injury blighted this midfielder though.

	Apps	Goals
1988-89	11 (3)	1
1989-90	2 (1)	0
Total	13 (4)	1

COWAN Tom

Rated a real prospect at his first club Clyde, Cowan, a left-back, never really fulfilled his potential, although played in the Championship decider of 90-91. Now in England.

	Apps	Goals
1988-89	3 (1)	0
1989-90	1 (2)	0
1990-91	4 (1)	0
Total	8 (4)	0

DALZIEL Gordon

Striker who didn't quite make the grade, but proceeded to become Raith Rovers' highest-ever scorer and won the hearts of Ibrox fans by equalising against Celtic in the 1994 Coca-Cola Final.

	Apps	Goals
1979-80	1	0
1980-81	0	0
1981-82	14 (3)	6
1982-83	7 (7)	3
Total	22 (10)	9

DAVIES Billy

Another who started at Rangers, was not quite up to scratch, but went on to carve a reasonable career with the likes of St Mirren, Dunfermline and Motherwell.

	Apps	Goals
1981-82	1 (3)	0
1982-83	2 (2)	0
1983-84	0 (3)	1
Total	3 (8)	1

DAWSON Ally

Solid servant for the club in defence, he captained Rangers and went on to play for Scotland five times, before leaving for a spell with Blackburn.

	Apps	Total
1975-76	3	0
1976-77	1	0
1977-78	1 (1)	0
1978-79	23	1
1979-80	32	0
1980-81	22	2
1981-82	25	1
1982-83	24 (1)	0
1983-84	28	0
1984-85	25 (1)	1
1985-86	23 (1)	0
1986-87	6 (1)	0
Total	213 (5)	

DENNY Jim

Now coaching at St Mirren, Denny's main moment of fame at Ibrox was when he amazingly made his debut as an unknown 21-year-old in the 1971 Cup Final replay, against Celtic, in front of 103,332.

	Apps	Goals
1975-76	6 (3)	0
1976-77	5	0
Total	11 (3)	0

DODDS Davie

Scotland cap who had a fine career at Dundee United and Aberdeen before a shock move to Ibrox late in his career. Now a vital member of the backroom staff.

	Apps	Goals
1989-90	4 (10)	4
1990-91	3	0
Total	7 (10)	4

DRINKELL Kevin

Popular striker, signed from Norwich, who was just that little bit short of establishing himself as an international. Finished top scorer in 1988-89, but later went to Coventry.

	Apps	Goals
1988-89	32	12*
1989-90	2 (2)	0
Total	34 (2)	12

DURIE Gordon

Came to prominence in Scotland with East Fife and Hibs, and had spells at Chelsea and Tottenham, who paid £2.2 million for him, before Walter Smith signed him to boost his Scottish contingent.

	Apps	Goals
1993-94	23 (1)	12
1994-95	16 (4)	5
Total	39 (5)	17

DURRANT Ian

One of the great Rangers, a local who made good in the cosmopolitan Ibrox of the late eighties. Career-threatening injury perhaps prevented worldwide fame.

	Apps	Goals
1984-85	5	0
1985-86	30	2
1986-87	39	4
1987-88	39 (1)	10
1988-89	8	2
1989-90	0	0
1990-91	3 (1)	1
1991-92	9 (4)	0
1992-93	19 (11)	3
1993-94	14 (9)	0
1994-95	16 (10)	4
Total	182 (36)	26

FALCO Mark

English striker who made a splash at Tottenham, but was a victim of Souness' revolving door policy. Highlight at Ibrox was a goal against Dynamo Kiev in the European Cup.

	Apps	Goals
1987-88	9 (5)	5
Total	9 (5)	5

FERGUSON Derek

Superbly skilled midfielder whose career was more of a case of what might have been. Hardliner Souness didn't approve of his indiscipline and he was offloaded to Hearts.

	Apps	Goals
1983-84	1	0
1984-85	7 (1)	0
1985-86	12 (7)	0
1986-87	26 (4)	1
1987-88	31 (1)	4
1988-89	12 (4)	2
1989-90	3 (2)	0
Total	92 (19)	7

FERGUSON Duncan

Signed for close-on £4 million from Dundee United, then a British record, his own off-field problems and Mark Hateley's form saw him off to Everton, for a profit, after a patchy spell at Ibrox.

	Apps	Goals
1993-94	7 (3)	1
1994-95	1 (3)	1
Total	8 (6)	2

FERGUSON Eric

The most popular surname of Rangers' time in the Premier, but sadly Eric Ferguson, once a promising striker, proved the least successful of the glut of Fergies.

	Apps	Goals
1983-84	2 (2)	0
1984-85	8 (1)	1
Total	10 (3)	1

FERGUSON Iain

Nomadic striker and another signing of the mid-eighties who failed to live up to his potential. More successful spells at Dundee United and Motherwell followed.

	Apps	Goals
1984-85	24 (4)	6
1985-86	1 (4)	0
Total	25 (8)	6

FERGUSON Ian

A Scottish Cup winning goal for St Mirren persuaded Graeme Souness to splash almost £1,000,000 for Fergie, who has proved his worth with some vital goals from midfield.

	Apps	Goals
1987-88	8	1

1988-89	30	6
1989-90	21 (3)	0
1990-91	10 (1)	1
1991-92	12 (4)	1
1992-93	29 (1)	4
1993-94	35	0
1994-95	13 (3)	1
Total	158 (12)	14

FLECK Robert

Nippy forward who showed no sign of becoming a prolific hitman under Jock Wallace. Graeme Souness arrived, the goals flowed and he was perhaps unwisely sold to Norwich.

	Apps	Goals
1983-84	1	0
1984-85	1 (7)	0
1985-86	9 (6)	3
1986-87	35 (5)	19
1987-88	15 (6)	7
Total	61 (24)	29

FORSYTH Alex

Played for Scotland with Partick Thistle and Man United, from where he was signed by John Greig. He was in the latter stages of career when at Ibrox, although he scored a few penalties.

	Apps	Goals
1978-79	16	4
1979-80	8	1
1980-81	1	0
Total	25	5

FORSYTH Tom

Valuable defender who played his part in many a Rangers triumph. Capped 22 times by Scotland, his finest moment at Ibrox came when scoring the winner in the 1973 Scottish Cup Final.

	Apps	Goals
1975-76	28	1
1976-77	25	0
1977-78	31	0
1978-79	17	0
1979-80	16	0
1980-81	15 (7)	0
1981-82	12	0
Total	144 (7)	1

FRANCIS Trevor

A pay as you play policy took Francis to Glasgow from Italy. Unbelievably, this England star failed to score during his time at Ibrox – apart from in a Skol final penalty shootout!

	Apps	Goals
1987-88	8 (10)	0
Total	8 (10)	0

FRASER Cammy

Combative midfielder, signed from Dundee, who didn't quite make the impact hoped. Another player to suffer from regular injury problems, he later went on to play for Dundee, Raith and Montrose.

	Apps	Goals
1984-85	27 (1)	3
1985-86	7 (1)	2
1986-87	16	1
Total	50 (2)	6

FRASER Scott

Full-back who filled in at right-back during the 1983-84 season, but found himself behind the likes of Ally Dawson, Hugh Burns and Jimmy Nicholl in his bid for regular first team football.

	Apps	Goals
1983-84	7	0
1984-85	0 (2)	0
Total	7 (2)	0

FYFE Graham

After coming to Ibrox from Motherwell in December 1968, this inside right enjoyed some good times with Rangers before leaving for Hibs in the deal which took Iain Munro to the club in April 1976.

	Apps	Goals
1975-76	1 (2)	0
Total	1 (2)	0

GINZBURG Bonni

Signed as back-up to Chris Woods, this Israeli goalkeeper never got much chance to show his undoubted skills, although one of his four games came in the special atmosphere of the Old Firm clash.

	Apps	Goals
1989-90	4	0
Total	4	0

GORAM Andy

Outstanding goalkeeper, signed from Hibs as more Scots were required for the Euro challenge – and won Player and Footballer of the Year in 1993-94.

	Apps	Goals
1991-92	44	0
1992-93	34	0
1993-94	8	0
1994-95	18 (1)	0
Total	104 (1)	0

GORDON Dale

Followed Chris Woods and Kevin Drinkell in signing from Norwich, but was not as big a hit as his predecessors and moved on to West Ham after a couple of seasons.

	Apps	Goals
1991-92	23	5
1992-93	18 (4)	1
Total	41 (4)	6

GOUGH Richard

Dundee United prodigy who signed via Spurs and led the side to, to date, seven successive championships as well as League and Scottish Cups.

	Apps	Goals
1987-88	31	5
1988-89	35	4
1989-90	26	0
1990-91	26	0
1991-92	33	2
1992-93	25	2
1993-94	37	3
1994-95	25	1
Total	238	17

GRAY Andy

Self-confessed Rangers fan who signed on at the tail end of a glittering career with Dundee United, Wolves, Everton and Aston Villa – and scored a few goals to justify his capture.

	Apps	Goals
1988-89	3 (10)	5
Total	3 (10)	5

GREIG John

Legendary captain of the club, now PR officer at Ibrox, who came to the end of his

playing days and stepped into the manager's seat – sadly with less success or
distinction.

	Apps	Goals
1975-76	36	2
1976-77	30	0
1977-78	28 (1)	2
Total	94 (1)	4

HAGEN David

Young, quick striker who filled in during McCoist and Hateley's absences but
could not find a regular place and went to Hearts for first-team football.

	Apps	Goals
1992-93	5 (3)	2
1993-94	4 (2)	1
1994-95	0 (2)	0
Total	9 (7)	3

HAMILTON Johnny

Was part of the Treble winning squad of 1975-76, although missed out on a League
Cup medal. Two years later he experienced the other side of the coin with a free
transfer.

	Apps	Goals
1975-76	22	1
1976-77	22 (1)	3
1977-78	3 (1)	0
Total	45 (2)	4

HATELEY Mark

Scepticism followed his capture from Monaco, but the big striker proved a massive
success, forming a great partnership with Ally McCoist and scoring more goals
himself than ever before.

	Apps	Goals
1990-91	30 (3)	10
1991-92	29 (1)	21
1992-93	36 (1)	19
1993-94	40 (2)	22
1994-95	23	13
Total	158 (7)	85

HENDERSON Martin

Finished second top scorer in the 75-76 championship team, but by 1977-78 he was
off on loan to Hibs before being transferred to Philadelphia Furies for £30,000.

	Apps	Goals
1975-76	23 (3)	10
1976-77	4 (3)	0
Total	27 (6)	10

HUISTRA Pieter

Lavishly skilled Dutch winger, who suffered through his own erratic performances. Left for Japan during 1994-95, ironically as he hit his most consistent form during his time with the club.

	Apps	Goals
1990-91	10 (17)	4
1991-92	25 (7)	5
1992-93	27 (3)	4
1993-94	10 (11)	6
1994-95	15	3
Total	87 (38)	22

HURLOCK Terry

Described by a Millwall fanzine as epitomising the 'true spirit' of the South London club with a hard reputation, he lasted one season and ended up the Premier's most booked player.

	Apps	Goals
1990-91	29	2
Total	29	2

JACKSON Colin

Another long-serving centre-half, he played for Scotland eight times and was the lynchpin of many a Blues success in the seventies.

	Apps	Goals
1975-76	33	2
1976-77	30	4
1977-78	35	3
1978-79	28	1
1979-80	29	2
1980-81	29	0
1981-82	21	0
Total	205	12

JARDINE Sandy

Superbly talented defender who appeared 38 times for Scotland and prolonged his career after leaving Ibrox by playing on with Hearts until his late thirties.

	Apps	Goals
1975-76	18 (7)	2

1976-77	36	2
1977-78	32	5
1978-79	35	0
1979-80	35	3
1980-81	29 (2)	3
1981-82	36	1
Total	221(9)	16

JOHNSTON Maurice

Formerly of Celtic, his arrival from Nantes provoked uproar in Glasgow, but he proved his quality with two splendid seasons before moving off for more money at Everton.

	Apps	Goals
1989-90	36	15
1990-91	29	11
1991-92	10 (1)	5
Total	75 (1)	31

JOHNSTON Willie

Nimble-toed winger whose finest moment came in the Cup-Winners' Cup final of 1972 and not in the second spell he had at the club in the twilight of his career.

	Apps	Goals
1980-81	21 (6)	2
1981-82	6 (2)	0
Total	27 (8)	2

JOHNSTONE Derek

Now a successful TV pundit in Scotland, DJ was just as adept at the back as he was up front, where he regularly finished top scorer for the club. A return to Ibrox was less fruitful.

	Apps	Goals
1975-76	31 (1)	15*
1976-77	27	15
1977-78	33	25*
1978-79	31	9
1979-80	31 (2)	14*
1980-81	23 (3)	4
1981-82	27 (1)	9
1982-83	18	6
1984-85	11	1
1985-86	8	0
Total	240 (7)	98

KENNEDY Andy

Pacy striker who looked the business when he burst on to the scene, but could not live up to the hopes and drifted about in England thereafter, with spells at Watford and Birmingham.

	Apps	Goals
1982-83	12 (1)	3
1983-84	0 (2)	3
Total	12 (3)	6

KENNEDY Stewart

Signed from Stenhousemuir, he alternated the goalkeeper's jersey with Peter McCloy and even made it into the Scotland team on five occasions – although he le in five against England!

	Apps	Goals
1975-76	12	0
1976-77	31	0
1977-78	22	0
Total	65	0

KIRKWOOD Davie

Signed from East Fife, but only ever appeared fleetingly in the first team. He disappeared to display his midfield skills at Hearts and Airdrie.

	Apps	Goals
1986-87	0 (1)	0
1987-88	3 (1)	0
1988-89	2	0
Total	5 (2)	0

KUZNETSOV Oleg

Tremendously talented Ukrainian defender who suffered a shocking leg injury in only his second game, at St Johnstone, which prevented him becoming the great he should have been.

	Apps	Goals
1990-91	2	0
1991-92	16 (2)	0
1992-93	8 (1)	0
1993-94	4 (2)	1
Total	30 (5)	1

LAUDRUP Brian

A European Championship winner with Denmark in 1992, this superbly skilled winger made a phenomenal impact in his first season, scooping Player of the Year honours.

	Apps	Goals
1994-95	33	10
Total	33	10

LYALL Kenny

Another prospect from the eighties who failed to blossom into the player many thought he should have, he enjoyed most success at Brechin City.

	Apps	Goals
1981-82	3	0
1982-83	2 (2)	0
1983-84	1	0
Total	6 (2)	0

MACKAY Billy

Injury interrupted career denied him the chance of staking a regular place in the Rangers line-up. Fitness problems later blighted him at Hearts.

	Apps	Goals
1977-78	1	0
1978-79	0 (1)	1
1979-80	0 (2)	0
1980-81	0 (6)	0
1981-82	1 (6)	1
1982-83	2 (2)	0
1983-84	1 (1)	0
Total	5 (18)	2

MacDONALD Alex

Doddie was a gritty midfielder, who chipped in with more than his fair share of goals. His no-nonsense style has been mirrored by Hearts and Airdrie in managerial spells.

	Apps	Goals
1975-76	34 (1)	4
1976-77	29 (1)	9
1977-78	34	3
1978-79	33	5
1979-80	23 (3)	1
Total	153 (5)	22

MacDONALD John

Regular scorer whose finest hour came in the 1981 Scottish Cup final replay against Dundee United when he scored twice in the 4-1 win. Faded in his later years.

	Apps	Goals
1978-79	0 (2)	0
1979-80	21 (5)	5

1980-81	26 (4)	11
1981-82	32 (3)	14*
1982-83	25 (3)	10*
1983-84	2 (16)	1
1984-85	8 (10)	3
1985-86	2	0
Total	116 (43)	44

MacDONALD Kevin

Highlander who won the Double with Liverpool down south, but enjoyed less success in the three games he had on loan with Rangers – they lost the pair he started!

	Apps	Goals
1988-89	2 (1)	0
Total	2 (1)	0

MacFARLANE Dave

Had a Skol Cup medal to show for his time at the club, but this defender-cum-midfielder never really made the mark and went to Kilmarnock before featuring in the junior ranks.

	Apps	Goals
1984-85	1 (1)	0
1985-86	0	0
1986-87	2 (2)	0
1987-88	1	0
Total	4 (3)	0

McADAM Colin

Signed from Partick Thistle for £160,000, this bustling striker was a success in his first season, when he was top scorer, but ended up playing in defence.

	Apps	Goals
1980-81	31	12
1981-82	15 (7)	2
1982-83	2 (2)	0
1983-84	8	1
Total	56 (9)	15

McCALL Ian

Skilled winger, who impressed whilst with Dunfermline, but let himself down with his own indiscipline at Rangers, and ended with a chequered career around a number of Scottish clubs.

	Apps	Goals
1987-88	8 (4)	1

1988-89	2 (3)	1
1989-90	2 (2)	0
total	12 (9)	2

McCALL Stuart

Industrious midfielder, he first came to prominence with Bradford, then Everton, before a move north. Relentless energy, he has been a key figure in the success of recent years.

	Apps	Goals
1991-92	35 (1)	1
1992-93	35 (1)	5
1993-94	34	3
1994-95	30	3
total	134 (2)	12

McCLELLAND John

Distinguished central defender, captain and Northern Ireland international who spent an all too brief time at the club. Went on to win an English championship medal with Leeds.

	Apps	Goals
1981-82	14	0
1982-83	35	2
1983-84	36	2
1984-85	11	0
total	96	4

McCLOY Peter

Known as 'The Girvan Lighthouse', this towering goalkeeper played more games than he missed, but was forever vying for the number one keeping position with a rival.

	Apps	Goals
1975-76	24	0
1976-77	5	0
1977-78	14	0
1978-79	36	0
1979-80	24	0
1980-81	26	0
1981-82	10	0
1982-83	17	0
1983-84	26	0
1984-85	21	0
1985-86	2	0
total	205	0

McCOIST Ally

Signed from Sunderland, McCoist is in touching distance of Bob McPhail's all tim
goals record for the club. Suffered under Souness, but exploded back to life under
Walter Smith.

	Apps	Goals
1983-84	32 (2)	9*
1984-85	22 (3)	12*
1985-86	33	24*
1986-87	44	33*
1987-88	40	31*
1988-89	18 (1)	9
1989-90	32 (2)	14
1990-91	15 (11)	11
1991-92	37 (1)	34*
1992-93	32 (2)	34*
1993-94	16 (5)	7
1994-95	4 (5)	1
Total	325 (32)	219

McDOUGALL Ian

A £15,000 transfer to Dundee in August 1977 failed to tell the whole story of this
winger's Ibrox career. Another one to suffer from injury.

	Apps	Goals
1975-76	3 (1)	1
1976-77	1 (3)	0
Total	4 (4)	1

McGINTY Brian

Promising striker whose 1994-95 appearance against Partick Thistle probably
surprised him as much as it did the fans and press. One to watch for the future.

	Apps	Goals
1994-95	1	0
Total	1	0

McGREGOR John

Snapped up from Liverpool, where he'd gone from Queen's Park. Knee problem
curtailed his playing career, but he is now a valued member of the coaching set-u

	Apps	Goals
1987-88	20 (5)	0
1988-89	0	0
1989-90	0	0
1990-91	0	0

| 1991-92 | 1 | 0 |
| Total | 21 (5) | 0 |

McINTYRE Jimmy

A regular in the reserves in the early eighties, but a sub appearance against Dundee, in front of a paltry 8,500, in the second last game of 81-82, was the pinnacle first-team wise.

	Apps	Goals
1981-82	0 (1)	0
Total	0 (1)	0

McKEAN Bobby

A tragic death in Barrhead overshadowed his considerable achievements as a player, which were also recognised on the international front where he won a full cap in 1976.

	Apps	Goals
1975-76	32 (1)	5
1976-77	14 (8)	2
1977-78	6 (4)	0
Total	52 (13)	7

McKINNON Dave

A surprise signing from Partick Thistle for £30,000, he made regular appearances at right-back before becoming yet another to fall in Graeme Souness' early regime.

	Apps	Goals
1982-83	30 (1)	1
1983-84	12 (5)	0
1984-85	30	0
1985-86	18 (6)	0
Total	90 (12)	1

McKNIGHT Paul

Star of Rangers' highly successful youth team, his potential was recognised in the last game of the 1994-95 season when he made his debut against Partick Thistle.

	Apps	Goals
1994-95	0 (1)	0
Total	0 (1)	0

McLAREN Alan

A resilient marker and useful defender who was captured from Hearts in a deal which took Dave McPherson and David Hagen to Tynecastle. A regular Scottish international.

	Apps	Goals
1994-95	24	2
Total	24	2

McLEAN Tommy

Yet another Ranger who has had success as a boss, notably at Motherwell before moving to Hearts. Signed from Killie, wee Tam was a skillful winger.

	Apps	Goals
1975-76	34 (1)	4
1976-77	36	1
1977-78	29 (2)	1
1978-79	34 (1)	1
1979-80	22 (6)	2
1980-81	23 (3)	0
1981-82	2 (1)	1
Total	180 (14)	10

McMINN Ted

Unorthodox winger, signed from Queen of the South, who would delight and exasperate in the same match. Remembered fondly at Ibrox for the entertainment provided.

	Apps	Goals
1984-85	13 (7)	1
1985-86	15 (13)	2
1986-87	26 (4)	1
Total	54 (24)	4

McPHERSON Dave

Up and down career with Rangers, where he had two spells. Didn't always please the fans, but proved himself a composed central defender. Exchanged for Alan McLaren in 1994-95.

	Apps	Goals
1982-83	15 (5)	1
1983-84	32 (4)	2
1984-85	27 (4)	0
1985-86	34	5
1986-87	42	7
1987-88	0	0
1988-89	0	0
1989-90	0	0
1990-91	0	0
1991-92	0	0

1992-93	34	2
1993-94	27 (1)	1
1994-95	9	0
Total	220 (14)	18

McSWEGAN Gary

Will always be remembered at Ibrox for a memorable Champions League goal against Marseille. But he also scored the goal which won the 1992-93 title at Airdrie, then left for Notts County.

	Apps	Goals
1987-88	0 (1)	0
1988-89	0 (1)	0
1989-90	1 (2)	0
1990-91	0 (4)	0
1991-92	8 (1)	4
Total	9 (9)	4

MAXWELL Ally

Respected goalkeeper who featured more than he might have expected because of Andy Goram's problems. Won every medal in the Scottish game, but prone to high profile mistakes.

	Apps	Goals
1992-93	10	0
1993-94	31 (1)	0
1994-95	10 (1)	0
Total	51 (2)	0

MIKHAILITCHENKO Alexei

Another Ukrainian, and a well-balanced midfielder with a deft left foot. Inconsistency marred his game, though, and he didn't contribute as much as it often appeared he could.

	Apps	Goals
1991-92	24 (3)	10
1992-93	16 (13)	5
1993-94	24 (10)	5
1994-95	4 (5)	2
Total	68 (31)	22

MILLER Alex

Reliable defender, who never really claimed a regular place, but was part of many triumphs. A fruitful managerial career, especially at Hibs, saw him appointed Scotland number two.

	Apps	Goals
1975-76	25 (2)	1
1976-77	17 (7)	4
1977-78	16 (8)	2
1978-79	10 (7)	0
1979-80	13 (5)	3
1980-81	24 (1)	0
1981-82	14 (2)	0
Total	119 (32)	10

MILLER Charlie

Supremely gifted midfielder-cum-forward who made the breakthrough in the 1994-95 season. One of the few Glaswegians in the present side, hailing from Castlemilk.

	Apps	Goals
1993-94	2 (1)	0
1994-95	21	3
Total	23 (1)	3

MILLER Colin

Canadian international who made the grade with Hamilton, before a move to St Johnstone then Hearts, where he scored to help knock Rangers out of the Scottish Cup last season.

	Apps	Goals
1985-86	1	0
Total	1	0

MITCHELL Dave

Rugged Australian striker whose impressive physique made him a real presence on the pitch, but not a regular. Later made more of a splash at Swindon and Millwall.

	Apps	Goals
1983-84	7 (5)	2
1985-85	11 (3)	4
Total	18 (8)	6

MOORE Craig

Aussie full-back, who began to stake a claim for a regular place in the 1994-95 campaign, despite picking up three suspensions after a number of bookings.

	Apps	Goals
1993-94	1	0
1994-95	19 (2)	2
Total	20 (2)	2

MORRIS Eric

A star in the junior ranks, where he won a Cup medal with Irvine Meadow.
Unfortunately, he found life at Ibrox somewhat tougher and failed to make the
grade.

	Apps	Goals
1976-77	1	0
1977-78	0	0
1978-79	1	0
Total	2	0

MORROW John

Young Ulsterman who has made it into Northern Ireland's squads, although not into
the side, despite a dearth of first-team action at Ibrox.

	Apps	Goals
1991-92	1	0
1992-93	0	0
1993-94	2	0
1994-95	0	0
Total	3	0

MUNRO Iain

Another ex-Ger who has made his mark as a boss at Dunfermline, Dundee and
Hamilton, his success as a player came with St Mirren, where he won Scotland
recognition, and not at Ibrox.

	Apps	Goals
1976-77	3 (2)	0
Total	3 (2)	0

MUNRO Stuart

Signed for £15,000 from Alloa, this left-back emerged as a surprise regular in the
Souness era, despite a number of players signed to replace him. Went to Blackburn,
then Bristol City.

	Apps	Goals
1983-84	2 (3)	0
1984-85	13	0
1985-86	29 (1)	0
1986-87	43	0
1987-88	16 (1)	0
1988-89	21 (1)	2
1989-90	36	1
1990-91	14	0
Total	174 (6)	3

MURRAY Neil

Initially seen as a right-back, this university graduate became more of a midfielder. Scored the first goal in the 1993 Scottish Cup final against Aberdeen.

	Apps	Goals
1992-93	11 (5)	0
1993-94	20 (2)	0
1994-95	14 (6)	1
Total	45 (13)	1

NICHOLL Jimmy

Another with two spells at Ibrox, he won 73 caps at right-back with Northern Ireland. Won renewed affection with the Light Blue hordes, steering Raith to Coca-Cola Cup success over Celtic.

	Apps	Goals
1983-84	17	0
1984-85	0	0
1985-86	0	0
1986-87	34 (1)	0
1987-88	21 (1)	0
1988-89	1	0
Total	73 (2)	0

NISBET Scott

Started off a striker, moved to the back, but finished off his career with an outrageous fluked goal against Bruges in the Champions League, before a bad injury ended his playing days.

	Apps	Total
1985-86	4 (1)	0
1986-87	0 (1)	0
1987-88	22 (3)	0
1988-89	5 (2)	1
1989-90	4 (3)	0
1990-91	15	0
1991-92	20	5
1992-93	10	0
Total	80 (10)	6

O'HARA Alex

Midfielder with an eye for goal, who enjoyed his best days before the birth of the Premier and departed for a career at Partick Thistle and Morton.

	Apps	Goals
1975-76	1 (3)	0
1976-77	5	2
Total	6 (3)	2

PARLANE Derek

Free-scoring forward, who surprisingly failed to convert his ability on the international stage for Scotland, where he netted only once. Left to join Leeds United.

	Apps	Goals
1975-76	17 (7)	5
1976-77	31 (2)	16*
1977-78	6 (16)	5
1978-79	21 (3)	4
1979-80	2 (1)	0
Total	77 (29)	30

PATERSON Craig

Signed from Hibs for a then club record fee of £225,000, but he failed to become the sort of Greig-like inspiration so obviously missing and was sold off to Motherwell, before a move to Killie.

	Apps	Goals
1982-83	20	0
1983-83	21	1
1984-85	22	2
1985-86	18	1
1986-87	2	0
Total	83	4

PHILLIPS Jimmy

One of a number of left-backs in the early Souness days at Ibrox, and like most of the others, he did not command a regular slot. Eventually made a career for himself down south.

	Apps	Goals
1986-87	0 (6)	0
1987-88	19	0
Total	19 (6)	0

PRESSLEY Steven

Stylish and confident centre-half, likened to Richard Gough, who became fed-up waiting for a regular place, slapped in a transfer request and saw himself move to Coventry in 1994-95.

	Apps	Goals
1991-92	0 (1)	0
1992-93	8	0
1993-94	17 (6)	1
1994-95	2	0
Total	27 (7)	1

PRYTZ Robert

Superbly creative midfielder, but like so many of John Greig's signings of this era, this Swede just could not produce the goods consistently, although he had a good career in Italy.

	Apps	Goals
1982-83	24 (6)	5
1983-84	22 (4)	4
1984-85	17 (4)	3
Total	63 (14)	12

REDFORD Ian

Signed for £210,000, Scottish record fee, he had an up and down career, scoring the winner in a League Cup Final, but missing a penalty in a Scottish Cup Final. Had Euro success with Dundee United.

	Apps	Goals
1979-80	13	0
1980-81	35	9
1981-82	20 (12)	2
1982-83	29 (4)	3
1983-84	28 (4)	4
1984-85	24 (2)	5
Total	149 (22)	23

REID Brian

Looked a fantastic prospect at Morton, and went straight into the team after his £300,000 capture. But a red card at Dunfermline and a bad ligament injury ruined his Ibrox career.

	Apps	Goals
1990-91	3	0
1991-92	0	0
1992-93	2	0
1993-94	0	0
1994-95	0	0
Total	5	0

RIDEOUT Paul

Short-term signing from Southampton to act as cover up front, he developed an unfortunate habit of hitting the post rather than the net, before leaving for Everton, where he scored the winner in the FA Cup Final.

	Apps	Goals
1991-92	7 (4)	1
1992-93	0 (1)	0
Total	7 (5)	1

ROBERTS Graham

A 100% committed defender or midfielder, Roberts, signed from Spurs, became a great favourite with the fans, but not Graeme Souness, who saw him out of the door after a massive bust-up.

	Apps	Goals
1986-87	18	2
1987-88	37	1
Total	55	3

ROBERTSON Chris

Brother of Hearts' John. This winger appeared only fleetingly in the Premier Division and made the traditional exit from Ibrox to Tynecastle.

	Apps	Goals
1976-77	7 (4)	1
1977-78	2 (1)	0
1978-79	0 (2)	1
Total	9 (7)	2

ROBERTSON David

Excellent value signing from Aberdeen, he immediately established himself at left-back and became a mainstay of the Rangers defence. Is now finally establishing himself with Scotland.

	Apps	Goals
1991-92	42	1
1992-93	39	3
1993-94	32	1
1994-95	23	3
Total	136	8

ROBERTSON Dougie

Weight problems proved a bugbear for this hefty striker, who, despite not making it at Ibrox, became a real favourite and regular scorer for Morton.

	Apps	Goals
1981-82	1 (1)	0
1982-83	2 (2)	0
Total	3 (3)	0

ROBERTSON Lee

Young midfielder whose appearances have come in meaningless end of the season matches. Was the victim of a bad foul which saw Aberdeen's Lee Richardson sent off.

	Apps	Goals
1991-92	1	0
1992-93	1	0
1993-94	0	0
1994-95	0 (1)	0
Total	2 (1)	0

ROBERTSON Sandy

Sandy found winning a regular place hard work, although injury problems contributed. Went to Coventry, but his one goal will be long-remembered as crucial to the 1991 title win.

	Apps	Goals
1988-89	1 (1)	0
1989-90	0 (1)	0
1990-91	7 (8)	1
1991-92	3 (3)	0
1992-93	0 (2)	0
Total	11 (15)	1

RUSSELL Robert

Magnificent passer of a ball from midfield, Russell amazingly was never awarded a Scotland cap. After his career at Ibrox waned, he enjoyed a brief revival at Motherwell.

	Apps	Goals
1977-78	33	3
1978-79	36	4
1979-80	22 (1)	7
1980-81	23 (5)	6
1981-82	32	6
1982-83	18 (3)	1
1983-84	27 (4)	4
1984-85	9 (9)	0
1985-86	17 (9)	0
1986-87	1	0
Total	218 (31)	31

SCOTT Alistair

Now heard occasionally on local radio in the west of Scotland, this bald eagle's statistics belie the fact he had two reasonable seasons prior to the Premier Division's launch.

	Apps	Goals
1975-76	1 (1)	0
Total	1 (1)	0

SCOTT Colin

Young goalkeeper who came into the equation as both Andy Goram and Andy Maxwell got injured in the 1993-94 campaign. Took him until 1994-95 to feature on a winning side though!

	Apps	Goals
1993-94	5 (1)	0
1994-95	3 (1)	0
Total	8 (2)	0

SMITH Gordon

Unfairly remembered down south for John Motson's "And Smith Must Score" commentary in the FA Cup final with Brighton, Smith had a super career with Rangers, before returning on loan.

	Apps	Goals
1977-78	34 (1)	20
1978-79	31 (2)	11*
1979-80	20 (10)	4
1980-81	0	0
1981-82	1 (1)	0
Total	86 (14)	35

SOUNESS Graeme

Revitalised the club when he arrived as player-manager in 1986, where his influence on the pitch was as valuable as it was off it. Won Leagues and Skol Cups, but never a Scottish Cup.

	Apps	Goals
1986-87	24 (1)	1
1987-88	14 (4)	2
1988-89	0 (6)	0
1989-90	0 (1)	0
Total	38 (12)	3

SPACKMAN Nigel

Arrived from Liverpool as a replacement for Ray Wilkins, and while he could not match the playmaking qualities of Butch, he became in integral part of Rangers in central midfield.

	Apps	Goals
1989-90	21	1
1990-91	35	0
1991-92	42	0
1992-93	2	0
Total	100	1

SPENCER John

Now with Nigel Spackman at Chelsea, Spenny, a diminutive striker, was another who got disillusioned waiting for his chance and moved south. Now a Scotland international.

	Apps	Goals
1990-91	3 (2)	1
1991-92	4 (4)	1
Total	7 (6)	2

STEELE Jimmy

Played for Southampton in their FA Cup final win over Manchester United in May 1976, and was on his way, on loan, to Rangers just months later. Was not signed after a month of games.

	Apps	Goals
1976-77	5	0
Total	5	0

STEIN Colin

Scored in Rangers' tremendous Cup-Winners Cup success of 1972, but was past his best by the days of the Premier. A prolific scorer who notched 10 times in 21 Scotland appearances.

	Apps	Goals
1975-76	3 (3)	1
1976-77	1 (1)	0
Total	4 (4)	1

STERLAND Mel

He came, he played in a few league games and a Scottish Cup Final, then he left. Signed from Sheffield Wednesday, he went back to Yorkshire with Leeds.

	Apps	Goals
1988-89	7 (2)	3
Total	7 (2)	3

STEVEN Trevor

Signed, like Gary Stevens, from Everton, a massive transfer to Marseille – for around £5 million – interrupted his Rangers career, and injury troubled him after his return.

	Apps	Goals
1989-90	34	3
1990-91	19	2
1991-92	2	1
1992-93	24	5

1993-94	32	4
1994-95	10 (1)	0
Total	121 (1)	15

STEVENS Gary

Durable and reliable right-back, who proved a vital cog in the regular trophy winning side of the early nineties. Signed from Everton, this England cap left for Tranmere.

	Apps	Goals
1988-89	35	1
1989-90	35	1
1990-91	36	0
1991-92	43	2
1992-93	9	0
1993-94	28 (1)	0
1994-95	0	0
Total	186 (4)	4

STRICKLAND Derek

A regular scorer for the reserves, he found the first team a tougher nut to track and signed for Leicester in the deal that took Gregor Stevens to Ibrox.

	Apps	Goals
1978-79	1	0
Total	1	0

STEVENS Gregor

Signed from Leicester, but a dreadful disciplinary record let him down, and a string of sendings-off and bookings saw him receive a six month ban from the SFA.

	Apps	Goals
1979-80	31	1
1980-81	7 (2)	0
1981-82	13	0
1982-83	10	0
1983-84	1	0
Total	62 (2)	1

STEWART Jim

Played for Scotland with Killie, but it was from Middlesbrough Rangers signed him. Never really established himself as keeper and was eventually freed.

	Apps	Goals
1980-81	10	0
1981-82	26	0

1982-83	18	0
1983-84	2	0
Total	56	0

THOMSON Billy

Another back-up keeper, signed from Motherwell, who couldn't have expected much on arrival, but found himself in the team after some Ally Maxwell mistakes.

	Apps	Goals
1994-95	5	0
Total	5	0

URQUHART Billy

Impressed John Greig when Rangers played Highland League Caley, and was signed for a record Highland fee. But he found the step up too great and was soon on his way to Wigan.

	Apps	Goals
1978-79	6 (4)	4
1979-80	4	2
Total	10 (4)	6

VINNICOMBE Chris

Rangers took the opportunity of snapping up his potential from Exeter, but UEFA restrictions on foreigners worked against him, and he was never a regular, before moving to Burnley.

	Apps	Goals
1989-90	1 (6)	0
1990-91	10	1
1991-92	1 (1)	0
1992-93	0	0
1993-94	2 (2)	0
Total	14 (9)	1

WALKER Nicky

Only had one season as first choice, this keeper ended up understudying Chris Woods. Made an unlikely Scotland appearance whilst with Hearts in 1993.

	Apps	Goals
1983-84	8	0
1984-85	14	0
1985-86	34	0
1986-87	2	0
1987-88	5	0
1988-89	12	0
Total	75	0

WALTERS Mark

Skillful winger who came from Aston Villa and started scoring and creating goals regularly. But another to fall foul of the restrictions on foreigners, and Souness took him to Liverpool.

	Apps	Goals
1987-88	18	7
1988-89	30 (1)	8
1989-90	27	5
1990-91	26 (4)	12*
Total	101 (5)	32

WATSON Kenny

Signed from Montrose, Watson was a skillful midfielder, with a spotty Ibrox career. In and out of the side before Partick Thistle moved in.

	Apps	Goals
1976-77	30	3
1977-78	2 (2)	0
1978-79	11 (2)	2
1979-80	12 (3)	0
Total	55 (7)	5

WATSON Steve

Scouse full-back who received a shock call-up to the full team at the latter end of the 1992-93 season. But later he was allowed to join St Mirren.

	Apps	Goals
1992-93	3	0
Total	3	0

WEST Colin

Claimed a bit of history as Graeme Souness's first signing, but an injury picked up against Hamilton in only his fourth game was to prevent the big striker's Ibrox career getting off the ground.

	Apps	Goals
1986-87	4 (5)	2
1987-88	0 (1)	0
Total	4 (6)	2

WILKINS Ray

An inspired signing from Paris St Germain, Wilkins enjoyed two golden years at Ibrox where he was idolised for his superb passing ability from midfield.

	Apps	Goals
1987-88	24	1
1988-89	30 (1)	1
1989-90	15	0
Total	69 (1)	2

WILLIAMSON Bobby

Hustling striker who was unlucky with injury after his capture from Clydebank. Was a relative success in England with WBA and Rotherham before moving to Kilmarnock.

	Apps	Goals
1983-84	16 (1)	6
1984-85	0 (1)	0
1985-86	20 (4)	6
Total	36 (6)	12

WISHART Fraser

Signed on a free from Falkirk, Wishart acquitted himself well any time he played, but could not command a regular place and was sold on to Hearts for £50,000.

	Apps	Goals
1993-94	5	0
1994-95	3 (1)	0
Total	8 (1)	0

WOODS Chris

The second big-money arrival at Ibrox under Graeme Souness, Woods was a superb keeper who only lost his place because of Walter Smith's need to find a Scottish number one.

	Apps	Goals
1986-87	42	0
1987-88	39	0
1988-89	24	0
1989-90	32	0
1990-91	36	0
Total	173	0

WOODS Neil

Souness saw some potential in this English forward, but proceeded to play him in the reserves rather than the first team, and he was soon discarded to move to Ipswich.

	Apps	Goals
1986-87	0 (3)	0
Total	0 (3)	0

YOUNG George

Signed from Stirling Albion for £10,000, this back-up keeper deputised twice for Peter McCloy, but was back in the second team after a 2-1 loss to Hibs.

	Apps	Goals
1979-80	2	0
Total	2	0

YOUNG Quinton

Not many Quintons have played for Rangers! Young was another whose better days preceded the Premier and this winger left Ibrox under a cloud in April 1976.

	Apps	Goals
1975-76	7 (1)	2
Total	7 (1)	2

All-time Records and Statistics

Year by Year League and Cup Records

Year	P	W	D	L	F	A	Pts	Pos	LC	SC	EC
Scottish League											
1890-91	18	13	3	2	58	25	29	1*	–	1R	–
1891-92	22	12	2	8	57	49	26	4	–	SF	–
1892-93	18	12	4	2	41	27	28	2	–	3R	–
1893-94	18	8	4	6	44	30	20	4	–	Won	–

* Championship shared with Dumbarton.

First Division											
1894-95	18	10	2	6	41	26	22	3	–	1R	–
1895-96	18	11	4	3	57	39	26	2	–	3R	–
1896-97	18	11	3	4	64	30	25	3	–	Won	–
1897-98	18	13	3	2	71	15	29	2	–	Won	–
1898-99	18	18	0	0	79	18	36	1	–	Final	–
1899-00	18	15	2	1	69	27	32	1	–	SF	–
1900-01	20	17	1	2	60	25	35	1	–	1R	–
1901-02	18	13	2	3	43	29	28	1	–	SF	–
1902-03	22	12	5	5	56	30	29	3	–	Won	–
1903-04	26	16	6	4	80	33	38	4	–	Final	–
1904-05	26	18	5	3	68	31	41	2	–	Final	–
1905-06	30	15	7	8	58	48	37	4	–	3R	–
1906-07	34	19	7	8	69	33	45	3	–	3R	–
1907-08	34	21	8	5	74	40	50	3	–	2R	–
1908-09	34	19	7	8	91	38	45	4	–	Final†	–
1909-10	34	20	6	8	70	35	46	3	–	2R	–
1910-11	34	23	6	5	90	34	52	1	–	3R	–
1911-12	34	24	3	7	86	34	51	1	–	2R	–
1912-13	34	24	5	5	76	41	53	1	–	3R	–
1913-14	38	27	5	6	79	31	59	2	–	3R	–

† Cup withheld after riot at the end of second replay between Celtic and Rangers.

Division A											
1914-15	38	23	4	11	74	47	50	3	–	n/c	–

Scottish League											
1915-16	38	25	6	7	87	39	56	2	–	n/c	–
1916-17	38	24	5	9	68	32	53	3	–	n/c	–
1917-18	34	25	6	3	66	24	56	1	–	n/c	–

Year	P	W	D	L	F	A	Pts	Pos	LC	SC	EC
1918-19	34	26	5	3	86	16	57	2	–	n/c	–
1919-20	42	31	9	2	106	25	71	1	–	SF	–
1920-21	42	35	6	1	91	24	76	1	–	Final	–

First Division

Year	P	W	D	L	F	A	Pts	Pos	LC	SC	EC
1921-22	42	28	10	4	83	26	66	2	–	Final	–
1922-23	38	23	9	6	67	29	55	1	–	2R	–
1923-24	38	25	9	4	72	22	59	1	–	3R	–
1924-25	38	25	10	3	77	27	60	1	–	SF	–
1925-26	38	19	6	13	79	55	44	6	–	SF	–
1926-27	38	23	10	5	85	41	56	1	–	4R	–
1927-28	38	26	8	4	109	36	60	1	–	Won	–
1928-29	38	30	7	1	107	32	67	1	–	Final	–
1929-30	38	28	4	6	94	32	60	1	–	Won	–
1930-31	38	27	6	5	96	29	60	1	–	2R	–
1931-32	38	28	5	5	118	42	61	2	–	Won	–
1932-33	38	26	10	2	113	43	62	1	–	3R	–
1933-34	38	30	6	2	118	41	66	1	–	Won	–
1934-35	38	25	5	8	96	46	55	1	–	Won	–
1935-36	38	27	7	4	110	43	61	2	–	Won	–
1936-37	38	26	9	3	88	32	61	1	–	1R	–
1937-38	38	18	13	7	75	49	49	3	–	SF	–
1938-39	38	25	9	4	112	55	59	1	–	3R	–

Division A

Year	P	W	D	L	F	A	Pts	Pos	LC	SC	EC
1946-47	30	21	4	5	76	26	46	1	2R	Won	–
1947-48	30	21	4	5	64	28	46	2	Won	SF	–
1948-49	30	20	6	4	63	32	46	1	Won	Won	–
1949-50	30	22	6	2	58	26	50	1	Won	SF	–
1950-51	30	17	4	9	64	37	38	2	2R	FQ	–
1951-52	30	16	9	5	61	31	41	2	4R	Final	–
1952-53	30	18	7	5	80	39	43	1	Won	SF	–
1953-54	30	13	8	9	56	35	34	4	SF	SF	–
1954-55	30	19	3	8	67	33	41	3	6R	QF	–
1955-56	34	22	8	4	85	27	52	1	7R	SF	–

First Division

Year	P	W	D	L	F	A	Pts	Pos	LC	SC	EC
1956-57	34	26	3	5	96	48	55	1	6R	FQ	1R A
1957-58	34	22	5	7	89	49	49	2	SF	Final	2R A
1958-59	34	21	8	5	92	51	50	1	3R	FQ	FQ B
1959-60	34	17	8	9	72	38	42	3	Won	FQ	SF A
1960-61	34	23	5	6	88	46	51	1	3R	Won	Fin B

273

Year	P	W	D	L	F	A	Pts	Pos	LC	SC	EC
1961-62	34	22	7	5	84	31	51	2	Won	Won	QF A
1962-63	34	25	7	2	94	28	57	1	SF	Won	2R B
1963-64	34	25	5	4	85	31	55	1	Won	Won	Pre A
1964-65	34	18	8	8	78	35	44	5	Final	3R	QF A
1965-66	34	25	5	4	91	29	55	2	Final	Won	FQ B
1966-67	34	24	7	3	92	31	55	2	Final	1R	Fin. B
1967-68	34	28	5	1	93	34	61	2	FQ	3R	QF C
1968-69	34	21	7	6	81	32	49	2	FQ	Final	SF C
1969-70	34	19	7	8	67	40	45	2	FQ	3R	2R B
1970-71	34	16	9	9	58	34	41	4	Won	Final	1R C
1971-72	34	21	2	11	71	38	44	3	FQ	SF	Won B
1972-73	34	26	4	4	74	30	56	2	SF	Won	Banned
1973-74	34	21	6	7	67	34	48	3	SF	4R	2R B
1974-75	34	25	6	3	86	33	56	1	FQ	3R	FQ B

Premier Division

Year	P	W	D	L	F	A	Pts	Pos	LC	SC	EC
1975-76	36	23	8	5	59	24	54	1	Won	Won	2R A
1976-77	36	18	10	8	62	37	46	2	SF	Final	1R A
1977-78	36	24	7	5	76	39	55	1	Won	Won	1R B
1978-79	36	18	9	9	52	35	45	2	Won	Won	QF A
1979-80	36	15	7	14	50	46	37	5	3R	Final	2R B
1980-81	36	16	12	8	60	32	44	3	2R	Won	FQ
1981-82	36	16	11	9	57	45	43	3	Won	Final	1R B
1982-83	36	13	12	11	52	41	38	4	Final	Final	2R D
1983-84	36	15	12	9	53	41	42	4	Won	5R	2R B
1984-85	36	13	12	11	47	38	38	4	Won	4R	2R D
1985-86	36	13	9	14	53	45	35	5	SF	3R	1R D
1986-87	44	31	7	6	85	23	69	1	Won	3R	3R D
1987-88	44	26	8	10	85	34	60	3	Won	4R	QF A
1988-89	36	26	4	6	62	26	56	1	Won	Final	2R D
1989-90	36	20	11	5	48	19	51	1	Final	4R	1R A
1990-91	36	24	7	5	62	23	55	1	Won	QF	2R A
1991-92	44	33	6	5	101	31	72	1	SF	Won	1R A
1992-93	44	33	7	4	97	35	73	1	Won	Won	ChL A
1993-94	44	22	14	8	74	41	56	1	Won	Final	1R A
1994-95	36	20	9	7	60	35	69	1	3R	4R	Pre A

n/c– No Competition   LC – League Cup   SC – Scottish Cup

QF – Quarter Finals   SF – Semi-Finals   Final – Beaten finalists

ChL – Champions League   FQ – Failed to qualify from section

EC – European Competition

     (A) – European Cup   (B) – European Cup Winners' Cup

     (C) – Fairs Cup   (D) – UEFA Cup

1946-47

Section	*v.* St Mirren	(h)	4-0	Cox, Stead, Arnison 2
Section	*v.* Queen's Park	(a)	4-2	Duncanson 2, Gillick, Thornton
Section	*v.* Morton	(h)	3-0	Duncanson, Thornton, Caskie
Section	*v.* St Mirren	(a)	4-0	Gillick 2, Thornton 2
Section	*v.* Queen's Park	(h)	1-0	Arnison
Section	*v.* Morton	(a)	2-0	Young pen., Thornton

Won section

1st Quarter Final	*v.* Dundee United	(h)	2-1	Waddell, Caskie
2nd Quarter Final	*v.* Dundee United	(a)	1-1	Duncanson
Semi-Final	*v.* Hibernian	(H)	3-1	Gillick, Thornton, Waddell
Final	*v.* Aberdeen	(H)	4-0	Gillick, Williamson, Duncanson 2

1947-48

Section	*v.* Celtic	(h)	2-0	Williamson 2
Section	*v.* Third Lanark	(a)	3-1	Williamson 2, Duncanson
Section	*v.* Dundee	(h)	3-0	Williamson, Gillick, Thornton
Section	*v.* Celtic	(a)	0-2	
Section	*v.* Third Lanark	(h)	3-0	Gillick, Findlay 2
Section	*v.* Dundee	(a)	1-1	Paton

Won section

Quarter Final	*v.* Stenhousemuir	(h)	2-0	Findlay, Thornton
Semi-Final	*v.* Falkirk	(H)	0-1	

1948-49

Section	*v.* Clyde	(h)	1-1	Findlay
Section	*v.* Hibernian	(a)	0-0	
Section	*v.* Celtic	(a)	1-3	Findlay
Section	*v.* Clyde	(a)	3-1	Waddell 3, 2 pen.
Section	*v.* Hibernian	(h)	1-0	Thornton
Section	*v.* Celtic	(h)	2-1	Williamson, Waddell

Won section

Quarter Final	*v.* St Mirren	(h)	1-0	Thornton

Semi-Final	v. Dundee	(H)	4-1	Rutherford, McColl, Duncanson, Thornton
Final	v. Raith Rovers	(H)	2-0	Gillick, Paton

1949-50

Section	v. Celtic	(a)	2-3	Waddell pen., Thornton
Section	v. St Mirren	(h)	5-1	Waddell 2 (1 pen.), Rutherford, Findlay, Thornton
Section	v. Aberdeen	(h)	4-2	Findlay 2, Duncanson 2
Section	v. Celtic	(h)	2-0	Findlay, Waddell
Section	v. St Mirren	(a)	1-1	Duncanson
Section	v. Aberdeen	(a)	1-1	Findlay
Won section				
1st Quarter Final	v. Cowdenbeath	(h)	2-3	Williamson, Marshall
2nd Quarter Final	v. Cowdenbeath	(a)	3-1 aet	Cox 2, Rutherford
Semi-Final	v. East Fife	(H)	1-2	Marshall

1950-51

Section	v. Morton	(a)	2-1	Rutherford, Findlay
Section	v. Aberdeen	(h)	1-2	Findlay
Section	v. Clyde	(h)	4-0	Thornton 3, Dunn OG
Section	v. Morton	(h)	6-1	Findlay 2, Thornton 2, Paton 2
Section	v. Aberdeen	(a)	0-2	
Section	v. Clyde	(a)	5-3	Thornton 2, Findlay 2, Paton

Second in section. Aberdeen qualified

1951-52

Section	v. East Fife	(a)	0-0	
Section	v. Aberdeen	(h)	2-1	Rutherford, Paton
Section	v. Queen of the South	(a)	3-0	Simpson 2, Waddell
Section	v. East Fife	(h)	4-1	Simpson 2, Waddell pen., Findlay
Section	v. Aberdeen	(a)	1-2	Simpson
Section	v. Queen of the South	(h)	5-2	Thornton 3, McColl, Simpson

Won section

1st Quarter Final	v. Dunfermline	(a)	0-1	
2nd Quarter Final	v. Dunfermline	(h)	3-1	Findlay 2, Gardiner
Semi-Final	v. Celtic	(H)	3-0	Thornton, Johnson, Findlay
Final	v. Dundee	(H)	2-3	Findlay, Young

1952-53

Section	v. Hearts	(a)	0-5	
Section	v. Motherwell	(h)	2-0	Thornton, Liddell
Section	v. Aberdeen	(h)	3-1	Grierson 2, Thornton
Section	v. Hearts	(h)	2-0	Thornton, Liddell
Section	v. Motherwell	(a)	3-3	Prentice, Thornton, Paton
Section	v. Aberdeen	(a)	2-1	Waddell, Thornton

Won section

1st Quarter Final	v. Third Lanark	(h)	0-0	
2nd Quarter Final	v. Third Lanark	(a)	2-0	Grierson, Thornton
Semi-Final	v. Kilmarnock	(H)	0-1	

1953-54

Section	v. Raith Rovers	(a)	4-0	Young pen., Prentice, Simpson, Grierson
Section	v. Hearts	(h)	4-1	Simpson, Hubbard, Young pen., Grierson
Section	v. Hamilton A	(h)	5-1	Grierson 3, Paton 2
Section	v. Raith Rovers	(h)	3-1	McCulloch, Paton 2
Section	v. Hearts	(a)	1-1	Grierson
Section	v. Hamilton A	(a)	5-0	Paton 4, Waddell

Won section

1st Quarter Final	v. Ayr United	(h)	4-2	Prentice 3, Grierson
2nd Quarter Final	v. Ayr United	(a)	2-3	Waddell pen., Paton
Semi-Final	v. Partick Th	(H)	0-2	

1954-55

Section	v. Stirling A	(a)	5-0	Prentice 2, Simpson 3
Section	v. Partick Th	(h)	1-1	Davidson OG
Section	v. Clyde	(h)	1-3	Grierson
Section	v. Stirling A	(h)	2-0	Paton, Hubbard pen.
Section	v. Partick Th	(a)	2-1	Prentice, Simpson
Section	v. Clyde	(a)	2-1	Simpson, Paton

Won section

1st Quarter Final	v. Motherwell	(a)	1-2	Prentice
2nd Quarter Final	v. Motherwell	(h)	1-1	Paton

1955-56

Section	v. Falkirk	(a)	5-0	Scott, Murray, Hubbard 2, McMillan
Section	v. Falkirk	(h)	4-3	Hubbard 2, Scott, Murray
Section	v. Queen of the South	(a)	2-1	Hubbard, Scott
Section	v. Celtic	(h)	1-4	Fallon og.
Section	v. Celtic	(a)	4-0	Baird 2, Simpson, Murray
Section	v. Queen of the South	(h)	6-0	Arnison 2, Hubbard Simpson, Scott 2
1st Quarter Final	v. Hamilton	(a)	2-1	Hubbard, Simpson
2nd Quarter Final	v. Hamilton	(h)	8-0	Scott 3, Simpson 2, Prentice, Hubbard 2
Semi-Final	v. Aberdeen	(H)	1-2	Hubbard

1956-57

Section	v. East Fife	(h)	3-0	Simpson 2, Hubbard pen.
Section	v. Celtic	(a)	1-2	Murray
Section	v. Aberdeen	(a)	6-2	Simpson 2, Murray 2, Shearer, Hubbard
Section	v. East Fife	(a)	4-1	Murray, Simpson, Hubbard pen., Rae
Section	v. Celtic	(h)	0-0	
Section	v. Aberdeen	(h)	4-1	Simpson 2, Hubbard pen., Scott

Second in section. Celtic qualified

1957-58

Section	v. St Mirren	(h)	6-0	Murray 3, Simpson 3
Section	v. Partick Th	(a)	1-0	Baird
Section	v. Raith Rovers	(h)	4-3	Scott, Leigh OG, Murray, Simpson
Section	v. St Mirren	(a)	4-0	Scott, Murray 2, Baird
Section	v. Partick Th	(h)	0-3	
Section	v. Raith Rovers	(a)	3-4	Scott 2, Hubbard pen.

Won section

1st Quarter Final	v. Kilmarnock	(a)	1-2	Kichenbrand
2nd Quarter Final	v. Kilmarnock	(h)	3-1	Hubbard pen., Scott, Simpson
Semi-Final	v. Brechin City	(H)	4-0	Melrose 2., Shearer pen., Paterson OG
Final	v. Celtic	(H)	1-7	Simpson

1958-59

Section	v. Hearts	(h)	3-0	Wilson, Hubbard, Milne OG
Section	v. Raith Rovers	(a)	1-3	Hubbard pen.
Section	v. Third Lanark	(h)	2-2	Brand, Murray
Section	v. Hearts	(a)	1-2	Hubbard pen
Section	v. Raith Rovers	(a)	6-0	Murray, Simpson 3, Wilson, Hubbard pen
Section	v. Third Lanark	(a)	3-0	Murray 3

Second in section. Hearts qualified

1959-60

Section	v. Hibernian	(a)	6-1	Brand 4, Matthew, Millar
Section	v. Motherwell	(h)	1-2	Scott
Section	v. Dundee	(h)	2-0	Brand, Wilson
Section	v. Hibernian	(h)	5-1	Baird, Wilson 2, Millar 2
Section	v. Motherwell	(a)	1-2	Millar
Section	v. Dundee	(a)	3-2	Millar, Wilson, Baird

Second in section. Motherwell qualified

1960-61

Section	v. Partick Th	(h)	3-1	Scott, Millar 2
Section	v. Third Lanark	(a)	1-2	Millar
Section	v. Celtic	(h)	2-3	Millar, Brand
Section	v. Partick Th	(a)	4-1	McMillan 2, Millar, Brand
Section	v. Third Lanark	(h)	3-2	Millar 2, and OG
Section	v. Celtic	(a)	2-1	Davis, Brand
Won section				
1st Quarter Final	v. Dundee	(h)	1-0	Scott
2nd Quarter Final	v. Dundee	(a)	4-3	Wilson, McMillan 2, Brand

Semi-Final	v. Queen of the South	(H)	7-0	Brand 3, Millar 2, McMillan, Scott
Final	v. Kilmarnock	(H)	2-0	Brand, Scott

1961-62

Section	v. Third Lanark	(a)	2-0	Wilson 2
Section	v. Dundee	(h)	4-2	Brand 2, Wilson, Millar
Section	v. Airdrie	(a)	2-1	Brand, Davis
Section	v. Third Lanark	(h)	5-0	Wilson 2, Brand, Millar, McGillivray OG
Section	v. Dundee	(a)	1-1	Brand
Section	v. Airdrie	(h)	4-1	Greig, Christie, Brand 2
Won section				
1st Quarter Final	v. East Fife	(h)	3-1	Davis, Christie 2
2nd Quarter Final	v. East Fife	(a)	3-1	Wilson, Scott, Brand
Semi-Final	v. St Johnstone	(Cel)	3-2	Wilson 2, Caldow pen.
Final	v. Hearts	(H)	1-1 aet	Millar
Replay	v. Hearts	(H)	3-1	Millar, Brand, McMillan

1962-63

Section	v. Hibernian	(a)	4-1	Henderson, Brand 2, 1 pen., Wilson
Section	v. Third Lanark	(h)	5-2	Millar 3, Scott, Wilson
Section	v. St Mirren	(a)	1-2	Murray
Section	v. Hibernian	(h)	0-0	
Section	v. Third Lanark	(a)	5-3	Millar 3, Scott 2
Section	v. St Mirren	(h)	4-0	Millar, Greig 3
Won section				
1st Quarter Final	v. Dumbarton	(a)	3-1	Millar, Greig, Watson pen.
2nd Quarter Final	v. Dumbarton	(h)	1-1	Greig
Semi-Final	v. Kilmarnock	(H)	2-3	Brand 2

1963-64

Section	v. Celtic	(a)	3-0	Forrest 2, McLean
Section	v. Queen of the South	(h)	5-2	McLean, Wilson 2, Forrest, Provan
Section	v. Kilmarnock	(a)	4-1	Henderson, McLean

280

				Brand 2
Section	v. Celtic	(h)	3-0	Wilson, Brand pen., Forrest
Section	v. Queen of the South	(a)	5-2	Forrest 4, Wilson
Section	v. Kilmarnock	(h)	2-2	Wilson, Forrest
Won section				
1st Quarter Final	v. East Fife	(a)	1-1	Forrest
2nd Quarter Final	v. East Fife	(h)	2-0	Brand pen., Forrest
Semi-Final	v. Berwick Rangers	(H)	3-1	Wilson, Brand, Forrest
Final	v. Morton	(H)	5-0	Forrest 4, Willoughby

1964-65

Section	v. Aberdeen	(h)	4-0	Forrest, McLean 2, Wilson
Section	v. St Mirren	(a)	0-0	
Section	v. St Johnstone	(a)	9-1	McLean 2, Forrest 4, Brand 2, Baxter
Section	v. Aberdeen	(a)	4-3	Forrest 3, Brand
Section	v. St Mirren	(h)	6-2	Baxter, Forrest, McLean, Brand, Henderson, Wilson
Section	v. St Johnstone	(h)	3-1	Forrest
Won section				
1st Quarter Final	v. Dunfermline	(a)	3-0	Forrest, Brand, McLean OG
2nd Quarter Final	v. Dunfermline	(h)	2-2	Millar, Forrest
Semi-Final	v. Dundee United	(H)	2-1 aet	Forrest 2
Final	v. Celtic	(H)	2-1	Forrest 2

965-66

Section	v. Hearts	(a)	2-4	Forrest 2, 1 pen., Wallace 2
Section	v. Clyde	(h)	3-0	Willoughby 2, Forrest
Section	v. Aberdeen	(a)	0-2	
Section	v. Hearts	(h)	1-0	Johnston
Section	v. Clyde	(a)	3-1	Johnston, Willoughby, Forrest
Section	v. Aberdeen	(h)	4-0	Forrest 3, McLean
Won section				
1st Quarter Final	v. Airdrie	(a)	5-1	Greig, McLean 2, Forrest, Willoughby

2nd Quarter Final	v. Airdrie	(h)	4-0	Forrest 3, McLean
Semi-Final	v. Kilmarnock	(H)	6-4	McLean 3, 1 pen
				Willoughby, Forrest,
				Henderson
Final	v. Celtic	(H)	1-2	Young OG

1966-67

Section	v. Hibernian	(h)	1-0	McLean
Section	v. Stirling A	(a)	8-0	Wilson, McLean 2,
				1 pen, Forrest 5
Section	v. Kilmarnock	(h)	0-0	
Section	v. Hibernian	(a)	2-3	McLean, A. Smith
Section	v. Stirling A	(h)	1-1	A. Smith
Section	v. Kilmarnock	(a)	1-0	Forrest
Won section				
1st Quarter Final	v. Ayr United	(a)	1-1	Johnston
2nd Quarter Final	v. Ayr United	(h)	3-0	McLean 2, Greig
Semi-Final	v. Aberdeen	(H)	2-2	Henderson 2
Replay	v. Aberdeen	(H)	2-0	Johnston, A. Smith
Final	v. Celtic	(H)	0-1	

1967-68

Section	v. Aberdeen	(a)	1-1	Persson
Section	v. Celtic	(h)	1-1	Penman
Section	v. Dundee United	(h)	1-0	Johansen pen.
Section	v. Aberdeen	(h)	3-0	Penman 2, Jardine
Section	v. Celtic	(a)	1-3	Henderson
Section	v. Dundee United	(a)	3-0	Ferguson 2,
				Johnston

Second in section. Celtic qualified

1968-69

Section	v. Celtic	(h)	0-2	
Section	v. Partick Thistle	(a)	5-1	A. Smith 2,
				Ferguson 2, Persson
Section	v. Morton	(h)	2-0	Jackson 2
Section	v. Celtic	(a)	0-1	
Section	v. Partick Thistle	(h)	2-1	Henderson, Jardine
Section	v. Morton	(a)	5-0	Jardine 2,
				Henderson 2,
				Penman

Second in section. Celtic qualified

1969-70

Section	*v.* Raith Rovers	(a)	3-2	Johansen, Stein, MacDonald
Section	*v.* Celtic	(h)	2-1	Persson, Johnston
Section	*v.* Airdrie	(a)	3-0	Persson, Jardine, Watson
Section	*v.* Celtic	(a)	0-1	
Section	*v.* Raith Rovers	(h)	3-3	Polland OG, Penman, MacDonald
Section	*v.* Airdrie	(h)	3-0	Stein, Johnston, Penman

Second in section. Celtic qualified

1970-71

Section	*v.* Dunfermline	(h)	4-1	Stein 2, Jardine, Johnston pen,
Section	*v.* Motherwell	(a)	2-0	Fyfe, Henderson
Section	*v.* Morton	(h)	0-0	
Section	*v.* Motherwell	(h)	2-0	Penman, Stein
Section	*v.* Dunfermline	(a)	6-0	Johnston 3, 1 pen Jackson, Fyfe, Stein
Section	*v.* Morton	(a)	2-0	Johnston, Conn
Won section				
1st Quarter Final	*v.* Hibernian	(a)	3-1	Conn, Fyfe 2
2nd Quarter Final	*v.* Hibernian	(a)	3-1	MacDonald, Greig, Fyfe
Semi-Final	*v.* Cowdenbeath	(H)	2-0	Johnston pen., Stein
Final	*v.* Celtic	(H)	1-0	Johnstone

1971-72

Section	*v.* Celtic	(a)	0-2	
Section	*v.* Ayr United	(h)	4-0	Johnstone 2, Stein, McLean pen.
Section	*v.* Morton	(h)	2-0	Johnstone, MacDonald
Section	*v.* Ayr United	(a)	4-0	Stein 2, MacDonald, Johnstone
Section	*v.* Celtic	(h)	0-3	
Section	*v.* Morton	(a)	1-0	Stein

Second in section. Celtic qualified

1972-73

Section	*v.* Clydebank	(h)	2-0	Conn, MacDonald
Section	*v.* St Mirren	(a)	4-0	Johnstone, Greig, Stein, Conn
Section	*v.* Ayr United	(h)	2-1	Johnston, Parlane
Section	*v.* St Mirren	(h)	1-4	Conn
Section	*v.* Clydebank	(a)	5-0	Greig, McLean pen., Smith, Stein, Johnstone
Section	*v.* Ayr United	(a)	2-1	Johnston, Johnstone

Won section

2nd Rnd, 1st Leg	*v.* Stenhousemuir	(a)	5-0	Johnstone 3, Parlane, Greig
2nd Rnd, 2nd Leg	*v.* Stenhousemuir	(h)	1-2	Fyfe
1st Quarter Final	*v.* St Johnstone	(h)	1-1	Parlane
2nd Quarter Final	*v.* St Johnstone	(a)	2-0	Young, Parlane pen.
Semi-Final	*v.* Hibernian	(H)	0-1	

1973-74

Section	*v.* Falkirk	(h)	3-1	Scott 2, Conn
Section	*v.* Arbroath	(a)	2-1	Conn, Parlane
Section	*v.* Celtic	(h)	1-2	McNeill OG
Section	*v.* Arbroath	(h)	3-0	MacDonald, Conn, Smith
Section	*v.* Celtic	(a)	3-1	MacDonald, Parlane, Conn
Section	*v.* Falkirk	(a)	5-1	O'Hara, McLean, Forsyth, Conn 2

Won section

2nd Rnd, 1st Leg	*v.* Dumbarton	(h)	6-0	Parlane 3, 1 pen., Young 2, Greig pen.
2nd Rnd, 2nd Leg	*v.* Dumbarton	(a)	2-1	Scott, Fyfe
1st Quarter Final	*v.* Hibernian	(h)	2-0	Greig, Schaedler OG
2nd Quarter Final	*v.* Hibernian	(a)	0-0	
Semi-Final	*v.* Celtic	(H)	1-3	MacDonald

1974-75

Section	*v.* St Johnstone	(h)	3-2	Scott, Jardine, Parlane
Section	*v.* Hibernian	(a)	1-3	Scott
Section	*v.* St Johnstone	(a)	6-3	Young 2, Jardine 2, Scott, Forsyth
Section	*v.* Dundee	(a)	2-0	Jardine, Fyfe
Section	*v.* Dundee	(h)	4-0	Jardine pen., Scott, Johnstone 2

Section	v. Hibernian	(h)	0-1	
Second in section. Hibs qualified				

1975-76

Section	v. Airdrie	(h)	6-1	Jardine 3, 2 pens., Stein, Parlane, Miller pen.
Section	v. Clyde	(a)	1-0	Johnstone
Section	v. Motherwell	(h)	1-1	Greig
Section	v. Clyde	(h)	6-0	Parlane 2, Jackson, Miller pen., Young, Johnstone
Section	v. Motherwell	(a)	2-2	Jardine, Miller pen.
Section	v. Airdrie	(a)	2-1	Johnstone, Young
Won section				
1st Quarter Final	v. Queen of the South	(h)	1-0	Johnstone
2nd Quarter Final	v. Queen of the South	(a)	2-2	Johnstone, MacDonald
Semi-Final	v. Montrose	(H)	5-1	Parlane, Johnstone, Miller pen., Scott, Jardine
Final	v. Celtic	(H)	1-0	MacDonald

1976-77

Section	v. St Johnstone	(h)	5-0	Jardine 2, Johnstone, Miller pen., Henderson
Section	v. Hibernian	(a)	1-1	Munro
Section	v. Montrose	(h)	4-0	Johnstone 2, Jardine, MacDonald
Section	v. Hibernian	(h)	3-0	Miller pen., Jardine, McLean.
Section	v. Montrose	(a)	3-0	Johnstone, Parlane, Jardine
Section	v. St. Johnstone	(a)	1-0	Jardine
Won section				
1st Quarter Final	v. Clydebank	(h)	3-3	Johnstone, MacDonald, Hamilton
2nd Quarter Final	v. Clydebank	(a)	1-1 aet	Greig
Replay	v. Clydebank	(h)	0-0 aet	
2nd Replay	v. Clydebank	(Fir)	2-1	Parlane, McKean
Semi-Final	v. Aberdeen	(H)	1-5	MacDonald

1977-78

2nd Rnd, 1st Leg	v. St Johnstone	(h)	3-1	Johnstone 2, Miller pen.
2nd Rnd, 2nd Leg	v. St Johnstone	(a)	3-0	Parlane, Miller pen., Smith
3rd Rnd, 1st Leg	v. Aberdeen	(h)	6-1	Smith 3, Johnstone, Miller pen., MacDonald
3rd Rnd, 2nd Leg	v. Aberdeen	(a)	1-3	Smith
1st Quarter Final	v. Dunfermline	(h)	3-1	Jackson, McLean 2
2nd Quarter Final	v. Dunfermline	(a)	3-1	Greig, Jardine pen., Johnstone
Semi-Final	v. Forfar	(H)	5-2 aet	Johnstone 2, Parlane 2, MacDonald
Final	v. Celtic	(H)	2-1 aet	Cooper, Smith

1978-79

1st Rnd, 1st Leg	v. Albion Rovers	(h)	3-0	Parlane, Johnstone, Smith
1st Rnd, 2nd Leg	v. Albion Rovers	(a)	1-0	Parlane
2nd Rnd, 1st Leg	v. Forfar	(h)	3-0	Cooper, McLean, Smith
2nd Rnd, 2nd Leg	v. Forfar	(a)	4-1	MacDonald, Cooper Smith 2
3rd Rnd, 1st Leg	v. St Mirren	(h)	3-2	Cooper, Miller, Johnstone
3rd Rnd, 2nd Leg	v. St Mirren	(a)	0-0	
1st Quarter Final	v. Arbroath	(h)	1-0	Wells OG
2nd Quarter Final	v. Arbroath	(a)	2-1	Smith, Russell
Semi-Final	v. Celtic	(H)	3-2 aet	Jardine, Jackson, Casey OG
Final	v. Aberdeen	(H)	2-1	MacDonald, Jackson

1979-80

2nd Rnd, 1st Leg	v. Clyde	(a)	2-1	Dawson, Robertson
2nd Rnd, 2nd Leg	v. Clyde	(h)	4-0	O'Neill OG Mackay 2, Smith
3rd Rnd, 1st Leg	v. Aberdeen	(a)	1-3	Johnstone
3rd Rnd, 2nd Leg	v. Aberdeen	(h)	0-2	

1980-81

1st Rnd, 1st Leg	v. Forfar	(a)	2-0	McAdam 2
1st Rnd, 2nd Leg	v. Forfar	(h)	3-1	Miller pen., Johnston,

				McAdam pen.
2nd Rnd, 1st Leg	v. Aberdeen	(h)	1-0	McAdam
2nd Rnd, 2nd Leg	v. Aberdeen	(a)	1-3	McAdam

1981-82

Section	v. Morton	(a)	1-1	McAdam
Section	v. Dundee	(h)	4-1	McAdam, Johnstone, Miller, MacDonald
Section	v. Raith Rovers	(h)	8-1	Jardine, Russell 2, McAdam, Redford 4
Section	v. Dundee	(a)	2-1	McGeachie OG, Stevens
Section	v. Morton	(h)	1-0	Johnstone
Section	v. Raith Rovers	(a)	3-1	Redford, Johnstone, MacDonald

Won section

1st Quarter Final	v. Brechin City	(a)	4-0	Russell, Jackson, McLean pen., Redford
2nd Quarter Final	v. Brechin City	(h)	1-0	MacDonald
1st Semi-Final	v. St Mirren	(H)	2-2	McAdam, MacDonald
2nd Semi-Final	v. St Mirren	(h)	2-1	Bett pen., MacDonald
Final	v. Dundee United	(H)	2-1	Cooper, Redford

1982-83

Section	v. Hibernian	(a)	1-1	MacDonald
Section	v. Airdrie	(h)	3-1	Bett, Paterson, Black
Section	v. Clydebank	(a)	4-1	Prytz, MacDonald 2, McClelland
Section	v. Airdrie	(a)	2-1	Dalziel, Paterson
Section	v. Hibernian	(h)	0-0	
Section	v. Clydebank	(h)	3-2	MacDonald, Prytz pen., Redford

Won section

1st Quarter Final	v. Kilmarnock	(a)	6-1	Cooper 4, MacDonald 2
2nd Quarter Final	v. Kilmarnock	(h)	6-0	MacDonald 2, Johnstone 2, Bett pen. McPherson
1st Semi-Final	v. Hearts	(h)	2-0	Cooper, Bett

2nd Semi-Final	v. Hearts	(a)	2-1	Bett pen., Johnstone
Final	v. Celtic	(H)	1-2	Bett

1983-84

2nd Rnd, 1st Leg	v. Queen of the South	(h)	4-0	Clark, MacDonald 2, Prytz pen.
2nd Rnd, 2nd Leg	v. Queen of the South	(a)	4-1	Mitchell, McKinnon, Cooper, McCoist
Section	v. Clydebank	(h)	4-0	McCoist 2, Russell, Prytz
Section	v. Hearts	(a)	3-0	Gauld OG, Clark 2
Section	v. St Mirren	(h)	5-0	Clark, McCoist 2, McClelland, Paterson
Section	v. Hearts	(a)	2-0	Prtyz, Mitchell
Section	v. Clydebank	(a)	3-0	Cooper, McCoist, McPherson
Section	v. St Mirren	(a)	1-0	Cooper
Won section				
1st Semi-Final	Dundee United	(a)	1-1	Mitchell
2nd Semi-Final	Dundee United	(h)	2-0	Clark, Redford
Final	v. Celtic	(H)	3-2 aet	McCoist 3, 1 pen

1984-85

2nd Round	v. Falkirk	(h)	1-0	McPherson
3rd Round	v. Raith Rovers	(h)	4-0	McCoist 2, 1 pen., Paterson, Redford
Quarter Final	v. Cowdenbeath	(a)	3-1	I. Ferguson, Russel Redford
1st Semi-Final	v. Meadowbank	(h)	4-0	McCoist 2, I. Ferguson, Fraser
2nd Semi-Final	v. Meadowbank	(a)	1-1	McCoist
Final	v. Dundee United	(H)	1-0	I. Ferguson

1985-86

2nd Round	v. Clyde	(h)	5-0	McCoist, Williamson 3, 1 pen., Paterson
3rd Round	v. Forfar	(a)	2-2	Cooper pen., Williamson
Rangers won 6-5 on penalties.				
Quarter Final	v. Hamilton	(a)	2-1	Williamson 2
1st Semi-Final	v. Hibernian	(a)	0-2	

2nd Semi-Final	v. Hibernian	(h)	1-0	Cooper

1986-87

2nd Round	v. Stenhousemuir	(a)	4-1	Souness, West, Cooper, McCoist
3rd Round	v. East Fife	(a)	0-0	

Rangers won 5-4 on penalties.

Quarter Final	v. Dundee	(h)	3-1 aet	Fraser, Souness, McMinn
Semi-Final	v. Dundee United	(H)	2-1	McCoist, McMinn
Final	v. Celtic	(H)	2-1	Durrant, Cooper pen.

1987-88

2nd Round	v. Stirling A	(a)	2-1	Falco, McCoist
3rd Round	v. Dunfermline	(a)	4-1	McCoist 3, 1 pen., Falco
Quarter Final	v. Hearts	(h)	4-1	Durrant 2, McCoist 2, 1 pen.
Semi-Final	v. Motherwell	(H)	3-1	Kirk OG, Fleck, Falco
Final	v. Aberdeen	(H)	3-3 aet	Cooper, Durrant, Fleck

Rangers won 5-3 on penalties.

1988-89

2nd Round	v. Clyde	(a)	3-0	Drinkell, Walters, D. Ferguson
3rd Round	v. Clydebank	(h)	6-0	Gough, Wilkins, Drinkell, McCoist, Durrant, Walters
4th Round	v. Dundee	(h)	4-1	McCoist, Walters, I. Ferguson, Forsyth OG
Semi-Final	v. Hearts	(H)	3-0	Walters 2, Nisbet
Final	v. Aberdeen	(H)	3-2	McCoist 2, I. Ferguson

1989-90

2nd Round	v. Arbroath	(h)	4-0	I. Ferguson, McCoist 3
3rd Round	v. Morton	(a)	2-1	Walters, Pickering OG
4th Round	v. Hamilton A	(a)	3-0	Walters 2, Steven
Semi-Final	v. Dunfermline	(H)	5-0	Steven, Johnston, McCoist 2, I. Ferguson pen.

| Final | v. Aberdeen | (H) | 1-2 | Walters pen. |

1990-91

2nd Round	v. East Stirling	(h)	5-0	Steven, Hateley 2, Walters, Johnston
3rd Round	v. Kilmarnock	(h)	1-0	Johnston
4th Round	v. Raith Rovers	(h)	6-2	McCoist 3, Johnston, Butcher, Steven
Semi-Final	v. Aberdeen	(H)	1-0	Steven
Final	v. Celtic	(H)	2-1 aet	Walters, Gough

1991-92

2nd Round	v. Queen's Park	(h)	6-0	Durrant, Johnston 4, Spackman
3rd Round	v. Partick Thistle	(a)	2-0	Johnston, Robertson
4th Round	v. Hearts	(a)	1-0	McCoist
Semi-Final	v. Hibernian	(H)	0-1	

1992-93

2nd Round	v. Dumbarton	(H)	5-0	Durrant, Gordon, Hateley, McCoist, Mikhailitchenko
3rd Round	v. Stranraer	(a)	5-0	McCoist 3, Hateley 2
4th Round	v. Dundee United	(a)	3-2	Gough, McCoist, Huistra
Semi-Final	v. St Johnstone	(H)	3-1	McCoist 3
Final	v. Aberdeen	(H)	2-1 aet	McCall, Smith OG

1993-94

2nd Round	v. Dumbarton	(h)	1-0	I. Ferguson
3rd Round	v. Dunfermline	(a)	2-0	Steven, I. Ferguson
4th Round	v. Aberdeen	(h)	2-1 aet	Hateley pen. I. Ferguson
Semi-Final	v. Celtic	(h)	1-0	Hateley
Final	v. Hibernian	(Cel)	2-1	Durrant, McCoist

1994-95

| 2nd Round | v. Arbroath | (a) | 6-1 | D. Ferguson 3, Hateley 2, McCall |
| 3rd Round | v. Falkirk | (h) | 1-2 | Laudrup |

Abbreviations

Abbreviations

H – Hampden   Fir – Firhill   Cel – Celtic

League Cup Winners – *at a glance*

Rangers	19	Dundee United	2
Celtic	9	Hibernian	2
Aberdeen	4	Motherwell	1
Hearts	4	Partick Thistle	1
Dundee	3	Raith Rovers	1
East Fife	3		

League Cup Winning Teams

5-4-47
RANGERS ....(3) 4   ABERDEEN...........(0) 0   Att. 82,684
Gillick, Williamson, Duncanson 2
Rangers: Brown, Young, Shaw, McColl, Woodburn, Rae, Rutherford, Gillick, Williamson, Thornton, Duncanson.

12-3-49
RANGERS ....(0) 2   RAITH ROVERS ...(0) 0   Att. 57,450
Gillick, Paton
Rangers: Brown, Young, Shaw, McColl, Woodburn, Cox, Gillick, Paton, Thornton, Duncanson, Rutherford.

29-10-60
RANGERS ....(1) 2   KILMARNOCK.....(0) 0   Att. 82,063
Brand, Scott
Rangers: Niven, Shearer, Caldow, Davis, Paterson, Baxter, Scott, McMillan, Millar, Brand, Wilson.

28-10-61
RANGERS ....(1) 1   HEARTS ....(0) 1†   Att. 90,000
Millar   Cumming pen.
Rangers: Ritchie, Shearer, Caldow, Davis, Paterson, Baxter, Scott, McMillan, Millar, Brand, Wilson.

† After Extra Time

Replay - 18-12-61
RANGERS ....(3) 3   HEARTS ....(1) 1   Att. 47,500
Millar, Brand, McMillan   Davidson
Rangers: Ritchie, Shearer, Caldow, Davis, Baillie, Baxter, Scott, McMillan, Millar, Brand, Wilson.

26-10-63
RANGERS ....(0) 5   MORTON..............(0) 0   Att. 105,907
Forrest 4, Willoughby
Rangers: Ritchie, Shearer, Provan, Greig, McKinnon, Baxter, Henderson, Willoughby, Forrest, Brand, Watson.

24-10-64
RANGERS ....(0) 2   CELTIC.................(0) 1   Att. 91,423
Forrest 2   Johnstone
Rangers: Ritchie, Provan, Caldow, Greig, McKinnon, Wood, Brand, Millar, Forrest, Baxter, Johnston.

24-10-70
RANGERS ....(1) 1   CELTIC.................(0) 0   Att. 106,263
Johnstone
Rangers: McCloy, Jardine, Miller, Conn, McKinnon, Jackson, Henderson, MacDonald, Johnstone, Stein, Johnston.

25-10-75
RANGERS ....(0) 1   CELTIC.................(0) 0   Att. 58,000
MacDonald
Rangers: Kennedy, Jardine, Greig, Forsyth, Jackson, MacDonald, McLean, Stein, Parlane, Johnstone, Young.

18-3-78
RANGERS ....(1) 2   CELTIC.................(0) 1†   Att. 60,168
Cooper, Smith   Edvaldsson
Rangers: Kennedy, Jardine, Jackson, Forsyth, Greig, Hamilton (Miller), MacDonald, Smith, McLean, Johnstone, Cooper (Parlane).

31-3-79
RANGERS ....(0) 2   ABERDEEN..........(0) 1   Att. 54,000
MacDonald, Jackson   Davidson
Rangers: McCloy, Jardine, Dawson, Johnstone, Jackson, A. MacDonald, McLean, Russell, Urquhart (Miller), Smith, Cooper (Parlane).

28-11-81
RANGERS ....(0) 2   DUNDEE UTD ......(0) 1   Att. 53,795
Cooper, Redford   Milne
Rangers: Stewart, Jardine, Miller, Stevens, Jackson, Bett, Cooper, Johnstone,
Russell, MacDonald, Dalziel (Redford).

25-3-84
RANGERS ....(1) 3   CELTIC ....(0) 2†   Att. 66,369
McCoist 3, 1 pen.   McClair, Reid pen.
Rangers: McCloy, Nicholl, Dawson, McClelland, Paterson, McPherson, Russell,
McCoist, Clark (McAdam), MacDonald (Burns), Cooper.

28-10-84
RANGERS ....(1) 1   DUNDEE UTD ......(0) 0   Att. 44,698
Ferguson
Rangers: McCloy, Dawson, McClelland, Fraser, Paterson, McPherson, Russell
(Prytz), McCoist, Ferguson (Mitchell), Redford, Cooper.

26-10-86
RANGERS ....(0) 2   CELTIC ....(0) 1   Att. 74,219
Durrant, Cooper pen.   McClair
Rangers: Woods, Nicholl, Munro, Fraser (MacFarlane), Dawson, Butcher,
Ferguson, McMinn (Fleck), Durrant, Cooper.

25-10-87
RANGERS ....(2) 3   ABERDEEN ....(1) 3†   Att. 71,961
Cooper, Durrant, Fleck   Bett, Falconer, Hewitt
Rangers: Walker, Nicholl, Munro, Roberts, Ferguson (Francis), Gough, McGregor
(Cohen), Fleck, McCoist, Durrant, Cooper.
Rangers won 5-3 on penalties.

3-10-88
RANGERS ....(1) 3   ABERDEEN ....(1) 2   Att. 72,122
McCoist 2, I. Ferguson   Dodds 2
Rangers: Woods, Stevens, Brown, Gough, Wilkins, Butcher, Drinkell, Ferguson,
McCoist, Cooper, Walters.

28-10-90
RANGERS ....(0) 2   CELTIC ....(0) 1   Att. 62,817
Walters, Gough   Elliott
Rangers: Woods, Stevens, Munro, Gough, Spackman, Brown, Steven, Hurlock
(Huistra), McCoist (I. Ferguson), Hateley, Walters.

25-10-92
RANGERS ....(1) 2   ABERDEEN..........(0) 1†   Att. 45,298
McCall, Smith OG   Shearer
Rangers: Goram, McCall, Robertson, Gough (Mikhailitchenko), McPherson,
Brown, Steven (Gordon), I. Ferguson, McCoist, Hateley, Durrant.

24-10-93
RANGERS ....(0) 2   HIBERNIAN..........(0) 1   Att. 47,632
Durrant, McCoist
Rangers: Maxwell, Stevens, Robertson, Gough, McPherson, McCall, Steven,
Ferguson, Durrant, Hateley, Huistra (McCoist).

Appearances in Finals

Rangers	25	Kilmarnock	3
Celtic	21	Dunfermline	2
Aberdeen	10	Motherwell	2
Hibernian	7	Raith Rovers	2
Dundee	5	Falkirk	1
Hearts	5	Morton	1
Dundee Utd	4	St Johnstone	1
Partick Th	4	St Mirren	1
East Fife	3	Third Lanark	1

Full Record in Scottish Cup

1874-75

1st Round	*v.* Oxford	(h)	2-0	Scorers unknown
2nd Round	*v.* Dumbarton	(a)	0-1	

1875-76

1st Round	*v.* First Lanark RV	(h)	7-0	Scorers unknown
2nd Round	*v.* Third Lanark	(h)	1-2	Scorer unknown

1876-77

1st Round	*v.* Queen's Park Jun	(h)	4-1	Scorers unknown
2nd Round	*v.* Towerhill	(h)	8-0	Scorers unknown
3rd Round	Bye			
4th Round	*v.* Mauchline	(h)	3-0	Scorers unknown
5th Round	*v.* Lennox	(h)	3-0	Scorers unknown
Semi-Final	Bye			

Final	v. Vale of Leven		1-1	McDougall OG

1877-78

1st Round	v. Possilpark	(h)	13-0	Maxwell, Watson, Rickatt, Campbell 2, plus 8 others
2nd Round	v. Alexandria A	(h)	8-0	Dunlop, P. Campbell 2, McNeil 3, J. Campbell 2
3rd Round	v. Uddingston	(h)	13-0	Scorers unknown
4th Round	v. Vale of Leven	(h)	0-0	
Replay	v. Vale of Leven	(a)	0-5	

1878-79

1st Round	v. Shaftesbury	(h)	3-0	Struthers (plus 2 others)
2nd Round	v. Whitefield	(h)	6-1	Scorers unknown
3rd Round	v. Parkgrove	(h)	8-2	Scorers unknown
4th Round	v. Alexandria A	(h)	3-0	Scorers unknown
5th Round	v. Partick	(h)	4-0	Scorers unknown
6th Round	v. Queen's Park	(a)	1-0	Dunlop
Semi-Final	Bye			
Final	v. Vale of Leven	(H)	1-1	Struthers

Rangers refused to replay because they claimed they had scored a second goal in this first match. Vale of Leven were awarded the Cup.

1879-80

1st Round	v. Queen's Park	(h)	0-0	
Replay	v. Queen's Park	(a)	1-5	Steel

1880-81

1st Round	v. Govan	(h)	4-1	Scorers unknown
2nd Round	v. Northern	(h)	1-0	Scorer unknown
3rd Round	v. Partick Th	(h)	3-0	Scorers unknown
4th Round	v. Clyde	(h)	11-0	Scorers unknown
5th Round	v. Hurlford	(a)	3-0	Scorers unknown
6th Round	v. Dumbarton	(h)	1-3	Scorer unknown

1881-82

1st Round	v. Third Lanark	(h)	2-1	Pringle plus 1 other
2nd Round	v. Harmonic			Opponents scratched
3rd Round	v. Alexandria A	(h)	3-1	Pringle 2, Hill
4th Round	v. Thornliebank	(a)	2-0	Henderson plus OG
5th Round	v. South Western	(a)	2-1	Scorers unknown

South Western protested about method of throw-in. Replay ordered.

Replay	v. South Western	(h)	4-0	Hill 2, McFarlane, Young
6th Round	v. Dumbarton	(a)	1-2	Scorer unknown

Rangers protested that full-time was not played. Replay ordered.

Replay	v. Dumbarton	(a)	1-5	McKinnon OG

1882-83

1st Round	v. Jordanhill	(a)	4-0	Scorers unknown
2nd Round	v. Queen's Park	(a)	2-3	McIntyre (plus 1 other)

1883-84

1st Round	v. Northern	(a)	1-0	Scorer unknown
2nd Round	v. Whitehill	(h)	14-2	McHardy (plus 13)
3rd Round	v. Falkirk	(h)	5-3	Scorers unknown
4th Round	v. Dunblane	(a)	6-0	Scorers unknown
5th Round	v. St. Bernard's	(a)	3-0	McHardy, Gossland, Pringle
6th Round	v. Cambuslang	(a)	5-1	Gossland 2, Pringle, Heggie, Inglis
Semi-Final	v. Vale of Leven	(a)	0-3	

1884-85

1st Round	v. Whitehill	(h)	11-0	
2nd Round	v. Third Lanark	(a)	2-2	Gossland, Morton
Replay	v. Third Lanark	(h)	0-0	

Both teams allowed into the next round.

3rd Round	v. Third Lanark	(a)	3-0	Laurie, Cook, Morton
4th Round	v. Arbroath	(a)	3-4	Morton, Gossland, McKenzie

Rangers protested at the small size of pitch. Replay ordered.

Replay	v. Arbroath	(a)	8-1	Scorers unknown
5th Round	Bye			
6th Round	v. Renton	(a)	3-5	Peacock (plus 2)

1885-86

1st Round	v. Clyde	(a)	0-1	

1886-87

1st Round	v. Govan Athletic	(h)	9-1	Scorers unknown
2nd Round	v. Westbourne	(h)	5-2	Laurie (plus 4 others)
3rd Round	v. Cambuslang	(h)	0-2	

1887-88

1st Round	*v.* Battlefield	(h)	4-1	White 2, J. Sellar, Brand
2nd Round	*v.* Partick Th	(a)	1-2	Brand

1888-89

1st Round	*v.* Partick Th	(h)	4-2	Wylie, Gow, Sloan 2
2nd Round	*v.* Clyde	(a)	2-2	Aird, Wylie
Replay	*v.* Clyde	(a)	0-3	

1889-90

1st Round	*v.* United Abstainers	(h)	6-2	Scorers unknown
2nd Round	*v.* Kelvinside A	(a)	13-0	Allan 2, McIntyre, Wylie 2, Mitchell Henderson 2, Robin, (plus 4 others)
3rd Round	*v.* Vale of Leven	(h)	0-0	
Replay	*v.* Vale of Leven	(a)	2-3	Wylie, Gow

1890-91 – First Scottish Cup after formation of Scottish League

1st Round	*v.* Celtic	(a)	0-1	

1891-92

1st Round	*v.* St Bernard's	(h)	5-1	Kerr, Blyth, McPherson, McBain, (plus 1 other)
2nd Round	*v.* Kilmarnock	(h)	0-0	
Replay	*v.* Kilmarnock	(a)	1-1	Kerr
2nd Replay	*v.* Kilmarnock		3-2	Henderson 2, J. McPherson
at Westmarch				
3rd Round	*v.* Annbank	(h)	2-0	Watt (plus 1 other)
Semi-Final	*v.* Celtic	(H)	3-5	Law, Henderson, Kerr

1892-93

1st Round	*v.* Annbank	(h)	7-0	N. Kerr 4, Clark H. McReadie 2
2nd Round	*v.* Dumbarton	(h)	1-0	H. McReadie
3rd Round	*v.* St Bernard's	(a)	2-3	Barker (plus 1 other)

1893-94

1st Round	*v.* Cowlairs	(h)	8-0	Boyd 3, McPherson, H. McReadie 2,

				Lamont OG, Kerr
2nd Round	v. Leith Athletic	(h)	2-0	Blyth, McPherson
3rd Round	v. Clyde	(a)	5-0	Steel 4, McPherson
Semi-Final	v. Queen's Park	(h)	1-1	Boyd
Replay	v. Queen's Park	(a)	3-1	McPherson, Steel, Smith
Final	v. Celtic	(H)	3-1	Barker, McPherson, H. McReadie

1894-95

1st Round	v. Hearts	(a)	1-2	Cowan

1895-96

1st Round	v. Dumbarton	(a)	1-1	Scorer unknown
Replay	v. Dumbarton	(h)	3-1	Smith 2, Oswald
2nd Round	v. St Mirren	(h)	5-0	Oswald 3, McPherson, McCreadie
3rd Round	v. Hibernian	(h)	2-3	Smith, McReadie

1896-97

1st Round	v. Partick Th	(a)	4-2	Gray OG, Hyslop 2 Gibson
2nd Round	v. Hibernian	(h)	3-0	Low 2, McPherson
3rd Round	v. Dundee	(a)	1-1	Smith

Match deemed a friendly because of state of pitch.

3rd Round	v. Dundee	(a)	4-0	Gibson, Hyslop, McCreadie, Millar
Semi-Final	v. Morton	(a)	7-2	Gibson, Millar, Hyslop, A. Smith, McPherson 2, Low
Final	v. Dumbarton	(H)	5-1	Millar, Hyslop 2, McPherson, A. Smith

1897-98

1st Round	v. Polton Vale	(h)	8-0	Smith, Hamilton, Millar 2, Neill, McPherson 2, Goudie
2nd Round	v. Cartvale	(h)	12-0	Smith 2, Gibson, Hamilton 4, Millar Mitchell, Neill pen Coulrough og, Kerr
3rd Round	v. Queen's Park	(a)	3-1	McPherson, Millar

				Hamilton
Semi-Final	v. Third Lanark	(h)	1-1	A. Smith
Replay	v. Third Lanark	(a)	2-2	Hamilton, A. Smith
2nd Replay	v. Third Lanark	(a)	2-0	McPherson, Gibson pen.
Final	v. Kilmarnock	(H)	2-0	A. Smith, Hamilton

1898-99

1st Round	v. Hearts	(h)	4-1	Gibson 2, Neill pen., Hamilton
2nd Round	v. Ayr Parkhouse	(a)	4-1	Hamilton, Campbell, A. Smith.
3rd Round	v. Clyde	(h)	4-0	Low, McPherson, Gibson pen., Hamilton
Semi-Final	v. St Mirren	(a)	2-1	McPherson, Millar
Final	v. Celtic	(H)	0-2	

1899-1900

1st Round	v. Morton	(h)	4-2	Wilkie, A. Smith McPherson 2
2nd Round	v. Maybole	(h)	12-0	Hamilton 4, Neil, Wilkie 3, A. Smith, Robertson, Hyslop, Gibson
3rd Round	v. Partick Thistle	(a)	6-1	Hamilton 2, Wilkie, McPherson, Smith, Graham
Semi-Final	v. Celtic	(h)	2-2	A. Smith, McPherson
Replay	v. Celtic	(a)	0-4	

1900-01

1st Round	v. Celtic	(a)	0-1	

1901-02

1st Round	v. Johnstone	(h)	6-1	Howie OG, Speedie, A. Smith, Hamilton Robertson, Graham
2nd Round	v. Inverness Caley	(h)	5-1	Wilkie, A. Smith 2, Campbell, Hamilton
3rd Round	v. Kilmarnock	(h)	3-0	Gibson, Hamilton 2

Match declared a friendly because of weather conditions.

3rd Round	v. Kilmarnock	(h)	2-0	Speedie, A. Smith
Semi-Final	v. Hibernian	(h)	0-2	

1902-03

1st Round	v. Auchterarder T	(h)	7-0	Hamilton, Speedie 3 McDonald ?, Gibson
2nd Round	v. Kilmarnock	(h)	4-0	Walker 2, Robertson, McDonald
3rd Round	v. Celtic	(a)	3-0	A. Smith, Walker, Hamilton
Semi-Final	v. Stenhousemuir	(a)	4-1	Robertson 2, Hamilton 2
Final	v. Hearts	(Cel)	1-1	Stark
Replay	v. Hearts	(Cel)	0-0	
2nd Replay	v. Hearts	(Cel)	2-0	Mackie, Hamilton

1903-04

1st Round	v. Hearts	(h)	3-2	Hamilton, J. Walker 2
2nd Round	v. Hibernian	(a)	2-1	Mackie, Walker
3rd Round	v. St Mirren	(a)	1-0	Hamilton
Semi-Final	v. Morton	(h)	3-0	Walker 2, Hamilton
Final	v. Celtic	(H)	2-3	Speedie 2

1904-05

1st Round	v. Ayr Parkhouse	(h)	2-1	Robertson, Chalmers
2nd Round	v. Morton	(a)	6-0	McColl 2, Walker, Speedie 2, 1 pen., Kyle
3rd Round	v. Beith	(h)	5-1	Chalmers 2, Kyle 2, Speedie
Semi-Final	v. Celtic	(h)	2-0	Speedie, Robertson

Result stood despite pitch invasion.

Final	v. Third Lanark	(H)	0-0	
Replay	v. Third Lanark	(H)	1-3	A. Smith

1905-06

1st Round	v. Arthurlie	(a)	7-1	Speirs 3, McColl, May, Dalrymple 2
2nd Round	v. Aberdeen	(a)	3-2	Dalrymple 2, Hamilton
3rd Round	v. Port Glasgow A	(a)	0-1	

1906-07

1st Round	v. Falkirk	(a)	2-1	Campbell pen.,

2nd Round	v. Galston	(a)	4-0	McPhie Fullarton OG, Livingstone 2, Speirs
3rd Round	v. Celtic	(h)	0-3	

1907-08

1st Round	v. Falkirk	(a)	2-2	Livingstone, May
Replay	v. Falkirk	(h)	4-1	Kyle 2, Smith 2
2nd Round	v. Celtic	(h)	1-2	Kyle

1908-09

1st Round	v. St Johnstone	(a)	3-0	Stark, Bennett, Campbell
2nd Round	v. Dundee	(a)	0-0	
Replay	v. Dundee	(h)	1-0	McPherson
3rd Round	v. Queen's Park	(h)	1-0	McPherson
Semi-Final	v. Falkirk	(a)	1-0	McPherson
Final	v. Celtic	(H)	2-2	Gilchrist, Bennett
Replay	v. Celtic	(H)	1-1	Gordon

Cup withheld after riot.

1909-10

1st Round	v. Inverness Thistle	(h)	5-1	Gilchrist, May, Reid plus 2 others
2nd Round	v. Clyde	(a)	0-2	

1910-11

1st Round	v. Kilmarnock	(h)	2-1	Hogg, Reid
2nd Round	v. Morton	(a)	3-0	Bowie, Reid 2
3rd Round	v. Dundee	(a)	1-2	Hogg

1911-12

1st Round	v. Stenhousemuir	(h)	3-1	Mawell, Kane OG Reid
2nd Round	v. Clyde	(a)	1-3	Hendry

Match abandoned after pitch invasion. Rangers conceded.

1912-13

2nd Round	v. Hamilton A	(a)	1-1	Reid
Replay	v. Hamilton A	(h)	2-0	Goodwin, Parker
3rd Round	v. Falkirk	(h)	1-3	Parker

1913-14

2nd Round	v. Alloa Athletic	(h)	5-0	Stewart 3, Brown, Bowie

3rd Round	v. Hibernian	(a)	1-2	Reid

1914-19 - No competition

1919-20

1st Round	v. Dumbarton	(h)	0-0	
Replay	v. Dumbarton	(h)	1-0	Cairns
2nd Round	v. Arbroath	(h)	5-0	Muirhead 2, Bowie, Archibald, Cunningham
3rd Round	v. Broxburn United	(h)	3-0	Muirhead, Arthur, Cunningham
4th Round	v. Celtic	(h)	1-0	Muirhead
Semi-Final	v. Albion Rovers	(Cel)	1-1	Paterson
Replay	v. Albion Rovers	(Cel)	0-0	
2nd Replay	v. Albion Rovers	(Cel)	0-2	

1920-21

2nd Round	v. Morton	(h)	2-0	Morton, Henderson
3rd Round	v. Alloa Athletic	(h)	0-0	
Replay	v. Alloa Athletic	(h)	4-1	Cairns 2, Archibald, Cunningham
4th Round	v. Dumbarton	(a)	3-0	Bowie, Henderson Cunningham
Semi-Final	v. Albion Rovers	(Cel)	4-1	Cairns 2, Archibald, Cunningham
Final	v. Partick Th	(Cel)	0-1	

1921-22

1st Round	v. Clachnacuddin	(a)	5-0	Henderson 3, McDiarmid, Morton
2nd Round	v. Albion Rovers	(a)	1-1	McColgan OG
Replay	v. Albion Rovers	(h)	4-0	Meiklejohn, Archibald, Morton 2
3rd Round	v. Hearts	(a)	4-0	Cunningham 2, Dixon, McDiarmid
4th Round	v. St Mirren	(h)	1-1	Henderson
Replay	v. St Mirren	(a)	2-0	Henderson, Cunningham
Semi-Final	v. Partick Thistle	(h)	2-0	Henderson, Archibald pen.
Final	v. Morton	(H)	0-1	

1922-23

1st Round	v. Clyde	(a)	4-0	Cunningham, Henderson, Morton

302

2nd Round	*v.* Ayr United	(a)	0-2	

1923-24

1st Round	*v.* Lochgelly United	(h)	4-1	Henderson 3, Craig
2nd Round	*v.* St Mirren	(a)	1-0	Henderson
3rd Round	*v.* Hibernian	(h)	1-2	Meiklejohn

1924-25

1st Round	*v.* East Fife	(a)	3-1	Archibald 2, Henderson
2nd Round	*v.* Montrose	(a)	2-0	Chalmers 2
3rd Round	*v.* Arbroath	(h)	5-3	Cairns, Cunningham Henderson 3
4th Round	*v.* Kilmarnock	(a)	2-1	Henderson, Cunningham
Semi-Final	*v.* Celtic	(H)	0-5	

1925-26

1st Round	*v.* Lochgelly Utd	(h)	3-0	Fleming 2, Archibald
2nd Round	*v.* Stenhousemuir	(h)	1-0	Henderson
3rd Round	*v.* Falkirk	(a)	2-0	McKay, Cunningham
4th Round	*v.* Morton	(a)	4-0	Morton 2, Fleming, Cunningham pen.
Semi-Final	*v.* St Mirren	(Cel)	0-1	

1926-27

1st Round	*v.* Leith Athletic	(a)	4-1	Morton 2, Fleming, Craig
2nd Round	*v.* St Mirren	(h)	6-0	Fleming 2, Morton 2, Archibald, Cunningham
3rd Round	*v.* Hamilton A	(h)	4-0	Fleming 2, Cunningham, Archibald
4th Round	*v.* Falkirk	(a)	2-2	Archibald, McCandless pen.
Replay	*v.* Falkirk	(h)	0-1 aet	

1927-28

1st Round	*v.* East Stirling	(a)	6-0	Fleming 3, McPhail pen., Archibald,

					Cunningham
2nd Round	*v.* Cowdenbeath	(h)	4-2	McPhail 3, Fleming
3rd Round	*v.* Kings Park	(h)	3-1	Morton 2, Cunningham
4th Round	*v.* Albion Rovers	(a)	1-0	Cunningham
Semi-Final	*v.* Hibernian	(T)	3-0	Archibald, McPhail, Simpson
Final	*v.* Celtic	(H)	4-0	Meiklejohn pen., McPhail, Archibald 2

1928-29

1st Round	*v.* Edinburgh City	(h)	11-1	Fleming 3, McPhail 2, Craig 2, 1 pen., Morton 2, Archibald Cunningham
2nd Round	*v.* Partick Th	(h)	5-1	Craig, Fleming 3, Morton
3rd Round	*v.* Clyde	(a)	2-0	Muirhead, Archibald
4th Round	*v.* Dundee United	(h)	3-1	Marshall, Fleming, McPhail
Semi-Final	*v.* St Mirren	(H)	3-2	Muirhead, Morton, Lilley OG
Final	*v.* Kilmarnock	(H)	0-2	

1929-30

1st Round	*v.* Queen's Park	(a)	1-0	McPhail
2nd Round	*v.* Cowdenbeath	(h)	2-2	Morton 2, 1 pen.
Replay	*v.* Cowdenbeath	(a)	3-0	Fleming 2, McPhail
3rd Round	*v.* Motherwell	(a)	5-2	Archibald, Fleming 2, McPhail 2
4th Round	*v.* Montrose	(h)	3-0	Morton 2, 1 pen., Brown
Semi-Final	*v.* Hearts	(H)	4-1	Fleming 3, McPhail
Final	*v.* Partick Th	(H)	0-0	
Final	*v.* Partick Th	(H)	2-1	Marshall, Craig

1930-31

1st Round	*v.* Armadale	(a)	7-1	Fleming 3, Morton, McPhail 2, Marshall
2nd Round	*v.* Dundee	(h)	1-2	Fleming

1931-32

1st Round	*v.* Brechin City	(h)	8-2	McPhail 2,

				Fleming 2, English 3, Marshall
2nd Round	v. Raith Rovers	(a)	5-0	Archibald, Fleming, English 3
3rd Round	v. Hearts	(a)	1-0	Marshall
4th Round	v. Motherwell	(h)	2-0	Murray, McPhail
Semi-Final	v. Hamilton A	(Cel)	5-2	Marshall 2, English 2, Archibald
Final	v. Kilmarnock	(H)	1-1	McPhail
Replay	v. Kilmarnock	(H)	3-0	Fleming, English, McPhail

1932-33

1st Round	v. Arbroath	(h)	3-1	Marshall 2, Smith
2nd Round	v. Queen's Park	(h)	1-1	English
Replay	v. Queen's Park	(a)	1-1 aet	Marshall
2nd Replay	v. Queen's Park	(a)	3-1	Marshall, Fleming, Smith
3rd Round	v. Kilmarnock	(a)	0-1	

1933-34

1st Round	v. Blairgowrie	(h)	14-2	Fleming 9, Venters 2, Marshall 2, Nicholson
2nd Round	v. Third Lanark	(a)	3-0	Smith 3
3rd Round	v. Hearts	(h)	0-0	
Replay	v. Hearts	(a)	2-1	Fleming, McPhail
4th Round	v. Aberdeen	(h)	1-0	Smith
Semi-Final	v. St Johnstone	(H)	1-0	Marshall
Final	v. St Mirren	(H)	5-0	Nicholson 2, Smith, McPhail, Main

1934-35

1st Round	v. Cowdenbeath	(h)	3-1	Gillick 2, Main
2nd Round	v. Third Lanark	(h)	2-0	Smith 2, 1 pen.
3rd Round	v. St Mirren	(h)	1-0	Gillick
4th Round	v. Motherwell	(a)	4-1	Smith 4
Semi-Final	v. Hearts	(H)	1-1	Gillick
Replay	v. Hearts	(H)	2-0	McPhail, Main
Final	v. Hamilton A	(H)	2-1	Smith 2

1935-36

| 1st Round | v. East Fife | (h) | 3-1 | Smith, Venters 2 |
| 2nd Round | v. Albion Rovers | (a) | 3-1 | Smith 3 |

3rd Round	v. St Mirren	(a)	2-1	McPhail, Smith
4th Round	v. Aberdeen	(a)	1-0	Thomson pen.
Semi-Final	v. Clyde	(H)	3-0	Meiklejohn, Main, McPhail
Final	v. Third Lanark	(H)	1-0	McPhail

1936-37

1st Round	v. Queen of the South	(a)	0-1	

1937-38

1st Round	v. Alloa Athletic	(a)	6-1	Venters, McPhail, Smith 3, Reid
2nd Round	v. Queen of the South	(h)	3-1	Reid, McPhail 2
3rd Round	Bye			
4th Round	v. Falkirk	(a)	2-1	Venters, Thornton
Semi-Final	v. Kilmarnock	(H)	3-4	Thornton, Venters 2

1938-39

1st Round	v. Raith Rovers	(a)	1-0	Venters
2nd Round	v. Hamilton A	(h)	2-0	Lyness, Venters
3rd Round	v. Clyde	(h)	1-4	Lyness pen.

1940-46 – No competition

1946-47

1st Round	v. Clyde	(h)	2-1	Duncanson, Thornton
2nd Round	Bye			
3rd Round	v. Hibernian	(h)	0-0	
Replay	v. Hibernian	(a)	0-2	

1947-48

1st Round	v. Stranraer	(a)	1-0	Thornton
2nd Round	v. Leith Athletic	(h)	4-0	Thornton, Waddell, Cox, Rutherford
3rd Round	v. Partick Th	(h)	3-0	Young pen., Duncanson, McGowan OG
4th Round	v. East Fife	(h)	1-0	Duncanson
Semi-Final	v. Hibernian	(H)	1-0	Thornton
Final	v. Morton	(H)	1-1	Gillick
Replay	v. Morton	(H)	1-0	Williamson

1948-49

1st Round	v. Elgin City	(h)	6-1	Thornton 2, Cox, Duncanson 2,

				Rutherford
2nd Round	v. Motherwell	(a)	3-0	Young pen., Paton, Thornton
3rd Round	Bye			
4th Round	v. Partick Th	(h)	4-0	Duncanson, Paton, Thornton 2
Semi-Final	v. East Fife	(H)	3-0	Thornton 3
Final	v. Clyde	(H)	4-1	Young 2 pens., Williamson, Duncanson

1949-50

1st Round	v. Motherwell	(a)	4-2	Williamson, Paton, McCulloch, Findlay
2nd Round	v. Cowdenbeath	(h)	8-0	McCulloch 2, Paton, Williamson 2, Johnston 2, Rutherford
3rd Round	Bye			
4th Round	v. Raith Rovers	(h)	1-1	Findlay
Replay	v. Raith Rovers	(a)	1-1 aet	Williamson
2nd Replay	v. Raith Rovers	(h)	2-0	Findlay, Cox
Semi-Final	v. Queen of the South	(H)	1-1	Rutherford
Replay	v. Queen of the South	(H)	3-0	Williamson, Findlay Young pen.
Final	v. East Fife	(H)	3-0	Findlay, Thornton 2

1950-51

1st Round	v. Queen of the South	(h)	2-0	Simpson, Waddell
2nd Round	v. Hibernian	(h)	2-3	Simpson 2

1951-52

1st Round	Bye			
2nd Round	v. Elgin City	(h)	6-1	Paton, Waddell, Liddell, Findlay 2, Thornton
3rd Round	v. Arbroath	(a)	2-0	Thornton 2
4th Round	v. Motherwell	(h)	1-1	Thornton
Replay	v. Motherwell	(a)	1-2	Thornton

1952-53

1st Round	v. Arbroath	(h)	4-0	Hubbard, Prentice, McCulloch, Simpson
2nd Round	v. Dundee	(a)	2-0	Grierson, Hubbard

3rd Round	v. Morton	(a)	4-1	Simpson, Prentice, Grierson 2
4th Round	v. Celtic	(h)	2-0	Grierson, Prentice
Semi-Final	v. Hearts	(H)	2-1	Grierson, Prentice
Final	v Aberdeen	(H)	1-1	Prentice
Final	v. Aberdeen	(H)	1-0	Simpson

1953-54

1st Round	v. Queen's Park	(h)	2-0	Waddell, Gardiner
2nd Round	v. Kilmarnock	(h)	2-2	Grierson, Gardiner
Replay	v. Kilmarnock	(a)	3-1	Paton 2, McCulloch
3rd Round	v. Third Lanark	(a)	0-0	
Replay	v. Third Lanark	(h)	4-4 aet	Prentice 2, Simpson 2
2nd Replay	v. Third Lanark	(h)	3-2	Caldow pen., Paton, Prentice
4th Round	v. Berwick R	(h)	4-0	Simpson, Paton, Liddell, Caldow pen.
Semi-Final	v. Aberdeen	(H)	0-6	

1954-55

5th Found	v. Dundee	(h)	0-0	
Replay	v. Dundee	(a)	1-0	Gallacher OG
6th Round	v. Aberdeen	(a)	1-2	Neillands

1955-56

5th Round	v. Aberdeen	(h)	2-1	Scott, Kichenbrand
6th Round	v. Dundee	(a)	1-0	Kichenbrand
7th Round	v. Hearts	(a)	0-4	

1956-57

5th Round	v. Hearts	(a)	4-0	Hubbard pen., Murray, Scott, Simpson
6th Round	v. Celtic	(a)	4-4	Morrison, Simpson, Hubbard pen., Murray
Replay	v. Celtic	(h)	0-2	

1957-58

1st Round	v. Cowdenbeath	(a)	3-1	Simpson, Murray 2
2nd Round	v. Forfar	(a)	9-1	Hubbard, Brand 2, Murray 3, McColl, Simpson 2
3rd Round	v. Dunfermline	(a)	2-1	Murray, Brand

4th Round	v. Queen of the South	(a)	4-3	Murray 2, Millar 2
Semi-Final	v. Hibernian	(H)	2-2	Millar, Murray
Replay	v. Hibernian	(H)	1-2	Baird pen.

1958-59

1st Round	v. Forfar	(a)	3-1	Murray, Millar, Scott
2nd Round	v. Hearts	(h)	3-2	Matthews 2, Kirk og
3rd Round	v. Celtic	(a)	1-2	Murray

1959-60

1st Round	v. Berwick R	(a)	3-1	Wilson 3
2nd Round	v. Arbroath	(h)	2-0	Scott, Brown OG
3rd Round	v. Stenhousem'r	(a)	3-0	Watson OG McMillan, Wilson
4th Round	v. Hibernian	(h)	3-2	Baird, Wilson, Millar
Semi-Final	v. Celtic	(H)	1-1	Millar
Replay	v. Celtic	(H)	4-1	Wilson 2, Millar 2
Final	v. Kilmarnock	(H)	2-0	Millar 2

1960-61

1st Round	Bye			
2nd Round	v. Dundee	(a)	5-1	Murray 2, Brand 2, Scott
3rd Round	v. Motherwell	(a)	2-2	Murray 2
Replay	v. Motherwell	(h)	2-5	Wilson, McMillan

1961-62

1st Round	v. Falkirk	(a)	2-1	Millar, Wilson
2nd Round	v. Arbroath	(h)	6-0	Millar 3, Brand 2 Glasgow og
3rd Round	v. Aberdeen	(a)	2-2	Caldow pen., Brand
Replay	v. Aberdeen	(h)	5-1	McMillan, Millar 2, Wilson, Brand
4th Round	v. Kilmarnock	(a)	4-2	Caldow pen., McMillan 2, Brand
Semi-Final	v. Motherwell	(H)	3-1	Murray 2, Wilson
Final	v. St Mirren	(H)	2-0	Brand, Wilson

1962-63

| 1st Round | Bye | | | |
| 2nd Round | v. Airdrie | (a) | 6-0 | Brand pen., Wilson 3, Henderson, |

				Thomson og
3rd Round	v. East Stirling	(h)	7-2	Brand 4, Wilson, Millar, McLean
4th Round	v. Dundee	(a)	1-1	Brand pen.
Replay	v. Dundee	(h)	3-2	Hamilton OG, Brand 2, 1 pen
Semi-Final	v. Dundee Utd	(H)	5-2	Millar 3, Brand, McLean
Final	v. Celtic	(H)	1-1	Brand
Replay	v. Celtic	(H)	3-0	Wilson, Brand 2

1963-64

1st Round	v. Stenhousemuir	(a)	5-1	Millar, Greig 2, Provan pen., Brand
2nd Round	v. Duns	(h)	9-0	Millar 4, Brand 3, McLean, Henderson
3rd Round	v. Partick Th	(h)	3-0	Wilson 2, Forrest
4th Round	v. Celtic	(h)	2-0	Forrest, Henderson
Semi-Final	v. Dunfermline	(H)	1-0	Wilson
Final	v. Dundee	(H)	3-1	Millar 2, Brand

1964-65

1st Round	v. Hamilton A	(h)	3-0	Brand, Millar, Forrest
2nd Round	v. Dundee Utd	(a)	2-0	Forrest 2
3rd Round	v. Hibernian	(a)	1-2	Hynd

1965-66

1st Round	v. Airdrie	(h)	5-1	Wilson, Johnston, McLean 3, 1 pen.
2nd Round	v. Ross County	(a)	2-0	Johnston, McLean
3rd Round	v. St Johnstone	(h)	1-0	Willoughby
Semi-Final	v. Aberdeen	(H)	0-0	
Replay	v. Aberdeen	(H)	2-1	Forrest, McLean
Final	v. Celtic	(H)	0-0	
Replay	v. Celtic	(H)	1-0	Johansen

1966-67

1st Round	v. Berwick R	(a)	0-1	

1967-68

1st Round	v. Hamilton A	(h)	3-1	Johnston, Greig 2
2nd Round	v. Dundee	(a)	1-1	Stewart OG
Replay	v. Dundee	(h)	4-1 aet	Persson, Watson 2, Easton OG

3rd Round	v. Hearts	(h)	1-1	Persson
Replay	v. Hearts	(a)	0-1	

1968-69

1st Round	v. Hibernian	(h)	1-0	Stein
2nd Round	v. Hearts	(h)	2-0	Johnston, Persson
3rd Round	v. Airdrie	(h)	1-0	Greig pen.
Semi-Final	v. Aberdeen	(H)	6-1	Penman 2, Henderson, Johnston 3
Final	v. Celtic	(H)	0-4	

1969-70

1st Round	v. Hibernian	(h)	3-1	MacDonald 2, Penman
2nd Round	v. Forfar	(a)	7-0	MacDonald, Stein, Jardine 3, Greig, Penman
3rd Round	v. Celtic	(a)	1-3	Craig og.

1970-71

3rd Round	v. Falkirk	(h)	3-0	Conn, Johnston 2
4th Round	v. St Mirren	(a)	3-1	Stein 2, Johnston pen.
5th Round	v. Aberdeen	(h)	1-0	Jackson
Semi-Final	v. Hibernian	(H)	0-0	
Replay	v. Hibernian	(H)	2-1	Henderson, Conn
Final	v. Celtic	(H)	1-1	Johnstone
Replay	v. Celtic	(H)	1-2	Callaghan OG

1971-72

3rd Round	v. Falkirk	(a)	2-2	Johnstone, Greig
Replay	v. Falkirk	(h)	2-0	Stein, McLean
4th Round	v. St Mirren	(a)	4-1	MacDonald, Stein, McLean 2, 1 pen.
5th Round	v. Motherwell	(a)	2-2	MacDonald, Stein
Replay	v. Motherwell	(h)	4-2	Stein 2, McLean, Fallon OG
Semi-Final	v. Hibernian	(H)	1-1	MacDonald
Replay	v. Hibernian	(H)	0-2	

1972-73

3rd Round	v. Dundee Utd	(h)	1-0	Young
4th Round	v. Hibernian	(h)	1-1	Johnstone
Replay	v. Hibernian	(a)	2-1	McLean 2, 1 pen.

5th Round	*v.* Airdrie	(h)	2-0	Parlane pen., Young
Semi-Final	*v.* Ayr United	(H)	2-0	Parlane 2
Final	*v.* Celtic	(H)	3-2	Parlane, Forsyth, Conn

1973-74

3rd Round	*v.* Queen's Park	(h)	8-0	Parlane 3, Scott, Morris, McLean 3
4th Round	*v.* Dundee	(h)	0-3	

1974-75

3rd Round	*v.* Aberdeen	(a)	1-1	Scott
Replay	*v.* Aberdeen	(h)	1-2 aet	McKean

1975-76

3rd Round	*v.* East Fife	(h)	3-0	MacDonald, Henderson, Hamilton
4th Round	*v.* Aberdeen	(h)	4-1	Johnstone, MacDonald, Henderson, Parlane
5th Round	*v.* Queen of the South	(a)	5-0	McKean 2, Johnstone 2, Henderson
Semi-Final	*v.* Motherwell	(H)	3-2	Miller pen., Johnstone 2
Final	*v.* Hearts	(H)	3-1	Johnstone 2, MacDonald

1976-77

3rd Round	*v.* Falkirk	(h)	3-1	Jardine pen., Johnstone, MacDonald
4th Round	*v.* Elgin City	(h)	3-0	Jackson, MacDonald McLean pen.
5th Round	*v.* Motherwell	(h)	2-0	McKean, Watson
Semi-Final pen.	*v.* Hearts	(H)	2-0	Jackson, Jardine
Final	*v.* Celtic	(H)	0-1	

1977-78

3rd Round	*v.* Berwick R	(a)	4-2	Johnstone 2, Jackson 2
4th Round	*v.* Stirling A	(h)	1-0	Johnstone
5th Round	*v.* Kilmarnock	(h)	4-1	Johnstone,

				Hamilton, MacDonald, Cooper pen.
Semi-Final	v. Dundee Utd	(H)	2-0	Johnstone, Greig
Final	v. Aberdeen	(H)	2-1	MacDonald, Johnstone

978-79

3rd Round	v. Motherwell	(h)	3-1	Johnstone, Cooper, Jackson
4th Round	v. Kilmarnock	(h)	1-1	MacDonald
Replay	v. Kilmarnock	(a)	1-0	Urquhart
5th Round	v. Dundee	(h)	6-3	Jardine pen., Smith, T. Forsyth, Russell, Cooper, McDonald
Semi-Final	v. Partick Th	(H)	0-0	
Replay	v. Partick Th	(H)	1-0	Johnstone
Final	v. Hibernian	(H)	0-0	
Replay	v. Hibernian	(H)	0-0	
2nd Replay	v. Hibernian	(H)	3-2	Johnstone 2, Duncan OG

979-80

3rd Round	v. Clyde	(a)	2-2	Jackson, Jardine pen
Replay	v. Clyde	(h)	2-0	J. MacDonald 2
4th Round	v. Dundee United	(h)	1-0	Johnstone
5th Round	v. Hearts	(h)	6-1	J. MacDonald 2, Jardine pen., Cooper, Russell, Johnstone
Semi-Final	v. Aberdeen	(Cel)	1-0	Johnstone
Final	v. Celtic	(H)	0-1 aet	

80-81

3rd Round	v. Airdrie	(a)	5-0	Stevens, Redford, Bett, Johnstone 2
4th Round	v. St Johnstone	(a)	3-3	McAdam, Redford 2
Replay	v. St Johnstone	(h)	3-1	McAdam 2, Stevens
5th Round	v. Hibernian	(h)	3-1	Russell, McAdam, MacDonald
Semi-Final	v. Morton	(Cel)	2-1	Jackson, Russell
Final	v. Dundee United	(H)	0-0 aet	
Replay	v. Dundee United	(H)	4-1	Cooper, Russell, MacDonald 2

313

1981-82

3rd Round	v. Albion Rovers	(h)	6-2	Johnstone, Russell, MacDonald, McAdam, Redford, McPherson pen.
4th Round	v. Dumbarton	(h)	4-0	Jardine 2, McAdam, Johnstone
5th Round	v. Dundee	(h)	2-0	Johnstone, McAdam
Semi-Final	v. Forfar	(H)	0-0	
Replay	v. Forfar	(H)	3-1	Johnstone, Bett, Cooper
Final	v. Aberdeen	(H)	1-4 aet	MacDonald

1982-83

3rd Round	v. Falkirk	(a)	2-0	Oliver OG, Kennedy
4th Round	v. Forfar	(h)	2-1	MacDonald 2
5th Round	v. Queen's Park	(a)	2-1	Dalziel, Cooper
Semi-Final	v. St Mirren	(Cel)	1-1	Clark
Replay	v. St Mirren	(H)	1-0 aet	Clark
Final	v. Aberdeen	(H)	0-1	

1983-84

3rd Round	v. Dunfermline	(h)	2-1	McAdam, McCoist
4th Round	v. Inverness Caley	(a)	6-0	Redford, McCoist, Williamson 2, Russell
5th Round	v. Dundee	(a)	2-2	McGeachie OG, Russell
Replay	v. Dundee	(h)	2-3	McClelland, McPherson

1984-85

3rd Round	v. Morton	(a)	3-3	Prytz, MacDonald, McPherson
Replay	v. Morton	(h)	3-1	Mitchell, Fraser, MacDonald
4th Round	v. Dundee	(h)	0-1	

1985-86

3rd Round	v. Hearts	(a)	2-3	McCoist, Durrant

1986-87

3rd Round	v. Hamilton A	(h)	0-1	

1987-88

3rd Round	v. Raith Rovers	(a)	0-0	
Replay	v. Raith Rovers	(h)	4-1	Durrant 2, 1 pen., McCoist, Walters
4th Round	v. Dunfermline	(a)	0-2	

1988-89

3rd Round	v. Raith Rovers	(a)	1-1	I. Ferguson
Replay	v. Raith Rovers	(h)	3-0	Walters, Drinkell, Fraser OG
4th Round	v. Stranraer	(h)	8-0	I. Ferguson, Walters, Drinkell 2, Brown 2, McCoist 2 1 pen.
Quarter Final	Dundee United	(a)	1-0	McCoist
Semi-Final	v. St Johnstone	(Cel)	0-0	
Replay	v. St Johnstone	(Cel)	4-0	Walters, Stevens, Drinkell, McCoist
Final	v. Celtic	(H)	0-1	

1989-90

3rd Round	v. St Johnstone	(h)	3-0	Johnston, Brown, Walters
4th Round	v. Celtic	(a)	0-1	

1990-91

3rd Round	v. Dunfermline	(h)	2-0	Huistra, Spackman
4th Round	v. Cowdenbeath	(h)	5-0	Hateley 2, Nisbet, McCoist, Walters pen.
Quarter Final	Celtic	(a)	0-2	

1991-92

3rd Round	v. Aberdeen	(a)	1-0	McCoist
4th Round	v. Motherwell	(h)	2-1	Mikhailitchenko 2
5th Round	v. St Johnstone	(a)	3-0	McCoist, Gough, Hateley
Semi-Final	v. Celtic	(H)	1-0	McCoist
Final	v. Airdrie	(H)	2-1	Hateley, McCoist

1992-93

3rd Round	v. Motherwell	(a)	2-0	McCoist 2
4th Round	v. Ayr United	(a)	2-0	McCoist, Gordon
Quarter Final	Arbroath	(a)	3-0	Hateley, Murray, McCoist pen.
Semi-Final	v. Hearts	(Cel)	2-1	McPherson,

| | | | | McCoist |
| Final | v. Aberdeen | (Cel) | 2-1 | Murray, Hateley |

1993-94

3rd Round	v. Dumbarton	(h)	4-1	Durie, Hateley pen., Steven, Robertson
4th Round	v. Alloa A	(h)	6-0	I. Ferguson, McPherson, McCoist 3, 1 pen., Newbigging OG
5th Round	v. Hearts	(h)	2-0	Brown, Hateley
Semi-Final	v. Kilmarnock	(H)	0-0	
Replay	v. Kilmarnock	(H)	2-1	Hateley 2
Final	v. Dundee United	(H)	0-1	

1994-95

| 3rd Round | v. Hamilton | (a) | 3-1 | Boli, Steven, Laudrup |
| 4th Round | v. Hearts | (a) | 2-4 | Durie, Laudrup |

Abbreviation

(Cel) – Celtic Park   (H) – Hampden Park   (T) – Tynecastle

Scottish Cup Winning Teams

17-02-1894
RANGERS .... (0) 3   CELTIC .... (0) 1   Att. 17, 000
Barker, H. McReadie, McPherson   Maley
Rangers: Haddow, Smith, Drummond, Marshall, A. McReadie, Mitchell, Steel, H. McReadie, Gray, McPherson, Barker.

20-3-97
RANGERS .... (1) 5   DUMBARTON ...... (0) 1   Att. 14, 000
Hyslop 2, Millar, McPherson, A. Smith.   W. Thomson
Rangers: Dickie, N. Smith, Drummond, Gibson, McCreadie, Mitchell, Low, McPherson, Millar, Hyslop, A. Smith.

26-3-98
RANGERS .... (0) 2   KILMARNOCK .... (0) 0   Att. 13,000
A. Smith, Hamilton
Rangers: Dickie, N. Smith, Drummond, Gibson, Neill, Mitchell, Miller, McPherson, Hamilton, Hyslop, A. Smith.

11-4-1903

RANGERS ....(0) 1   HEARTS ....(0) 1   Att. 30,000
Stark   R. Walker

Rangers: Dickie, Fraser, Drummond, Gibson, Stark, Robertson, McDonald, Speedie, Hamilton, J. Walker, A. Smith.

Replay – 18-4-03

RANGERS ....(0) 0   HEARTS ....(0) 0   Att. 35,000

Rangers: Dickie, Fraser, Drummond, Gibson, Stark, Robertson, McDonald, Speedie, Hamilton, J. Walker, A. Smith.

2nd Replay – 25-4-03

RANGERS ....(1) 2   HEARTS ....(0) 0   Att. 30,000
Mackie, Hamilton

Rangers: Dickie, Fraser, Drummond, Henderson, Stark, Robertson, Mackie, McDonald, Hamilton, Speedie, A. Smith.

14-4-28

RANGERS ....(0) 4   CELTIC.................(0) 0   Att. 118,115
Meiklejohn pen, McPhail, Archibald 2

Rangers: T. Hamilton, Gray, R. Hamilton, McDonald, Meiklejohn, Craig, Archibald, Marshall, Fleming, McPhail, Morton.

12-4-30

RANGERS ....(0) 0   PARTICK T ....(0) 0   Att. 107,475

Rangers: T. Hamilton, Gray, R. Hamilton, Buchanan, Meiklejohn, Craig, Archibald, Marshall, Fleming, McPhail, Nicholson.

Replay – 16-4-30

RANGERS ....(1) 2   PARTICK T ....(0) 1   Att. 103,688
Marshall, Craig   Torbet

Rangers: T. Hamilton, Gray, R. Hamilton, McDonald, Meiklejohn, Craig, Archibald, Marshall, Fleming, McPhail, Morton.

16-4-32

RANGERS ....(0) 1   KILMARNOCK.....(1) 1   Att. 112,000
McPhail   Maxwell

Rangers: Hamilton, Gray, McAuley, Meiklejohn, Simpson, Brown, Archibald, Marshall, English, McPhail, Morton.

Replay – 20-4-32

RANGERS ....(1) 3   KILMARNOCK.....(0) 0   Att.104,600

Fleming, English, McPhail
Rangers: Hamilton, Gray, McAuley, Meiklejohn, Simpson, Brown, Archibald, Marshall, English, McPhail, Fleming.

21-4-34
RANGERS ....(2) 5   ST. MIRREN.........(0) 0   Att. 113,43
Nicholson 2, McPhail, Main, Smith
Rangers: Hamilton, Gray, McDonald, Meiklejohn, Simpson, Brown, Main, Marshall, Smith, McPhail, Nicholson.

20-4-35
RANGERS ....(1) 2   HAMILTON A.......(0) 1   Att. 87,74
Smith 2   Harrison
Rangers: Dawson, Gray, McDonald, Kennedy, Simpson, Brown, Main, Venters, Smith, McPhail, Gillick.

18-4-36
RANGERS ....(1) 1   THIRD LANARK ..(0) 0   Att. 88,85
McPhail
Rangers: Dawson, Gray, Cheyne, Meiklejohn, Simpson, Brown, Fiddes, Venters, Smith, McPhail, Turnbull.

17-4-48
RANGERS ....(1) 1   MORTON..............(1) 1†   Att. 129,1
Gillick   Whyte
Rangers: Brown, Young, Shaw, McColl, Woodburn, Cox, Rutherford, Gillick, Thornton, Findlay, Duncanson.
† *After Extra Time*

Replay – 21-4-48
RANGERS ....(0) 1   MORTON..............(0) 0†   Att. 133,7
Williamson
Rangers: Brown, Young, Shaw, McColl, Woodburn, Cox, Rutherford, Gillick, Thornton, Williamson, Duncanson.
† *After Extra Time*

23-4-49
RANGERS ....(2) 4   CLYDE..................(0) 1   Att. 108,4
Young 2 pens., Williamson, Duncanson   Galletly
Rangers: Brown, Young, Shaw, McColl, Woodburn, Cox, Waddell, Duncanson, Thornton, Williamson, Rutherford.

2-4-50
ANGERS ....(1) 3   EAST FIFE.............(0) 0   Att. 118,262
indlay, Thornton 2

angers: Brown, Young, Shaw, McColl, Woodburn, Cox, Rutherford, Findlay,
hornton, Duncanson, Rae.

5-4-53
ANGERS ....(1) 1   ABERDEEN...........(0) 1†   Att. 129,761
entice   Yorston

angers: Niven, Young, Little, McColl, Stanners, Pryde, Waddell, Grierson, Paton,
entice, Hubbard.
After Extra Time

eplay – 29-4-53
ANGERS ....(1) 1   ABERDEEN...........(0) 0   Att. 113,700
mpson

ngers: Niven, Young, Little, McColl, Woodburn, Pryde, Waddell, Grierson,
ton, Simpson, Hubbard.

-4-60
ANGERS ....(1) 2   KILMARNOCK.....(0) 0   Att. 108,017
llar 2

ngers: Niven, Caldow, Little, McColl, Paterson, Stevenson, Scott, McMillan,
llar, Baird, Wilson.

-4-62
ANGERS ....(1) 2   ST MIRREN...........(0) 0   Att. 127,940
nd, Wilson

ngers: Ritchie, Shearer, Caldow, Davis, McKinnon, Baxter, Henderson,
Millan, Millar, Brand, Wilson.

-63
NGERS ....(1) 1   CELTIC.................(1) 1†   Att. 129,643
nd   Murdoch

gers: Ritchie, Shearer, Provan, Greig, McKinnon, Baxter, Henderson, McLean,
lar, Brand, Wilson.
fter Extra Time

lay – 15-5-63
NGERS ....(2) 3   CELTIC.................(0) 0   Att. 120,273
son, Brand 2

gers: Ritchie, Shearer, Provan, Greig, McKinnon, Baxter, Henderson,
Millan, Millar, Brand, Wilson.

25-4-64
RANGERS ....(1) 3   DUNDEE ....(0) 1   Att. 120,9?
Millar 2, Brand   Cameron
Rangers: Ritchie, Shearer, Provan, Greig, McKinnon, Baxter, Henderson, McLea
Millar, Brand, Wilson.

23-4-66
RANGERS ....(0) 0   CELTIC.................(0) 0† Att. 126,5
Rangers: Ritchie, Johansen, Provan, Greig, McKinnon, Baxter, Henderson, Forre
Miller, Johnston, Wilson.
† *After Extra Time*

Replay – 27-4-66
RANGERS ....(0) 1   CELTIC.................(0) 0   Att. 98,2
Johansen
Rangers: Ritchie, Johansen, Provan, Greig, McKinnon, Baxter, Henderson,
McLean, Miller, Johnston, Wilson.

5-5-73
RANGERS ....(1) 3   CELTIC.................(1) 2   Att. 122,7
Parlane, Conn, Forsyth   Dalglish, Connolly pen.
Rangers: McCloy, Jardine, Mathieson, Greig, Johnstone, MacDonald, McLean,
Forsyth, Parlane, Conn, Young.

1-5-76
RANGERS ....(2) 3   HEARTS ....(0) 1   Att. 85,3
Johnstone 2, MacDonald   Shaw
Rangers: McCloy, Miller, Greig, Forsyth, Jackson, MacDonald, McKean, Hamil
(Jardine), Henderson, McLean, Johnstone.

6-5-78
RANGERS ....(1) 2   ABERDEEN...........(0) 1   Att. 61,?
MacDonald, Johnstone   Ritchie
Rangers: McCloy, Jardine, Greig, Forsyth, Jackson, MacDonald, McLean, Russe
Johnstone, Smith, Cooper (Watson).

12-5-79
RANGERS ....(0) 0   HIBERNIAN.........(0) 0 † Att. 50,
Rangers: McCloy, Jardine, Dawson, Johnstone, Jackson, MacDonald (Miller),
McLean, Russell, Parlane, Smith, Cooper.
† *After Extra Time*

Replay – 16-5-79
RANGERS ....(0) 0   HIBERNIAN ....(0) 0 †   Att. 33,504
Rangers: McCloy, Jardine, Dawson, Johnstone, Jackson, MacDonald, McLean
(Miller), Russell, Parlane, Smith, Cooper.
† *After Extra Time*

2nd Replay – 28-5-79
RANGERS ....(1) 3   HIBERNIAN ....(1) 2†   Att. 30,602
Johnstone 2, Duncan OG   Higgins, McLeod pen.
Rangers: McCloy, Jardine, Dawson, Johnstone, Jackson, Watson (Miller), McLean
(Smith), Russell, Parlane, MacDonald, Cooper.
† *After Extra Time*

9-5-81
RANGERS ....(0) 0   DUNDEE UTD ......(0) 0 †   Att. 53,000
Rangers: Stewart, Jardine, Dawson, Stevens, Forsyth, Bett, McLean, Russell,
McAdam (Cooper), Redford (W. Johnstone) (J. MacDonald), A. MacDonald.
† *After Extra Time*

Replay – 12-5-81
RANGERS ....(3) 4   DUNDEE UTD ......(1) 1   Att. 43,099
Cooper, Russell, MacDonald 2   Dodds
Rangers: Stewart, Jardine, Dawson, Forsyth, Stevens, Bett, Cooper, Russell,
D. Johnstone, Redford, J. MacDonald.

9-5-92
RANGERS ....(2) 2   AIRDRIE................(0) 1   Att. 44,045
Hateley, McCoist   Smith
Rangers: Goram, Stevens, Robertson, Gough, Spackman, Brown, Durrant
(Gordon), McCall, McCoist, Hateley, Mikhailitchenko.

29-5-93
RANGERS ....(2) 2   ABERDEEN...........(0) 1   Att. 50,715
Murray, Hateley   Richardson
Rangers: Goram, McCall, Robertson, Gough, McPherson, Brown, Murray,
Ferguson, Durrant, Hateley, Huistra (Pressley).

Rangers in Europe – *European Cup*

4-10-56 – First Round
RANGERS ....(1) 2   OGC NICE ....(1) 1   Att. 65,000
Murray, Simpson   Faivre
Rangers: Niven, Shearer, Caldow, McColl, Young, Logie, Scott, Simpson, Murray,
Baird, Hubbard.

14-11-56 – First Round Second Leg

OGC NICE ....(0) 2   RANGERS ....(1) 1   Att. 5,000

Bravo, Foix   Hubbard pen.

Rangers: Niven, Shearer, Caldow, McColl, Young, Logie, Scott, Simpson, Murray, Baird, Hubbard.

3-3 on aggregate

28-11-56 – First Round Play-Off in Paris

OGC NICE ....(1) 3   RANGERS ....(0) 1   Att. 15,000

Foix, Muro, Faivre   Bonvin OG

Rangers: Niven, Shearer, Caldow, McColl, Davis, Logie, Scott, Simpson, Murray, Baird, Hubbard.

4-9-57 – First Round

RANGERS ....(1) 3   ST ETIENNE ....(1) 1   Att. 85,000

Kichenbrand, Scott, Simpson   Mekloufi

Rangers: Niven, Shearer, Caldow, McColl, Davis, Baird, Scott, Simpson, Kichenbrand, Murray, Hubbard.

25-9-57 – First Round Second Leg

ST ETIENNE ....(1) 2   RANGERS ....(0) 1   Att. 35,000

Oleksiak, Fevrier   Wilson

Rangers: Ritchie, Shearer, Caldow, McColl, Valentine, Millar, Scott, Simpson, Murray, Baird, Wilson.

Rangers won 4-3 on aggregate

27-11-57 – Second Round

RANGERS ....(1) 1   AC MILAN ....(0) 4   Att. 85,000

Murray   Grillo 2, Baruffi, Bean

Rangers: Ritchie, Little, Caldow, McColl, Telfer, Millar, Scott, Simpson, Murray, Baird, Hubbard.

11-12-57 – Second Round Second Leg

AC MILAN ....(1) 2   RANGERS ....(0) 0   Att. 2,000

Baruffi, Galli

Rangers: Niven, Shearer, Caldow, McColl, Telfer, Baird, Scott, Millar, Kichenbrand, Wilson, Hubbard.

Milan won 6-1 on aggregate

16-9-59 – Prelim Round

RANGERS ....(2) 5   ANDERLECHT .....(0) 2   Att. 80,000

Millar, Scott, Matthew pen.,   Stockman, De Waele

Baird 2, 1 pen.

Rangers: Niven, Shearer, Little, Davis, Telfer, Stevenson, Scott, McMillan, Millar, Baird, Matthew.

23-9-59 – Prelim Round Second Leg

ANDERLECHT .....(0) 0   RANGERS ....(0) 2   Att. 40,000
                                    Matthew, McMillan

Rangers: Niven, Shearer, Little, Davis, Telfer, Stevenson, Scott, McMillan, Wilson, Baird, Matthew.

Rangers won 7-2 on aggregate

11-11-59 – First Round

RANGERS ....(2) 4   RED STAR BELGRADE...(2) 3   Att. 80,000
McMillan, Scott, Wilson, Millar   Scherer 2, Dolinsky

Rangers: Niven, Caldow, Little, Davis, Telfer, Stevenson, Scott, McMillan, Millar, Baird, Wilson.

18-11-59 – First Round Second Leg

RED STAR BELGRADE...(0) 1   RANGERS ....(0)1   Att. 60,000
Tichy   Scott

Rangers: Niven, Shearer, Little, Davis, Telfer, Stevenson, Scott, McMillan, Millar, Baird, Wilson.

Rangers won 5-4 on aggregate

9-3-60 – Second Round

SPARTA ROTTERDAM ...(1) 2   RANGERS ....(2) 3   Att. 50,000
De Vries 2   Wilson, Baird, Murray

Rangers: Niven, Caldow, Little, Davis, Paterson, Stevenson, Scott, McMillan, Murray, Baird, Wilson.

16-3-60 – Second Round Second Leg

RANGERS ....(0) 0   SPARTA ROTTERDAM ...(0) 1   Att. 82,587
                                   Van Ede

Rangers: Ritchie, Caldow, Little, Davis, Paterson, Stevenson, Scott, Baird, Millar, Brand, Wilson.

3-3 on aggregate

30-3-60 – Second Round Play-Off (at Highbury)

RANGERS ....(1) 3   SPARTA ROTTERDAM ...(1) 2   Att. 34,176
Verhoeven OG, Baird, Van Der Lee OG   Verhoeven, Bosselaar pen.

Rangers: Niven, Caldow, Little, Davis, Paterson, Stevenson, Scott, McMillan, Millar, Baird, Wilson.

13-4-60 – Semi-Final

ENTRACHT FRANKFURT ...(1) 6   RANGERS ....(1) 1   Att. 70,000
Kinka, Pfaff 2, Lindner 2, Stein   Caldow pen.

Rangers: Niven, Caldow, Little, Baird, Paterson, Stevenson, Scott, McMillan, Murray, Millar, Wilson.

5-5-60 – Semi-Final Second Leg

RANGERS ....(1) 3   EINTRACHT FRANKFURT ...(3) 6   Att. 70,000

McMillan 2, Wilson   Lindner 2, Pfaff 2, Meier 2

Rangers: Niven, Caldow, Little, Davis, Paterson, Stevenson, Scott, McMillan, Millar, Baird, Wilson.

Eintracht won 12-4 on aggregate

5-9-61 – Preliminary Round

AS MONACO ....(0) 2   RANGERS ....(2) 3   Att. 7,000

Hess, Carlier pen.   Baxter, Scott 2

Rangers: Ritchie, Shearer, Caldow, Davis, Paterson, Baxter, Scott, McMillan, Millar, Brand, Wilson.

12-9-61 – Preliminary Round, Second Leg

RANGERS ....(0) 3   AS MONACO ....(1) 2   Att. 65,000

Christie 2, Scott   Hess 2

Rangers: Ritchie, Shearer, Caldow, Davis, Paterson, Baxter, Scott, McMillan, Christie, Brand, Wilson.

Rangers won 6-4 on aggregate

15-11-61 – First Round

ASK VORWAERTS .....(1) 1   RANGERS ....(2) 2   Att. 20,000

Kohle   Caldow pen., Brand

Rangers: Ritchie, Shearer, Caldow, Davis, Paterson, Baxter, Scott, McMillan, Millar, Brand, Wilson.

22-11-61 – First Round Second Leg

Match played in Malmo, Sweden. The East Germans were refused visas.

RANGERS 1   ASK VORWAERTS 0   Att. 4,000

Henderson

Rangers: Ritchie, Shearer, Caldow, Davis, Paterson, Baxter, Scott, McMillan, Millar, Brand, Wilson.

Abandoned after 45 minutes due to fog.

23-11-61 – First Round, Second Leg. Rearranged Game in Malmo.

RANGERS ....(0) 4   ASK VORWAERTS .....(0) 1   Att. 1,78

Kalinke OG, McMillan 2, Henderson   Caldow OG

Rangers: Ritchie, Shearer, Caldow, Davis, Paterson, Baxter, Henderson, McMillan, Millar, Brand, Wilson.

Rangers won 6-2 on aggregate

7-2-62 – Quarter-Final

STANDARD LIEGE ....(2) 4　　　　RANGERS ....(1) 1　Att. 37,000

Claesson, Crossan 2, Vliers　　　　Wilson

Rangers: Ritchie, Shearer, King, Davis, Paterson, Baxter, Henderson, Greig, Millar, Brand, Wilson.

14-2-62 – Quarter-Final Second Leg

RANGERS ....(1) 2　　　　STANDARD LIEGE ....(0) 0　Att. 76,000

Brand, Caldow pen.

Rangers: Ritchie, Shearer, Caldow, Davis, Baillie, Baxter, Scott, McMillan, Millar, Brand, Wilson.

Standard Liege won 4-3 on aggregate

25-9-63 – Preliminary Round

RANGERS ....(0) 0　　　　REAL MADRID ....(0) 1　Att. 80,000

　　　　　　　　　　　　　　　　Puskas

Rangers: Ritchie, Shearer, Provan, Greig, McKinnon, Baxter, Henderson, McLean, Forrest, Brand, Wilson.

-10-63 – Preliminary Round Second Leg

REAL MADRID ....(4) 6　　　　RANGERS ....(0) 0　Att. 80,000

Puskas 3, Evariste, Gento, Ruiz

Rangers: Ritchie, Shearer, Provan, Greig, McKinnon, Baxter, Henderson, Willoughby, Forrest, McLean, Watson.

Real Madrid won 7-0 on aggregate

-9-64 – First Round First Leg

RANGERS ....(1) 3　　　　RED STAR BELGRADE...(0) 1　Att. 80,000

Brand 2, Forrest　　　　Djazic

Rangers: Ritchie, Hynd, Provan, Greig, McKinnon, Baxter, Henderson, McLean, Forrest, Brand, Wilson.

-9-64 – First Round Second Leg

RED STAR BELGRADE...(1) 4　　　　RANGERS ....(1) 2　Att. 70,000

Sincevic 2, Kostic, Melic.　　　　Greig, McKinnon

Rangers: Ritchie, Shearer, Provan, Greig, McKinnon, Baxter, Henderson, Millar, Forrest, Brand, Wilson.

5 on aggregate

-11-64 – First Round Play-Off. At Highbury

RANGERS ....(2) 3　　　　RED STAR BELGRADE...(0) 1　Att. 34,428

Forrest 2, Brand　　　　Kop

Rangers: Ritchie, Provan, Caldow, Greig, McKinnon, Wood, Brand, Millar, Forrest, Baxter, Johnston.

18-11-64 – Second Round
RANGERS ....(1) 1   RAPID VIENNA....(0) 0   Att. 60,000
Wilson
Rangers: Ritchie, Provan, Caldow, Greig, McKinnon, Wood, Wilson, Millar,
Forrest, Baxter, Johnston.

8-12-64 – Second Round Second Leg
RAPID VIENNA....(0) 0   RANGERS ....(1) 2   Att. 70,000
                                       Forrest, Wilson
Rangers: Ritchie, Provan, Caldow, Greig, McKinnon, Wood, Johnston, Millar,
Forrest, Baxter, Wilson.
Rangers won 3-0 on aggregate

17-2-65 – Quarter-Final
INTER MILAN ......(0) 3   RANGERS ....(0) 1   Att. 49,520
Suarez, Peiro 2   Forrest
Rangers: Ritchie, Provan, Caldow, Wood, McKinnon, Greig, Henderson, Millar,
Forrest, Brand, Wilson.

3-3-65 – Quarter-Final
RANGERS ....(1) 1   INTER MILAN ......(0) 0   Att. 77,200
Forrest
Rangers: Ritchie, Provan, Caldow, Greig, McKinnon, Hynd, Henderson, Millar,
Forrest, McLean, Johnston.

17-9-74 – First Round
RANGERS ....(2) 4   BOHEMIANS ....(1) 1   Att. 24,000
Fyfe, Burke OG, O'Hara, Johnstone   Flanagan
Rangers: McCloy, Denny, Miller, Greig, Jackson, Johnstone, Fyfe, O'Hara,
Parlane, Stein, Young.

1-10-74 – First Round Second Leg
BOHEMIANS ....(0) 1   RANGERS ....(1) 1   Att. 8,000
O'Connor   Johnstone
Rangers: McCloy, Miller, Dawson, Greig, Jackson, Young, McLean, MacDonald,
Parlane, Johnstone, Fyfe.
Rangers won 5-2 on aggregate

22-10-74 – Second Round
ST ETIENNE ....(1) 2   RANGERS ....(0) 0   Att. 28,390
Revelli, Bathenay
Rangers: Kennedy, Jardine, Miller, Greig, Jackson, Forsyth, McLean, Stein,
Parlane, MacDonald, Johnstone.

5-11-74 – Second Round Second Leg

RANGERS ....(0) 1   ST ETIENNE ....(0) 2   Att. 45,000
MacDonald   Rocheteau, Revelli

Rangers: Kennedy, Jardine, Greig, Forsyth, Jackson, MacDonald, McLean, Stein, Parlane, Johnstone, Young.

St Etienne won 4-1 on aggregate

15-9-76 – First Round

RANGERS ....(1) 1   FC ZURICH ....(1) 1   Att. 35,000
Parlane   Cucinotta

Rangers: McCloy, Miller, Greig, Forsyth, Denny, MacDonald, McLean, Jardine, Parlane, McKean, Johnstone.

29-9-76 – First Round Second Leg

FC ZURICH ....(1) 1   RANGERS ....(0) 0   Att. 28,500
Martinelli

Rangers: McCloy, Miller, Greig, Forsyth, Jackson (Denny), Jardine, MacDonald, Hamilton (McKean), McLean, Parlane, Johnstone.

Zurich won 2-1 on aggregate

13-9-78 – First Round

JUVENTUS............(1) 1   RANGERS ....(0) 0   Att. 62,000
Virdis

Rangers: McCloy, Jardine, A. Forsyth, T. Forysth, Jackson, A. MacDonald, Miller, Russell, Parlane, Smith, Watson.

27-9-78 – First Round Second Leg

RANGERS ....(1) 2   JUVENTUS............(0) 0   Att. 44,000
A. MacDonald , Smith

Rangers: McCloy, Jardine, A. Forsyth, T. Forsyth, Jackson, A. MacDonald, McLean, Russell, Parlane, Johnstone, Smith.

Rangers won 2-1 on aggregate

18-10-78 – Second Round

RANGERS ....(0) 0   PSV EINDHOVEN ...(0) 0   Att. 44,000

Rangers: McCloy, Jardine, A. Forsyth, T. Forsyth, Jackson, A. MacDonald, McLean, Russell, Parlane (Cooper), Johnstone, Smith.

-11-78 – Second Round Second Leg

PSV EINDHOVEN ...(1) 2   RANGERS ....(0) 3   Att. 28,000
ubse, Deykers   MacDonald, Johnstone, Russell

Rangers: McCloy, Jardine, A. Forsyth, T. Forsyth, Johnstone, A. MacDonald, McLean, Russell, Parlane, Smith, Watson.

Rangers won 3-2 on aggregate

327

6-3-79 – Quarter-Final
COLOGNE.............(0) 1   RANGERS ....(0) 0   Att. 45,000
Muller
Rangers: McCloy, Jardine, Dawson, T. Forsyth, Jackson, A. MacDonald, McLean,
Russell, Parlane (Urquhart), Smith, Denny (Miller).

21-3-79 – Quarter-Final Second Leg
RANGERS ....(0) 1   COLOGNE.............(0) 1   Att. 44,000
McLean   Muller
Rangers: McCloy, Jardine, Dawson (Johnstone), T. Forsyth, Jackson, A.
MacDonald, McLean, Russell, Urquhart (Parlane), Smith, Cooper.
Cologne won 2-1 on aggregate

16-9-87 – First Round
DYNAMO KIEV ...(0) 1   RANGERS ....(0) 0   Att. 100,000
Mikhailitchenko pen.
Rangers: Woods, Nicholl, Butcher, McGregor, Phillips, Roberts, Souness,
Ferguson, Cohen, Durrant, McCoist.

30-9-87 – First Round Second Leg
RANGERS ....(1) 2   DYNAMO KIEV ...(0) 0   Att. 44,500
Falco, McCoist
Rangers: Woods, Nicholl, Phillips, McGregor, Souness, Butcher, Francis (Fleck),
Falco, McCoist, Durrant, Cohen (Kirkwood).
Rangers won 2-1 on aggregate

21-10-87 – Second Round
RANGERS ....(3) 3   GORNIK ZABRZE(0) 1   Att. 41,36
McCoist, Durrant, Falco   Urban
Rangers: Woods, Nicholl, Phillips, Roberts, Ferguson (Cohen), Butcher, Francis
(Fleck), Falco, McCoist, Durrant, Souness.

4-11-87 – Second Round Second Leg
GORNIK ZABRZE(0) 1   RANGERS ....(1) 1   Att. 23,35
Orzeszek   McCoist pen.
Rangers: Woods, Nicholl, Phillips, Roberts, Souness, Butcher, McGregor, Durrant
Ferguson, McCoist (Fleck), Cooper.
Rangers won 4-2 on aggregate

2-3-88 – Quarter-Finals
STEAUA BUCHAREST .(1) 2   RANGERS ....(0) 0   Att. 30,00
Piturca, Iovan
Rangers: Woods, Gough, Munro, Roberts, Wilkins, Nisbet (D. Ferguson), Nicholl,
Souness, McCoist (Francis), Durrant, Cooper.

328

16-3-88 – Quarter-Finals Second Leg

RANGERS ....(2) 2   STEAUA BUCHAREST .(1) 1   Att. 44,000

Gough, McCoist pen.   Lacatus

Rangers: Woods, Nisbet (Francis), Munro, Roberts, Wilkins, Gough, D. Ferguson, Souness, McCoist, Durrant, Cooper.

Steau Bucharest won 3-2 on aggregate

13-9-89 – First Round

RANGERS ....(1) 1   BAYERN MUNICH .....(1) 3   Att. 40,135

Walters pen.   Kogl, Thon pen., Augenthaler

Rangers: Woods, Stevens, Munro, Nisbet, Wilkins, Butcher, Steven, I. Ferguson, D. Ferguson, Johnston, Walters.

27-9-89 – First Round Second Leg

BAYERN MUNICH .....(0) 0   RANGERS ....(0) 0   Att. 43,000

Rangers: Ginzburg, Stevens, Munro, Gough, Wilkins, Butcher, Steven, I. Ferguson, Cowan (Drinkell), Johnston, Walters.

Bayern Munich won 3-1 on aggregate

19-9-90 – First Round

VALLETTA ....(0) 0   RANGERS ....(1) 4   Att. 8,000

                         McCoist pen., Hateley, Johnston 2

Rangers: Woods, Stevens, Munro (Brown), Gough, Spackman, Butcher, Steven, McCoist, Hateley, Johnston, Walters.

2-10-90 – First Round Second Leg

RANGERS ....(4) 6   VALLETTA ....(0) 0   Att. 20,627

Dodds, Spencer, Johnston 3, 1 pen., McCoist

Rangers: Woods, Stevens, Munro, Cowan (Robertson), Dodds (McCoist), Brown, Steven, Walters, Spencer, Johnston, Huistra.

Rangers won 10-0 on aggregate

24-10-90 – Second Round

RED STAR BELGRADE...(1) 3   RANGERS ....(0) 0   Att. 82,000

Brown OG, Prosinecki, Pancev

Rangers: Woods, Stevens, Munro, Gough, Spackman, Brown, Steven, Ferguson, Walters, Johnston, Huistra (McCoist).

7-11-90 – Second Round Second Leg

RANGERS ....(0) 1   RED STAR BELGRADE...(0) 1   Att. 23,821

McCoist   Pancev

Rangers: Woods, Stevens, Munro, Gough (Nisbet), Spackman, Brown, Steven, Dodds (Robertson), McCoist, Hateley, Walters.

Red Star won 4-1 on aggregate

17-9-91 – First Round
SPARTA PRAGUE......(1) 1   RANGERS ....(0) 0   Att. 11,053
Nemec
Rangers: Goram, Stevens, D. Robertson, Gough, Spackman, Nisbet, McCall, I.
Ferguson, McCoist (Brown), Hateley, Huistra.

2-10-91 – First Round Second Leg
RANGERS ....(0) 2   SPARTA PRAGUE(0) 1†   Att. 34,260
McCall 2   Nisbet OG
Rangers: Goram, Stevens, D. Robertson, Brown (Durrant), Spackman, Nisbet,
Kuznetsov, McCall, McCoist (Spencer), Johnston, Mikhailitchenko.
2-2 on aggregate. Sparta Prague won on away goals after extra time

16-9-92 – First Round
RANGERS ....(1) 2   LYNGBY ....(0) 0   Att. 40,036
Hateley, Huistra
Rangers: Goram, McPherson, D. Robertson, Gough, Brown, Durrant,
Mikhailitchenko, Ferguson, McCoist, Hateley, Huistra.

30-9-92 – First Round Second Leg
LYNGBY ....(0) 0   RANGERS ....(0) 1   Att. 4273
                                  Durrant
Rangers: Goram, McCall, D. Robertson, Durrant, McPherson, Brown, Steven,
Ferguson, McCoist, Hateley, Huistra.
Rangers won 3-0 on aggregate

21-10-92 – Second Round
RANGERS ....(2) 2   LEEDS UNITED....(1) 1   Att. 44,000
Lukic OG, McCoist   McAllister
Rangers: Goram, McCall, D. Robertson, Gough, McPherson, Brown, Steven
(Huistra), Ferguson, McCoist, Hateley, Durrant.

4-11-92 – Second Round Second Leg
LEEDS UNITED....(0) 1   RANGERS ....(1) 2   Att. 25,518
Cantona   Hateley, McCoist
Rangers: Goram, McCall, D. Robertson, Gough, McPherson, Brown, Gordon
(Mikhailitchenko), Ferguson, McCoist, Hateley, Durrant.
Rangers won 4-2 on aggregate

Champions League – Group A
25-11-92 – Match 1
RANGERS ....(0) 2   MARSEILLE ....(1) 2   Att. 41,624
McSwegan, Hateley   Boksic, Voller
Rangers: Goram, Murray, D. Robertson, Gough (Pressley), McPherson, Brown,
Steven (McSwegan), McCall, Durrant, Hateley, Mikhailitchenko.

330

9-12-92 – Match 2 in Bochum, Germany
CSKA MOSCOW ..(0) 0   RANGERS ....(1) 1   Att. 9,000
                                   Ferguson
Rangers: Goram, McCall, D. Robertson, Durrant, McPherson, Brown, Steven, Ferguson, McCoist, Hateley, Mikhailitchenko.

3-3-93 – Match 3
FC BRUGGE..........(1) 1   RANGERS ....(0) 1   Att. 19,000
Dziubinski   Huistra
Rangers: Goram, Nisbet (Pressley), D. Robertson, Murray, McPherson, Brown, Mikhailitchenko, McCall, McCoist, Hateley, Huistra.

17-3-93 – Match 4
RANGERS ....(1) 2   FC BRUGGE..........(0) 1   Att. 42,731
Durrant, Nisbet   Staelens
Rangers: Goram, Nisbet, Murray, Gough, McPherson, Brown, Steven, McCall, Durrant, Hateley, Mikhailitchenko.

7-4-93 – Match 5
MARSEILLE ....(1) 1   RANGERS ....(0) 1   Att. 40,000
Sauzee   Durrant
Rangers: Goram, McCall, D. Robertson (Murray), Gough, McPherson, Brown, Steven, Ferguson, McCoist, Durrant, Huistra (McSwegan).

21-3-93 – Match 6
RANGERS ....(0) 0   CSKA MOSCOW ..(0) 0   Att. 43,142
Rangers: Goram, McCall, D. Robertson, Gough, McPherson, Brown, Steven (McSwegan), Ferguson, McCoist, Durrant, Huistra.

Final Table

	P	W	D	L	F	A	Pts
1. Marseille	6	3	3	0	14	4	9
2. Rangers	6	2	4	0	7	5	8
3. FC Brugge	6	2	1	3	5	8	5
4. CSKA Moscow	6	0	2	4	2	11	2

15-9-93 – First Round
RANGERS ....(1) 3   LEVSKI SOFIA .....(0) 2   Att. 37,013
McPherson, Hateley 2   Borimirov, Todorov
Rangers: Maxwell, Stevens, D. Robertson, McCall, McPherson, Pressley, Steven, I. Ferguson, Durrant (Morrow), Hateley, D. Ferguson.

29-9-93 – First Round Second Leg
LEVSKI SOFIA .....(1) 2   RANGERS ....(1) 1   Att. 50,000

Sirakov, Todorov   Durrant

Rangers: Maxwell, Stevens, Wishart, Gough, McPherson, McCall, Steven, I. Ferguson, Durrant, Hateley, Hagen.

4-4 on aggregate. Levski Sofia won on away goals

10-8-94 – First Round
AEK ATHENS ....(1) 2   RANGERS ....(0) 0   Att. 30,000
Saravakos 2

Rangers: Goram, Stevens, Robertson, Gough, Pressley, McCall, Laudrup, I. Ferguson, Durie (Durrant), Hateley, Murray.

24-10-94 – First Round Second Leg
RANGERS ....(0) 0   AEK ATHENS ....(1) 1   Att. 44,789
Saveski

Rangers: Goram, McCall, D. Robertson, Gough, Boli, McPherson, Durie (Durrant), I. Ferguson, D. Ferguson, Hateley, Laudrup.

AEK Athens won 3-0 on aggregate

Rangers in Europe – European Cup-Winners' Cup

28-9-60 – First Round
RANGERS ....(0) 4   FERENCVAROS ...(1) 2   Att. 36,000
Davis, Millar 2, Brand   Orosz, Friedmansky

Rangers: Ritchie, Shearer, Caldow, Davis, Paterson, Baxter, Scott, McMillan, Millar, Brand, Wilson.

12-10-60 – First Round Second Leg
FERENCVAROS ...(1) 2   RANGERS ....(0) 1   Att. 25,000
Orosz, Friedmansky   Wilson

Rangers: Ritchie, Shearer, Caldow, Davis, Paterson, Baxter, Scott, McMillan, Millar, Brand, Wilson.

Rangers won 5-4 on aggregate

15-11-60 – Second Round
B. MOENCHENGLADBACH.....(0) 0   RANGERS................(2) 3   Att. 50,000
Millar, Scott, McMilland

Rangers: Niven, Shearer, Caldow, Davis, Paterson, Baxter, Scott, McMillan, Millar, Brand, Wilson.

30-11-60 – Second Round Second Leg
RANGERS ....(5) 8   B. MOENCHENGLADBACH ..(0) 0   Att. 38,174
Baxter, Brand 3, Pfeffier og, Millar 2,

Davis
Rangers: Niven, Shearer, Caldow, Davis, Paterson, Baxter, Scott, McMillan,
Millar, Brand, Wilson.
Rangers won 11-0 on aggregate

29-3-61 – Semi-Final
RANGERS ....(1) 2   WOLVES ....(0) 0   Att. 80,000
Scott, Brand
Rangers: Ritchie, Shearer, Caldow, Davis, Paterson, Baxter, Scott, Wilson, Baillie,
Brand, Hume.

19-4-61 – Semi-Final Second Leg
WOLVES ....(0) 1   RANGERS ....(1) 1   Att. 45,163
Broadbent   Scott
Rangers: Ritchie, Shearer, Caldow, Davis, Paterson, Baxter, Wilson, McMillan,
Scott, Brand, Hume.
Rangers won 3-1 on aggregate

17-5-61 – Final – First Leg
RANGERS ....(0) 0   FIORENTINA ....(1) 2   Att. 80,000
                                      Milan 2
Rangers: Ritchie, Shearer, Caldow, Davis, Paterson, Baxter, Wilson, McMillan,
Scott, Brand, Hume.

27-5-61 – Final – Second Leg
FIORENTINA ....(1) 2   RANGERS ....(0) 1   Att. 40,000
Milan, Hamrin   Scott
Rangers: Ritchie, Shearer, Caldow, Davis, Paterson, Baxter, Scott, McMillan,
Millar, Brand, Wilson.
Fiorentina won 4-1 on aggregate

5-9-62 – First Round
RANGERS ....(2) 4   SEVILLE................(0) 0   Att. 65,000
Millar 3, Brand
Rangers: Ritchie, Shearer, Caldow, Davis, McKinnon, Baxter, Henderson, Greig,
Millar, Brand, Wilson.
26-9-62 – First Round Second Leg
SEVILLE................(2) 2   RANGERS ....(0) 0   Att. 25,000
Dieguez, Mateos
Rangers: Ritchie, Shearer, Caldow, Davis, McKinnon, Baxter, Henderson, Greig,
Millar, Brand, Wilson.
Rangers won 4-2 on aggregate

31-10-62 – Second Round
TOTTENHAM H ...(4) 5   RANGERS ....(2) 2   Att. 58, 859

White, Greaves, Allen, Shearer OG,   Henderson, Millar
Norman
Rangers: Ritchie, Shearer, Caldow, Davis, McKinnon, Baxter, Henderson,
McMillan, Millar, Brand, Wilson.

11-12-62 – Second Round Second Leg
RANGERS ....(0) 2   TOTTENHAM H ...(1) 3   Att. 80,000
Brand, Wilson   Greaves, Smith 2
Rangers: Ritchie, Shearer, Caldow, Davis, McKinnon, Baxter, Henderson,
McMillan, Millar, Brand, Wilson.
Spurs won 8-4 on aggregate

27-9-66 – First Round
GLENTORAN ....(0)1   RANGERS ....(1) 1   Att. 40,000
Sinclair   McLean
Rangers: Ritchie, Johansen, Provan, Millar, McKinnon, D. Smith, Henderson,
Greig, McLean, A. Smith, Johnston.

5-10-66 – First Round Second Leg
RANGERS ....(2) 4   GLENTORAN ....(0) 0   Att. 40,000
Johnston, D. Smith, Setterington, McLean
Rangers: Ritchie, Johansen, Provan, Greig, McKinnon, D. Smith, Henderson, A.
Smith, McLean, Setterington, Johnston.
Rangers won 5-1 on aggregate

23-11-66 – Second Round
RANGERS ....(1) 2   BORUSSIA DORTMUND .(1) 1   Att. 65,000
Johansen, A. Smith   Trimholdt
Rangers: Martin, Johansen, Provan, Greig, McKinnon, D. Smith, Henderson,
Watson, Forrest, A. Smith, Johnston.

6-12-66 – Second Round Second Leg
BORUSSIA DORTMUND .(0) 0   RANGERS ....(0) 0   Att. n/a
Rangers: Martin, Johansen, Provan, Jardine, McKinnon, Greig, Henderson,
Willoughby, A. Smith, D. Smith, Wilson.
Rangers won 2-1 on aggregate
1-3-67 – Third Round
RANGERS ....(2) 2   REAL ZARAGOZA .....(0) 0   Att. 65,000
D. Smith, Willoughby
Rangers: Martin, Johansen, Provan, Jardine, McKinnon, Greig, Henderson,
Willoughby, A. Smith, D. Smith, Wilson.

22-3-67 – Third Round Second Leg
REAL ZARAGOZA .....(1) 2   RANGERS ....(0) 0   Att. 35,000

Lapetra, Santos pen.
Rangers: Martin, Johansen, Provan, Jardine, Jackson, Greig, Henderson, Willoughby, A. Smith, D. Smith, Wilson.
Rangers won on toss of coin.

19-4-67 – Semi-Final
SLAVIA SOFIA.....(0) 0   RANGERS ....(1) 1   Att. n/a
                                         Wilson
Rangers: Martin, Johansen, Provan, Jardine, McKinnon, Greig, Henderson, Willoughby, A. Smith, D. Smith, Wilson.

3-5-67 – Semi-Final Second Leg
RANGERS ....(1) 1   SLAVIA SOFIA.....(0) 0   Att. 70,000
Henderson
Rangers: Martin, Johansen, Provan, Jardine, McKinnon, Greig, Henderson, A. Smith, Hynd, D. Smith, Johnston.
Rangers won 2-0 on aggregate

31-5-67 – Final
RANGERS ....(0) 0   BAYERN MUNICH.....(0) 1†   Att. 65,000
                                         Roth
Rangers: Martin, Johansen, Provan, Jardine, McKinnon, Greig, Henderson, A. Smith, Hynd, D. Smith, Johnston.

17-09-69 – First Round
RANGERS ....(2) 2   STEAUA BUCHAREST .(0) 0   Att. 43,346
Johnston 2.
Rangers: Neef, Johansen, Provan, Greig, McKinnon, Baxter, Henderson, Jardine, Stein, Johnston, Persson (Smith).

1-10-69 – First Round Second Leg
STEAUA BUCHAREST .(0) 0   RANGERS ....(0) 0   Att. 90,000
Rangers: Neef, Johansen, Provan, Greig, McKinnon, Baxter, Henderson, Watson (Smith), Stein, Jardine, Johnston.
Rangers won 2-0 on aggregate
† *After Extra Time*
12-11-69 – Second Round
GORNIK ZABRZE...(2) 3   RANGERS ....(0) 1   Att. 60,000
Lubanski, Szoltysik, Lubanski   Persson
Rangers: Neef, Johansen, Heron, Greig, McKinnon, Baxter, Henderson, Penman, Stein, Johnston, Persson.

26-11-69 – Second Round Second Leg
RANGERS ....(1) 1   GORNIK ZABRZE(0) 3   Att. 63,000

335

Baxter   Olek, Lubański, Skowronek
Rangers: Neef, Johansen, Heron, Greig, McKinnon, Baxter, Henderson, Penman,
Stein, Johnston, Persson (MacDonald).
Gornik won 6-2 on aggregate

15-9-71 – First Round
RENNES ....(0) 1   RANGERS ....(0) 1   Att. 20,000
Redon   Johnston
Rangers: McCloy, Jardine, Mathieson, Greig, McKinnon, Jackson, McLean,
MacDonald, Stein (Denny), Penman, Johnston.

28-9-71 – First Round Second Leg
RANGERS ....(1) 1   RENNES ....(0) 0   Att. 40,000
MacDonald
Rangers: McCloy, Jardine, Mathieson, Greig, McKinnon, Jackson, Henderson,
Conn, Stein, MacDonald, Johnston.
Rangers won 2-1 on aggregate

20-10-71 – Second Round
RANGERS ....(3) 3   SPORTING LISBON ....(0) 2   Att. 50,000
Stein 2, Henderson   Chico, Gomes
Rangers: McCloy, Greig, Mathieson, Jardine, McKinnon, Smith, Henderson,
Penman (Conn), Stein, Fyfe, MacDonald.

3-11-71 – Second Round Second Leg
SPORTING LISBON ....(2) 4   RANGERS ....(1) 3†   Att. 60,000
Yazalde, Tome, Gomes, Perez   Stein 2, Henderson
Rangers: McCloy, Greig, Mathieson, Jardine, McKinnon (Smith), Jackson,
Henderson, Conn, Stein, Johnston (McLean), MacDonald.
6-6 on aggregate. Rangers won on away goals after extra time

8-3-72 – Quarter-Final
TORINO ....(0) 1   RANGERS ....(1) 1   Att. 35,000
Toschi   Johnston
Rangers: McCloy, Jardine, Mathieson, Greig, Jackson, Smith, McLean, D.
Johnstone, Stein, MacDonald, Johnston.
22-3-72 – Quarter-Final Second Leg
RANGERS ....(0) 1   TORINO ....(0) 0   Att. 65,000
MacDonald
Rangers: McCloy, Jardine, Mathieson, Greig, Jackson, Smith, McLean, D.
Johnstone, Stein, MacDonald, Johnston.
Rangers won 2-1 on aggregate

5-4-72 – Semi-Final
BAYERN MUNICH..(1) 1 **RANGERS** ....(0) 1 Att. 40,000
Breitner Zobel OG
Rangers: McCloy, Jardine, Mathieson, Greig, Jackson, Smith, McLean, D. Johnstone, Stein, MacDonald, Johnston.

19-4-72 – Semi-Final Second Leg
RANGERS ....(2) 2 **BAYERN MUNICH..(0) 0** Att. 80,000
Jardine, Parlane
Rangers: McCloy, Jardine, Mathieson, Parlane, Jackson, Smith, McLean, D. Johnstone, Stein, MacDonald, Johnston.
Rangers won 3-1 on aggregate

24-5-72 – Final in Barcelona
RANGERS ....(2) 3 **MOSCOW DYNAMO ..(0) 2** Att. 35,000
Stein, Johnston 2 Eschtrekov, Makovikov
Rangers: McCloy, Jardine, Mathieson, Greig, D. Johnstone, Smith, McLean, Conn, Stein, MacDonald, W. Johnston.

19-9-73 – First Round
ANKARAGUCU ...(0) 0 **RANGERS** ....(1) 2 Att. 30,000
Conn, McLean
Rangers: McCloy, Jardine, Mathieson, Greig, Jackson, Smith, McLean, Forsyth, Parlane, Conn, Young.

3-10-73 – First Round Second Leg
RANGERS ....(1) 4 **ANKARAGUCU ...(0) 0** Att. 30,000
Greig 2, O'Hara, Johnstone
Rangers: McCloy, Jardine, Mathieson, Greig, Johnstone, MacDonald, McLean, Forsyth, O'Hara, Conn, Houston.
Rangers won 6-0 on aggregate

21-10-73 – Second Round
B. MOENCHENGLADBACH ..(1) 3 **RANGERS** ....(0) 0 Att. 33,000
Heynckes 2, Rupp
Rangers: McCloy, Jardine, Johnstone, Forsyth, Mathieson, Greig, MacDonald, Houston, McLean, Parlane (O'Hara), Conn.

7-11-73 – Second Round Second Leg
RANGERS ....(2) 3 **B. MOENCHENGLADBACH ..(1) 2** Att. 40,000
Conn, Jackson, MacDonald Jensen 2
Rangers: McCloy, Jardine, Mathieson, Greig, Jackson, MacDonald, McLean, Forsyth (Young), O'Hara, Conn, Houston.
Borussia Moenchengladbach won 5-2 on aggregate

17-8-77 – Preliminary Round
RANGERS ....(1) 1   YOUNG BOYS BERNE..(0) 0   Att. 39,000
Greig
Rangers: McCloy, Jardine, Greig, Forsyth, Jackson, MacDonald, McLean
(Mackay), Russell, Parlane (Smith), Robertson, Cooper.

31-8-77 – Preliminary Round Second Leg
YOUNG BOYS BERNE..(0) 2   RANGERS ....(1) 2   Att. 17,000
Jackson OG, LeuzingerJohnstone, Smith
Rangers: McCloy, Jardine, Greig, Forsyth, Jackson, MacDonald, McLean
(McKean), Russell (Miller), Johnstone, Smith, Cooper.
Rangers won 3-2 on aggregate

14-9-77 – First Round
RANGERS ....(0) 0   TWENTE ENSCHEDE .(0) 0   Att. 33,000
Rangers: McCloy, Jardine, Miller, Forsyth, Jackson, Watson, McKean, Russell,
Henderson, Smith, Cooper.

28-9-77 – First Round Second Leg
TWENTE ENSCHEDE .(2) 3   RANGERS ....(0) 0   Att. 20,000
Gritte, Muhren, Van der Vall
Rangers: Kennedy, Jardine, Miller, Forsyth, Jackson, MacDonald, McKean,
Russell, Parlane, Smith, Cooper.
Twente won 3-0 on aggregate

21-8-79 – Preliminary Round
RANGERS ....(1) 1   LILLESTROM ....(0) 0   Att. 25,000
Smith
Rangers: McCloy, Jardine, Dawson, Smith, Jackson, Watson, McLean (J.
MacDonald), Russell, Johnstone (Robertson), A. MacDonald, Cooper.

5-9-79 – Preliminary Round Second Leg
LILLESTROM ....(0) 0   RANGERS ....(1) 2   Att. 6,175
                                 A. MacDonald, Johnstone
Rangers: McCloy, Miller, Dawson, Jardine, Jackson, Watson, McLean (Cooper),
Russell, Johnstone, A. MacDonald, Smith.
Rangers won 3-0 on aggregate
19-9-79 – First Round
RANGERS ....(0) 2   FORTUNA DUSSELDORF ..(0) 1   Att. 30,000
A. MacDonald, McLean.   Wenzel
Rangers: McCloy, Miller, Dawson, Jardine, Jackson, A. MacDonald, McLean,
Russell (Watson), Johnstone, Smith, Cooper.

3-10-79 – First Round Second Leg
FORTUNA DUSSELDORF ..(0) 0   RANGERS ....(0) 0   Att. 40,000
Rangers: McCloy, Miller (A. Forsyth), Dawson, Jardine, Jackson, A. MacDonald, McLean, Watson, Johnstone, Smith (Cooper), Parlane.
Rangers won 2-1 on aggregate

24-10-79 – Second Round
VALENCIA ....(1) 1   RANGERS ....(1) 1   Att. 45,000
Kempes   McLean
Rangers: McCloy, Miller, Jardine, Johnstone, A. Forsyth, A. MacDonald, Watson, Smith, McLean (Parlane), Urquhart, Cooper (Dawson).

7-11-79 – Second Round Second Leg
RANGERS ....(1) 1   VALENCIA ....(2) 3   Att. 36,000
Johnstone   Jardine OG, Kempes 2
Rangers: McCloy, Jardine, A. Forsyth, Miller, Watson, A. MacDonald, McLean, Smith, Johnstone, Urquhart (Parlane), Cooper (Mackay).
Valencia won 4-2 on aggregate

16-9-81 – First Round
DUKLA PRAGUE ....(1) 3   RANGERS ....(0) 0   Att. 22,500
Rada, Stambachr, Nehoda
Rangers: McCloy, Jardine, Dawson, Forsyth, Jackson (Stevens), McClelland, Bett, McLean, Russell, McAdam, Johnstone (Redford).

30-9-81 – First Round Second Leg
RANGERS ....(2) 2   DUKLA PRAGUE.(1) 1   Att. 20,000
Bett, MacDonald   Stambachr
Rangers: Stewart, McClelland (Redford), Dawson, Jardine, Forsyth, Bett, Cooper, Russell, McAdam (Johnstone), MacDonald, Johnston.
Dukla Prague won 4-2 on aggregate

14-9-83 – First Round
VALETTA ....(0) 0   RANGERS ....(6) 8   Att. 18,213
                          McPherson 4, Paterson, Prytz 2, 1 pen., MacDonald
Rangers: McCloy, Dawson, McClelland, McPherson, Paterson, McKinnon, Prytz, McCoist (Davies), Clark (D. Ferguson), MacDonald, Cooper.

28-9-83 – First Round Second Leg
RANGERS ....(5) 10   VALETTA ....(0) 0   Att. 11,500
Mitchell 2, MacDonald 3, 1 pen., Dawson, Mackay, Redford 2, Davies
Rangers: Stewart, Dawson, McClelland, McPherson, Paterson (D. Ferguson), Redford, Prytz (Mackay), Davies, Mitchell, MacDonald, Cooper.
Rangers won 18-0 on aggregate

19-10-83 – Second Round
RANGERS ....(1) 2   PORTO..................(0) 1   Att. 28,000
Clark, Mitchell   Jacques
Rangers: McCloy, Dawson, McClelland, McPherson, Paterson, Redford, Prytz
(Mitchell), McCoist, Clark, Russell, Cooper (MacDonald).
2-11-83 – Second Round Second Leg
PORTO..................(0) 1   RANGERS ....(0) 0   Att. 60,000
Gomes
Rangers: McCloy, McKinnon, McClelland, Paterson, Dawson, McPherson,
Cooper, Russell, Prytz (McCoist), Redford, Clark (Mitchell).
2-2 on aggregate. Porto won on away goals

Rangers in Europe – Fairs/UEFA Cup

20-9-67 – First Round
DYNAMO DRESDEN..(0) 1   RANGERS ....(0) 1   Att. 48,000
Reidel   Ferguson
Rangers: Sorensen, Johansen, Greig, Jardine, McKinnon, D. Smith, Henderson,
Penman, Ferguson, Persson, Johnston.

4-10-67 – First Round Second Leg
RANGERS ....(1) 2   DYNAMO DRESDEN..(0) 1   Att. 50,000
Penman, Greig   Kreische
Rangers: Sorensen, Johansen, Mathieson, Greig, McKinnon, D. Smith, Henderson,
Penman, Ferguson, Persson, Johnston.
Rangers won 3-2 on aggregate

8-11-67 – Second Round
RANGERS ....(0) 3   COLOGNE.............(0) 0   Att. 54,000
Ferguson 2, Henderson
Rangers: Sorensen, Johansen, Mathieson, Greig (A. Smith), McKinnon, D. Smith,
Henderson, Penman, Ferguson, Johnston, Persson.

28-11-67 – Second Round Second Leg
COLOGNE.............(1) 3   RANGERS ....(0) 1†   Att. n/a
Overath, Weber, Ruhl   Henderson
Rangers: Sorensen, Johansen, Mathieson, Greig, McKinnon, D. Smith, Henderson,
Penman, Ferguson (Watson), Johnston, Persson.
Rangers won 4-3 on aggregate after extra time

26-3-68 – Quarter-Final
RANGERS ....(0) 0   LEEDS UNITED....(0) 0   Att. 80,000
Rangers: Sorensen, Johansen, Mathieson, Greig, McKinnon, D. Smith, Henderson,
A. Smith, Ferguson, Johnston, Persson.

9-4-68 – Quarter-Final Second Leg
LEEDS UNITED....(2) 2   **RANGERS** ....(0) 0   Att. 50, 498
Giles pen., Lorimer
Rangers: Sorensen, Johansen, Mathieson, Greig, McKinnon, D. Smith, Henderson,
Willoughby (Penman), Ferguson, Johnston, Persson.
Leeds won 2-0 on aggregate

18-9-68 – First Round
RANGERS ....(1) 2   **VOJVODINA** ....(0) 0   Att. 65,000
Greig pen., Jardine
Rangers: Martin, Jackson, Mathieson, Greig, McKinnon, Hynd, Henderson,
Penman, Jardine, Johnston, Persson.

2-10-68 – First Round Second Leg
VOJVODINA ....(0) 1   **RANGERS** ....(0) 0   Att. 7,000
Nikezic
Rangers: Martin, Jackson, Mathieson, Greig, McKinnon, Hynd, Henderson,
Penman (D. Smith), Jardine, Johnston, Persson.
Rangers won 2-1 on aggregate

0-10-68 – Second Round
RANGERS ....(2) 6   **DUNDALK** ....(1) 1   Att. 26,000
Henderson 2, Greig, Ferguson 2,   Murray pen.
Brennan OG
Rangers: Martin, Johansen, Mathieson, Greig, McKinnon, D. Smith, Henderson,
Penman, Ferguson, Johnston, Persson.

3-11-68 – Second Round Second Leg
DUNDALK ....(0) 0   **RANGERS** ....(1) 3   Att. n/a
Mathieson, Stein 2
Rangers: Martin, Johansen, Mathieson, Hynd, Jackson, D. Smith, Henderson,
Ferguson (Conn), Stein, Johnston, Persson.
Rangers won 9-1 on aggregate

15-1-69 – Third Round
DWS AMSTERDAM....(0) 0   **RANGERS** ....(1) 2   Att. 18,000
                                     Johnston, Henderson
Rangers: Martin, Johansen, Mathieson, Greig, McKinnon, Watson, Henderson,
Penman, Stein, Johnston, Persson (Stein).

2-1-69 – Third Round – Second Leg
RANGERS ....(2) 2   **DWS AMSTERDAM....(1) 1**   Att. 51,000
Smith, Stein   Guertsen

341

Rangers: Martin, Johansen, Greig, Watson, McKinnon, D. Smith (Jardine), Henderson, Penman, Stein, MacDonald, Johnston.
Rangers won 4-1 on aggregate

19-3-69 – Quarter-Final
RANGERS ....(2) 4   ATLETICO BILBAO....(1) 1   Att. 63,00
Ferguson, Penman, Persson, Stein   Clemente
Rangers: Martin, Johansen, Mathieson, Greig, McKinnon, D. Smith, Henderson, Penman, Stein, Ferguson (Persson), Johnston.

2-4-69 – Quarter-Final Second Leg
ATLETICO BILBAO....(1) 2   RANGERS ....(0) 0   Att. 40,00
Estefano, Ibanez
Rangers: Martin, Johansen, Mathieson, Greig, McKinnon, D. Smith, Henderson, Jackson, Stein, Ferguson, Johnston.
Rangers won 4-3 on aggregate

14-5-69 – Semi-Final
RANGERS ....(0) 0   NEWCASTLE UTD..(0) 0   Att. 70,00
Rangers: Neef, Johansen, Provan, Greig, Jackson, D. Smith, Henderson, Penman, Stein, Jardine, Persson.

21-5-69 – Semi-Final Second Leg
NEWCASTLE UTD..(0) 2   RANGERS ....(0) 0   Att. 60,00
Scott, Sinclair
Rangers: Neef, Johansen, Mathieson, Greig, McKinnon, D. Smith, Henderson, Penman, Stein, Johnston, Persson.
Newcastle won 2-0 on aggregate

16-9-70 – First Round
BAYERN MUNICH..(1) 1   RANGERS ....(0) 0   Att. 27,0
Beckenbauer
Rangers: McCloy, Jardine, Miller, Greig, McKinnon, Jackson, Fyfe, Conn, Stein (Henderson), MacDonald, Johnston.

30-9-70 – First Round Second Leg
RANGERS ....(0) 1   BAYERN MUNICH..(0) 1   Att. 83,0
Stein   Muller
Rangers: McCloy, Jardine, Miller, Greig, McKinnon, Jackson (D. Johnstone), Fy (Henderson), Conn, Stein, MacDonald, Johnston.
Bayern Munich won 2-1 on aggregate

1-9-82 – First Round
BORUSSIA DORTMUND .(0) 0   RANGERS ....(0) 0   Att. 54,0

Rangers: Stewart, McKinnon, Dawson, McClelland, Paterson, Bett, Cooper, Prytz (Miller), Johnstone, Russell, Redford.

29-9-82 – First Round Second Leg
RANGERS ....(1) 2   BORUSSIA DORTMUND .(0) 0   Att. 44,000
Cooper, Johnstone
Rangers: Stewart, McKinnon, McClelland, Paterson, Dawson, Russell (Redford), Bett, Prytz, Cooper, Johnstone, MacDonald.
Rangers won 2-0 on aggregate

20-10-82 – Second Round
RANGERS ....(1) 2   COLOGNE............(0) 1   Att. 32,000
Johnstone, McClelland   Allofs
Rangers: Stewart, McKinnon, McClelland, Paterson (Stevens), Dawson (MacDonald), Bett, Prytz, Russell, Cooper, Johnstone, Redford.

3-11-82 – Second Round Second Leg
COLOGNE............(4) 5   RANGERS ....(0) 0   Att. 61,000
Littbarski, Engels 2, Fischer, Allofs
Rangers: Stewart, McKinnon, McClelland, Stevens, Dawson, Russell, Prytz, Bett, Redford (McAdam), Cooper (MacDonald), Johnstone.
Cologne won 6-2 on aggregate

18-9-84 – First Round (First entry into UEFA Cup)
BOHEMIANS ....(2) 3   RANGERS ....(2) 2   Att. 10,000
O'Brien 2, Lawless   McCoist, McPherson
Rangers: Walker, McKinnon, Dawson, McClelland, Paterson, Redford, McPherson, Fraser, Clark (I. Ferguson), McCoist (MacDonald), Cooper.

3-10-84 – First Round Second Leg
RANGERS ....(0) 2   BOHEMIANS ....(0) 0   Att. 31,000
Paterson, Redford
Rangers: McCloy, McKinnon, Dawson, McClelland, Paterson, Redford, Russell, McPherson, I. Ferguson (Mitchell), McCoist (C. Fraser), Cooper.
Rangers won 4-3 on aggregate

24-10-84 – Second Round
INTER MILAN ......(1) 3   RANGERS ....(0) 0   Att. 65,591
Sabato, Causio, Rumminegge
Rangers: McCloy, Dawson, McClelland, McPherson, Paterson, Redford, Russell (I. Ferguson), Fraser, McCoist (Fleck), Prytz, Cooper.

7-11-84 – Second Round Second Leg
RANGERS ....(2) 3   INTER MILAN ......(1) 1   Att. 30,000
Mitchell, I. Ferguson 2   Altobelli

Rangers: McCloy, Dawson, McClelland, McPherson, Paterson, Redford, McKinnon, Fraser, Mitchell, I. Ferguson (McCoist), Prytz (Munro).
Inter won 4-3 on aggregate

18-9-85 – First Round
RANGERS ....(1) 1   ATLETICO OSASUNA ..(0) 0   Att. 29,479
Paterson
Rangers: Walker, Burns, Munro, McPherson, Paterson, Bell, McCoist, D. Ferguson, Williamson, Durrant, Cooper.

2-10-85 – First Round Second Leg
ATLETICO OSASUNA ..(2) 2   RANGERS ....(0) 0   Att. 26,000
Ripodas, Martin
Rangers: Walker, Burns, Munro, McPherson, Paterson, Bell, McCoist, Russell (McMinn), Johnstone, Durrant, Cooper (Williamson).
Atletico Osasuna won 2-1 on aggregate

17-9-86 – First Round
RANGERS ....(2) 4   ILVES TAMPERE ....(0) 0   Att. 27,436
Fleck 3, McCoist
Rangers: Woods, Nicholl, Munro, Souness (McMinn), McPherson, Butcher, Fraser, Fleck, McCoist, Durrant, Cooper.

1-10-86 – First Round Second Leg
ILVES TAMPERE ....(0) 2   RANGERS ....(0) 0   Att. 210
Hjelm pen., Uimonen
Rangers: Woods, Nicholl, Munro, Miller, McPherson, Butcher, Russell, Fleck, McCoist, Durrant (Bell), Cooper (Nisbet).
Rangers won 4-2 on aggregate

23-10-86 – Second Round
RANGERS ....(2) 2   BOAVISTA............(1) 1   Att. 38,77
McPherson, McCoist   Tonanha
Rangers: Woods, Nicholl, Munro, Souness (McMinn), McPherson, Butcher, Ferguson, Fleck (Nisbet), McCoist, Durrant, Cooper.
4-11-86 – Second Round Second Leg
BOAVISTA............(0) 0   RANGERS ....(0) 1   Att. 23,00
                                  Ferguson
Rangers: Woods, Nicholl, Munro, Fraser, McPherson, Butcher, Ferguson, Bell, McCoist (Fleck), Durrant, Cooper.
Rangers won 3-1 on aggregate

26-11-86 – Third Round
RANGERS ....(1) 1   B. MOENCHENGLADBACH ..(1) 1   Att. 44,00
Durrant   Rahn

Rangers: Woods, Nicholl, Munro, Ferguson, McPherson, Butcher, Fraser (West), McMinn, McCoist, Durrant, Cooper.

10-12-86 – Third Round Second Leg
B. MOENCHENGLADBACH ..(0) 0   RANGERS ....(0) 0   Att. 34,000
Rangers: Woods, Dawson, Munro, Souness, McPherson, Butcher, Ferguson, Bell (West), McCoist, McMinn, Cooper.
Aggregate 1-1. Borussia Moenchengladbach won on away goals

7-9-88 – First Round
RANGERS ....(0) 1   GKS KATOWICE ..(0) 0   Att. 41,120
Walters
Rangers: Woods, Stevens, Brown, Gough, Wilkins, Butcher, Drinkell, I. Ferguson, Cooper, Durrant (D. Ferguson), Walters.

21-9-88 – First Round Second Leg
GKS KATOWICE ..(1) 2   RANGERS ....(2) 4   Att. 35,000
Furtok, Kubisztal   Butcher 2, Durrant, I. Ferguson
Rangers: Woods, Stevens, Gough, Butcher, Munro, Walters, Wilkins, I. Ferguson, Cooper, Durrant (McGregor), McCoist.
Rangers won 5-2 on aggregate

26-10-88 – Second Round
COLOGNE ....(0) 2   RANGERS ....(0) 0   Att. 42,000
Jenssen, T. Allofs
Rangers: Woods, Stevens, Munro, Gough, Wilkins, Butcher, Drinkell, I. Ferguson, McCoist, D. Ferguson, Walters (Nisbet).

9-11-88 – Second Round Second Leg
RANGERS ....(0) 1   COLOGNE ....(0) 1   Att. 42,204
Drinkell   Jenssen
Rangers: Woods, Stevens, Munro, Gough, Nicholl (McCall), Butcher, Cooper (Nisbet), I. Ferguson, Drinkell, D. Ferguson, Walters.
Cologne won 3-1 on aggregate

Competition Representation

EUROPEAN CUP	16 times	Best – Semi-Final 1960
		2nd Champions League 1993
EUROPEAN CUP-WINNERS CUP	10 times	Best – Winners 1972
FAIRS CUP	3 times	Best – Semi-Finals 1969
UEFA CUP	5 times	Best – Third Round 1987

Competition Representation – *Country by Country*

The following table is a country-by-country breakdown of Rangers' performances in European competition, based on the Light Blues' results against that nation's clubs.

For the purpose of the league, German clubs have been split into West and East German categories, as most of Rangers' ties were played prior to re-unification. Russians CSKA Moscow, who Rangers played in the Champions League, are considered from the Soviet Union.

		P	W	D	L	F	A	%
1	MALTA	4	4	0	0	28	0	100
2	TURKEY	2	2	0	0	6	0	100
3	AUSTRIA	2	2	0	0	3	0	100
	DENMARK	2	2	0	0	3	0	100
	NORWAY	2	2	0	0	3	0	100
6	EAST GERMANY	4	3	1	0	9	4	87.5
7	REPUBLIC of IRELAND	6	4	1	1	18	6	75
8	BELGIUM	6	4	1	1	13	8	75
9	NORTHERN IRELAND	4	3	1	0	5	1	75
10	BULGARIA	4	3	1	0	6	4	75
11	SOVIET UNION	5	3	1	1	6	3	70
12	HOLLAND	9	5	2	2	13	11	66.7
13	PORTUGAL	6	4	0	2	11	9	66.7
14	ROMANIA	4	2	1	1	4	3	62.5
15	POLAND	6	3	1	2	11	9	58.3
16	YUGOSLAVIA	9	4	2	3	16	15	55.6
17	FRANCE	13	5	3	5	20	21	50
18	SWITZERLAND	4	1	2	1	4	4	50
19	CZECHOSLOVAKIA	4	2	0	2	4	6	50
20	FINLAND	2	1	0	1	4	2	50
21	HUNGARY	2	1	0	1	5	4	50
22	WEST GERMANY	29	9	10	10	38	41	48.3
23	ENGLAND	10	3	3	4	11	15	45
24	SPAIN	12	4	1	7	13	20	37.5
25	ITALY	12	4	1	7	11	19	37.5
26	GREECE	2	0	0	2	0	3	0

If percentages are the same, the country against whose teams Rangers have played more often is given higher status.

European Competition – *Club by Club*

Rangers have played a total of 63 different teams from 26 countries in European competition. The following list details which sides they have crossed swords with, and how they fared. (W) denotes progression into the next round of a European competition, or success in a final, or a better two game aggregate in the Champions League. (L) denotes elimination, defeat in a final or a worse two game aggregate in the Champions League.

AUSTRIA	Rapid Vienna (W).
BELGIUM	Anderlecht (W); Brugge (W); Standard Liege (L).
BULGARIA	Levski Sofia (L); Slavia Sofia (W).
CZECHOSLOVAKIA	Dukla Prague (L); Sparta Prague (L).
DENMARK	Lyngby (W).
EAST GERMANY	Dynamo Dresden (W); Vorwaerts (W).
ENGLAND	Leeds United (2 -W,L); Newcastle United (L); Tottenham Hotspur (L); Wolverhampton Wanderers (W).
FINLAND	Ilves Tampere (W).
FRANCE	Marseille (L); Monaco (W); Nice (L); Rennes (W); St Etienne (2 - W,L).
GREECE	AEK Athens (L).
HOLLAND	DWS Amsterdam (W); PSV Eindhoven (W); Sparta Rotterdam (W); Twente Enschede (L).
HUNGARY	Ferencvaros (W).
IRELAND	Bohemians (2 - W2); Dundalk (W).
ITALY	AC Milan (L); Fiorentina (L); Internazionale (2 - L2); Juventus (W); Torino (W).
MALTA	Valletta (2 - W2).
NORTHERN IRELAND	Glentoran (W).
NORWAY	Lillestrom (W).
POLAND	Gornik Zabrze (2 - L,W); Katowice (W).
PORTUGAL	Boavista (W); Porto (L); Sporting Lisbon (W).
ROMANIA	Steau Bucharest (2 - W,L).
SOVIET UNION	CSKA Moscow (W); Dynamo Kiev (W); Moscow Dynamo (W).
SPAIN	Atletico Bilbao (W); Osasuna (L); Real Madrid (L); Real Zaragoza (W); Seville (W); Valencia (L).
SWITZERLAND	FC Zurich (L); Young Boys of Berne (W).
TURKEY	Ankargucu (W).
WEST GERMANY	Bayern Munich (4 - W1,L3); Borussia Dortmund (2 - W2); Borussia Moenchengladbach (3 - W1, L2); Cologne (4 - W1, L3); Eintracht Frankfurt (L) Fortuna Dusseldorf (W).
YUGOSLAVIA	Red Star Belgrade (3 - W2, L1); Vojvodina (W).

Scottish Player of the Year Awards

1977-78	Derek Johnstone	1992-93	Andy Goram
1991-92	Ally McCoist	1993-94	Mark Hateley
		1994-95	Brian Laudrup

Scottish Young Player of the Year Awards

1979-80	John MacDonald	1986-87	Robert Fleck
		1994-95	Charlie Miller

Scottish Football Writers Footballer of the Year

1965-66	John Greig	1988-89	Richard Gough
1971-72	Dave Smith	1991-92	Ally McCoist
1974-75	Sandy Jardine	1992-93	Andy Goram
1975-76	John Greig	1993-94	Mark Hateley
1977-78	Derek Johnstone	1994-95	Brian Laudrup

RECORD BREAKING RANGERS

Over a third of Scottish league clubs' record attendance has come against Rangers.
Below is a complete list of those who have the Light Blues to thank for their most
memorable paydays.

1	Celtic	92,000	January 1938
2	Hearts	53,496	February 1932
3	Clyde	52,000	November 1908
4	Partick Thistle	49,838	February 1922
5	Dundee	43,024	February 1953
6	Motherwell	35,632	March 1952
7	Kilmarnock	34,246	August 1963
8	Albion Rovers	27,381	February 1936
9	Cowdenbeath	25,586	November 1949
10	Ayr United	22,225	September 1969
11	Arbroath	13,510	February 1952
12	Berwick Rangers	13,365	January 1967
13	Forfar	10,800	February 1970
14	Ross County	8,000	February 1966
15	Stranraer	6,500	January 1948

3-Year Form & Fixture Guide

Here's your guide to the 1995-96 season. It includes details of previous Premier Division encounters plus a few pointers as to what you can expect from the match. Dates are subject to change what with Cup matches, TV requirements and bad weather – so always double check along with kick-off times. Enjoy the games!

No	Date	Opponents	92/3	93/4	94/5	95/6

1. 26-8-95   KILMARNOCK (h)   -   1-2   2-0
Killie have posed problems in the past, but with the championship flag being presented, it has to be a flying start to the season.

22. 9-9-95   RAITH ROVERS (h)   -   2-2   -
Promoted clubs have more to prove at the start of the season, so expect a stiff test before the points are claimed.

3. 16-9-95   Falkirk (a)   2-1   -   2-0
The Bairns like to attack, especially at Brockville, and that should ensure enough gaps for a slender victory.

4. 23-9-95   HIBERNIAN (h)   1-0   2-1   2-0
Hibs' shocking away record is down to a dismal lack of ambition; expect an easy win.

5. 30-9-95   Celtic (a)   1-0   0-0   3-1
Gazza's first Old Firm clash will be a real eye opener. And after the poor 3-0 defeat in the last derby of 1994-95, Rangers have revenge firmly in mind.

6. 3-10-95   MOTHERWELL (h)   4-2   1-2   2-1
Motherwell usually put up a good fight, meaning their visits, once dreaded under the negative Tommy McLean, can now mean decent games.

7. 7-10-95   Aberdeen (a)   1-0   0-2   2-2
There would have been a lot of laughter if Aberdeen had been relegated. But the Dons regularly provide stiff opposition at Pittodrie, and those fixtures would have been missed.

8. 14-10-95   Partick Thistle (a)   4-1   1-1   2-0
Thistle can scrap and fight, but it's generally no substitute for Rangers' skill and class.

9. 21-10-95   HEARTS (h)   2-0   2-1   3-0
Supposedly one of Scotland's big clubs, there is rarely evidence of that when they visit Ibrox. Another comfortable win seems a certainty.

10. 28-10-95   Raith Rovers (a)   -   1-1   -
Stark's Park is a tight little ground, and Rovers have frustrated Rangers there before. And it will be interesting to see how signing target Steve Crawford fares.

11. 4-11-95   FALKIRK (h)   4-0   -   1-1
A cup win and two draws last season on the Gers' patch for Falkirk. They're certainly not daunted by the atmosphere, but a defeat is long overdue.

12. 8-11-95 Kilmarnock (a)   -   2-0   2-1

Alex Totten, an ex-Ibrox number two, loves pitting his wits against his former club. They could make it difficult.

13. 11-11-95 ABERDEEN (h)   3-1   2-0   1-0

Long gone are the days when Aberdeen used to come to Ibrox to win. Their mental block about playing Rangers in Glasgow should mean another three points.

14. 19-11-95 CELTIC (h)   1-1   1-2   0-2

An Ibrox drubbing for the old rivals must be on the cards. Celtic's recent Ibrox form has been a real frustration.

15. 25-11-95 Hibernian (a)   0-0   1-0   1-2

Hi-bees are a different proposition at Easter Road, even if they still seem reluctant to attack. Few goals likely.

16. 2-12-95 Hearts (a)   1-1   2-2   1-1

Hearts had not beaten Rangers for years, prior to their Scottish Cup win last year. Then they did it again in the League. That could give them confidence at Tynecastle.

17. 9-12-95 PARTICK THISTLE (h)   3-0   1-1   3-0

Christmas is normally the time when Rangers start to extend their lead in the league. This match might be the start of an important run.

18. 19-12-95 Motherwell (a)   4-1   2-0   1-2

Well will be among the challengers again, but if they fail to win their home matches against Rangers, they can't expect to win anything. And they won't.

19. 26-12-95 KILMARNOCK (h)   3-0   3-0

This Boxing Day clash could prove a bit of a mis-match – as long as Gascoigne hasn't eaten too much festive turkey.

20. 30-12-95 HIBERNIAN (h)   3-0   2-0   3-1

The last home game of the year, a chance to thank the fans for their support – and send Hibs back to Edinburgh for anything but a happy Hogmanay.

21. 3-1-95 Celtic (a)   1-2   4-2   0-3

Don't be deceived by the above statistics; they relate to the second away fixture of the season at Celtic. When it's the New Year clash, as it was in 93-94, Rangers are usually up for the occasion.

2. 6-1-96 Falkirk (a)   2-1   -   3-2

This is the sort of fixture the likes of Laudrup and Gascoigne are supposed not to fancy; Brockville on a cold January Saturday. Maurice Johnston will certainly be out to prove a point.

3. 13-1-96 RAITH ROVERS (h)   -   4-0   -

The corresponding fixture in 1993-94 led to Duncan Ferguson in court for assault. There'll be no trouble this time – no butts about it.

4. 20-1-96 HEARTS (h)   2-1   2-2   1-0

The Ibrox old-boys – McPherson, Hagen, Colin Miller – make another visit, most likely to show why the club moved them on.

No	Date	Opponents	92/3	93/4	94/5	95/6

25. 3-2-96 Partick Thistle (a)   0-3   2-1   1-1

Discount that 3-0 defeat at Firhill in 1992-93, which came once the title was clinched. The Jags just aren't sharp enough to sting the Light Blues.

26. 10-2-96 MOTHERWELL (h)   1-0   2-1   0-2

Hopefully, attentions will be focused on Europe at this stage – so this may be a rare dropped home point!

27. 24-2-96 Aberdeen (a)   0-1   0-0   0-2

The results speak for themselves; by the second away clash of the season, whether chasing a UEFA place or battling relegation, the Dons at Pittodrie are unwelcoming.

28. 2-3-96 Hibernian (a)   4-3   0-1   1-1

March is usually when the title gets wrapped up. This could be a key match in the championship run-in…

29. 17-3-96 CELTIC (h)   1-0   1-1   1-1

And wouldn't it be marvellous to end Celtic's challenge with another Old Firm win?

30. 23-3-96 FALKIRK (h)   5-0   -   2-2

By this point, who knows where Falkirk will be in the Premier – they could be anywhere from second to bottom. Their position will determine how difficult this match is.

31. 30-3-96 RAITH ROVERS (a)   -   2-1   -

Ian Ferguson and Gordon Durie scored the goals here the last time Rangers played. In fact, his strike against Celtic in the New Year match last season was the last League goal Fergie scored.

32. 6-4-96 Hearts (a)   3-2   2-1   1-2

Hearts away generally means two things; three points and Mark Hateley on the scoresheet.

33. 13-4-96 PARTICK THISTLE (h)   3-1   5-1   1-1

Wouldn't it be nice this season if the title celebration comprised of a few thrashings? This has to be an ideal candidate.

34. 20-4-96 Motherwell (a)   4-0   1-2   3-1

But with one eye on the European Cup and Scottish Cup finals, this match with the Steelmen could prove an awkward distraction.

35. 27-4-96 ABERDEEN (h)   2-0   1-1   3-2

A full house, community singing, Gazza's comedy breasts, Laudrup collecting his player of the year awards. Sounds like a good day!

36. 4-5-96 Kilmarnock (a)   -   0-1   1-0

The blue and white of Killie on Saturday, with the blue and white of Blackburn in battle of Britain Champions Cup showdown to come? Don't bet against it – and don't forget Hampden either for the Scottish Cup Final.

Enjoy the season!